"In *The ELL Teacher's Toolbox*, readers will find powerful, research-based instructional methods and practical classroom ideas that are tried and true. This is a must-have resource for all teachers!"

—*Valentina Gonzalez, Professional Development Specialist for ELLs, Katy Independent School District, Texas*

"This collection of immediately usable strategies is a godsend for teachers of English Language Learners, which should be no surprise to fans of Ferlazzo and Sypnieski. This is a book you'll want to put on the desk of all the ELL teachers you know."

—*Shanna Peeples, 2015 National Teacher of the Year*

"A grab-and-go book of strategies for teachers of English learners. With this book, all educators can be both teachers of content and language at the same time. *The ELL Teacher's Toolbox* turns principles into practices."

—*Tan Huynh, teacher, consultant, blogger at EmpoweringELLs.com*

"This book combines clear strategies by teachers for teachers in real classrooms. It includes a research base, points out connections to standards, and has tips on what to watch out for. A genuine all-in-one approach that's a winning formula for the classroom!"

—*Giselle Lundy-Ponce, American Federation of Teachers*

*The ELL Teacher's Toolbox* is just that. A box full of tools that you will want to have at your fingertips all year long. If you teach any English learners, you'll be grateful to have this practical guide and all the reproducible resources packed into it!

—*Carol Salva, Seidlitz Education, author, Boosting Achievement: Reaching Students with Interrupted Or Minimal Education*

# The ELL Teacher's Toolbox

# The ELL Teacher's Toolbox

## Hundreds of Practical Ideas to Support Your Students

LARRY FERLAZZO AND KATIE HULL SYPNIESKI

**JB** JOSSEY-BASS™
A Wiley Brand

Published by Jossey-Bass
A Wiley Brand
One Montgomery Street, Suite 1000, San Francisco, CA 94104-4594—www.josseybass.com

Published simultaneously in Canada.

For general information on our other products and services or for technical support, please contact our Customer Care Department within the United States at (800) 762-2974, outside the United States at (317) 572-3993 or fax (317) 572-4002.

Wiley publishes in a variety of print and electronic formats and by print-on-demand. Some material included with standard print versions of this book may not be included in e-books or in print-on-demand. If this book refers to media such as a CD or DVD that is not included in the version you purchased, you may download this material at http://booksupport.wiley.com. For more information about Wiley products, visit www.wiley.com.

*Library of Congress Cataloging-in-Publication Data:*

Names: Ferlazzo, Larry, author. | HullSypnieski, Katie, 1974- author.
Title: The ELL teacher's toolbox : hundreds of practical ideas to support
   your students / by Larry Ferlazzo, Katie Hull Sypnieski.
Description: Hoboken, New Jersey : John Wiley & Sons, 2018. | Includes index.
   | Identifiers: LCCN 2017057348 (print) | LCCN 2017061783 (ebook) | ISBN
   9781119364986 (pdf) | ISBN 9781119364955 (epub) | ISBN 9781119364962 (pbk.)
Subjects: LCSH: English language—Study and teaching—Foreign
   speakers—Handbooks, manuals, etc.
Classification: LCC PE1128.A2 (ebook) | LCC PE1128.A2 F44 2018 (print) | DDC
   428.0071—dc23
LC record available at https://lccn.loc.gov/2017057348

Cover Design: Wiley
Cover Image: ©ThomasVogel/iStockphoto

Printed in the United States of America
FIRST EDITION

*PB Printing*   10 9 8 7 6 5 4 3 2 1

# Contents

## 8. Language Experience Approach (LEA)

## 9. Jigsaw

## 28. Using Photos or Other Images in Speaking and Listening ....275

## 29. Video ...................................................................279

## 43. Beginning and Ending of Class ......................... 415

## 44. Textbooks ...................................................... 423

## 45. Using Technology .......................................... 427

# Introduction

If you have an important point to make, don't try to be subtle or clever.
Use a pile driver. Hit the point once. Then come back and hit it again.
Then hit it a third time.

*Winston Churchill*

We are, indeed, again hitting the important point that we must look at English language learners through the lens of assets and not deficits in this, our third book.

*The ESL/ELL Teacher's Survival Guide* (2012), our first book, looked through this positive lens and was categorized by *themes* and *genres*. In our second book, *Navigating the Common Core with English Language Learners* (2016), we applied this same lens to approaching the ELL classroom and used *standards* to organize our recommendations.

We're now ready to hit it a third time and share *instructional strategies* that again build on the assets of ELLs.

What is our definition of an instructional strategy? We define it loosely as a teaching tactic, technique, or method that can be used in a class as part of multiple lessons and across content areas. We are not saying that *every* strategy we discuss can be used in *all* lessons or in *all* content areas. However, we *are* saying that each strategy can be used in a number of different classroom lessons.

The names of each of the 45 strategies we discuss, though, don't always reflect this loose definition, but the one- to five-word titles are less important than the practical classroom ideas included under each one.

We can say with confidence, however, that everything in this book does fit the definition of the root word of *strategy*—*ag*, which means to "draw out or forth, move"

(Strategy, n.d.). We apply these ideas to assist students to *draw out* the gifts and tools they already possess and to provide them with new ones so that they can *move* forward in their academic, social-emotional, and professional-economic lives.

There are hundreds of specific ideas contained within these 45 broader strategies, including scores of reproducible student handouts. They all reflect our commitment to supporting language acquisition (being able to actually use the target language in a practical way) and not just language learning (being able to complete a worksheet on a grammar concept but not being able to apply it in a conversation). In addition, these strategies recognize and build on the gifts our ELL students (and, in fact, all our students) bring to the classroom. Finally, they all promote a classroom culture of active learning and not passivity.

These are truly teacher-tested strategies that we have used day-in and day-out during our combined 35 years of teaching experience. The majority of the lesson ideas we discuss have not appeared in our previous books. Others were present in them, but they are updated with improvements or revised student handouts. One percent of the book is lifted verbatim from our first two books because we felt it was just too good to leave out.

Each strategy follows a similar outline. First, we explain what it is, followed by a short analysis about why we like it. Next, we provide research supporting its use with English language learners and list the Common Core Anchor Standards that the strategy can help meet (we've also reprinted those standards as an Appendix at the end of this book). The Application section contains the meat of the strategy, where we describe different ways to apply it in class. We then talk about what could go wrong in these lessons—and, believe us, we speak from much direct experience in this part! Next, we share various ways to integrate technology. Then, we recognize the contribution of other educators to the ideas we have discussed. Last, we share the related figures (these reproducibles and a complete list of links to technology resources discussed in the book can be accessed online at our book's website, www .wiley.com/go/ellteachertools). The 45 strategies are divided into three sections. The first section's focus relates to reading and writing; the second to speaking and listening; and the third, for lack of a better term, we're calling *additional key strategies* that don't quite fit under either of the first two labels. We also recognize that even the first two categories are somewhat artificial labels because most classroom lessons involve all four domains.

Though this book's focus is on English language learners, we also want to make clear that we use all these strategies, or variations of them, with our English-proficient students. Good ELL teaching is good teaching for everyone, and we hope you will read our book and implement its suggestions in that spirit!

# PART 1

# Reading and Writing

## STRATEGY 1

# Independent Reading

### What Is It?

Independent reading, also called *free voluntary reading, extensive reading, leisure or pleasure reading,* and *silent sustained reading,* is the instructional strategy of providing students with time in class on a regular basis to read books of their choice. Students are also encouraged to do the same at home. In addition, no formal responses or academic exercises are tied to this reading.

### Why We Like It

We believe the best way for our ELL students to become more motivated to read and to increase their literacy skills is to give them time to read and to let them read what they like! That being said, we *don't* just stand back and watch them read. We *do* teach reading strategies, conduct read alouds to generate interest, take our classes to the school library, organize and maintain our classroom library, conference with students during reading time, and encourage our students to read outside the classroom, among other things. All of these activities contribute to a learning community in which literacy is valued and reading interest is high.

### Supporting Research

Research shows there are many benefits of having students read self-selected books during the school day (Ferlazzo, 2011, February 26; Miller, 2015). These benefits include enhancing students' comprehension, vocabulary, general knowledge, and empathy, as well as increasing their self-confidence and motivation as readers. These benefits apply to English language learners who read in English and in their native languages (International Reading Association, 2014).

Encouraging students to read in their home language, as well as in English, can facilitate English language acquisition and build literacy skills in both languages (Ferlazzo, 2017, April 10). Extensive research has found that students increasing their first language (L1) abilities are able to transfer phonological and comprehension skills as well as background knowledge to second language (L2) acquisition (Genessee, n.d.).

## Common Core Connections

According to the Common Core ELA Standards, "students must read widely and deeply from among a broad range of high-quality, increasingly challenging literary and informational texts" in order to progress toward career and college readiness (Common Core State Standards Initiative, n.d.b). The lead authors of the Common Core advocate for daily student independent reading of self-selected texts and specifically state that students should have access to materials that "aim to increase regular independent reading of texts that appeal to students' interests while developing their knowledge base and joy in reading" (Coleman & Pimentel, 2012, p. 4).

## Application

Our students are allowed to choose whatever reading material they are currently interested in and are given time to read every day (depending on the day's schedule they spend anywhere from 10 to 20 minutes per day). Our students' use of digital reading materials in the classroom has dramatically increased in the past few years, and we discuss this in the Technology Connections section.

In order for this time to be effective—for our ELL students to experience the various benefits of independent reading discussed in the research section—we scaffold the independent reading process in several ways.

### SELECTING BOOKS

At the beginning of the year, we familiarize our students with the way our classroom libraries are organized—ours are leveled (beginner, intermediate, advanced) and categorized (fiction, nonfiction, bilingual). We organize our books in this way so that students don't have to waste time looking through many books that are obviously not accessible to them. For example, a newcomer having to thumb through 10 intermediate or advanced books before he or she finds a readable one can easily lead to a feeling of frustration, not anticipation. Students, however, are free to choose a book from any section of the library, even if that means selecting a book at a higher reading level than we would select for them. That being said, we do our best to help students find books they are interested in that are also accessible to them.

We also teach our students how to identify whether a book is too hard, too easy, or just right by reading the first couple of pages and noticing if most of the words seem unfamiliar (too hard right now), if they know the majority of the words (too easy), or if some of the words are familiar and some are new (just right). We also emphasize to students the importance of challenging themselves to improve (using a sports analogy works well—if you want to get better at basketball, you don't just work on the same shot every day) by sometimes practicing a little out of their comfort zones. We do allow students to use their phones or classroom dictionaries to look up words, but we also explain that having to look up every word usually indicates a book is too hard for now.

If you are facing a situation-like we have at times-when your new ELL student knows no English, doesn't have a cell phone, you don't have a peer tutor to help him or her read, there's no computer available in the classroom, and no bilingual book using that student's home language, then we make sure to get a bilingual dictionary (ideally, with pictures) that students can read. These can easily be found online for most languages, though they can be expensive. It's not ideal, but it's something.

## STUDENT-TEACHER CHECK-INS

We use independent reading time to check in with individual students about their engagement, comprehension, and future reading interests. These are not formal assessments but are brief, natural conversations about reading ("Why did you choose this book? What is your favorite part so far? Which part is most confusing? How are you feeling about reading in English?"). We may also use the time to help students find new books, listen to students practice reading aloud, talk about new words they are learning, discuss which reading strategies they are using (see Strategy 10: Reading Comprehension), and glean information about their reading interests, strengths, and challenges.

## WRITING AND TALKING ABOUT BOOKS

Sometimes we may ask students to respond to their daily reading in a quickwrite, a drawing, or talking with a partner. Other times we ask students to respond to their reading in their writer's notebooks (see Strategy 18: Writer's Notebook for a more detailed explanation of how we use them for reader response). We may also have students participate in one of the activities described in Strategy 2: Literary Conversations, such as creating a book trailer, conducting a book interview, or identifying and writing about a golden line.

## PUBLISHING STUDENT SUCCESSES

We have our students keep track of the books they have read in English and in their home language, not as an accountability measure but as a celebration of their growth as readers. When they finish a book of any length, we give them a colored sticky note and they write their name, the title of the book, the number of pages, and a four- to five-word rating, or blurb (e.g., "sad, but good ending" or "best graphic novel I've read!"). Students then stick their notes on the finished books wall (made of a large piece of colored paper).

We also have students keep a list of finished books in their writer's notebooks (see Strategy 18). We remind our students that it's not a race for who can finish the most books, but that the most important goal is that each student is making his or her own progress.

At the end of each quarter, we ask students to reflect on their independent reading (see Figure 1.1: End-of-Quarter Reading Reflection). At the end of the year, we celebrate all the reading our students have done with a visual project called *My Year of Reading*. Students use their sticky notes and lists of finished books in their notebooks to create a list of all the books they've read. Then they design a visual representation of their reading journey (a chart, a time line, a map, a bookshelf, etc.). See Figure 1.2: My Year of Reading Visual Project for the directions and Figure 1.3: My Year of Reading Student Example.

## WORKING WITH STUDENTS NOT LITERATE IN THEIR HOME LANGUAGE

Independent reading can be especially challenging with English language learners who are preliterate, not literate, or who have low literacy skills in their home language. However, new research (which we share with our students and their families) shows that learning to read creates deeper, stronger, and faster connections in the brain, even for those who are late to reading (Sparks, 2017). We frequently do lessons with all our students about how learning new things changes and strengthens the brain (Ferlazzo, 2011, November 26).

In our experience, one of the best ways to engage students facing these challenges and to build their literacy skills is through online reading activities. The online sites we have found most useful are interactive and contain leveled texts, bilingual stories, visualizations, and audio support in which words are pronounced aloud in English and in the student's home language. Many of our students especially enjoy sites that incorporate music lyrics and videos. For teachers who have limited technology in the classroom, another option is to access printable books online at sites such as Learning A-Z or edHelper. See the Technology Connections for a list of the sites we have found most useful. In addition, explore Strategy 35: Supporting ELL Students with Interrupted Formal Education (SIFE) for other ideas.

## Student Handouts and Examples

Figure 1.1: End-of-Quarter Reading Reflection

Figure 1.2: My Year of Reading Visual Project

Figure 1.3: My Year of Reading Student Example

# What Could Go Wrong?

Providing ELL students with access to high-interest books at their English proficiency levels can be challenging. Children's books, although often well written and available in multiple languages, are not always of high interest to adolescent learners. We've found that purchasing popular young adult fiction in English and in various home languages works especially well for our intermediate students. They can read the English version and use their home language copy as a reference—to check their understanding or to identify similarities and differences. As we stated previously, digital texts are another engaging option for adolescent ELLs and provide many features that support literacy development—glossaries, animations, audio tools, and so on (see Technology Connections for resources on digital reading).

Independent reading is a very important component of English language instruction; however, it is not a substitute for explicit reading instruction (see Strategy 10: Reading Comprehension). Ideally, it is a time when students can apply the reading skills and strategies they are learning in class to the texts they are reading independently. The teacher plays a big role in helping students reach this goal by consistently providing guidance and encouragement. It can quickly become an ineffective practice if students are not supported as they select books, read them, and interact with them. Teachers can fall into the trap of using student independent reading time to plan or catch up on paperwork. We certainly have done this and still do it now at times, but we try to resist the urge and we hope you do, too.

# Technology Connections

There are numerous online sites that provide free, high-interest reading materials for all levels of ELLs. Links to these sites can be found here:

The Best Websites to Help Beginning Readers (http://larryferlazzo.edublogs .org/2008/01/22/the-best-websites-to-help-beginning-readers/)

The Best Websites for Beginning Older Readers (http://larryferlazzo.edublogs .org/2008/01/23/the-best-websites-for-beginning-older-readers/)

The Best Online Resources for Teachers of Preliterate ELLs (http://larryferlazzo .edublogs.org/2008/12/06/the-best-online-resources-for-teachers-of-pre-literate-ells/)

The Best Websites for Intermediate Readers (http://larryferlazzo.edublogs.org/2008/01/26/the-best-websites-for-intermediate-readers/)

The Best Sources for Free and Accessible Printable Books (http://larryferlazzo.edublogs.org/2009/07/31/the-best-sources-for-free-accessible-printable-books/)

## Attribution

Portions of this section are adapted from our books, *The ESL/ELL Teacher's Survival Guide* (Ferlazzo & Sypnieski, 2012, p. 125–127) and *Navigating the Common Core with English Language Learners* (Ferlazzo & Sypnieski, 2016, p. 95–97).

## Figures

1. How many books did you read this quarter? List the titles (look at your sticky notes and your list in your writer's notebook). How do you feel about this number of books?

2. How do you feel about your progress in reading (what is getting easier, what is still challenging)?

3. What was your favorite book you read this quarter? Give at least three reasons why it was your favorite.

4. Are you reading mostly fiction books, nonfiction books, or a mix of both? Why do you think this is?

5. What strategies are you using to help you understand your book (summarizing, looking up new words, asking questions, etc.)?

6. What changes will you make as a reader next quarter (read more-challenging books, ask for book recommendations, read at home, etc.)?

7. What help do you need from your teacher or your classmates to become an even better reader (finding books, a quiet place to read in class, a partner to talk about my book with, starting a book club, etc.)?

8. Complete the following statement:

Reading is _____ because _____.

**Figure 1.1** End-of-Quarter Reading Reflection

You have read many good books this year! You will demonstrate evidence of your reading and celebrate it by completing a final visual project. Follow this guide to complete your My Year of Reading Visual Project:

- Look back over your finished books list in your writer's notebook and your sticky notes from the finished books wall.

- Look at the titles you have read and think about how you might like to tie all of these books together.

- You may present your books on a poster in the form of a map, time line, game board, video game, advertisement, list, or any other creative way you want. You must include the title of each book.

- Complete a quick draft on a piece of scratch paper to show me your plan *before* I give you the final poster paper.

- On the poster paper, *sketch* your design with pencil before you use ink or color.

- You may use a combination of colored pens and colored pencils to complete your poster.

**Figure 1.2**  My Year of Reading Visual Project

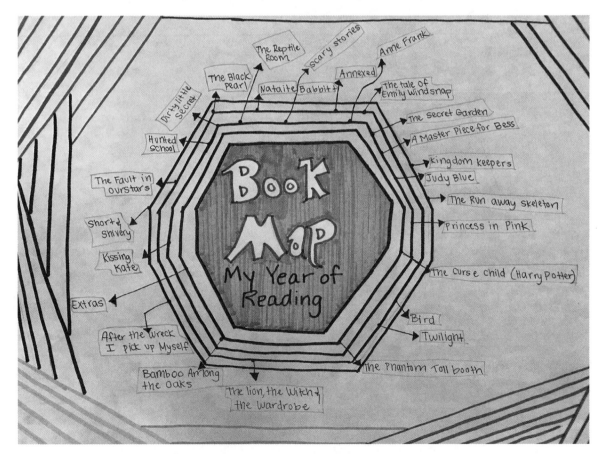

**Figure 1.3**  My Year of Reading Student Example

# STRATEGY 2

# Literary Conversations

## What Is It?

We provide our students with the opportunity to read high-interest books independently (see Strategy 1: Independent Reading). Literary conversations, written and oral, help them interact with these texts while creating a classroom culture of shared literacy. We apply these strategies primarily to independent reading books, but they can also be used with texts we are reading together as a class.

## Why We Like It

The activities we list in this strategy all serve to encourage student investment in reading while gaining authentic writing and speaking practice. In addition, they reinforce literary terms and concepts. We want our students to discuss their reading in meaningful and engaging ways, not in ways that feel obligatory, monotonous, or always tied to a grade. The following activities provide students with the opportunity to share their reading in creative, fun ways. They also reflect how readers talk about books outside the classroom—we don't know many people who write a book report every time they finish a book!

## Supporting Research

Much research confirms the benefits of having students read books of their own choice and giving them time to read these books during the school day (Calkins & Ehrenworth, n.d.; Russ on Reading, 2016).

Research also indicates that students are more motivated to read and discuss their books when they know they will be discussing them with their peers (Bedee, 2010, p. 64).

In addition, students tend to be more invested in the task if they are writing for authentic audiences, as opposed to just for the teacher (Ferlazzo, 2009, April 1). Research has found that mandatory reading logs, however, can have a detrimental effect on students' motivation for reading (Pak & Weseley, 2012, p. 260; Reischer, 2016).

Further, studies show that having students simulate actions and skills they will be using in the future, such as self-selected reading and discussing their insights with others, increases the chance of transferring these behaviors to situations outside the classroom (Perkins & Salomon, n.d., 1992).

## Common Core Connections

The Addendum for English Language Learners published in the Common Core State Standards states that ELLs must have access to "opportunities for classroom discourse and interaction that are well-designed to enable ELLs to develop communicative strengths in language arts" (Council of Chief State Officers and the National Governors Association, n.d., p. 2). Literary conversations provides these opportunities. It can also support several of the Common Core State Reading Standards as students draw conclusions about a text and support their inferences with evidence. This strategy can also be used to support several of the Listening and Speaking Standards under "Comprehension and Collaboration."

## Application

The following activities are a few of the alternatives to traditional reading logs or book reports that we use in class. Many more can be found on the sites listed in Technology Connections. These activities can be modified for different English proficiency levels and can either incorporate technology or be done as low-tech versions. In Strategy 1: Independent Reading, we discussed providing our students with the opportunity to read books of their choice during independent reading time. We have found they are more motivated to engage in conversations about these types of high-interest, self- selected books. However, the following activities could also be used with a text that the class is reading together.

### BOOK TRAILERS

Book trailers are an engaging way to help students write and talk about their reading. This strategy also invites students to practice elements of argumentation as they present a claim and back it up with specific reasons and evidence.

The teacher can begin by showing students some examples of book trailers (see Technology Connections) and asking students to write down what these examples have in common. The teacher might ask, "Do they summarize the whole book or just describe some elements of the story?" "Do they offer reasons why someone should read the book?" "How do the images appeal to readers?" After studying the examples, students then choose a favorite book and begin creating their own trailer. The teacher can give students a handout listing the elements that the book trailer must include (see Figure 2.1: Book Trailer for an example) or the teacher and students can come up with a list together.

Students can do a low-tech version by displaying their book while they read their trailer in front of the class, in small groups, or when visiting another classroom. They could also create a book trailer poster (similar to a movie poster) with the title, main characters' names, images representing the story, and a rating (e.g., five stars). Students could then display their posters and take turns sharing their book trailers in small groups or as a class.

Creating digital book trailers can be even more engaging for students and results in a living archive where students can go for inspiration. There are several great tools students can use to create digital book trailers (see Technology Connections).

## BOOK TALKS

Book talks are another great way for students to interact with their reading and gain valuable speaking practice. The teacher can give students questions to answer about the books they are reading (e.g., "Why did you choose this book?" "What do you like about this book?" "Why should another student read this book?"). Students answer the questions in writing and then use them to do a book talk with a partner, in a small group, or for the whole class (we would recommend doing one or two a day, rather than having students listen to 30 book talks in a row!). This activity enables classmates to hear about other interesting books their classmates are reading and helps to build a classroom culture of shared literacy (see Figure 2.2: Book Talk for an example of the directions we give to students).

## PARTNER READING

Reading self-selected books in pairs is another activity that builds engagement in literacy. It provides student choice; reading, speaking, listening, and writing practice; an authentic audience; and immediate feedback.

Once a week in our combined beginner-intermediate class, students pair up—primarily, but not exclusively, with one beginner and one intermediate (we have found that pairing students up in this way is less frustrating for the beginner and more confidence-boosting for the intermediate). We post Figure 2.3: Partner-Reading Instructions and students are given a couple of minutes to choose a book. Then we explain to students they will read one paragraph at a time aloud to each other. After reading (we usually give students about ten minutes of reading time), they choose three new words they encountered, write them down on a piece of paper, and learn what they mean. In addition, they draw a picture that represents what they read and write a sentence that explains why they liked or didn't like the book. Students then can either present to groups of other students or we record their presentation using one of many apps (see Technology Connections).

## BOOK INTERVIEWS

Book interviews are another way for students to interact with the books that they and their classmates are reading. In this activity, students work in pairs to interview each other about the books they are currently reading. We give students Figure 2.4: Book Interview, where they can take notes as they ask their partner questions about his or her book. The teacher can create the questions for the form or students can come up with their own. After partners are finished interviewing each other, they can use their notes to prepare a short presentation about their partner's book, which they can present to the class, in small groups, or record them to post on a class blog.

## GOLDEN LINES

This activity, which we were first introduced to by the WRITE Institute (https://writeinstitute.sdcoe.net/), can be used to instantly generate students to think, write, and discuss their reading. It involves students reading a text and identifying a "golden line"—a sentence that is surprising, descriptive, thought-provoking, meaningful, and so on. Students can copy this golden line onto a piece of paper and write why they selected it. Sometimes we have students illustrate it as well. Then students share their golden lines with each other in pairs, small groups, or as a class. They can also be posted on the classroom wall or shared online.

## CREATIVE RESPONSE PROMPTS

Traditional reading strategies, such as making a prediction, asking a question, summarizing, and so on (see Strategy 10: Reading Comprehension), are obviously important for students to practice. However, when we want to spice things up, we'll provide students with more-creative response prompts. We've found these types of prompts promote more intrinsically motivating reading responses and sharing among our students while building higher-order thinking. The following prompts include some of the possibilities:

- **Plot Twist:** Choose a part of the book you have read and explain how you would change the story. Why would you make these changes?

- **Be a Therapist:** Give advice to one of the book's characters. What would you tell him or her to do, and why?

- **Dear Diary:** Pick a character from your book and write an entry in his or her diary.

- **Texting or Tweeting:** Choose two characters from your book and write a conversation they might have through text messages or on Twitter. Think about what emojis they might use, what their Twitter names might be, and what hashtags they might use.

- **Trading Card:** Choose a character and make a trading card. On one side draw a picture of the character and on the other side write important facts and traits about this character.

- **Rename It:** Write a new title for your book, and explain why you chose this title.

- **What If...?:** Write a question about your book that begins with "What if...?" (for example, in *The Hunger Games,* "What if Katniss didn't volunteer as a tribute?") and then write a response to your question.

Some of these prompts were modified from a list by Ross Cooper (2015).

## Student Handouts and Examples

Figure 2.1: Book Trailer
Figure 2.2: Book Talk
Figure 2.3: Partner-Reading Instructions
Figure 2.4: Book Interview

## What Could Go Wrong?

As we stated, these activities represent alternatives to required reading logs, which often squash student interest in reading. However, even engaging, meaningful activities can become rote or less motivating when tied to external motivators (i.e., grades, rewards, mandates) (Ferlazzo, 2010, May 17a). Keeping the end goal of creating lifelong readers in mind means balancing accountability with choice and recognizing individual students' circumstances.

Some teachers may be hesitant to ask their beginning-level students to have literary conversations. However, our beginners have been able to do so with modifications, such as drawing and sharing pictures about their books and using teacher-provided sentence stems (such as the ones in Figure 2.4: Book Interview) to scaffold book discussions.

## Technology Connections

Social media apps provide a highly engaging way for students to share their reading with their peers. Students can create and share book snaps using Snapchat or Instagram by simply snapping a picture of text and adding their own annotations, highlighting, and other visual representations. For further explanation and how-to videos on booksnaps see #BookSnap—Snapping for Learning (www.tarammartin .com/booksnaps-snapping-for-learning/) and 15 Second Book Talks Take 1 (https://sharpread.wordpress.com/2017/04/17/15-second-book-talks-take-1/).

Tools for creating and sharing digital book trailers, along with many examples, can be found at The Best Posts on Books: Why They're Important & How to Help Students Select, Read, Write, and Discuss Them (http://larryferlazzo.edublogs .org/2010/05/30/my-best-posts-on-books-why-theyre-important-how-to-help-students-select-read-write-discuss-them/).

Specific ideas on using Instagram and other online tools for book trailers can be found at The Best Resources for Learning to Use the Video Apps "Vine" & Instagram (http://larryferlazzo.edublogs.org/2013/02/18/the-best-resources-for-learning-to-use-the-video-app-twine/).

Online tools for recording and sharing student presentations on books (book talks, book interview, partner reading poster) can be found at The Best Sites to Practice Speaking English (http://larryferlazzo.edublogs.org/2008/03/17/the-best-sites-to-practice-speaking-english).

Students can create simple videos using Shadow Puppet (http://larryferlazzo .edublogs.org/2014/11/07/heres-a-new-reading-activity-i-tried-out-today-that-went-pretty-well/), Apple Clips (http://larryferlazzo.edublogs.org/2017/04/06/ apples-new-video-editing-app-clips-is-much-more/), and Adobe Spark (http:// larryferlazzo.edublogs.org/2017/01/24/video-adobe-spark-is-excellent-tool-for-ells/).

What-if questions and responses can be used to further critical thinking and language development in any subject area. For a list of resources, including sample what-if projects for social studies, see The Best Resources for Teaching "What If" History Lessons (http://larryferlazzo.edublogs.org/2012/05/19/the-best-resources-for-teaching-what-if-history-lessons/).

## Attribution

Portions of this section originally appeared in our books, *The ESL/ELL Teacher's Survival Guide* (Ferlazzo & Sypnieski, 2012, p. 127,131–132) and *Navigating the Common Core with English Language Learners* (Ferlazzo & Sypnieski, 2016, p. 96–98).

# Figures

Use this guide to create a book trailer about a favorite book that you read this semester. Remember, a trailer is like a commercial—you are trying to sell this book to your classmates. You will need to give specific reasons *why* they should read this book. Your trailer should be no more than two minutes long and should include the following:

- A brief, but catchy introduction that includes the title, author, and genre of the book
- A one-sentence summary of the book
- Two specific reasons why your classmates should read this book (be convincing, but don't give away any secrets!)
- Share either your favorite character or a favorite line from the book and include why you like him, her, or it

**Figure 2.1** Book Trailer *Source:* Modified from Ferlazzo & Sypnieski, *The ESL/ELL Teacher's Survival Guide* (2012, p. 131–132).

**First**, answer the following questions about your book:

1. What is the title of your book?
   The title of my book is _____.

2. Who is the author of the book?
   The author is _____.

3. Why did you choose to read this book?
   I chose this book because _____.

4. What is the book about?
   This book is about _____.

5. What do you like about this book?
   I like this book because _____.

6. Write down an important sentence from your book and explain why you picked it.
   An important sentence in my book is "_____."
   I picked this sentence because _____.

**Second**, use your answers above to **practice** doing a book talk with a partner.

**Third**, find a new partner and give your book talk. Remember to hold up your book while you are talking.

**Figure 2.2**  Book Talk *Source:* Modified from Exhibit 5.4 in *The ESL/ELL Teacher's Survival Guide* (Ferlazzo & Sypnieski, 2012, p. 131).

1. Find someone you want to read with and sit next to him or her—30 seconds

2. Pick a book you want to read together—2 minutes

3. Get one piece of paper for each pair of students—30 seconds

4. Read the book aloud to each other, taking turns. You will read together for 10 minutes.

5. On the piece of paper, write (for 10 minutes):
   - Your names
   - The title of your book
   - Three words that are new to you in the book
   - What those words mean, in your own words
   - A picture representing the book
   - Finish one of these sentences:

     "We liked this book because_____." "We didn't like this book because _____."

6. Practice presenting your poster, with each person saying about half of what you wrote.

7. You will present in small groups and/or record it for the class blog.

**Figure 2.3** Partner-Reading Instructions *Source:* Reprinted from Ferlazzo & Sypnieski, *Navigating the Common Core with English Language Learners* (2016, p. 98).

My name: _____

My partner's name: _____

Ask your partner the following questions and write down his or her answers:

1. What is the title of your book? Who is the author?

2. Have you read any other books written by this author? If yes, which books?

3. Is your book fiction or nonfiction? How do you know this?

4. What is your book about?

5. Why did you choose to read this book?

6. Would you recommend this book to a friend? Why or why not?

**Figure 2.4**   Book Interview

# STRATEGY 3

# Graphic Organizers

## What Is It?

A graphic organizer is a visual display or template used to scaffold students' reading, writing, listening, and speaking activities. They support students in tackling demanding cognitive and linguistic tasks.

Although there are many different types of graphic organizers, some of the most common ones are story maps, KWL charts, Venn diagrams, concept maps, idea webs, cause-and-effect diagrams, and flow charts.

## Why We Like It

The strategy of using graphic organizers is an essential part of our daily instruction. We use them often to promote active learning and engagement. They serve as critical scaffolds to move students toward more-complex tasks, such as writing academic essays or giving formal presentations. We've found that ELL students especially need the visual processing opportunities that graphic organizers provide, along with the academic language and structures contained in them. We try to give students practice with a variety of organizers and encourage them to reflect on which ones are more effective and why. We also provide time for students to create their own graphic organizers. We want students to be able to produce their own when we're not around to support their learning in future ELA classes and in other content areas. Most important, graphic organizers promote students' self-efficacy so they can take on increasingly more-challenging academic tasks.

## Supporting Research

Many studies support the use of graphic organizers in all subject areas to increase students' reading comprehension and vocabulary knowledge (Strangman et al., 2004, p. 6–7).

In addition, research has shown that they can be specifically beneficial to English language learners (Sam D & Rajan, 2013, p. 166–167).

Studies also point to many positive effects of graphic organizers on student writing. When used in the prewriting process, they can have a major impact on students' ability to clarify and organize their thoughts before writing (Brown, 2011, p. 9).

Their use can also promote increased student motivation for writing (Tayib, 2015, p. 1).

## Common Core Connections

Graphic organizers can be used to support a variety of learning tasks that can meet any of the Common Core Anchor Standards in all four domains! The graphic organizers shared in the Application section specifically support the Standards for narrative writing.

## Application

In this section we will share how we scaffold a unit on story with our beginning English language learners (see our previous book, *Navigating the Common Core with English Language Learners,* 2016, for examples of how we scaffold a unit on argument with ELL students at all levels). We teach this unit a few months into the school year, after first focusing on survival and core English skills.

### READING

We start by providing our students with Figure 3.1: Narrative Word Chart to introduce our students to key words related to the genre. Word charts are critical tools used to support students in acquiring the vocabulary and academic language needed to access reading and writing tasks. Teachers and students can create different formats of word charts, which students can access in their binders or folders. Larger versions can be posted on the classroom wall.

We first read *The Story of Ferdinand* (Leaf, 1977). We read it aloud as students follow along in their own copies of the book and identify new words that they think are important to know. Then, after every third or fourth page we stop and ask students to write down three words that are new to them on Figure 3.2: Identifying

Words While Reading. Students can work together and use an online dictionary to find the meanings. We remind them to try to restate the meaning using their own words and not just copy the definition.

Then, students get into small groups or pairs to complete a dictation activity for the pages we just read. They are given mini-whiteboards and markers, and they take turns reading a few sentences of the story to each other while the other writes the words down on the board (if necessary, students can "cheat" by looking at the book). The reader checks the accuracy of the writer. We then come back together as a class and repeat the process with the next few pages. Depending on student engagement, we may continue the process through the rest of the story or vary the process by simply reading a few pages without doing the vocabulary or dictation activities (see Strategy 24: Dictation).

In order to keep interest high with our teenage students (remember this example is a children's book), we encourage students to make connections between themselves and the text. For example, you may remember that Ferdinand has his favorite spot under the cork tree. At that point in the story, we pause and provide students with this sentence starter: "My favorite spot is because ____." They create mini-posters on white copy paper and share them in small groups.

Next, we complete a story map together as a class—there are a zillion versions of story maps that can be found online. We make sure that the story map we select contains the genre-related words we are focusing on (see Figure 3.1: Narrative Word Chart) and is visually simple with enough space for students to write. We have found the most-challenging part of the story map is helping our students understand *theme* and, to a lesser extent, *protagonist-antagonist*. To reinforce these concepts, we ask students to create a quick poster for three of their favorite movies or stories and to identify the theme and the protagonists and antagonists in each (we provide a teacher model as well).

We have students go back into the story and make a list of sensory words and details used in the text. We then work together to add additional related words to each column on Figure 3.2: Five Senses Chart. See Figure 3.3 for a student-completed example of this chart.

Next, we read the book *The Teacher from the Black Lagoon* (Thaler, 2000) using a similar process. We find this book is engaging and supports critical school vocabulary.

## WRITING

After our reading, we revisit the narrative word chart to reinforce our understanding of the vocabulary and to make note of any new learnings. Students are then ready to apply their knowledge of these concepts to writing their own stories.

So, do we hand out the prompt and take a seat? No, we do not (though on some days it may be more tempting than others). We do hand out graphic organizers that support students as they progress through the writing process.

We often use backwards mapping or planning when developing a unit for our students. In other words, we think about what the culminating task will be (in this case, writing a story) and what instructional steps and scaffolding students will need to get there.

Here are some universal questions that we ask ourselves when creating or choosing graphic organizers to support students in navigating complex learning tasks. Following each question is an explanation of how we address it within the context of our unit on story.

1. What prior knowledge do students possess about the learning task? Is it necessary to build more background knowledge?

   In this instance, students have already built background knowledge by reading the two books and completing story maps and sensory detail charts.

2. What are the key elements students need to know in order to achieve the complex learning task?

   In this unit, students need to develop their own story with a setting, characters (including a protagonist and an antagonist), a plot containing conflict and a resolution, and a theme. They must also employ the narrative strategies of using imagery and dialogue. The graphic organizers we use (Figures 3.3–3.12) enable students to develop their ideas and language for each story element one at a time. This process increases motivation and decreases anxiety as students gradually build their writing skills and confidence. It also enables students to see how each organizer is connected and develops from the previous one. This steady advancement builds on research showing that one of the key factors in developing intrinsic motivation is seeing progress in one's work (also known as the progress principle, www .progressprinciple.com/).

3. What is the vocabulary level of students?

   A student's English proficiency level must be taken into consideration when developing a graphic organizer. For example, this unit is designed for beginners, so several of the graphic organizers (see Figures 3.5–3.8) contain a box for students to draw their ideas. After drawing, students can label the items they know and seek assistance from other students and the teacher to identify the English words that are new to them. Students can then use this bank of words to write sentences on the lines below their drawing.

4. What organizational structures or language techniques do students need to know in order to achieve the learning task?

In the story unit, students need to sequence the events in their story and include a conflict and a resolution. Figure 3.10: Story Events provides a visual tool on which students can write the events of their story in order. Students also need to employ the narrative strategies of using imagery and dialogue. Figure 3.10: Story Events also asks students to incorporate sensory details from Figure 3.3: Five Senses Chart. Figure 3.11: Dialogue encourages students to create a dialogue between two characters and gives them an opportunity to practice structuring it with quotation marks. All of this practice boosts their confidence and serves to prepare them for the final task of writing a story.

## Student Handouts and Examples

Figure 3.1: Narrative Word Chart

Figure 3.2: Identifying Words While Reading

Figure 3.3: Five Senses Chart

Figure 3.4: Five Senses Chart Student Example

Figure 3.5: Setting

Figure 3.6: Main Characters

Figure 3.7: Supporting Characters

Figure 3.8: Theme

Figure 3.9: Conflict Map

Figure 3.10: Story Events

Figure 3.11: Dialogue

Figure 3.12: Write Your Story

## What Could Go Wrong?

Providing students with graphic organizers without any instruction or modeling in how to use them can render them ineffective and result in student frustration. Graphic organizers that are overly complicated or have complex directions can have the same results. Have we ever passed out a graphic organizer without modeling it first? Of course! Have we used a mediocre graphic organizer because we didn't have time to make a better one? Yes! However, we try to minimize these situations and we hope you will, too.

A note of further caution: Don't hand out a big packet of graphic organizers, no matter how cool you think they are. This will be a disaster and you may be greeted with expressions of disbelief. Having students complete them *one at a time* over several class periods will result in more-engaged students and better-quality work. In addition, as students complete the graphic organizers, be sure to stop periodically so that they can share with partners what they have done. Teachers can also encourage students with higher English proficiency to help their classmates.

## Technology Connections

We haven't found any huge benefits for our students in completing graphic organizers online as opposed to with pencil and paper. That said, we sometimes have our students use online versions of graphic organizers for a change of pace. For a list of what we think are some of the better mind-mapping and flow chart tools (all free and all accessible to English language learners) and sources for hard-copy graphic organizers, see The Best List of Mindmapping, Flow Chart Tools, & Graphic Organizers at https://larryferlazzo.edublogs.org/2009/02/09/not-the-best-but-a-list-of-mindmapping-flow-chart-tools-graphic-organizers/comment-page-1/.

## Attribution

We were introduced to using *The Story of Ferdinand* (Leaf, 1977) in a genre-based short story unit by the WRITE Institute, though the series of lessons shared in this section are substantially different. For information on WRITE and their curriculum resources see https://writeinstitute.sdcoe.net/. Figure 3.5 was also inspired by a graphic organizer from the WRITE Institute.

## Figures

| Word | Meaning in English | Meaning in Home Language | Picture |
|------|--------------------|-----------------------|---------|
| Protagonist | | | |
| Antagonist | | | |
| Characters | | | |
| Setting | | | |
| Conflict | | | |
| Events | | | |
| Dialogue | | | |
| Resolution | | | |
| Theme | | | |

**Figure 3.1** Narrative Word Chart

| Page Number Word | Definition In English Using My Own Words | Definition in Home Language and/or Picture | My Own Sentence |
|---|---|---|---|
|  |  |  |  |
|  |  |  |  |
|  |  |  |  |
|  |  |  |  |

**Figure 3.2**  Identifying Words While Reading

| Name_____  **Five Senses Chart** | Sights |
|---|---|
| **Sounds** | **Smells** |
| **Tastes** | **Touch** |

**Figure 3.3**  Five Senses Chart

Name_____

# Five
# Senses
# Chart

**Sights**

- green grass
- beautiful flowers
- red cape
- huge arena with many people
- colorful flags

**Sounds**

- quiet under the cork tree
- a bumble bee buzzing
- puffing and snorting
- people yelling
- people clapping
- music playing

**Smells**

- fresh flowers
- grass
- dust
- food cooking
- animals

**Tastes**

- sweet grass
- delicious food
- salty
- sweet

**Touch**

- cool breeze
- soft grass
- painful sting
- hot sun

**Figure 3.4** Five Senses Chart Student Example

Your Name _____

**Setting**

When does your story take place? _____

Where does your story take place? Draw it and use as many details as possible. What do the characters in your story see? What is the weather like? What objects, animals, are there? What colors do they see?

Describe the setting and include adjectives (colors, size, shape, temperature, smells, sounds, etc.). *Examples:* There is a blue sky. The school is big. The park is shaped like a square. The weather is very hot. It smells like bread. A dog is barking:

_____

_____

_____

_____

_____

_____

**Figure 3.5** Setting

Your Name _____

**Main Characters**

What is the name of the protagonist? _____

Draw the protagonist:

| | Describe your protagonist: How old is he or she? What does he or she look like? How does he or she feel? What kind of clothes is she or he wearing? What is her or his hair color? |
|---|---|

What is the name of the antagonist? _____

Draw the antagonist:

| | Describe your protagonist: How old is he or she? What does he or she look like? How does he or she feel? What kind of clothes is she or he wearing? What is her or his hair color? |
|---|---|

**Figure 3.6** Main Characters

Your Name _____

Who are the other characters?

Name _____          Name _____

_____        _____

_____        _____

_____        _____

_____        _____

Name _____          Name _____

_____        _____

_____        _____

_____        _____

_____        _____

**Figure 3.7** Supporting Characters

Your Name _____

## Theme

What is the theme of your story? Circle one or create your own:

Good beats evil.

Love conquers all.

Be true to yourself.

Friendship is important.

Beauty is on the inside.

Being brave is better than being a coward.

Racism is bad.

It is important to be kind.

We should try new things.

Other theme: _____

How will your story show that theme? Draw it:

Describe the picture (for example, The strong man kills the monster. That shows that good is better than bad.):

_____

_____

_____

**Figure 3.8** Theme

## Conflict Map

**What is the conflict?**

**What are some ways the conflict could be resolved?**

**Why does this conflict occur?**

**Figure 3.9** Conflict Map *Source:* Reproduced with the permission of NCTE/ReadWriteThink. This resource was provided by ReadWriteThink.org, a website developed by the National Council of Teachers of English.

Your Name _____

**Story Events**

Describe what happens. Please try to include words from the Five Senses sheet.

First:

Second:

Third:

Fourth:

Fifth:

Sixth:

Resolution:

**Figure 3.10** Story Events

Your Name _____

**Dialogue**

What is a dialogue at least two of your characters can have and in which event (First? Second? Third? . . .)?

Be sure to use quotation marks!

This dialogue takes place in Event Number _____

Name of character:
_____

Name of character:
_____

Name of character:
_____

Name of character:
_____

Name of character:
_____

Name of character:
_____

**Figure 3.11** Dialogue

Your Name _____

You may use a lined sheet of paper. Please write it in this order, using paragraphs:

**1.** Describe the setting.

**2.** Introduce the protagonist and antagonist.

**3.** Tell about the different events. Be sure to include a dialogue.

**4.** Write the resolution.

**Figure 3.12** Write Your Story

# STRATEGY 4

# Vocabulary

## What Is It?

Many of the other strategies we've discussed in this book are related to learning vocabulary—Strategy 1: Independent Reading, Strategy 9: Jigsaw, Strategy 11: Inductive Learning, Strategy 17: Using Photos or Other Images in Reading and Writing, and Strategy 23: Learning Games for Reading and Writing—just to name a few. We thought it would also be important to share examples of several other strategies we use, and provide a big-picture look at what generally works for English language learners in vocabulary instruction.

Respected education researcher Robert Marzano (2009) developed a widely used and research-backed six-step process for effective vocabulary instruction. We use it with minor modifications, and all the strategies listed under Application fit into at least one of the steps.

Here is that model with our personal tweaks:

1. First, the teacher pronounces the word—whether it's in the context of pre-teaching words needed for an upcoming text or unit, saying it while doing a read aloud, or introducing it as part of a cline or word web (see the Application section). We usually write it on the board or overhead, as well. Marzano doesn't explicitly point out the act of pronunciation in the six-step process. However, it's a crucial step for ELLs.

2. Next, the teacher describes the word using various examples—with an image or using different sentences.

3. Third, the student needs to actively process the word through writing his or her own definition (in English or in a home language) and drawing an image. Students can use an online dictionary for ideas, but they need to be reminded not to copy a definition word-for-word. Of course, this takes teacher modeling and student practice. We also encourage students to use the word in an original sentence.

These first three steps are completed right on the same day that the new vocabulary is introduced.

The following three activities are done within the next few days and beyond—reinforcing exercises (some of our favorites are categorization, clines, word webs and online exercises), student discussions, and games.

It's clear that multiple exposures to new words in different contexts (Thornbury, 2013, describes this as the principal of re-contextualization and the principle of multiple encounters) is critical, though there is not universal agreement about the exact number of repetitions needed before the word is fully learned. Some researchers suggest eight to ten times in different contexts will do the trick (Rossiter et al., 2016).

Similar to Marzano, we're big fans of games for reinforcing new vocabulary, and there is no shortage of different options in Strategy 23: Learning Games for Reading and Writing.

## Why We Like It

The strategies we list in the Application section are engaging to our students and can fit within the Marzano framework. Many of these strategies work in just about any instance or allotted amount of time. None of them require extensive teacher prep.

## Supporting Research

Extensive research supports the importance of using multiple methods of vocabulary instruction rather than focusing on one or two (Ford-Connors & Paratore, 2015; National Reading Technical Assistance Center, 2010). These methods should include explicit instruction (prior to and during reading of the text), active student participation (such as writing their own sentences using the word and drawing images as part of their definitions), repeated exposure to words in different contexts (Rossiter et al., 2016), and wide reading (Feldman & Kinsella, 2005, p. 4). Marzano's (2009) six steps, which include many of these elements, have been shown to be widely effective.

## Common Core Connections

There are four Standards under the heading "Vocabulary Acquisition and Use" in Language. Each of the applications we share meet one or more of these Standards.

# Application

Here are nine specific instructional strategies that we use in vocabulary instruction.

## FOUR WORDS SHEET

We ask that students identify four new words they learned that week during class or outside of class—and that they think are important—and complete Figure 4.1: Four Words Sheet. Every Friday, students share them with a partner using the question and sentence starters on Figure 4.2: Question and Sentence Starters List. This list roughly starts at easy and progresses to more difficult with the latter ones using academic language. Students choose which ones they want to use. After all students have shared with a partner, they each make a poster for one word to teach to the entire class and add it to the interactive word wall (see that section).

## WORD CHART

A word chart is a simple graphic organizer used to pre-teach important vocabulary that students will encounter in an upcoming text or writing genre. The teacher identifies ten or so key words and either provides a copy of a word chart graphic organizer with the words already printed or with blank spaces for students to write them. Figure 4.3 is the Narrative Word Chart we use in our story unit (see Strategy 3: Graphic Organizers).

The teacher pronounces two or three words at a time and then gives students several minutes to access any prior knowledge and then look up the meanings online. Students write the definition in their home language and in English (with the admonition to put it in their own words and not copy it from a dictionary). In addition, students draw an image that represents the word.

Students then share with a partner, make any needed revisions, and then the entire class reviews those words with the teacher calling on individual students to share what they wrote and drew.

The process is then repeated until all the words are reviewed. Afterward, we'll sometimes divide up the words and ask students to make a small poster for each word that we'll tape up on an interactive word wall (see that topic later in Application).

## TEACHING NEW WORDS DURING READING

The research cited previously finds that explicit instruction of new vocabulary before and during the reading of a text is an effective teaching and learning strategy. When we are reading a short text (e.g., a read aloud or think aloud; see Strategy 10: Reading Comprehension) we might see a word we suspect is new to many students and attempt to seamlessly teach it (e.g., "It was difficult [very hard, not easy] to do."). Many of these words end up on students' four words sheets.

When we are reading a short book together, such as *The Story of Ferdinand* (Leaf, 1977) or *The Teacher from the Black Lagoon* (Thaler, 2000), we'll show the pages on the document camera and read them aloud. We will quickly and explicitly teach key words that we think might be new to students and are crucial to understanding the story. We do not stop and teach *every* word. Then, we have students stop after we've read three or four pages and choose three words that are new to them. Next, they add these words to Figure 4.4: Identifying Words While Reading. They generally use an online dictionary and, as usual, we remind students to not copy what it says and, instead, use their own words. We next have students get into groups of two or three to share what they wrote and make any appropriate revisions. They then do a dictation activity with mini-whiteboards on the pages we just read together (see Strategy 24: Dictation) before we reconvene as a class and proceed to the next few pages.

Interestingly, no clear connection has yet been found in the research on vocabulary instruction suggesting that spending a lengthy period of time on teaching the meaning of a word (e.g., two to three minutes) is more effective than spending one or two minutes on it (Wright & Cervetti, 2016, p. 11). We are not surprised at this finding based on Larry's experience of falling asleep during a professional development training session in which the trainer spent 30 minutes teaching the word *expedition*. The only exception to our time rule is when we teach academic language in a humorous and engaging manner that includes active student processing and physical movement.

## ACADEMIC VOCABULARY

As you probably know, the authors of the Common Core Standards rely on research (Common Core State Standards Initiative, n.d.a, p. 33) dividing words into three categories, called Tiers 1, 2, and 3. Tier 1 is composed of words used often in typical oral conversation, Tier 2 includes general academic vocabulary often found in many different kinds of school texts (e.g., *vary, accumulated, request*). Tier 3 are domain-specific words found in content textbooks (e.g., *photosynthesis, legislature*).

When it comes time to teach academic vocabulary, we mainly focus on Tier 2 words because we feel we can get a bigger bang for the buck. These words will make more texts accessible to our students than Tier 3 words.

We take vocabulary word lists (the Technology Connections section has suggestions of where to obtain them online for free) and teach 8 to 12 Tier 2 words from them each week. We give students a copy of one page of the word list to paste in their writer's notebook (see Strategy 18: Writer's Notebook). We pronounce a word, define it, and then write a humorous question and answer:

> *Would you **compare** Mr. Ferlazzo to an egg?*
> *Yes, I would **compare** Mr. Ferlazzo to an egg because his bald head is smooth.*

We write the question on the document camera, say it, have students repeat it, and then do the same with the answer. We do the same for two more words, and then students break into small groups of two or three to practice asking and answering the same questions. In addition, they write their own questions and responses using the same words and share them. Each time we do this process, they also practice some of the words, questions, and answers from previous lessons. This is always a high-interest activity, and students particularly look forward to developing sentences that make fun of Larry!

Another common strategy for helping students learn and apply academic vocabulary is through the use of sentence starters. We discuss the use of sentence starters throughout this book (particularly in Strategy 14: Writing Frames and Writing Structures), and you can find links to downloadable word lists in the Technology Connections section.

## CLINES

Clines are scales, or spectrums, of words that go from one extreme to the other (e.g., freezing, cold, room temperature, warm, hot, boiling). Two examples can be found in Figure 4.5: Clines.

We prefer to teach clines by first taping up words from the cline in different sections of the room. Then, we show a blank cline (just the line without the words) on the document camera and have students copy it down in their writer's notebook. Next, we ask students a series of questions, which they answer by going to the appropriately labeled part of the room (e.g., in the love-hate cline, we ask questions such as "How do you feel about Justin Bieber?" or "How do you feel about our school's cafeteria food?" Or, if you're feeling brave, you can ask "How do you feel about your teacher?"). We ask different questions quickly so students are moving relatively fast from one section of the room to another. Then, students return to their seats and we complete the cline on the overhead together.

As a follow-up, students could create their own unique clines tied to their interests (e.g., "I hate beets"; "I love salsa picante"). Time permitting, students can then orally share what they wrote with a partner.

There are many other word groupings suitable for clines. English teacher Jonny Ingham (n.d.) has several on his website: https://eflrecipes.com/2014/03/18/clines/.


## WORD WEBS

*Word webs, semantic mapping, word maps* are the names given to graphic organizers that in some way map connections between words. Teachers use them in all sizes and in varying degrees of complexity; search the web and you'll see what we mean. They typically have one word in the middle with lots of words connected to that central one as well as others branching off from each other.

In the picture word inductive model (PWIM) (see Strategy 11: Inductive Learning), we have students essentially do the same thing when they categorize words from the picture and add new ones. We just have them divide their papers into columns instead of creating a word web. We've never seen any advantage to having students write them as a map while using the PWIM. However, as in everything we do, we always remain open to learning how to do things in a better way.

We keep our word webs simple when we use them and generally they are in preparation for a writing assignment. We might use a version to help students identify words that fit under the five senses (see Strategy 3: Graphic Organizers). Or we'll identify an important word that is key to a text they are reading and that they will be writing about (e.g., the word *scared*) and have them identify synonyms in a word web. We use the word *web organizer* because it can be a nice change of pace for students, not because we believe it has any major advantage over a chart or list. That said, a word web or map can sometimes make connections between words more visible to some students. We want to provide our students with a variety of learning and organizational tools so they can choose what works best for them now and in the future.

There are several online tools that are ideal for ELLs to use when generating these kinds of word webs, which we discuss in the Technology Connections section.


## INTERACTIVE WORD WALL

Many teachers are familiar with the idea of a word wall, though fewer might know the term *interactive word wall.* The traditional definitions for both, and their real-life uses, can vary widely. There's strong research supporting the idea that any version can assist vocabulary development by helping to create a print-rich classroom (Harmon et al., 2009; Southerland, 2011).

Because there is such a wide variance among them (just search *word wall* and *interactive word wall* online), we'll use this section to explain what it means to us and how we apply it in our classrooms.

Generally, the idea of an *interactive* word wall means that students interact with it in some way—it's not just a bunch of words stuck on the wall for decoration. Our interactive word walls typically have five elements (depending on the English levels of our students) and are often located in different parts of the classroom so they don't all just blend into each other. Some things they all have in common, however, are that the words are organized in some way, clearly written so they can be seen from most parts of the classroom, always being modified, and accompanied by an image (at least, most of the time).

The five elements of our interactive word wall are as follows:

- A labeled picture used with the weekly PWIM theme (see Strategy 11: Inductive Learning). This picture is almost always in the front of the classroom; these themes could be home, school, health, holidays, and so on; if we are in a classroom that has the appropriate physical layout we'll put retired labeled PWIM photos on the wall near the ceiling

- A chart of irregular verb conjugations

- A section devoted to total physical response (TPR) (see Strategy 26) words; easier words are regularly removed

- A section devoted to important words related to the writing genre we are using at the time, such as the words in a narrative word chart (see Figure 4.3)

- A section devoted to new words identified by students as part of their four words sheet assignment (see Figure 4.1)

Many of the words and pictures illustrating them—particularly for the writing genre and four words sheets—are created by students following these simple guidelines (with exemplars to demonstrate them):

- The words are written on a 4″× 11″ piece of construction paper.

- The letters need to be as large as possible, and they must contrast clearly with the background of the construction paper.

- Students can choose the color of the paper, and they must also devote at least some thought to considering if the color helps communicate the meaning of the word (e.g., blue for the word *ocean*).

- A simple and colorful picture representing the meaning of the word must be drawn on the last three or so inches of the paper.

Trust us, having exemplars and these precise instructions are not overdoing it!

We don't want to have too many words on our walls. They can blend in and end up looking more like clutter instead of a scaffold. We retire words from the four words sheet every Friday; however, we retire them in a productive way—last week's words are turned around and shown through our window so the hundreds of students who walk past each day can see them. Knowing that their word posters will have an authentic audience also motivates students to do a particularly good job on them!

## COGNATES

Cognates are words in different languages that have some similarity in spelling, meaning, and pronunciation. Although English does not have many cognates in most languages, it is estimated that more than 30% of English words have similar ones in Spanish (www.colorincolorado.org/article/using-cognates-develop-comprehension-english). These connections can provide a big benefit to our Spanish-speaking ELLs.

We don't do specific lessons on cognates or the small number of false cognates (words that have similar spelling and pronunciation but don't share the same meaning). We feel that teaching cognates in isolation is equally as ineffective as teaching any vocabulary out of context. However, because we both speak Spanish, it is easy for us to identify and highlight cognates when we see them in the course of our teaching (however, usually our Spanish-speaking students beat us to it). For teachers who don't speak Spanish, it's a great opportunity to do a quick lesson on cognates and give a few examples (there are many lists online). Then, invite and regularly remind students that you would love it if they would point out words that they believe are cognates in the texts the class is reading or that they are reading independently. Everyone can learn together!

## FROM CLUES TO WORDS

This is a fun activity that we use occasionally in conjunction with the theme we're teaching with the PWIM. We first ask each student to think about words in his or her home language that are connected to the theme, but which he or she has not yet learned. We ask that each student write down four words in his or her home language. For example, if we are studying *home*, students might write down the words *bathtub, tablecloth, attic,* and *basement* in their home language, because we probably have not already reviewed these less-common words.

Next, students get into groups of two to four students who share the same home language. Students who don't have classmates who speak the same language often seem fine doing these next parts alone. The groups each decide on one word they want to learn, and they develop several clues that would help others who don't speak their language identify the word in English. Students can use drawing, drama, pantomime, and so on. They just cannot say the word in their home language. Each group performs their clues in front for all the other small groups. Every group has a mini-whiteboard. After each performance is finished, student groups can talk together to see if they know the English word (they can't use their smartphones!).

Once they think they know the answer, they write it on their board. The teacher can provide the answer if no student knows the correct word.

This activity can also be used as a game with points being awarded to each group who writes the correct answer on their board within a minute. We haven't done so—students seem to have a lot of fun with this as it is. But it's certainly easy to make that modification.

## Student Handouts and Examples

Figure 4.1: Four Words Sheet

Figure 4.2: Question and Sentence Starters List

Figure 4.3: Narrative Word Chart

Figure 4.4: Identifying Words While Reading

Figure 4.5: Clines

## What Could Go Wrong?

Don't overdo it! Don't put a zillion words on the classroom walls, don't overwhelm students with too many words at one time, and don't re-create Larry's nightmare of spending a half-hour teaching one word.

Also, even though it's important for students to apply the new words they are learning, remember that it might be difficult for them to immediately use every one in an original sentence. During Larry's career as a community organizer, he learned community organizer Saul Alinsky's iron rule: "Never do for others what they can do for themselves. Never!" It would be a misinterpretation of that rule if you insist that ELLs immediately develop sentences using words they learned a few seconds earlier. Plan on providing lots of models and sentence frames for students who need that extra support.

## Technology Connections

Technology offers a gold mine of ways to support vocabulary instruction:

- **Students creating 15-second videos:** We often have students easily create short narrated videos teaching new words with images and sentences. Some of their creations have even been featured on the *New York Times* website! See tons of examples, along with instructions, at The Best Resources for Learning to Use the Video Apps "Vine" & Instagram (http://larryferlazzo.edublogs.org/2013/02/18/the-best-resources-for-learning-to-use-the-video-app-twine/).

- **Students monitoring their increasing vocabulary knowledge:** When students see obvious progress it enhances intrinsic motivation and supports the development of a growth mind-set showing that success comes from effort (www.ascd.org/publications/educational-leadership/sept10/vol68/num01/Even-Geniuses-Work-Hard.aspx). One tool we use to make this happen is having students periodically taking online vocabulary tests and noting their scores. Invariably, they increase as the school year continues. We like one called Test Your Vocab (http://testyourvocab.com/), but there are many others that you can find by searching that same phrase: *test your vocabulary.*

- **There are many accessible and free online tools designed for vocabulary instruction:** These sites not only offer explicit instruction but also provide engaging and reinforcing games. Quizlet (https://quizlet.com/) is probably the most well-known one, and you can find others at A Collection of "Best . . ." Lists on Vocabulary Development (http://larryferlazzo.edublogs.org/2013/01/05/a-collection-of-best-lists-on-vocabulary-development/).

- **There are several online tools that easily and visually show synonyms and antonyms:** We use them when students are creating word maps. We have several listed on The Best Reference Websites for English Language Learners (http://larryferlazzo.edublogs.org/2008/11/13/the-best-reference-websites-for-english-language-learners-2008/).

- **There are many word lists we use for teaching academic vocabulary:** They can be found at The Best Websites for Developing Academic English Skills & Vocabulary (http://larryferlazzo.edublogs.org/2008/04/06/the-best-websites-for-developing-academic-english-skills-vocabulary/). This list also contains links to downloadable sentence frames using academic vocabulary.

## Attribution

Versions of some of these ideas appeared in our book, *The ESL/ELL Teacher's Survival Guide* (Ferlazzo & Sypnieski, 2012, p. 132), and in our book, *Navigating the Common Core with English Language Learners* (Ferlazzo & Sypnieski, 2016, p. 259).

Thanks to English teacher Jonny Ingham for his great ideas on using clines: https://eflrecipes.com/2014/03/18/clines/.

Our from clues to words activity was inspired by a somewhat similar idea that English teacher Judit Fehér (2015, p. 64) wrote about in *Creativity in the English Language Classroom* (www.teachingenglish.org.uk/sites/teacheng/files/F004_ELT_Creativity_FINAL_v2%20WEB.pdf).

Figure 4.4 was inspired by a graphic organizer from the WRITE Institute. For information on WRITE and their curriculum resources see https://writeinstitute.sdcoe.net/.

# Figures

| Word and Definition in English | Word and Definition in English |
|---|---|
| _____ | _____ |
| _____ | _____ |
| Definition in Primary Language | Definition in Primary Language |
| _____ | _____ |
| Picture | Picture |
| | |
| Sentence | Sentence |
| _____ | _____ |
| _____ | _____ |
| _____ | _____ |
| Word and Definition in English | Word and Definition in English |
| _____ | _____ |
| _____ | _____ |
| Definition in Primary Language | Definition in Primary Language |
| _____ | _____ |
| Picture | Picture |
| | |
| Sentence | Sentence |
| _____ | _____ |
| _____ | _____ |
| _____ | _____ |

**Figure 4.1** Four Words Sheet *Source:* Reprinted from Ferlazzo & Sypnieski, *Navigating the Common Core with English Language Learners* (2016, p. 75).

Please take turns and ask your partner about their words using one or more of these questions.

## Questions

1. Can you tell me a word you learned this week?
2. Please tell me a word you learned this week.
3. Please teach me a new word.
4. Please help me learn new words.
5. What is a word you learned this week?
6. Can you share a new word with me?
7. Can you teach me some new vocabulary?
8. Can you tell me about an interesting word you learned this week?
9. Please tell me a word you decided was important to learn this week.
10. Can you tell me about an interesting word you learned this week?
11. Can you share a new word with me that you think is useful?
12. Please tell me a word you decided was important to learn this week.
13. Can you review your new words with me?
14. What new words did you collect this week?
15. Let's examine your new words now. What is your first one? What is your second one? What is your third one? What is your fourth one?
16. Can you point out your new words to me and tell me what they mean?
17. What are your new words and what are their definitions?
18. Let's discuss new words. Can you please start with your list?

## Answers

1. _____ is a new word I learned this week. It means _____ _____. I used it in this sentence: _____ _____.

2. I learned the word _____ this week. I read or heard it when _____ _____. It means _____. This is the sentence I used: _____.

3. _____ is a new word I learned this week. I read or heard it when _____. Its definition is _____. I used it in this sentence: _____ _____.

**Figure 4.2**  Question and Sentence Starters List

| Word | Meaning in English | Meaning in Home Language | Picture |
|------|--------------------|-------------------------|---------|
| Protagonist | | | |
| Antagonist | | | |
| Characters | | | |
| Setting | | | |
| Conflict | | | |
| Events | | | |
| Dialogue | | | |
| Resolution | | | |
| Theme | | | |

**Figure 4.3** Narrative Word Chart

| Page Number Word | Definition In English Using My Own Words | Definition in Home Language and/or Picture | My Own Sentence |
|---|---|---|---|
| | | | |
| | | | |
| | | | |
| | | | |

**Figure 4.4** Identifying Words While Reading

**Temperature Cline**

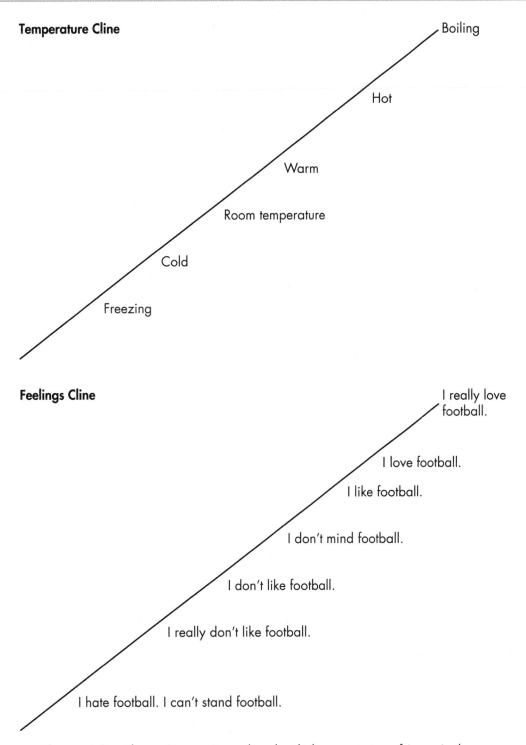

**Feelings Cline**

**Figure 4.5** Clines *Source:* Reproduced with the permission of Jonny Ingham.

# Activating Prior Knowledge

## What Is It?

Activating prior knowledge, also known as *activating schema,* is a well-known learning and teaching strategy of connecting students' prior or background knowledge to new concepts in order to promote deeper learning. In an ELL classroom, students possess varying levels of prior knowledge in English and academic content. Students also bring with them valuable funds of knowledge created through their cultural, family, and general life experiences outside of school (González et al., 2005; Lindahl, 2015). In order to help students maximize the language and content learning in a lesson, teachers must help them draw on their prior knowledge, including these funds of knowledge, and make connections to new learning.

We can't determine how to best help students build their understanding of a topic or concept until we find out what knowledge they already have about it. In other words, we need to identify what they know, what they don't know, and what they think they know.

Once we've determined what they know, we can then decide how much additional background building they need to understand new content. Building this background knowledge, however, does not mean pre-teaching all the information contained in a text or giving students the answers to upcoming questions on a topic. Instead, as educator Lauren Keppler (2016) says, it means giving students "experience with a foundational concept from which to build further knowledge" (para. 6).

In summary, activating prior knowledge means eliciting from students what they already know *and* building initial knowledge that they need in order to access upcoming content.

## Why We Like It

We have found this strategy to be essential to our students' acquisition of English language skills and content knowledge. To go even further, this strategy lies at the heart of our teaching philosophy—our students *already* possess a wealth of knowledge and experiences that they can build on as they encounter new learning. It is up to us to facilitate this process by developing relationships with our students so that we learn what they already know and ensure that they feel comfortable sharing it.

## Supporting Research

Research on the brain confirms it is easier to learn something new when we can attach it to something we already know (Carnegie Mellon University, 2015). Much research supports the idea that activating prior knowledge is a critical step in the learning process and a major factor in reading comprehension (Shanahan, 2013).

Additional research specifically with English language learners finds that activating and building prior knowledge plays a big role in improving their academic literacy (Short & Echevarria, 2004–2005).

## Common Core Connections

Educators and researchers, along with the Common Core authors, recognize that activating prior knowledge is a necessary step in accessing complex texts, whether in the form of written words, images, charts, or other text types. However, you can have too much of a good thing. As the Common Core authors say, "Student background knowledge and experiences can illuminate the reading but should not replace attention to the text itself" (Coleman & Pimentel, 2005, p. 7).

The activities that follow serve to activate and build background knowledge as a support, not as a bypass, for students in meeting the Common Core Standards. We are confident that all of our suggestions here function as the kind of support encouraged by the Common Core.

## Application

What follows is a variety of ways to activate students' prior knowledge and build further background knowledge in preparation for new learning. Activities for tapping prior knowledge are typically designed for use before reading activities, but we have used the ones listed here to also help students access writing, speaking, and listening tasks.

## KWL CHARTS

Of course, the tried-and-true KWL chart is always an effective way of gauging student background knowledge about a topic or concept. Students write and share what they already know about the topic in the *K* (what I know) section. They then add questions in the *W* (what I want to know) section and write their learnings in the *L* section (what I learned) as they uncover new information through written and digital texts.

Variations of KWL extend the chart to include columns for how students can find answers to their questions (online searches, personal interviews), what actions they might take after learning this new information (apply it, teach someone else, create something new), and what new questions they have based on what they've learned (Corbitt, 2016). Personally, we're old school when it comes to KWL and we like the original, simple version. More power to you if you want to expand your KWL horizons!

## ANTICIPATION GUIDES

Anticipation guides ask students to think, write, and talk about their opinions on key themes or big ideas contained in upcoming texts and units of study. They are often organized as a list of statements that students have to agree or disagree with. This can be done in writing or speaking.

It can be helpful to have students revisit their anticipation guides at the end of a unit in order to reflect on changes in their thinking and in preparation for writing an essay. Figure 5.1: Anticipation Guide is an example of one we've used with our students during a mini-unit on sports drinks.

For a more kinesthetic version of an anticipation guide, students can respond to a series of agree or disagree statements by standing and placing themselves on a continuum (strongly agree on one side of the room, strongly disagree on the other, and other opinions at other places along the continuum). This is also called a *cline* (see Strategy 4: Vocabulary). We have also used the well-known four corners strategy by posting four statements in different parts of the classroom. We then ask students which statement they agree with most and tell them to go that corner. Once there, students share with each other why they agree with that statement and then one student from each corner shares out to the whole class. This thinking and talking results in language building and developing curiosity about what is coming next.

## MULTIMEDIA

The old saying "a picture is worth a thousand words" can really ring true in an ELL classroom! Many times before we start a new unit or text, we will show students a related video (with English subtitles), slideshow, or display a photograph on the document camera. Asking students to write or talk about it with a partner is a great way to instantly gauge prior knowledge, build background, and spark interest. A simple prompt could be "What did you notice?" or "What did you find interesting?" So many resources are now at one's fingertips—listening to music from an era being studied, viewing a newscast about a famous event, watching an interview with an author—and can be used to build background in an engaging way.

## QUICKWRITES

Asking students to write to a quick prompt (e.g., "What do you think of when you hear the word *immigration*"?) related to a new topic of study (an immigration unit) is another way to activate and build student knowledge. Sharing these responses can be helpful in generating a class list of what is known and what questions students would like to find the answers to. Newcomers can respond to quickwrites in their home language or through drawing pictures of what they already know about the topic.

## PREPARATORY TEXTS

Providing simpler, preparatory texts in anticipation of a more-complex reading task can be very helpful in building ELLs' background knowledge and reading confidence. We often use the same text written in different lexile levels. There are many resources available online that make it easy to find or create these types of accessible texts (see Technology Connections). We're not suggesting that teachers simplify the complex text they are planning to use for close reading. Instead, teachers can provide simplified texts addressing similar topics or themes in the complex text *as a way* to build background knowledge.

In Strategy 10: Reading Comprehension we also share strategies that students can employ *while* reading, which prepare them to access complex texts. Obviously we're not going to ask our newcomers to read a complex text, but that doesn't mean they aren't making their way toward this goal. They can employ the same pre-reading and reading strategies higher proficiency ELLs are using, but with simpler texts or texts in their home language.

## FIELD TRIPS—REAL OR VIRTUAL

Taking students on field trips in order to build background knowledge is an ideal strategy—nothing compares to real, hands-on learning. As education researcher Robert Marzano (2004) states, "The most straightforward way to enhance students' academic background knowledge is to provide academically enriching experiences" (p. 14). Marzano lists field trips as one of those "academically enriching experiences," and we wholeheartedly agree with him.

However, we know it isn't always possible to secure the funds or support to make these trips possible. Another option, though definitely not as effective as a real trip, is a virtual field trip. There are many online resources for finding and creating these types of virtual adventures for your students (see Technology Connections).

## Student Handout and Example

Figure 5.1: Anticipation Guide

## What Could Go Wrong?

Just because you can build students' background knowledge on a topic doesn't mean you always should. Many teachers talk too much and get caught in the cycle of explaining every word, concept, or topic to their students. This nonstop yakking becomes background noise instead of background knowledge. Students can end up tuning out instead of tuning in.

It is also dangerous to assume that a student doesn't have prior knowledge of a concept or possesses incorrect understanding just because it *differs* from the teacher's prior knowledge. For example, asking students from different cultural backgrounds to write what they know about weddings or funerals may elicit very different responses from one written by the teacher.

Teachers should also be wary of assuming all students from a certain country or cultural background have the same prior knowledge or experiences. Nor should they put students in the role of ambassador and expect a student to be the sole resource on a whole culture, country, or ethnic background (Lundgren & Lundy-Ponce, n.d.). However, this doesn't mean however that individual students, with preparation and their permission, can't be lifted up to share their unique cultural experiences at appropriate times.

## Technology Connections

For an updated list of tools for simplifying texts, providing different leveled versions of the same text, and different leveled texts on the same topic, see The Best Places to Get the "Same" Text Written for Different "Levels" (http://larryferlazzo.edublogs .org/2014/11/16/the-best-places-to-get-the-same-text-written-for-different-levels/).

Providing ELLs with texts or videos in their home language can be another way to promote background knowledge. You can find resources for this at The Best Multilingual & Bilingual Sites for Math, Social Studies, & Science (http:// larryferlazzo.edublogs.org/2008/10/03/the-best-multilingual-bilingual-sites-for-math-social-studies-science/).

For helpful information on virtual field trips and virtual reality experiences, see The Best Resources for Finding and Creating Virtual Field Trips (http://larryferlazzo .edublogs.org/2009/08/11/the-best-resources-for-finding-and-creating-virtual- field-trips/) and A Beginning List of the Best Resources on Virtual Reality in Education (http://larryferlazzo.edublogs.org/2017/02/27/a-beginning-list-of-the- best-resources-on-virtual-reality-in-education/).

# Figure

---

### Sports Drinks Versus Water

Read each statement. Think about *to what extent* (how much) you agree or disagree with the statement. Make a mark on the line to show your opinion. Then, write down any reasons for your opinion below the line.

1. Kids should only be allowed to drink water and low fat-milk.

_____

_____

*Strongly*                                                     *Strongly*

*Agree*                                                        *Disagree*

Why I think this:


2. Kids need to drink sports drinks when they are exercising or playing sports.

_____

_____

*Strongly*                                                     *Strongly*

*Agree*                                                        *Disagree*

Why I think this:

---

**Figure 5.1** Anticipation Guide

3. Schools should not sell sports drinks on campus.

_____

_____

*Strongly*                                    *Strongly*

*Agree*                                        *Disagree*

Why I think this:

4. Sports drinks are better for you than soda.

_____

_____

*Strongly*                                    *Strongly*

*Agree*                                        *Disagree*

Why I think this:

**Figure 5.1**   *(Continued)*

*STRATEGY 6*

# Sequencing

## What Is It?

Sequencing activities—cutting up text and having students put them back in the correct order—is a common language-learning task in the ELL classroom. But its value is not limited to English language learners: Benjamin Franklin famously developed his writing style by regularly cutting apart essays he liked and going back to them weeks or months later to challenge himself to put them back together again (Public Broadcasting System, n.d.).

There are several different types of sequencing activities. Strip stories are divided passages that, when reordered correctly, show an accurate story. Sentence scrambles (see Strategy 23: Learning Games for Reading and Writing) mix up words and punctuation in one sentence and challenge the learner to put them back in order. A third common sequencing task uses comic strips.

## Why We Like It

We like this strategy for many reasons. One reason is these activities are clearly puzzles and, as we discuss in the Supporting Research section, can encourage participants to move into a state of *flow,* which is the highest form of intrinsic motivation. Second, strip stories in particular can let us hit two birds with one stone; it encourages the development of literacy skills *and* the content can be related to what we are studying at the time (US history, school vocabulary, argument writing, etc.). Third, sentence scrambles are easy for teachers to create and can be a central part of lessons or easily fill up any extra time that might be left before the bell. And, fourth, students themselves can easily create all three—strip stories, sentence scrambles, and comic strips—for use by their classmates.

Just having students complete the activities can be beneficial to learning. However, why we *really* like this strategy is that we add an additional step most of the time that challenges students to develop higher-level thinking skills and metacognition. We do this by insisting—most of the time—they note *why* they put the items in that order. In other words, what were the clues they used that led them to the correct response?

## Supporting Research

Teachers can frame sequencing activities as puzzles. Researcher Mihaly Csikszentmihalyi and others have found that looking at learning tasks and challenges as puzzles can promote the development of flow (Shernoff, 2013). Csikszentmihalyi (2008) suggests that an even better flow activity would be having students create their own puzzles that others can then solve (p. 129).

There is a substantial amount of research demonstrating the positive impact strip stories can have on English language acquisition (Kiftiah, n.d.). As far as we can tell, however, there have been no studies specifically done on sentence scrambles and reordering comic strips. However, because their process closely mirrors strip stories, we don't believe it's a stretch to say that research can also support these two versions of sequencing activities.

Research supports the benefits of students explaining their thinking to classmates or their teacher (Williams & Lombrozo, 2010) as well as explaining it to themselves (Ferlazzo, 2017, May 5).

## Common Core Connections

Sequencing activities support the Reading Standards of understanding conventions and using context clues for understanding. Combining those two attributes with the fact that analyzing and interpreting text (found under the Language Standards) are the essence of sequencing activities, it's clear that sequencing lessons hit a Common Core home run.

## Application

Here are specific how-to directions reflecting the steps we use to implement sequencing lessons in our classrooms.

### STRIP STORIES

In some classes, strip stories are often a text that is cut into strips. The strips are then divided among students with instructions to discuss and determine the correct order.

We do it differently.

We like to give each student (sometimes they can work in pairs) a sheet with numbered passages out-of-order (the numbers are important because it makes it easier to review—as in "What number do you think is first?"). Next, we have students cut each one out and read them. Then, with a highlighter in hand they mark the clues they are using to determine the order for each strip. They then begin placing the strips on another piece of paper. Students will eventually glue the strips there, but only after we've checked to make sure they are correct. We will usually show students the first correct strip and model highlighting the clue word. After we see that most students have completed the second one, we'll have students check their answer with a classmate and ask for someone to share the number, and their clue, with the entire class. We then continue that process down the line.

Figure 6.1: First Day of School Strip Story is an example we use with ELL high beginners, and Figure 6.2 is the teacher answer key. Figure 6.3: Mexico Strip Story is an example we use with intermediate ELLs, and Figure 6.4 is the teacher answer key. You will notice that some answers are very obvious by the time or date, and others require a more careful reading of context clues to determine their position. As we mentioned previously, each strip is numbered to make it easier to have a classroom discussion about which ones go in what order (be sure to remind students not to order the strips based on their numbers!).

These strip stories can be simplified even further and made far more complicated with full paragraphs on each strip. We have also created versions that give a list of questions, and then the strip story is composed of the answers. For high intermediates and advanced ELLs, it can be made more challenging by making more than one strip as part of the same answer. In other words, we divide an answer into two separate strips so that not only do students have to connect the correct answer to the question but also they have to use context clues to determine the correct order of the sentences in the answer. We also talk in Strategy 25: Conversation Practice about how we use this sequencing strategy with dialogues.

In addition, we have our intermediate students create strip stories on topics of interest to them (newspaper stories on big soccer games are easy ones). They can copy and paste text off the web (with attribution, of course) after making sure there are clues, divide them into strips, and create an answer sheet and one that is out of order for their classmates to use. See Figure 6.5 for student instructions on how to create them (those are the steps we use to create strip stories, too!). The instructions contain several steps. Students should create their strip stories only after having completed a number of teacher-created ones. Then, as always, it would be important for teachers to model the instructional steps as well.

## SENTENCE SCRAMBLES

As we've mentioned, sentence scrambles are just that—a sentence that has the words and punctuation scrambled and students have to put them in the correct order. These can be sentences that have been seen in previous text (e.g., ones written by the class using the Strategy 8: Language Experience Approach in or sentences in stories read by the class), sentences reinforcing a convention that we've recently taught, or a new fun sentence (e.g., "class love . this I").

They are great for games, which is why we talk about them in Strategy 23: Learning Games for Reading and Writing. They also are good formative assessment tools, and we often include them in periodic tests. And, as we explain in Strategy 23: Learning Games for Reading and Writing, it is also easy for students to create their own. When making sentence scrambles, though, we encourage students to copy sentences that are already written somewhere—a book, a text in their folder, and so on—and not create their own because of potential grammar or spelling errors.

## COMIC STRIPS

The use of comic strips almost explains itself. Identify comics with accessible language, cut them up, and have students put them back in order. Students can highlight clue words or be given a sentence starter to complete:

This box goes first because _____.

This box goes second because _____.

This box goes third because _____.

This box goes fourth because _____.

Students can even create their own comic strips for classmates to put in order. They don't have to be funny—they could be as simple as an event they experienced in the past or just their morning routine.

# Student Handouts and Examples

Figure 6.1: First Day of School Strip Story (Student Handout)

Figure 6.2: First Day of School Strip Story (Teacher Answer Key)

Figure 6.3: Mexico Strip Story (Student Handout)

Figure 6.4: Mexico Strip Story (Teacher Answer Key)

Figure 6.5: Strip Story Instructions

## What Could Go Wrong?

When it comes to strip stories, the main problem is that it can take some students sooooooooooo looooong to cut up the strips. We try to deal with that issue by telling the class at the beginning that they only have a certain period of time to cut them (we don't threaten them with a consequence if they do not finish, but we will periodically announce the minutes as they count down). That usually does the trick.

Precutting the strips deals with that problem, but doing that can create other issues: It takes time to pass them out one at a time, it takes teacher time to cut them up, and they're harder to store for students who are absent that day.

A problem related to sentence scrambles is that ELLs will sometimes miss copying down a word or punctuation mark. So, we usually spot-check student-created scrambles before they are taught to their classmates.

## Technology Connections

If you don't want to create your own strip stories, you can find some freely available online at http://esolonline.tki.org.nz/ESOL-Online/Teacher-needs/Pedagogy/ESOL-teaching-strategies/Oral-language/Teaching-approaches-and-strategies/Speaking-Listening/Strip-stories.

If you're making sentence scrambles for your students, it's easy for teachers to make a mistake and miss a word or punctuation mark (that's not an error limited to students). There are several free online tools that will automatically create them for you at The Best Sites for Creating Sentence Scrambles (http://larryferlazzo.edublogs.org/2010/03/29/the-best-sites-for-creating-sentence-scrambles/).

If, as a change of pace, you want students to create their own comic strips online, they can use one of the tools at The Best Ways to Make Comic Strips Online http://larryferlazzo.edublogs.org/2008/06/04/the-best-ways-to-make-comic-strips-online/).

## Attribution

Versions of some of these ideas appeared in our book, *Navigating the Common Core with English Language Learners* (Ferlazzo & Sypnieski, 2016, p. 199).

The Strip Story instructions were modified from a document in Larry's book, *Helping Students Motivate Themselves* (Ferlazzo, 2011, p. 110).

# Figures

1. Her second class was Math.

2. She liked her first day of class and was happy to tell her parents about it when she went home.

3. PE was her fourth class.

4. Consuelo was excited about her first day of school.

5. She liked that class because she liked to learn about the past.

6. Her brother drove her to the school in the morning.

7. Then she ate lunch with her new friends.

8. She liked that class because she liked to play.

9. She liked that class because she liked to draw.

10. Her fifth class was Science.

11. She first went to English class.

12. History was her third class.

13. She met her English teacher, Mr. Ferlazzo, who seemed very nice.

14. Her last class was Art.

15. She liked that class because she liked numbers.

**Figure 6.1**  First Day of School Strip Story (Student Handout)

**4.** Consuelo was excited about her first day of school.

**6.** Her brother drove her to the school in the morning.

**11.** She first went to English class.

**13.** She met her English teacher, Mr. Ferlazzo, who seemed very nice.

**1.** Her second class was Math.

**15.** She liked that class because she liked numbers.

**12.** History was her third class.

**5.** She liked that class because she liked to learn about the past.

**3.** PE was her fourth class.

**8.** She liked that class because she liked to play.

**7.** Then she ate lunch with her new friends.

**10.** Her fifth class was Science.

**14.** Her last class was Art.

**9.** She liked that class because she liked to draw.

**2.** She liked her first day of class and was happy to tell her parents about it when she went home.

**Figure 6.2**  First Day of School Strip Story (Teacher Answer Key)

1. Mexico became an independent country in 1821.

2. In 1521, the Aztecs were overthrown by Hernán Cortés and other people who lived in Mexico but who did not like the Aztecs.

3. Spain made people who lived there slaves, and 24 million of them died by 1605.

4. The United States won, and took what is now California, Utah, Nevada, Arizona, and New Mexico from Mexico.

5. The Olmecs were the first society in the area we call Mexico and lived there over 3,000 years ago.

6. The Civil War lasted 10 years.

7. Even though it has these problems, many people still think Mexico can be "The Next Great Power" in the world.

8. From 1846 to 1848, Mexico fought a war with the United States.

9. In 1910, people revolted against a dictatorship in Mexico and began a civil war.

10. Spain then took over the Aztec Empire.

11. The Mayans were the most powerful people in Mexico between 250 and 900 AD.

12. Hernán Cortés came to Mexico from Spain in 1519.

13. In 1810, a priest named Miguel Hidalgo y Costilla called for the people of Mexico to revolt against Spain.

14. It has many factories, and many tourists, but faces many problems, including drugs.

15. Mexico now has a population of over 125 million people spread over 31 states.

**Figure 6.3** Mexico Strip Story (Student Handout)

The clues, however, are fairly obvious for students who have been studying English for a few months. A cloze like this is not appropriate for a newcomer. Figure 7.2 is the teacher answer key for this cloze.

Figure 7.3: Cloze with No Answers Shown—Art and Music (Student Handout) is another example of a cloze without a word bank. This one is slightly more difficult than Figure 7.2: Cloze with No Answers Shown—Jobs because some of the clues are found in sentences following the blank. In Figure 7.2, clues preceded each blank. In addition, the vocabulary is more challenging. We use it as part of a unit on art and music and have already pre-taught the vocabulary through words and pictures—sometimes we're even able to get our school's music teacher and one of his classes to invite us over for a lesson! Figure 7.4 is the teacher answer key for this cloze.

Figure 7.5 is a cloze on Helen Keller's life and contains a word bank below the text. We ask students to identify clue words even with a word bank. Figure 7.6 is the teacher answer key for this cloze.

Figure 7.7 is a cloze on Cesar Chavez and offers a different twist on clozes. Here, the emphasis is on teaching prepositions. In addition, the word bank is a series of two-word choices following each blank. Instead of highlighting or underlining the clues, we ask students to choose one of their answers and use a sentence frame to share the evidence they used to pick their answer. Figure 7.8 is the teacher answer key for this cloze.

Figure 7.9 is a fictional story about Juan and Maria. The blanks are short lines corresponding to the number of letters in the correct word and the first letter is provided to students. The ending to this story tends to be enjoyed by adolescent readers. In addition to the usual clue-identification process, we'll often ask students to write their own ending. Figure 7.10 is the teacher answer key for this cloze.

Figure 7.11 is a particularly challenging type of cloze. We would only use it with higher-proficiency ELLs. In this cloze, which is about the history of the United States, we place the answer words at the end of sentences. However, we do not have any blanks—students have to identify where that answer word goes. They write the word where they think it goes in the space above the sentence with an arrow showing its correct location. You'll notice that the cloze is written double-spaced for that purpose. Instead of highlighting or underlining the clues, we ask students to pick two of their answers and use sentence frames to share the evidence they used to pick their answer. Figure 7.12 is the teacher answer key for this cloze.

As we discussed in *The ESL/ELL Teacher's Survival Guide* (Ferlazzo & Sypnieski, 2012, p. 137), clozes can also serve as models of writing that students will be expected to produce. The teacher can have students do a cloze that models their next writing assignment. Students can then mimic this style on their own. Figure 7.13: Persuading My Parents Cloze and Mimic Write is a cloze and writing frame modeling argument writing, and Figure 7.14: Persuading My Parents Student Sample is a paragraph produced by a student using that cloze as the model.

We give students Figure 7.15: Instructions for Making a Cloze when they are creating ones to teach their classmates. We use this assignment after they have had quite a bit of experience completing ones in class. It reflects a similar process we use to create our own clozes.

## Student Handouts and Examples

Figure 7.1: Cloze with No Answers Shown—Jobs (Student Handout)

Figure 7.2: Cloze with No Answers Shown—Jobs (Teacher Answer Key)

Figure 7.3: Cloze with No Answers Shown—Art and Music (Student Handout)

Figure 7.4: Cloze with No Answers Shown—Art and Music (Teacher Answer Key)

Figure 7.5: Cloze with Word Bank—Helen Keller (Student Handout)

Figure 7.6: Cloze with Word Bank—Helen Keller (Teacher Answer Key)

Figure 7.7: Cloze with Word Bank at End of Sentences—Cesar Chavez (Student Handout)

Figure 7.8: Cloze with Word Bank at End of Sentences—Cesar Chavez (Teacher Answer Key)

Figure 7.9: Cloze with Letter Blanks—Juan and Maria (Student Handout)

Figure 7.10: Cloze with Letter Blanks—Juan and Maria (Teacher Answer Key)

Figure 7.11: Cloze with No Blanks—US History (Student Handout)

Figure 7.12: Cloze with No Blanks—US History (Teacher Answer Key)

Figure 7.13: Persuading My Parents Cloze and Mimic Write

Figure 7.14: Persuading My Parents Student Sample

Figure 7.15: Instructions for Making a Cloze

## What Could Go Wrong?

We've learned from three common problems we've encountered using clozes. First, before we begin a cloze activity, we explain that there will be blanks in sentences and that students will need to decide which words belong in them. We then tell them that we will model two different ways of reading these sentences and they will vote on which version they think is most effective, in other words, which one helps them best figure out the correct word. We read the sentence the first time and say the sound "hmmmmm" when we reach the blank. The second time we read it, we say the word *blank* when we reach that space. Students generally pick the first option because in the second option saying the word *blank* can be confusing because it is a word! Once we start reading the cloze, we often get more than one student who wants to join us in saying "hmmmmm" in an exaggerated way, which distracts students from the text. We minimize this problem by addressing it before we start reading by saying, "Please remember that I am the only person who can say 'hmmmmm.' Raise your hand if you agree." We may not do this every time, but we always *remind* students of their prior agreement.

Second, when we ask students to create their own texts, some students or even entire classes do better if we pick six or seven texts ahead of time and let them choose from that selection. It is sometimes overwhelming and distracting to be given the entire Internet from which to choose, especially for middle school classes.

Finally, remember you can have too much of a good thing. Don't use the same kind of cloze all the time! We offer five different kinds (and we're sure there are more out there), so, please, mix it up!

## Technology Connections

When it comes to clozes, technology offers two ways to be helpful and one way not to be helpful. First, there are sites available that let you and students create their own clozes and complete them online. In addition, there are other tools that make it a little easier to create clozes to print out by letting you paste text and just click on words to create a word bank at the bottom. A selection of both kinds of sites can be found at The Best Tools for Creating Clozes (Gap-Fills) (http://larryferlazzo .edublogs.org/2012/04/30/the-best-tools-for-creating-clozes-gap-fills/).

If you search for *clozes* or *gap-fills* online, you'll get a zillion hits. This is where technology can become *not* helpful. Most of the online variations do not appear to have strategically placed blanks, and, instead, the gaps are either in arbitrary locations or are placed automatically after a certain number of words. Don't be seduced by the ease of their availability! We think it's better for everybody to make his or her own.

## Attribution

Versions of some of these ideas appeared in our book, *The ESL/ELL Teacher's Survival Guide* (Ferlazzo & Sypnieski, 2012, p. 136–138).

# Figures

People need to earn money to pay for food to eat and a place to live. People work at _____ to get money. Most adults work at jobs. The _____ you get to work at a job is called a wage or a salary.

If you work at the same kind of job for a long time then you have a career. Most people have more than one _____ during their lives.

People who graduate from high school make more money than people who do not _____ from high school. You can make even more _____ if you go to college.

It is important to work at a job to make money. It is also _____ to work at a job you like. Some people find a job they like to do. Some people do not like to work for somebody else. They start their own business.

**Figure 7.1**   Cloze with No Answers Shown—Jobs (Student Handout)

People need to earn money to pay for food to eat and a place to live. People work at **jobs** to get money. Most adults work at jobs. The **money** you get to work at a job is called a wage or a salary.

If you work at the same kind of job for a long time then you have a career. Most people have more than one **job** during their lives.

People who graduate from high school make more money than people who do not **graduate** from high school. You can make even more **money** if you go to college.

It is important to work at a job to make money. It is also **important** to work at a job you like. Some people find a job they like to do. Some people do not like to work for somebody else. They start their own business.

**Figure 7.2**   Cloze with No Answers Shown—Jobs (Teacher Answer Key)

Musicians play instruments. There are many different kinds of _____. You blow into flutes, horns, and tubas. You also blow _____ the trombone.

A violin has _____. A guitar also has _____. You hit drums to make music. You also _____ a xylophone to make sounds.

A large _____ of musicians playing instruments is called an orchestra. A smaller group of musicians is _____ a band.

Artists can draw, work with clay, and _____. Painters use different colors to paint a picture.

**Figure 7.3**   Cloze with No Answers Shown—Art and Music (Student Handout)

Musicians play instruments. There are many different kinds of **instruments**. You blow into flutes, horns, and tubas. You also blow **into** the trombone.

A violin has **strings**. A guitar also has **strings**. You hit drums to make music. You also **hit** a xylophone to make sounds.

A large **group** of musicians playing instruments is called an orchestra. A smaller group of musicians is **called** a band.

Artists can draw, work with clay, and **paint**. Painters use different colors to paint a picture.

**Figure 7.4** Cloze with No Answers Shown—Art and Music (Teacher Answer Key)

Helen Keller was born in Alabama in 1880. She lived on a farm. She got very sick when she was 18 months old. The _____ caused her to lose her sight and her hearing. *Blind* is another word for not being able to see. *Deaf* is _____ word for not being able to hear anything.

Helen was angry that she could not see or _____ anything. She would _____ people and throw things. Helen's parents hired a teacher named Anne Sullivan to work with Helen. Sullivan would put things in one of Helen's _____. Then, Sullivan would spell out the letters of the word on Helen's other _____. So she would put a doll in one hand and then spell out *d-o-l-l* on Helen's other hand. Helen learned English this way.

Helen learned to read using Braille, which are small bumps on pages. The _____ are letters and words.

Helen also learned to talk. She wrote about her life and became very famous. Helen spent her life trying to help people.

| hands | hear | hand | bumps | sickness | another | hit |
|-------|------|------|-------|----------|---------|-----|

**Figure 7.5** Cloze with Word Bank—Helen Keller (Student Handout)

Helen Keller was born in Alabama in 1880. She lived on a farm. She got very sick when she was 18 months old. The **sickness** caused her to lose her sight and her hearing. *Blind* is another word for not being able to see. *Deaf* is **another** word for not being able to hear anything.

Helen was angry that she could not see or **hear** anything. She would **hit** people and throw things.

Helen's parents hired a teacher named Anne Sullivan to work with Helen. Sullivan would put things in one of Helen's **hands**. Then, Sullivan would spell out the letters of the word on Helen's other **hand**. So she would put a doll in one hand and then spell out *d-o-l-l* on Helen's other hand. Helen learned English this way.

Helen learned to read using Braille, which are small bumps on pages. The **bumps** are letters and words.

Helen also learned to talk. She wrote about her life and became very famous. Helen spent her life trying to help people.

**Figure 7.6** Cloze with Word Bank—Helen Keller (Teacher Answer Key)

Cesar Chavez was born in 1917. He worked in the fields as a farmworker when he was a child. He began a labor union _____ (for, to) farmworkers in 1962. The union wanted farmworkers to get more money and work in safer conditions. The union changed its name to the United Farm Workers. Many of the growers did not want to work _____ (of, with) the union.

Chavez and the union tried to get people not to buy grapes the growers grew. They did this _____ (to, two) pressure the growers to work with the union. Chavez also stopped eating for many days to show support for the farmworkers. This kind of action is called a *hunger strike*.

Many growers did agree to work with the union _____ (for, by) signing a contract saying they would pay the workers more and make it safer for them to work in the fields.

Chavez died in 1993. Many states celebrate his birthday on March 31st every year. The headquarters of the United Farm Workers was named a national monument, which is like a national park, in 2012.

Choose one of your answers and explain the clue you used to figure it out:

I chose _____ as the correct word because

_____.

**Figure 7.7** Cloze with Word Bank at End of Sentences—Cesar Chavez (Student Handout)

Cesar Chavez was born in 1917. He worked in the fields as a farmworker when he was a child. He began a labor union **for** farmworkers in 1962. The union wanted farmworkers to get more money and work in safer conditions. The union changed its name to the United Farm Workers. Many of the growers did not want to work **with** the union.

Chavez and the union tried to get people not to buy grapes the growers grew. They did this **to** pressure the growers to work with the union. Chavez also stopped eating for many days to show support for the farmworkers. This kind of action is called a *hunger strike.*

Many growers did agree to work with the union **by** signing a contract saying they would pay the workers more and make it safer for them to work in the fields.

Chavez died in 1993. Many states celebrate his birthday on March 31st every year. The headquarters of the United Farm Workers was named a national monument, which is like a national park, in 2012.

**Figure 7.8**   Cloze with Word Bank at End of Sentences—Cesar Chavez (Teacher Answer Key)

It was snowing very hard, and Juan and Maria were alone in the woods. "I'm scared," s_ _ _ Juan. "Don't worry," replied Maria, "I know how to get home." The wind was blowing v_ _ _ hard, and it was very cold. It was almost the end of the day, so it was getting d_ _ _. Juan had lost his cellphone, and Maria's battery had died. They had no way to call for help, and they had nothing they could use for light. Juan followed Maria as she w_ _ _ _ _ through the snow. Juan tripped and fell. He got very wet. Maria h_ _ _ _ _ him, and they began walking again. Finally, they saw lights from houses. They were very happy. T_ _ _ were almost out of the woods. But then a big monster came and ate both of them.

**Figure 7.9**   Cloze with Letter Blanks—Juan and Maria (Student Handout)

It was snowing very hard, and Juan and Maria were alone in the woods. "I'm scared," said Juan. "Don't worry," replied Maria, "I know how to get home." The wind was blowing very hard, and it was very cold. It was almost the end of the day, so it was getting dark. Juan had lost his cellphone, and Maria's battery had died. They had no way to call for help, and they had nothing they could use for light. Juan followed Maria as she walked through the snow. Juan tripped and fell. He got very wet. Maria helped him, and they began walking again. Finally, they saw lights from houses. They were very happy. They were almost out of the woods. But then a big monster came and ate both of them.

**Figure 7.10**   Cloze with Letter Blanks—Juan and Maria (Teacher Answer Key)

The United States first became a country in 1776. People who lived here fought a war with Great Britain to become independent. The people who lived here that war in 1783. (won)

The United States was a lot smaller than it is now. There were only 13 states in the eastern part of the country.

The country got a lot bigger by Native Americans, who lived here first, to move. (forcing)

The United States bought land from France and Russia. The United States fought a war with Mexico and got more land.

Many people came to the United States from other countries for a better life. (looking)

A large number of people from Africa were to come to the United States to work as slaves. (forced)

A war called The Civil War was fought between the northern part of the United States and the southern part of the United States. The South to keep slaves. (wanted)

The North won, and the country slavery. (ended)

Many whites still did not treat African Americans well. This is still a problem today. Now, over 300 million people live in the United States.

Choose two of your answers and explain the clues you used to figure it out:

I put _____ between _____ and _____
because _____.

I put _____ between _____ and _____
because _____.

**Figure 7.11**  Cloze with No Blanks—US History (Student Handout)

The United States first became a country in 1776. People who lived here fought a war with Great Britain to become independent. The people who lived here **won** that war in 1783. The United States was a lot smaller than it is now. There were only 13 states in the eastern part of the country. The country got a lot bigger by **forcing** Native Americans, who lived here first, to move. The United States bought land from France and Russia. The United States also fought a war with Mexico and got more land. Many people came to the United States from other countries **looking** for a better life. A large number of people from Africa were **forced** to come to the United States to work as slaves. A war called The Civil War was fought between the northern part of the United States and the southern part of the United States. The South **wanted** to keep slaves. The North won, and the country **ended** slavery. Many whites still did not treat African Americans well. This is still a problem today. Now, over 300 million people live in the United States.

**Figure 7.12**   Cloze with No Blanks—US History (Teacher Answer Key)

Sometimes I need to persuade my parents to let me do things that I want to do. Last week, when I wanted to _____ up late and watch a movie, I had to convince my parents that it was a good idea. First, I had to think of a convincing _____ and support this reason with facts. For example, I told them that the reason I _____ be able to watch a movie is because I already completed my homework and set my alarm clock. My parents disagreed with me and presented an _____ viewpoint. They argued that if I stayed up to watch a movie, then I would be too tired to _____ up on time and get ready for school in the morning. I reminded them that just last week I stayed up late finishing my homework and the next _____ when my alarm clock went off at 6:00 a.m., I got up and got ready for _____ on time. This was a great counterargument because they were convinced and they agreed to let me watch my movie!

Sometimes I need to persuade _____ to let me do things that I want to do. Last week, when I wanted to _____, I had to convince _____ that it was a good idea. First, I had to think of a convincing reason and support this reason with facts. For example, I told them that the reason I should be able to _____ is because _____ disagreed with me and presented an opposing viewpoint. _____ argued that if I _____, then I _____ _____. I presented a counterargument when I said

_____

_____

_____

_____.

**Figure 7.13**   Persuading My Parents Cloze and Mimic Write   *Source:* Reprinted from L. Ferlazzo & K.H. Sypnieski, *ESL/ELL Teacher's Survival Guide* (2012, p. 138).

## Persuade My Parents

One time I tried to persuade my parent to let me do things that I want to do. Last week, I wanted to wake up early to play basket in my brother school. I had to convince my parents that it was a good idea. One reason I used was it help me to get exercise and my body get stronger. Another reason was I already finished cleaning the house and I already did my homework.

**Figure 7.14** Persuading My Parents (Student Sample) *Source:* Reprinted from L. Ferlazzo & K.H. Sypnieski, *ESL/ELL Teacher's Survival Guide* (2012, p. 139).

---

1. Look for a passage online that seems interesting to you and is related to the topic we are studying in class. It should have at least 15 sentences, but not be longer than one page.

2. Copy and paste the original passage onto a Word document or a Google Doc and cite the author. Title this *Cloze Answer Key.*

3. Copy and paste it again on another Word document or a Google Doc. Title this *Cloze.*

4. Read the passage carefully and select ten words that you will replace with blanks. Do not have a blank in the first or last sentence of the passage and do not have more than one blank in the same sentence. Be sure that there are clue words for each blank. Circle the clue words on your Cloze Answer Key.

5. Place the answer words on the bottom of the page. Be sure that they are not in the correct order.

6. Print out one copy of your Cloze Answer Key and six copies of your Cloze.

---

**Figure 7.15** Instructions for Making a Cloze

# *STRATEGY 8*

# Language Experience Approach (LEA)

## What Is It?

The language experience approach (LEA) describes the process of the entire class doing an activity and then discussing and writing about it in a teacher-led process. The completed sentences can then be used in multiple follow-up activities to reinforce language learning.

## Why We Like It

LEA can be a low-prep, high-energy lesson focused on student interests. It can be easily adapted to different subjects and, though it is most often used with ELL beginners, students at various degrees of English proficiency can benefit from its use.

## Supporting Research

The LEA is one of the most widely used and effective instructional strategies in ELL classes. Substantial research has shown its positive impact on writing (Arvin, 1987), reading comprehension, and student motivation (Rahayu, 2013). It is often described as a best practice for ELL instruction (Howard Research, 2009, p. 30).

## Common Core Connections

Using this strategy can assist students as they begin developing the skills to write informative, explanatory, and narrative text. In addition, it supports students in gaining an understanding of English conventions. Finally, it supports the Speaking and Listening Standard of "building on others' ideas" (Common Core State Standards Initiative, n.d.c).

# Application

The LEA describes the process of the entire class doing an activity and then discussing and writing about it (however, a tutor working with a student one-on-one or in a smaller group could also use it). Here are the steps involved when we use it (portions of Steps 1 through 4 also appeared in *The ESL/ELL Teacher's Survival Guide*, Ferlazzo & Sypnieski, 2012, p. 55):

1. The class does a teacher-planned activity, such as one of the following:
   - Watching a short video clip
   - Taking a walk around the school
   - Making a simple musical instrument
   - Doing a simple science experiment
   - Creating a piece of art (we've used clay, painting, and origami)
   - Going on a field trip
   - Playing a board game
   - Creating a puppet or toy
   - Preparing a food
   - Playing Frisbee, soccer, or basketball outside
   - Performing a simple dance
   - Working in a school garden
   - Inventing and performing a short silent play (pantomime)
   - Just about anything else you can think of!

2. Immediately following the activity, students can be given a short time to write down notes about what they did (very early beginners can draw). Then, the teacher calls on students to share what the class did—usually, though not always—in chronological order ("What did we do first?"). The teacher then writes down what is said on a document camera, overhead projector, or easel paper. It is sometimes debated if the teacher should write down exactly what a student says if there are grammar or word errors or if the teacher should say it back to the student and write it correctly—without saying the student was wrong. We use the second strategy and feel that as long as students are not being corrected explicitly ("That's not the correct way to say it, Eva; this is"), it is better to model accurate grammar and word usage. Figure 8.1: Language Experience Approach Model shows an example of what we wrote after playing basketball outside for 15 minutes.

3. The class can chorally repeat each sentence after the teacher reads it aloud. Students can copy down the sentences and can add their own illustrations. Because the text comes out of their own experience, it is much more accessible because they already know its meaning. Instead of doing an activity, it is also possible to use common experiences already shared by all students in the class—for example, a folktale that might be known if all students come from the same home culture, a popular movie that everyone has seen, a major world event, or even what has happened in class that day.

4. The text can subsequently be used for different follow-up activities, including as a cloze (removing certain words and leaving blanks that students have to complete), a sentence scramble (taking individual sentences and mixing up the words for learners to sequence correctly), or mixing up all the sentences in the text and having students put them back in order. Students can also read the sentences out loud with partners and without looking at the text (ideally), take turns writing down what the other is reading. In addition, students could be assigned a sentence to illustrate and practice prior to reading it to the class while showing their drawing (time to practice would be essential—we never want to demand that beginning students speak without time to prepare).

Students can create categories for words in the sentences (verbs, nouns, words that begin with *r,* etc.) and add new words to the categories using their prior knowledge and a dictionary. Simple grammar lessons can be taught either during the original sentence writing (only if they can be done quickly—for example, that *went* is the past tense of *go*) or later.

Students with higher English proficiency can be asked to add more sentences on their own to the group-created ones or use the text as a model for writing another text about one of their personal experiences (e.g., playing soccer, cooking a meal, what happened in a different movie they saw, etc.).

## Student Handout and Example

Figure 8.1: Language Experience Approach Model

## What Could Go Wrong?

Writing down too many sentences or ones that are too complex can be frustrating to beginners, particularly students with little school experience or who are unfamiliar with the English alphabet. Keep the length of sentences short, the vocabulary simple, and the number of them low—not more than 6 to 10.

## Technology Connection

Students can convert their sentences into an audio-narrated and illustrated slideshow online. See The Best Ways to Create Online Slideshows (http://larryferlazzo .edublogs.org/2008/05/06/the-best-ways-to-create-online-slideshows/).

## Attribution

Portions of this section originally appeared in our book, *The ESL/ELL Teacher's Survival Guide* (Ferlazzo & Sypnieski, 2012, p. 54).

## Figure

> *First, we walked outside.*
>
> *Second, we walked to the basketball court.*
>
> *Third, we played basketball.*
>
> *Fourth, Juan bounced the basketball.*
>
> *Fifth, Julia threw the basketball.*
>
> *Sixth, we drank water.*
>
> *Seventh, we ran back to the classroom.*

**Figure 8.1** Language Experience Approach Model

# STRATEGY 9

# Jigsaw

## What Is It?

The jigsaw strategy can be implemented with a number of different variations. Most, though, involve students becoming experts in a section of a text or an element of a broader topic (e.g., learning about different times of a famous person's life), which they then teach to other students who have become experts in different portions of the text. All students take turns teaching their classmates.

## Why We Like It

There are so many reasons to like the jigsaw strategy! It generally produces high student engagement in all four domains—reading, writing, speaking, and listening; it is a great tool for differentiation (beginners can be given easier portions of the text); it can be used for any topic; and it can require minimal teacher preparation.

## Supporting Research

Researchers share our enthusiasm for the jigsaw strategy. In fact, well-known education researcher John Hattie says that it is the *only* strategy that scores high in *all* sections of his newer four-quadrant model of learning: acquiring surface learning, consolidating surface learning, acquiring deep learning, and consolidating deep learning (Schwartz, 2017).

Other researchers have also found a number of academic benefits attributable to the jigsaw strategy for mainstream (National Association of Geoscience Teachers, n.d.) and ELL students (Sabbah, 2016).

Several studies have specifically found that the expectation to teach material has a positive impact on learning (Ferlazzo, 2012, April 22; Nestojko et al., 2014).

A jigsaw is also called an *information gap activity* (see Strategy 24: Dictation), a broader strategy used in many ELL classrooms. The idea behind an information gap activity is that one student is required to obtain information from a classmate in order to complete an activity. In other words, he or she has to bridge the gap. It uses what researchers identify as a primary lever of motivation—the "curiosity gap" (Dean, n.d.a).

## Common Core Connections

Apart from some of the Writing Standards, you can check off just about every other Standard with the jigsaw strategy—depending on the complexity of the text. Jigsaw can support students meeting the Writing Standards, too, if you have students use the process to kick off further writing about their topic.

# Application

There are several different ways we use the jigsaw strategy in our classrooms, depending on the English proficiency level of our students, the time we have available for the lesson, and if we are teaching English or social studies.

### BEGINNERS AND LOW-INTERMEDIATES

The teacher first prepares the materials. Figure 9.1: Driver's License Jigsaw is an example we have used with our beginners. It's simply a short article divided into five sections. We often create our own jigsaw materials or modify ones we've downloaded online (see Technology Connections for suggested resources).

After the teacher prepares the materials, he or she needs to decide which vocabulary words are critical to pre-teach. In the case of Figure 9.1, we first taught these words or phrases: *driver's license, drive, car, one-half years old, prove, safely, live.*

After providing vocabulary instruction, the teacher divides the class into groups. For our lesson, we divided the class into five groups of three students each. We had cut the five sections in Figure 9.1 prior to the class and gave the number 1 section to Group 1, the number 2 section to Group 2, and so on. We were, however, strategic in determining which students would go into what group—here is where the differentiation ability of the jigsaw strategy shines. The students with the lowest English proficiency were in group 1 and the highest were in group 5. Middle-level students were in the other groups.

Students were then asked to practice reading their sentence(s) within their groups, working on their pronunciation and their understanding of the text. They first would seek the help of their group members and then ask the teacher. They were told they were going to teach classmates their text and that they would do it in a small group. Making it clear that they would be teaching in a small group was important to lower the stress level—we didn't want students to think they would have to read in front of the entire class. Students were able to refer to their written text when they taught it, but we also told them that the less they had to refer to it, the better.

While students were practicing reading their text aloud by taking turns in their small group, the teacher circulated and gave a letter to each student. Every group had one student who was a letter *A,* a letter *B,* and a letter *C.* If one group was a student short, the teacher would have filled in for him or her.

After students spent five to seven minutes practicing, they moved into their letter groups. Students then read their passages in the numbered order of the sections with group members softly applauding after each one read.

Last, after everyone had read their text, we asked them to put their sections away and gave them Figure 9.2: Driver's License Activity, a cloze–gap-fill using the entire text, along with three true-false statements and one question to answer. Students were asked to circle clues they used to determine the right answers to the cloze. For example, the answer for the first blank is *license* and the clue is the word *license* in the first sentence.

Students were asked to spend a few minutes completing the sheet silently. Then, after that time, we told them to share their answers with one or two other members of the group. We then reviewed the answers as a class.

To summarize, here are the seven steps to the jigsaw process that we follow (after we prepare the materials):

1. Teach the vocabulary needed for comprehension of the jigsawed text.

2. Divide the class into expert groups and distribute the appropriate texts.

3. Expert groups practice reading the text together.

4. Groups are then formed with one person from each expert group represented.

5. Experts teach their text to the new group.

6. Students complete a follow-up task (which could also be creating a poster summarizing the article, planning a role-play to perform, etc.).

7. The teacher reviews the follow-up task with the entire class.

Figures 9.3: Nina's Break-In Part 1: Jigsaw and 9.4: Nina's Break-In Part 2: Questions About the Story come from Nancy Callan at ESL Jigsaws (www.esljigsaws .com/) and provide an idea of what a more-complex text and follow-up task might look like. Figure 9.5: Nina's Break-In: How to Use This Jigsaw contains a nice visualization of the jigsaw process that she uses in her classroom. We were inspired by her model and adapted it for our classroom situation.

We also sometimes use this kind of jigsaw to introduce new words before starting a new a unit or theme. In that case, instead of distributing sections of text, we give students a portion of a word list (e.g., one group of four receives the same words; another receives the next few from the list). They then have to create draft posters with their words. These have to include the words, a definition (not just copying it down from the dictionary), a sentence using the word, and a picture. They then work with their expert groups (the students who have the same word or words) to revise their draft posters and practice their presentations. Next, they teach their word(s) to the new group. We then might distribute mini-whiteboards to all students for a follow-up formative assessment activity in which the teacher calls out words and students write down definitions or vice versa.

## HIGH-INTERMEDIATES AND ADVANCED

Texts for students with a higher English proficiency could obviously be more complex. Here are examples of broader topics and the categories that could be used in jigsaws about them:

- Geography reports on countries: economy, culture, history, famous people, famous sites, politics, natural resources
- Biography reports on famous people: childhood, family as an adult, accomplishments, challenges, later years, and death
- Different wars: weapons, famous battles, leaders, causes, beginning and end
- Different sections of any lengthy article; there are many resources to obtain free articles that provide different versions depending on student English proficiency level, which is an easy way to differentiate jigsaws (see the Technology Connections section for online links)
- Different sports: how invented, famous players in the past, famous players in the present, key rules
- Articles published in different countries discussing the same current event (see the Technology Connections section for resources)
- Types of figurative language: metaphors, similes, personification
- Articles on different animals: habitat, diet, physical characteristics, behavior

The jigsaw process we use with high-intermediate and advanced ELLs is a bit different, because they tend to have a higher level of well-placed confidence in their English literacy and oral ability. This increased English proficiency enables them to do more on their own and complete more-complex tasks.

As we do with beginners, we first identify the materials students will read (here, we generally use articles already written and not needing modification) and determine if any vocabulary needs to be pre-taught.

We determine group members—who is going to read what article. However, in this case, instead of immediately bringing group members together, we ask that students read it on their own and take preliminary notes for the presentation they will eventually make when they teach the article (see Figure 9.6: Student Jigsaw Instructions). First, they prepare their draft presentation on their own. Next, they meet with others who read the same article and share their initial plans. Third, students make revisions based on their expert group discussion. Finally, students get into mixed groups and teach their classmates.

We generally give guidelines about what students should include in their presentations. Figure 9.6 is one example for instructions we might provide students. Another example could be any variation of the versatile 3–2–1 structure. The instructions for a 3–2–1 poster could be "Write three words and why they're important, two phrases and why they're important, one sentence and why it's important, and draw a picture" (see the Technology Connections section for links to many other 3–2–1 ideas). We may sometimes provide a 3–2–1 graphic organizer. In addition, we remind students to paraphrase and not copy what the article says (see Strategy 15: Quoting, Summarizing, and Paraphrasing).

Next, students teach their article to the mixed groups (again, see Figure 9.6). Our follow-up activity to this process is often a simple one (e.g., asking students to write down what was the most interesting thing they learned and *why* they found it most interesting).

This process of a student first creating a draft on their own, then meeting with others to share and discuss how to improve it, and then revising their original work based on those discussions promotes the concept of *collaborative* learning supported by the Common Core Standards (Ferlazzo & Sypnieski, 2016, p. 125). This contrasts with the cooperative learning that often appears in classrooms (including ours!) when student groups might be given directions to do a project together. There is also often a need for newcomers to work with a more-proficient ELL student in the jigsaw process and in other tasks in order to receive immediate peer support. In that case, cooperation can help newcomers develop the skills and self-efficacy to move toward more collaboration.

We should also note that collaboration also can mean two or more people working together in order to create new knowledge (Wisconsin Center for Education Research, n.d.) or something better than they could have created separately. We think this type of collaborative process is trickier to apply and demonstrate, though we do use it in Strategy 16: Cooperative Writing.

## Student Handouts and Examples

Figure 9.1: Driver's License Jigsaw

Figure 9.2: Driver's License Activity

Figure 9.3: Nina's Break-In Part 1: Jigsaw

Figure 9.4: Nina's Break-In Part 2: Questions About the Story

Figure 9.5: Nina's Break-In: How to Use This Jigsaw

Figure 9.6: Student Jigsaw Instructions

## What Could Go Wrong?

Time, time, time! Do we follow the outlined jigsaw steps exactly all the time? Of course not! We've got a lot of ground to cover, there is only so much available time, and lots of unplanned events occur during the course of a school day. Sometimes we'll skip the follow-up activity, other times we'll shorten the time students can work on their own, or we'll not have people ask questions of the expert presenters. Flexibility is the rule—for this strategy and for all of them!

Students can get distracted, so jigsaw lessons are not a time for teachers to work on their computer and get caught up on grading. We need to be circulating around the room, listening, providing guidance, and offering support.

Lengthy step-by-step instructions can sometimes be more helpful to the teacher than for the students. However, it can work better and be less overwhelming to students if you place a sheet such as Figure 9.6: Student Jigsaw Instructions on the overhead or document camera, cover it up, and unveil each step as you progress through the activity.

## Technology Connections

It's easy for teachers to create their own jigsaw materials, though we generally either modify materials we download from edHelper.com (https://edhelper.com/) or Enchanted Learning (www.enchantedlearning.com/Home.html), which require a very low-cost subscription, or use ready-made materials we purchase from ESL Jigsaws (www.esljigsaws.com/).

In addition, you can find many different variations of how students can construct 3–2–1 posters when presenting as experts at The Best Ways To Use "3–2–1" as an Instructional Strategy (http://larryferlazzo.edublogs.org/2015/09/19/the-best-ways-to-use-3–2–1-as-an-instructional-strategy/).

Teachers can find articles from different countries covering the same topic at The Best Tools to Help Develop Global Media Literacy (http://larryferlazzo.edublogs .org/2009/03/12/the-best-tools-to-help-learn-global-media-literacy/) and articles about the same topic at different lexile levels at The Best Places to Get the "Same" Text Written for Different "Levels" (http://larryferlazzo.edublogs.org/2014/11/16/ the-best-places-to-get-the-same-text-written-for-different-levels/).

## Attribution

Professor Elliot Aronson originated the jigsaw strategy at the University of Texas and the University of California during the early 1970s (www.jigsaw.org/).

Nancy Callan at ESL Jigsaws (www.esljigsaws.com/) has developed many ideas and materials related to applying jigsaws in ELL classes.

## Figures

**1.** You need a license to drive a car.

**2.** You can get a driver's license in California when you are 16 years old.

**3.** If you are less than 17 ½ years old, you must take a driver's education class before you can get a license.

**4.** If you are over 17 ½ years old, you do not have to take a driver's education class.

**5.** You have to take a test where you write the answers down on paper. You also have to drive a car and show that you know how to drive safely. In addition, you must prove that you live in California. There are many ways to show that you live here.

**Figure 9.1** Driver's License Jigsaw

## Cloze

You need a license to drive a car. You can get a driver's _____ in California when you are 16 years old. If you are less than 17 ½ years old, you must take a driver's education class before you can get a license. If you are over 17 ½ years old, you do not have to take a driver's _____ class. You have to take a test where you write the answers down on paper. _____ also have to drive a car and show that you know how to drive safely. In addition, you must prove that you live in _____. There are many ways to show that you live here.

True or False (circle T or F):

**1.** You can get a driver's license in California when you are 15.         T    F
**2.** You can live in another state and get a California driver's license.    T    F
**3.** You have to take a test where you write the answers down on paper. T    F

## Question

Do you want to get a driver's license? If your answer is yes, explain why. If your answer is no, explain why not.

I want to get a driver's license because _____

_____.

I do not want to get a driver's license because _____

_____.

**Figure 9.2**  Driver's License Activity

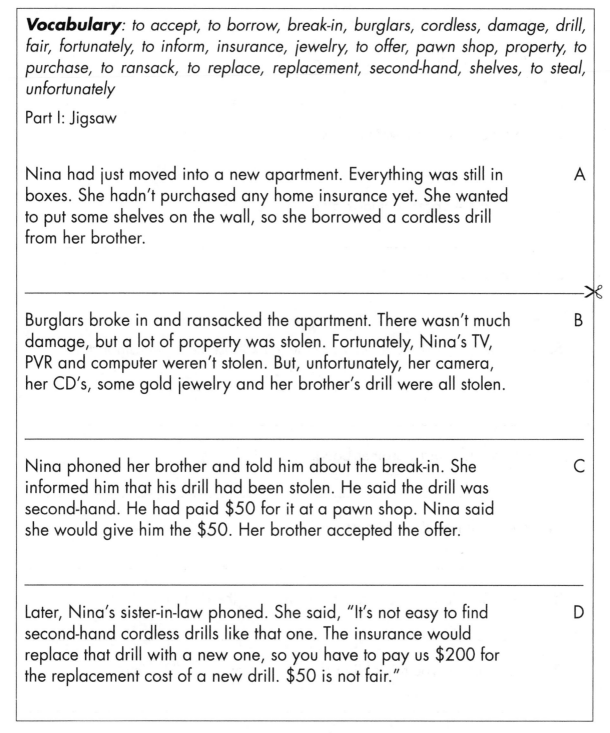

***Vocabulary***: *to accept, to borrow, break-in, burglars, cordless, damage, drill, fair, fortunately, to inform, insurance, jewelry, to offer, pawn shop, property, to purchase, to ransack, to replace, replacement, second-hand, shelves, to steal, unfortunately*

Part I: Jigsaw

Nina had just moved into a new apartment. Everything was still in boxes. She hadn't purchased any home insurance yet. She wanted to put some shelves on the wall, so she borrowed a cordless drill from her brother.

A

✂

Burglars broke in and ransacked the apartment. There wasn't much damage, but a lot of property was stolen. Fortunately, Nina's TV, PVR and computer weren't stolen. But, unfortunately, her camera, her CD's, some gold jewelry and her brother's drill were all stolen.

B

Nina phoned her brother and told him about the break-in. She informed him that his drill had been stolen. He said the drill was second-hand. He had paid $50 for it at a pawn shop. Nina said she would give him the $50. Her brother accepted the offer.

C

Later, Nina's sister-in-law phoned. She said, "It's not easy to find second-hand cordless drills like that one. The insurance would replace that drill with a new one, so you have to pay us $200 for the replacement cost of a new drill. $50 is not fair."

D

**Figure 9.3** Nina's Break-In Part 1: Jigsaw *Source:* Reproduced with permission of Nancy Callan (http://esljigsaws.com/).

*Please answer in full sentences together with your group.*

**1.** Why didn't Nina have insurance?

_____

**2.** Why did Nina borrow the drill?

_____

**3.** How did the apartment look after the break-in?

_____

**4.** What was stolen?

_____

**5.** What wasn't stolen and why do you think those items were not stolen?

_____

_____

**6.** Where had Nina's brother bought the drill?

_____

**7.** How much had the drill cost?

_____

**8.** How much did Nina's sister-in-law want for the drill and why?

_____

**9.** How much do you think Nina should pay for the drill? Why?

_____

_____

**Figure 9.4** Nina's Break-In Part 2: Questions About the Story  *Source:* Reproduced with permission of Nancy Callan (http://esljigsaws.com/).

## Nina's Break-In
Sample jigsaw courtesy of www.esljigsaws.com
1-888-ESL-BOOK

How to use this jigsaw:

**Step One:** (Teacher Preparation Stage): Photocopy 1/4 the number of copies of the jigsaw text and pictures as you have students. Cut each sheet of text and pictures into the 4 parts. Photocopy the follow-up task sheets (to be given out later).

**Step Two:** Preteach any new vocabulary, put students into groups, and give out an identical section of text to all members of a group. For a class of sixteen, your classroom should look like this:

A A     B B     C C     D D
A A     B B     C C     D D

Ask students to work together to memorize their section of text.
When students indicate that they're ready, take back the text passages.

**Step Three:** Regroup students into heterogeneous groups. Explain that they will be teaching the others their part of the story. At this point, for a class of sixteen, your classroom should look like this:

A B     A B     A B     A B
C D     C D     C D     C D

Go over comprehension checks before students begin telling their stories, such as:
*Do you understand me? Should I repeat anything? What does that word mean? etc.*

Ask students to begin telling their part of the story, starting with person A. Circulate to assist with any problems and to check comprehension.

**Step Four:** Once students have finished telling all parts of the story, distribute the group exercises and stress that the group should work on them together. When all groups have finished, take them up with the whole class.

**Figure 9.5** Nina's Break-In: How to Use This Jigsaw *Source:* Reproduced with permission of Nancy Callan (http://esljigsaws.com/).

1. Write the number of your article at the top of the first page.

2. Read the article silently on your own.

3. Make notes:

   - The three most important points made in the article

   - A picture illustrating a main idea of the article

   - Do you agree with the author? Why or why not?

   - Prepare a thoughtful question to ask your audience about the topic of the article.

4. Meet with other classmates who are reading the same article (your teacher will assign the groups). In that meeting, share your notes and learn from others. You will also be given a letter.

5. Take your notes (and any changes you have made after hearing your classmates) and make a simple poster. You will have ten minutes to create your poster.

6. Take your poster and meet with your letter group (the students who have the same letter as you). Take turns being the teacher and presenting your poster—starting with article number one and ending with the last article number.

7. After each teacher presents, all group members have 30 seconds to write down a question about the article. The teacher chooses one person to ask his or her question and then the teacher answers it.

**Figure 9.6** Student Jigsaw Instructions

# STRATEGY 10

# Reading Comprehension

## What Is It?

The word *comprehension* comes from the Latin word *comprehendere,* meaning "to seize or take in the mind" (Comprehend, n.d.). Although the word *seize* may seem a bit dramatic when applied to reading, for many ELLs it feels like quite a victory when they have "seized" the meaning from a text in English!

There are several ways we help build the reading comprehension skills of ELLs so they can gain small victories every day. We discuss some of these ways as separate strategies, such as Strategy 3: Graphic Organizers, Strategy 4: Vocabulary, Strategy 5: Activating Prior Knowledge, and Strategy 11: Inductive Learning. In this section, we will describe other key methods that help our students increase their understanding of texts while developing skills and metacognitive tools they can apply in future reading situations. We refer to metacognition in several places in this book and like the definition we used in our last book:

> It is the self-awareness to know what our strengths and weaknesses are, and how and when to apply the former and compensate for the latter. Broadly explained, learners applying metacognitive strategies plan in advance for effective learning, monitor and make adjustments during the lesson/activity to maximize their learning, and reflect afterwards about which learning strategies worked and which did not for them. (Ferlazzo & Sypnieski, 2016, p. 31)

# Why We Like It

We know, and research confirms, that students who are "actively engaged in their learning have better reading outcomes than do passive learners" (National Reading Technical Assistance Center, 2010, p. 12).

Therefore, the following strategies serve dual purposes—they help students become aware of the thinking processes that can build comprehension *and* keep them actively engaged as they are reading and learning.

# Supporting Research

### READING STRATEGIES

Many researchers have found that explicit instruction in reading strategies (such as monitoring for understanding, summarizing, asking and answering questions, etc.) can benefit comprehension (Education Endowment Foundation, n.d.). Some also offer the reasonable caution that continuous reading strategy instruction taught day after day can "take a process that could bring joy, and turn it into work" (Willingham, 2012).

Most of the research on the effectiveness of teaching reading comprehension strategies has been focused on mainstream students, not ELLs, and particularly not ELLs at the middle or high school level (Snyder et al., 2016, p. 143). However, a study on ELL college students did indicate that higher reading abilities were related to the ELL's awareness and use of strategies while reading (Nordin et al., 2013, p. 476).

Our experience in the classroom corroborates what Stanford researcher Claude Goldenberg (2013) states: "It seems highly likely that we can help ELLs improve their comprehension by teaching comprehension skills directly, although if done in English, the impact will probably depend on English proficiency level" (p. 28).

We have indeed found that ELL students benefit from instruction in reading strategies, especially if they haven't been exposed to them in previous learning experiences. They also need additional time to practice how and when to apply them.

Taking all this into account, it's not entirely clear *how* reading comprehension strategy instruction directly affects reading outcomes for ELLs. However, limited research, common sense, and our own classroom experience strongly suggest that teaching comprehension strategies promotes engagement in the reading and language acquisition process.

**READ ALOUDS AND THINK ALOUDS**

Reading aloud is a foundational strategy linked to literacy development (Gold & Gibson, n.d.). Findings suggest that conducting read alouds and think alouds can help students improve their reading comprehension, vocabulary, and listening skills while increasing their engagement in reading (Clark & Andreason, 2014, p. 174–175).

**CLOSE READING**

Research has linked the close reading of text by readers at all ability levels to increased reading proficiency. It has also been found to be an important part of college and career readiness (Boyles, 2012/2013). Reading a complex text that is challenging to understand can also help students to build stamina and persistence (Fisher & Frey, 2012).

However, although close reading can assist students in building valuable skills, it should be viewed as just one tool in the toolbox. As teacher-researchers Douglas Fisher and Nancy Frey (2012) state, "Close reading must be accompanied by other essential instructional practices that are vital to reading development: interactive read-alouds and shared readings, teacher modeling and think-alouds" (p. 180).

## Common Core Connections

The methods described in this section focus on building students' reading comprehension skills as they work toward meeting the Reading Standards. The section on Close Reading offers instructional moves to assist students in working with the types of complex texts called for in the Standards.

## Application

**READING STRATEGIES**

As we stated previously, and as we have said in our first two books, we believe reading strategies are important scaffolds to support our students' comprehension of texts. We focus on several strategies recommended by the National Reading Panel Report of 2000 as most effective in assisting student reading comprehension. These include comprehension monitoring, cooperative learning, graphic and semantic organizers, story structure, question answering, question generation, summarization, and multiple-strategy use.

We also teach our students to use other common strategies, such as predicting, visualizing, making connections, evaluating, and inferring, in order to enhance their understanding of text. This is not a comprehensive list, however, and it is important to keep in mind what literacy expert Jennifer Serravallo (2010) says: "a strategy is never a single word or phrase—it's a series of actionable steps, a process to help readers tackle a skill that is not yet automatic for them." It is our goal to demonstrate these steps or processes for our students so they can practice them when faced with challenging text.

We introduce these strategies to our lower English proficiency students as well as to more advanced ELLs. Even though our beginning ELLs may not have the language to access higher level texts in English, we can give them access to strategies they can apply to understand more simple texts in English or texts in their native language.

Figure 10.1: Reading Strategies Word Chart is one way we help familiarize students with different reading strategies. For each word, students (with the teacher as a guide) draw what it means and then chorally read the sentence stems for using the strategy. We've also found it helpful to create hand gestures or body movements for each strategy. For example, when teachers are demonstrating the strategy of *making a connection* they can link their fingers together to create a connected chain or the teachers can close their eyes and point to their head to show *visualizing*. Students can then practice making the gestures with each other and even come up with their own versions. Research has confirmed many positive correlations between movement and increased learning (Ferlazzo, 2011, June 2).

As a follow-up to this activity, we use a reading strategies text data set (featured in our book *Navigating the Common Core with English Language Learners,* 2016) with our intermediate ELLs. See the Technology Connections section for the link to download this data set and see Strategy 11: Inductive Learning for more on text data sets.

Throughout the year, we model these reading strategies and provide students opportunities to practice them collaboratively and individually. Students often demonstrate their use of strategies in their independent reading through their reading response entries in their writer's notebooks (see Strategy 18: Writer's Notebook). We also periodically ask students to show us how they use reading strategies by writing one on a mini-whiteboard and sharing it with the class. In the upcoming sections, we describe how we model and encourage this strategy use through read alouds and think alouds, whole-class readings, and close reading.

Of course, the ultimate goal is for students to be able to identify which strategies are most effective in certain reading contexts and for these strategies to become automatic and transferrable as they read independently. Having this end goal in mind can help teachers to look for opportunities to ask their students to reflect on which strategies they are finding most helpful in which reading contexts.

## READ ALOUDS AND THINK ALOUDS

We conduct read alouds with our students in order to spark their interest in reading; to model fluent, prosodic reading; and to increase their language development. Reading with prosody means reading aloud with proper intonation, expression, and rhythm. Recent research on the explicit teaching of prosody to students indicates it can improve fluency skills and reading comprehension (Calet et al., 2017, p. 7).

The read aloud process involves selecting a well-written, short piece of text (usually one to three paragraphs) related to our unit of study. We read it aloud to students and they follow along silently on their copy of the text. We may briefly supply a synonym or quick definition of an advanced word, but otherwise we do not stop to make any comments. Students can then respond to a variety of writing or speaking prompts that ask them to go back into the text and provide support for their answers (such as "What does the author mean by ?" or "Do you agree or disagree with and why?").

Sometimes we use read alouds to provide background knowledge or to pique student interest on an upcoming topic of study. Other times we give our students the chance to conduct their own read aloud with a partner or small group. They can choose their own texts, practice reading it aloud focusing on pronunciation and prosody, and create a writing or speaking prompt for their classmates.

Reading aloud, when structured carefully, can help less-proficient ELLs better understand what they are reading. We were introduced to an activity by educator Scott Thornbury (2017) called *Reading Aloud (Heads Up)*. In this method, students are given a sentence to read aloud. Then, instead of looking down at the page and reading it aloud, they must read it silently, look up, and then say the sentence aloud. Therefore, students must "hold the material in the mind in such a way that its meaning is processed, and then recall it meaningfully" (Thornbury, 2017). Students can say the sentence to another student, to a small group, or to the teacher, which naturally provides an authentic audience—a key to any meaningful language learning activity.

Think alouds, sometimes known as *interactive read alouds,* serve as a great opportunity for teachers to demonstrate their use of reading strategies. We do think alouds with many different types of texts—fiction and nonfiction.

In this strategy, the teacher again reads a text aloud demonstrating prosody but also pauses every so often to share his or her thinking. We find it most effective for

ELL students if we place the text on the document camera and demonstrate our use of reading strategies by writing annotations in the margins (we sometimes just share our comments orally with our most advanced ELLs). In other words, we may pause after reading the title and write down a question that comes to mind. Then we may read the first paragraph and pause to write a connection or summary statement in the margin.

Figure 10.2 is an example of a think aloud that Katie did with intermediate ELL students at the middle school level, but it could easily be used with older students. She worked with expert literacy teacher Dana Dusbiber to develop a unit examining the benefits of reading. The comments in italics have been inserted where the teacher broke from the text to share her thinking with students. The teacher also wrote her comments down on the copy of the think aloud under the document camera in order to make her thinking even more explicit to students.

Students can then practice making annotations on their own copies of the text, share them with a partner, and discuss them as a class. As with read alouds, students can develop their own think alouds by writing their thoughts in the margins, reading the text to a partner, and pausing to share their thoughts aloud.

Modeling our metacognitive processes of deciding which reading strategies to use and when to use them can assist students in employing these processes on their own (Boulware-Gooden et al., n.d.; Williams & Atkins, 2009, p. 39).

## WHOLE-CLASS READINGS

We often use the following process when we are going to read a text (an article, a poem, a story). Although this is definitely not an exhaustive list of reading support activities, it does represent what we generally do.

### Before Reading

#### Vocabulary

Before reading a text with ELLs, we determine any key words or concepts that students will need to know in order to access the text. Sometimes we simply provide students with the words and their meanings. Other times we may give students a word chart (see Strategy 4: Vocabulary for an example of a word chart and further vocabulary strategies).

#### Activating and Building Prior Knowledge

We also consider ways to activate or build students' background knowledge in order to aid their comprehension and increase engagement. If the teacher knows the class is familiar with the topic of the text, he or she may simply provide students with the topic and ask them to share what they know with a partner and then with the class. If more explanation is needed, students could then do any or all of the following activities—start a KWL chart, do an anticipation guide, respond to a quickwrite, or watch a short video (see Strategy 5: Activating Prior Knowledge for more detailed explanations and examples of these activities).

### *Previewing Text Structure*

We often ask students to scan the text we will be reading and look for what they notice about the text's structure. For example, we might ask, "Are there headings or any bold words? If so, what does that tell us?" "Does the text include quotations and what does that tell us?" This helps ELLs begin to notice the differences in text structures of different genres and to make predictions about the upcoming text.

### *Setting a Purpose*

It is also helpful for ELL students to set a purpose for their reading, in other words, having a *why* for reading. Sometimes readers have multiple purposes—to learn new vocabulary and new information or to figure out an author's claim and find the evidence used to support it. Other times, a reader's purpose may simply be to read for enjoyment or to learn the steps of how to do something. In whole-class readings, we will often set the purpose so students know what to look for as we are reading (e.g., looking for describing words in the passage or identifying the author's claims and evidence).

### During Reading

### *Reading the Text*

We have found it most effective to read the text aloud to ELL students as they follow the words on their own copy of the text. This enables us to model pronunciation and prosody and frees students to focus on comprehension. As we described in Strategy 3: Graphic Organizers, sometimes we stop periodically and have students take turns dictating sentences from the text to a partner who writes it on a mini-whiteboard. This gives students the chance to practice reading the text aloud and builds their listening and speaking skills.

Providing our students with a variety of texts (whether they are written texts, digital texts, photographs, videos, infographics, etc.) and with a balance of highly accessible and more challenging texts are two key instructional goals we strive to meet. We also find it most effective to teach thematically—when all the texts in a unit are related to an engaging, meaningful theme. Thematic instruction is supported by research indicating its positive impact on student learning (Northwest Regional Educational Laboratory, 2012).

Figure 10.2: Think Aloud Example, which we discussed in the section Read Alouds and Think Alouds, is one of the texts used in a thematic unit for intermediates on the benefits of reading. Another text we used in this unit is Figure 10.3: Benefits of Reading Data Set. For this activity, we read the first few items of the data set aloud to students and then they took turns reading the rest with a partner. Then students reread each item and added an annotation (see next section). We then gave students the categories for the data set. They worked with a partner to determine which items fit into which category and either highlighted evidence in the text or wrote a sentence supporting their opinion. See Strategy 11: Inductive Learning for more information on inductive data sets.

### *Annotating the Text*

As we read text with students, we often model using various reading strategies through annotation. For example, after reading a paragraph or two, we may pause and write a summary statement in the margin. We might underline a particularly descriptive sentence and draw a quick sketch in the margin of what we are visualizing as we read it. We encourage students to make their own annotations by marking up the text itself or, if this isn't an option, writing on sticky notes. We may model a specific strategy and then ask students to do it when they are new to the process. Once they've had practice with multiple strategies and when to use them, students can apply the ones that are most helpful.

A note about highlighting: We model how to use highlighting as a tool for readers. It can help the reader focus on key ideas and stay engaged while reading. We also show students how effective highlighting can save them time when rereading in preparation for writing about the text. Instead of having to reread every word, students can quickly locate key ideas that are highlighted. We explicitly teach our students these dos and don'ts: *Do* highlight key words that express the main ideas. *Don't* highlight unnecessary words such as *and, but, it, the,* and so on or highlight all the words in a sentence. It takes modeling and practice, but we do notice improvement in our students' highlighting over time.

Recently, some researchers have questioned the effectiveness of highlighting as a studying tool (Paul, 2013). Researcher Daniel Willingham (2016) has said that when teachers compare their classroom practice to research findings they should ask themselves, "How am I using this practice differently than it's been tested?" After examining these recent studies, we are confident in saying that our use of highlighting in the classroom is substantially different from how it has been used in the research. Test results have been the primary measure of effectiveness in those studies (Dunlosky et al., 2013). They have not measured the goals of improved writing quality and engagement, which, in our opinion, are more important than standardized test results.

### Using Graphic Organizers

As we've described in our previous books and in this book, graphic organizers are a key scaffold for ELL's (see Strategy 3: Graphic Organizers). They are critical for supporting comprehension and sustaining student engagement in the reading process. Depending on the text and the goals of the lesson, we use a variety of graphic organizers that students complete during and after reading. For example, if we are reading an argument piece, we may provide students with a graphic organizer that contains boxes where students can write in the author's claims and evidence. Students can complete a story map when reading a story. It is helpful to use organizers that reflect the text's structure and for students to be actively involved in completing them (not just copying the teacher's model). Graphic organizers for a variety of text structures can easily be found online.

### After Reading

#### Summarizing the Text

We often have students practice the important skill of summarizing what they've read. This can be done while students are reading by having them work in pairs or on their own to write summary statements for different sections of text. Students can then use these annotations to write a paragraph summary of the whole text after reading. In our second book, *Navigating the Common Core with English Language Learners* (2016, p. 122–124), we explain how we have students create a visual summary for a text they've read, which helps students and teachers monitor comprehension. Here are the quick steps for doing a visual summary activity:

1. Teacher divides the text into numbered sections and creates a simple chart containing the same number of boxes.

2. The teacher models rereading the first section of the text (referring to any highlighting or annotations as a support). Then he or she draws an image (pictures or symbols) to represent the key ideas in that section. The teacher can also add key words, phrases, or a one-sentence summary of the ideas in that section.

3. Students then do the same process, either working with a partner or individually.

4. The teacher circulates offering assistance and selecting helpful student examples to display on the document camera.

A new application related to visually summarizing text comes from Katie's work with Dana Dusbiber. We previously referred to the think aloud (Figure 10.2) and the data set (Figure 10.3) they used with intermediate ELLs in a unit on the benefits of reading. After reading multiple texts on this topic and viewing several video clips, Katie and Dana provided students with Figure 10.4: "What People Say About . . ." Graphic Organizer to capture the key claims in each text. It can be completed following class reading of each text or it can be given to students after all the readings are finished. This type of tool helps students gather the key claims made in each text on one page in preparation for writing their own argument. Here is the writing prompt used in the Benefits of Reading Unit:

> According to the texts and videos we've studied in class, what are the benefits of reading books regularly? Do you agree with these claims and the evidence given to support them? To support your opinion, you may use examples from your own experiences, your observations of others, and anything you've read or watched (including the benefits of reading data set).

In Figure 10.4, each author or source studied during the unit is represented by an image (a stick figure, a book, a video screen) with an accompanying speech bubble. Teachers can first model how to put an author's main claim into their own words and then write it in the speech bubble. Students can work in pairs or small groups to write the main claims of the other authors or sources in the corresponding speech bubbles. Another option is to have students identify and copy a direction quotation representing the author's claim into the speech bubble. This graphic organizer helps to scaffold the process of including quotations from multiple sources, especially by providing space for the authors' names and the titles of the texts.

This organizer can be modified depending on the writing task. We've found it is very helpful for ELL students to see the different authors and their opinions all on one page—they can actually point to the claims with which they agree or disagree. Students can then use this organizer as a writing resource. For even more on summarizing, see Strategy 15: Quoting, Summarizing, and Paraphrasing.

### *Responding to the Text*

Students can develop and demonstrate their comprehension by responding to a variety of speaking or writing prompts after reading. See Strategy 2: Literary Conversations for a list of creative response prompts and other helpful activities.

See Strategy 25: Conversation Practice and Strategy 30: Oral Presentations for ways students can demonstrate reading comprehension while building their listening and speaking skills.

**CLOSE READING**

We've written extensively about how we do close reading with ELLs in *Navigating the Common Core with English Language Learners* (2016). In this section, we will summarize the process we use and introduce some new ideas we've come across since writing that book.

We use close reading once or twice during a unit to support our ELL students in accessing complex texts and applying reading comprehension strategies in more-sophisticated ways. Close reading differs from the other types of reading we do in class because we purposely choose increasingly complex texts. We also work on slowing down so that students have multiple touches with these texts. In other words, students read the text more than once and for different purposes—to comprehend the text on a basic level, to examine word choice and structure, to analyze the central ideas, and so on.

The other difference in close reading is that we tend to focus more on the Common Core–supported strategy of asking text-dependent questions when students are required to look for evidence in the text to support their answers. We are also more careful about building background knowledge before close reading. We try to make sure that any background provided is truly necessary for students to access the text. We don't want it to act as a substitute for what can be learned through close reading the text itself.

It is also important for the teacher to identify the purpose for close reading. In other words, asking, "What are the conceptual goals for students?" (e.g., identifying claims and evidence, finding figurative language and why it is being used) and "What are the language-learning goals?" (e.g., learning three new words based on the use of context clues). Then teachers can select a text that is appropriate for both goals. Another key consideration is text length. With ELLs we recommend that the text for close reading be anywhere between one paragraph and two pages, though we have had more success using texts on the shorter end of that range.

The close-reading sequence that follows appeared in our last book, *Navigating the Common Core with English Language Learners* (2016), and contains the process of close reading we usually do with students. This sequence is a summary containing a few examples of questions and answer frames. We have also added a final step we recently learned from literacy experts Douglas Fisher and Nancy Frey. See the Technology Connections section for a link to our *Navigating* book's website where you can download *all* the figures, including sentence frames, for free.

**Step 1: Previewing the Text—What the Text Might Say**

We teach our students to survey a text on seeing it for the first time and to ask themselves questions that can help them make some predictions. We provide students with questions and answer frames. For example:

1. What type of text is this (a story, an article, a poem, etc.)? How do I know this?

   ("I think this text is _____ because _____.")

2. What is the title of this text? What predictions can I make about the text based on the title?

   ("The title is _____. Based on this title, I predict and _____.")

3. Who is this text written for (who is the audience)? What makes me think this?

   ("I believe the text is written for _____ because _____.")

**Step 2: Basic Comprehension and Decoding—What the Text Says**

The short headings in Steps 2, 3, and 4 come from literacy expert Timothy Shanahan (n.d.).

In this step, students read the text for the *first time* with the purpose of developing a basic understanding of it. The teacher can read aloud while students follow along on their copy of the text. At this time, the teacher can encourage students to underline a few unfamiliar words or jot down a couple of questions that come to mind. To assist students in understanding the text on a basic level, we provide literal-type questions along with sentence frames for student responses and encourage them to develop their own as well. After this first reading, students can work to answer a selection of teacher-provided questions along with any they generated on their own. Students should be encouraged to find evidence in the text to support their answers.

Here are two examples that work for fiction:

1. What is the setting of the text (setting means both place and time)?

   ("I think the text is set in _____ during _____. I think that because the author writes .")

2. Is there a conflict or problem in the text?

   ("I think a conflict or problem is _____ because the author writes _____.")

Here are two examples for nonfiction:

1. What is the text about?

   ("I think the text is about _____. The clues I see in the text are _____ and _____.")

2. What questions does the text make you wonder about?

   ("I wonder what/how/when/if/who because _____.")

**Step 3: More In-Depth Meaning—Figure Out How the Text Works**

Students read the text a *second time* in this step in order to dig a little deeper into the text and focus more on the text's structure and language. This time, students can read with partners (taking turns every few sentences or every other paragraph) or read on their own. After reading, they again can choose from a selection of teacher-generated questions that push them to gain a greater understanding of the text. For example:

1. What is a context clue to the meaning of ?

   ("I think means because the author writes _____.")

2. Is there dialogue (people talking) in the text? If so, why do you think the author uses it?

   ("I think the author uses dialogue because he or she wants to . For example, he or she wrote _____.")

3. What did the author mean by ?

   ("I think when the author wrote he or she meant _____.")

**Step 4: Picking It Apart—Analyze and Compare the Text**

Students now read the text again on their own and choose one question to answer from a list of more analytical questions. For example:

1. Is the author pushing a particular position and, if so, what evidence does he or she give to support that position?

   ("I think the author believes . I think the evidence he or she uses to support his or her belief is . I think that evidence is valid/invalid because _____.")

2. Does this text remind you in some way of another text you have read? How?

   ("This text reminds me of because that text also _____.")

As part of this step, students can be given another text from the same author, in the same genre, or on the same topic. The text could be printed words, a close-captioned video, a comic strip, an infographic, and so forth. Students could repeat Steps 2, 3, and the beginning of Step 4 with the second text and then work to compare the two texts by answering a variation of the following question:

> Why do you think Text A contained certain information, text structures, or certain vocabulary while Text B did not?

Students could also use a graphic organizer, such as a Venn diagram, to compare the two texts.

### Step 5: Taking Action—What the Text Inspires You to Do Now

We were introduced to the thinking behind this last step by Douglas Fisher and Nancy Frey (2016) in their *Edutopia* blog post "Questioning That Deepens Comprehension."

They explain that once students deeply understand a complex text, they can be inspired to act on the new information or insights they've gained. This action can take many forms and can look different for each student. Some ideas they suggest are writing about the text, presenting to the class, conducting further research on a topic, and participating in a debate, among others. We have offered our students these options along with several others:

- Writing a letter to the author of the text
- Creating a digital book summarizing the new information learned
- Forming a book club to read other texts by the author or a different author in the same genre
- Writing and illustrating a comic book based on the text
- Creating a video

Looking for opportunities for our students to take action can promote a sense of agency—a feeling that students are active participants in their lives and not just reactors to, or observers of, others, in other words, being the driver of a car and not just a passenger in it. This is particularly important to ELLs, many of whom have arrived in this country with little input into the decision to move.

**Important note to teachers:** Remember, the close-reading process can and should be applied to other types of texts—photographs, charts, infographics, close-captioned videos, and so on. See Strategy 17: Using Photos or Other Images in Reading and Writing for ideas on helping students to do close reading with images. In Strategy 21: Problem-Posing we discuss a version of close reading we do with beginners that also leads to taking action, primarily in the community.

## Student Handouts and Examples

Figure 10.1: Reading Strategies Word Chart

Figure 10.2: Think Aloud Example

Figure 10.3: Benefits of Reading Data Set

Figure 10.4: "What People Say About . . ." Graphic Organizer

## What Could Go Wrong?

Be strategic about the purpose and frequency of close reading with students. We like educator Laurie Elish-Piper's statement, "Close reading is like broccoli. It's good for you, but only in moderation" (Gallagher, 2015).

Doing a close reading of every text not only can overwhelm students but also can quickly squash their interest in reading. In addition, you can sometimes do a close read of a text *without* following every single step we list in the sequence, and we often do just that. As community organizers often say, "We live in the world as it is, not as we would like it to be." Time constraints and other real-life events force us to regularly modify our meticulously thought-out plans.

Asking students to think and read at higher levels, while keeping engagement high, is not an easy task for teachers. Research cautions that students may appear "busiest and most involved with material they already know" (Hendrick, 2015). We need to use strategies and texts that promote our students' curiosity and engagement in reading, but we also need to observe and assess their comprehension skills to ensure they are growing in reading and English proficiency.

## Technology Connections

Students can practice applying the reading strategies they are learning in class to online text. There are many sites where students can annotate and highlight while reading online. See a list of them at The Best Applications for Annotating Websites (http://larryferlazzo.edublogs.org/2008/12/18/best-applications-for-annotating-websites/).

Teachers can also set up virtual classrooms where students can read and annotate and teachers can see their progress. You can find links to these sites at The Best Sites That Students Can Use Independently and Let Teachers Check On Progress (http://larryferlazzo.edublogs.org/2008/05/21/the-best-sites-that-students-can-use-independently-and-let-teachers-check-on-progress/).

For more on close reading with various types of texts see The Best Resources on Close Reading Paintings, Photos & Videos (http://larryferlazzo.edublogs.org/2015/08/05/the-best-resources-on-close-reading-paintings-photos-videos/) and The Best Resources on "Close Reading" (http://larryferlazzo.edublogs.org/2013/05/13/the-best-resources-on-close-reading-help-me-find-more/).

You can download Exhibit 5.3: Reading Strategies Data Set along with all the figures in *The ESL/ELL Teacher's Survival Guide* (Ferlazzo & Sypnieski, 2012) at that book's website (www.wiley.com/WileyCDA/WileyTitle/productCd-1118095677.html).

You can download Exhibit 3.3: Question and answer starter list for close reading at our *Navigating the Common Core with English Language Learners* (Ferlazzo & Sypnieski, 2016) website (www.wiley.com/WileyCDA/WileyTitle/productCd-1119023009.html).

If you'd like to access many of the resources we used to create the benefits of reading unit, see http://larryferlazzo.edublogs.org/2013/07/13/the-best-videos-articles-where-athletes-explain-how-reading-writing-well-has-helped-their-career-help-me-find-more/ and http://larryferlazzo.edublogs.org/2016/08/13/the-best-resources-on-the-study-finding-that-reading-books-makes-you-live-longer/.

## Attribution

Versions of some of these ideas appeared in our book *Navigating the Common Core with English Language Learners* (Ferlazzo & Sypnieski, 2016, p. 100–107, 122–123, 128–130).

Our thanks to Douglas Fisher and Nancy Frey for their exceptional *Edutopia* blog post "Questioning That Deepens Comprehension" (www.edutopia.org/blog/questioning-that-deepens-comprehension-douglas-fisher-nancy-frey?utm_source=twitter&utm_medium=socialflow).

Our thanks to Dana Dusbiber for her excellent work on the benefits of reading unit.

Our thanks to Sean Banville (n.d.) for his article "People Who Read Live Longer" (www.breakingnewsenglish.com/1608/160810-reading.html). His sites for English language learners offer a wealth of materials for students and teachers.

# Figures

| Strategy | My Drawing or Translation | How It Works and How I Can Use It |
|---|---|---|
| Asking questions | | I wonder _____.<br>Why . . . ?<br>Will . . . ?<br>What does _____mean? |
| Making predictions | | I predict _____ because _____.<br>Based on _____, I think that _____. |
| Visualizing | | When I read _____, I picture _____.<br>I visualize _____ because _____. |
| Summarizing | | This story is about _____.<br>The main idea is _____.<br>From the text I learned _____ about _____. |
| Making connections | | This reminds me of _____ because _____.<br>_____ and _____ are similar because_____. |
| Evaluating | | I agree (or disagree with) _____ because _____.<br>In my opinion, _____. |
| Inferring | | The text says _____ and I know _____, therefore I guess that _____.<br>I infer _____ based on _____. |

**Figure 10.1** Reading Strategies Word Chart

## People Who Read Live Longer [That's an interesting title—how does reading help you live longer?]

New research shows that people who read a lot live longer. The study was carried out by researchers from Yale University in the USA. The researchers said reading keeps the mind active, helps reduce stress, and makes us take better care of our health.

*[This reminds me of the quote we read by President Obama about how reading helps him manage stress.]* The researchers said that books help the brain more than newspapers and magazines, but any kind of reading will help us to live longer. *[I wonder why books are better?]* Even reading for half an hour a day could help us to live longer. In the study, researchers looked at the lifestyles of 3,500 men and women over a 12-year period. They looked at their reading habits, health, lifestyle and their education. All of the people were at least 50 years old at the start of the research.

The study is in the journal *Social Science and Medicine*. It found that people who read for up to 3.5 hours a week were 17 percent less likely to die during the study's 12-year research period than those who read no books. Those who read for more than 3.5 hours a week were 23 percent less likely to die. Researcher Becca Levy said: "Older individuals, regardless of gender, health, wealth or education, showed the survival advantage of reading books." *[So I think she's saying that no matter how old you are or how rich you are, reading will help you live longer.]* She suggested people swap watching TV for reading to live longer. *[Oh no! But I love "America's Got Talent"!]* She said: "Individuals over the age of 65 spend an average of 4.4 hours per day watching television. Efforts to redirect leisure time into reading books could prove to be beneficial."

### SOURCES

http://www.dailymail.co.uk/health/article-3726386/Why-reading-help-live-longer-Immersing-good-story-mind-active-ease-stress.html

http://www.huffingtonpost.com/entry/those-who-read-books-live-longer-than-those-who-dont-study-finds_us_57a358c8e4b0104052a17cd2

https://www.rawstory.com/2016/08/a-new-study-has-found-that-avid-readers-appear-to-live-a-longer-life/

**Figure 10.2** Think Aloud Example *Source:* This article is reprinted here with the permission of Sean Banville (www.breakingnewsenglish.com/1608/160810-reading.html)

(1) "Books showed me there were possibilities in life, that there were actually people like me living in a world I could not only aspire to, but attain. Reading gave me hope. For me, it was the open door."
—Oprah Winfrey

(2) "At an early age, I always felt there was something relaxing and enjoyable about reading . . . and I still feel that way today: Reading is the best way for me to clear my mind and slow down."
—Andrew Luck

(3) "If you are a reader, then you have the ability to educate yourself. When you have the ability to be a lifelong learner, there are no limits on what you can acquire in terms of knowledge and information. It represents the ultimate freedom of humankind."
—LeVar Burton

(4) "It is not enough to simply teach children to read; we have to give them something worth reading . . . something that will help them make sense of their own lives and encourage them to reach out toward people whose lives are quite different from their own."
—Katherine Paterson

(5) "Reading has given me an opportunity, just for those . . . 25 minutes before the game . . . to read and think about something else and get a sense of what else is going on besides the game of basketball. It's made me comfortable . . . It's just something that I decided to do at the beginning of the postseason, and it's worked for me."
—LeBron James

(6) "Reading gave me the ability to slow down, get perspective, and walk in somebody else's shoes."
—President Barack Obama

**Figure 10.3** Benefits of Reading Data Set

(7) "Reading in some small way makes me a more productive athlete, and being a pro athlete makes me enjoy the serenity that reading provides just a little bit more."

—Dan Grunfeld

(8) "Whether reading books has made me a better president I can't say. But what I can say is that [reading books] has allowed me to sort of maintain my balance during the course of eight years."

—President Barack Obama

## Categories

- Stress Management or Comfort
- The Power of Reading
- Empathy and Understanding Others
- Reading and Athletic Performance

**Figure 10.3** (*Continued*)

**Figure 10.4** "What People Say About . . ." Graphic Organizer

# *STRATEGY 11*

# Inductive Learning

## What Is It?

When inductive methods are used in teaching and learning, students are presented with examples and are challenged to identify patterns in them. Inductive teaching uses a progression of going from the specific to the general. This instructional strategy contrasts with deductive teaching and learning in which the teacher presents the rule or concept and then reinforces with examples. In other words, it applies a sequence of going from the general to the specific.

For example, an inductive phonics lesson on differentiating between the long and short *a* sound might start by showing a series of words, supported by images, using the patterns of *ai, a-e,* and *ay*. Students could be asked to categorize those words, identify additional ones that fit into those patterns, say the words to a partner, and develop rules for those patterns as they practice the language. A subsequent lesson would do the same with words using a short *a* sound.

A deductive lesson, however, might begin with a teacher listing the patterns where a long *a* is present, sharing a list of those words, and having students practice writing and saying them.

## Why We Like It

We are proponents of the inductive method in many cases because it is more student-led than teacher-led. In addition, Duke psychology professor Dan Ariely (2016) often talks about the "IKEA effect"—we tend to value something more highly when we are involved in its creation as opposed to being presented with a finished product.

## Supporting Research

Substantial research (Prince & Felder, 2007) finds that this kind of guided discovery or enhanced discovery teaching (Ferlazzo, 2016, October 2) not only enhances student autonomy and motivation but also results in greater learning of content, retention (Stafford, 2011), and ability to transfer and apply knowledge to new situations (Ferlazzo, 2015, June 19). The pattern-seeking that is supported by inductive learning has been found to be especially effective in acquiring first (University of Sydney, 2016) and new languages (Association for Psychological Science, 2013). Interestingly enough, this ability to recognize patterns is also being sought more and more by employers, as well (Wilson, 2015).

## Common Core Connections

Inductive teaching specifically supports the Common Core State Standards. Induction is basically a strategy of noticing and seeking patterns. The Common Core explicitly promotes pattern-seeking—in word, sentence, and text structures; in oral discourse (Morrow et al., 2012); and in literature analysis (Common Core State Standards Initiative, n.d.e).

## Application

Under the instructional strategy umbrella of inductive learning, we will explore several specific ways to implement this method in the English language learner classroom: the picture word inductive model, data sets, and concept attainment. We will discuss concept attainment—plus (Strategy 12) as a separate instructional strategy because it requires a more lengthy explanation.

### PICTURE WORD INDUCTIVE MODEL (PWIM)

The PWIM (Calhoun, 1999) is a multistep language-development strategy that we use primarily with beginning English language learners. The steps and sequence can vary, but the following describes the general week-long process we use.

It begins with the teacher first choosing an image (including many different objects and people) based on the lesson theme (home, school, food, etc.). Figure 11.1: Man in the Kitchen is an example of an image we use in our unit on home. The photo is enlarged and laminated, and smaller paper copies are made for each student. Later, after students become familiar with the process, the class can be given the option to help choose the images.

> **Day 1:** All students come up to the large image and help label the objects by taking turns sharing the words they know. The teacher writes them, asking students to repeat each letter and then the word. The teacher adds new words that students do not know. The students return to their seats and copy down the words on their copy of the photo.

Students work in pairs to categorize the words—either by word structure (words that start with the letter *r*) or by broader subjects (things, people, colors) and then add new words that fit into those categories. Categories can either be student- or teacher-generated.

**Day 2:** After reviewing the words on the picture as a class, students are given a series of clozes or gap-fill sentences (see Figure 11.2: Kitchen Picture Cloze Sentences) describing the picture using some of the labeled words. Students complete the sentences, cut them out, and arrange the strips into categories on their desk (being sure to highlight the evidence they are using to support their being placed in a particular category). For example, in the case of Figure 11.2, two categories could be "things that are not living" and "things that are living." Next, students glue the cloze sentences on paper underneath the category title and leave space for additional sentences. They then begin to write new sentences (if they have a high-enough English proficiency level) describing the photo, which they add to their categories.

**Day 3:** Again, after reviewing the words on the picture, students complete writing new sentences and then turn the sentences (the cloze sentences and their own) into paragraphs. By the end of the day, they have several parts of a simple essay completed.

**Days 4 and 5:** These activities depend on the English proficiency level of the students. Newcomers can write a list of potential titles for their essay and choose one to write at the top or complete paragraph frames for simple introduction and conclusion paragraphs. Others can learn to write simple topic sentences for paragraphs ("There are many things in the kitchen."). Higher-level English-proficient students can learn to write introductory paragraphs including hooks and thesis statements, along with conclusions.

**Extensions:** As students advance, many modifications can be made to the PWIM:

- Instead of clozes, teachers can provide questions to students that they have to answer in sentences and then categorize their responses.

- Students can create clozes themselves that their classmates have to complete and categorize.

- Instead of providing cloze sentences, teachers can create paragraphs about the images with blanks needing to be filled in by students.

- Teachers can identify a somewhat similar image to one being used and have students create a Venn diagram comparing and contrasting one to the other.

- Students can develop thought bubbles for the people or animals in the picture or conversations between people in the image. Our students enjoy this activity.

- Assuming the image is hanging on a whiteboard, students draw what they imagine could be happening in other parts of the image if it were larger (Ferlazzo, 2016, September 23). Our students also have had a lot of fun with this particular extension.

Ways to incorporate technology in the PWIM are discussed in the Technology Connections section.

## TEXT, PHONICS, AND PICTURE DATA SETS

In the context of inductive learning, data sets are collections of texts, words, or pictures with a common theme.

### Text Data Sets

Figures 11.3: International New Year's Traditions Data Set (for Intermediates), 11.4: John F. Kennedy Data Set (for Intermediates), and 11.5: Seasons of the Year Data Set (for Beginners) show three examples of text data sets. These data sets are composed of a series of one-sentence examples. Other data sets can be made lengthier and more complex depending on student English proficiency (such as the benefits of reading data set shared previously).

Here is a typical sequence we use while teaching a text data set:

**Step 1:** Teachers read each sentence or word aloud. For higher-level English-proficient students, texts can be more complex and not necessarily read aloud by the teacher. Instead, students can read them individually or in pairs. Teachers also can add a further step—having students apply a reading comprehension strategy such as summarizing, visualizing, or asking a question of each text item.

**Step 2:** Students categorize the sentences or words while highlighting evidence supporting their category placement. Teachers can supply the categories or ask students to develop their own. Students then cut and paste the sentences under the category names—this action can make it easier to do the next step. However, we sometimes skip this step due to time constraints and have students simply write the category name next to each sentence.

**Step 3:** Students add information to their categories either through prior knowledge or through further research (reading, video).

**Step 4:** Students can either turn those categories into paragraphs (and, ultimately, an entire essay) or be asked to create a poster summarizing the main points of each category and drawing a representative picture. In the latter case, students can subsequently present their posters in small groups.

After students become familiar with the process, we often have students create their own text data sets about topics of high interest (see Figure 11.6: Data Set Instructions for a student guide to create data sets). They then teach an inductive lesson to their classmates in small groups.

Text data sets can also be used to teach language skills and vocabulary, for example, one showing different examples of how punctuation can be used (question marks, exclamation points, quotation marks, etc.). Instead of using those sentences to create essays, students can make posters explaining the rules they have developed from the categorization activity. Or a data set describing events that take place during different parts of the day can be used to teach the concepts of morning, afternoon, and evening.

**Phonics Data Sets**

Phonics instruction is particularly important for students with interrupted formal education. We teach phonics inductively, and the easiest resource available for this activity is the book *Sounds Easy!* by Sharron Bassano (2002). A sample page from that book teaching the long *a* sound can be found in Figure 11.7. We follow the instructional directions found in the book, which include teachers showing an image on an overhead, saying the word that describes that image, and giving students a few seconds to write it down. Then, the teacher writes the correct word so students can see it and check their work.

We then have students extend this activity to include an inductive process similar to how we use a text data set. Students work in pairs to look for patterns among the words (e.g., *cake, gate, grape, rake*), categorize them (words that have the pattern "consonant-*a*-consonant-*e*"), and identify the appropriate rules (e.g., if the pattern is "consonant-*a*-consonant-*e*" then the word has a long *a* sound). They then consider other words they know or research new ones that follow the same rules. Next, they create posters listing their words and the appropriate rules to share with the class.

An additional extension activity we use is having students draw a picture using as many objects or actions as they can from the *Sounds Easy!* page or from their new ones. Then, they write sentences describing their picture or a story about it.

It is also important to follow up this kind of phonics instruction with phonemic-awareness activities, which we discuss in Strategy 35: Supporting ELL Students with Interrupted Formal Education (SIFEs). In addition, the first two games listed in Strategy 23: Learning Games for Reading and Writing are ones we often use as part of our phonics instruction, and we discuss how we play them there.

**Picture Data Sets**

Picture data sets can be used in similar ways to text and phonics data sets. They are most easily done online with thematically based categories that are created either by the teacher or student. For example, while studying signs, students can search online for signs fitting into these categories: labels or names, warnings, instruction, and information. There are many free online tools that enable users to create virtual corkboards, where students can easily copy and paste images of signs into categories (see Technology Connections). Students can also write the sign's message in their own words (e.g., "This sign says, do not drive fast."). Transportation is another easy theme for creating this kind of picture data set (e.g., public, cars, sea, air, people-powered, etc.). Students can even use their phones to take photos to add to their categories. Of course, similar projects can also be done by cutting out pictures from magazines and pasting them in categories on poster paper.

Follow-up activities include students presenting their picture data sets to a partner, a small group, or the entire class.

## CONCEPT ATTAINMENT

The following explanation, except for the new figures, originally appeared in the *ELL/ESL Teacher's Survival Guide* (Ferlazzo & Sypnieski, 2012).

Concept attainment, originally developed by Jerome Bruner and his colleagues (Bruner, Goodnow, & Austin, 1956) is a form of inductive learning in which the teacher identifies "good" and "bad" examples of the intended learning objective (ideally, either taken from student work—with the names removed, of course—or teacher-created based on review of student writing).

First, the teacher develops sheets similar to the ones in Figures 11.8 and 11.9. Figure 11.8: Concept Attainment Example on Adjectives and Periods is designed to teach that adjectives come before nouns and that periods are placed at the end of sentences. Figure 11.9: Concept Attainment Example on *Has* and *Have* teaches when to use *has* and *have* correctly. The teacher would place the sheet on a document camera or overhead projector. At first, everything would be covered except for the *yes* and *no* titles. Then, the teacher would explain that he or she is going to give various examples, and students will identify why certain ones are under *yes* and others are under *no*.

After the first *yes* and *no* examples are shown, students are asked to think about them, and share with a partner why they think one is a *yes* and one is a *no*. After the teacher calls on people, if no one can identify the reason(s) (e.g. *have* is used with *they*), he or she continues uncovering one example at a time. The think-pair-share process continues until students identify the correct reason. Then students are asked to correct the *no* examples and write their own *yes* ones. Last, students can be asked to generate their own *yes* examples and share them with a partner or the class. This inductive learning strategy can be used effectively to teach countless lessons, including ones on grammar, spelling, and composition (Ferlazzo & Sypnieski, *The ESL/ELL Teacher's Survival Guide*, 2012, p. 53).

## Student Handouts and Examples

Figure 11.1: A Man in the Kitchen

Figure 11.2: Kitchen Picture Cloze Sentences

Figure 11.3: International New Year's Traditions Data Set (for Intermediates)

Figure 11.4: John F. Kennedy Data Set (for Intermediates)

Figure 11.5: Seasons of the Year Data Set (for Beginners)

Figure 11.6: Data Set Instructions

Figure 11.7: Page from *Sounds Easy! Phonics, Spelling, and Pronunciation Practice*

Figure 11.8: Concept Attainment Example on Adjectives and Periods

Figure 11.9: Concept Attainment Example on *Has* and *Have*

## What Could Go Wrong?

Of course, as with every instructional strategy, inductive learning can have a down side. In this case, inductive learning obviously can take a longer period of class time than a deductive lesson. Do we teach everything inductively? Of course not. When it comes to vocabulary, we might sometimes make a pedagogical decision to translate a word into a student's home language instead of spending an extra few minutes to find an image or act it out with gestures and objects. In other words, sometimes we decide that the time saved by teaching a concept explicitly and not inductively creates space for other better learning opportunities.

In addition, another problem of induction is that the conclusions reached through the process are based only on limited examples and do not take exceptions into account. Larry teaches this problem in his International Baccalaureate theory of knowledge classes using the famous example of many people believing all swans were white for many years until black swans were "discovered" in New Zealand. He also uses a more-recent example of playing basketball for years with his friend Don. Larry defends him well because Don almost always drives to the basket with his right hand. However, every now and then Larry is embarrassed on the court when Don chooses to go to his left.

Because there are so many exceptions to just about every rule in English, we cover ourselves by regularly telling our students that they will find exceptions to everything and that English is crazy. Most of the time, our students have already figured that out.

## Technology Connections

Technology makes it as easy as pie for intermediate ELLs students to create their own text data sets (which they can then teach to their classmates) or to add to their already-created categories from teacher-created ones. All they have to do is use the copy-and-paste function for online text, along with including the URL address of their source. See Figure 11.6: Data Set Instructions, which is a student handout describing this process.

Picture data sets can be easily created by beginning ELLs by using any of many free and easy-to-use sites to create bulletin boards (http://larryferlazzo.edublogs.org/2011/03/30/the-best-online-virtual-corkboards-or-bulletin-boards/). You can see examples at Larry's class blog (http://larryferlazzo.edublogs.org/?s=padlet). Images can be found via Google or at other sites we recommend (http://larryferlazzo.edublogs.org/2016/08/14/the-all-time-best-sources-of-online-images/).

Additional information on inductive teaching and learning, including many other examples, can be found at The Best Resources About Inductive Learning & Teaching (http://larryferlazzo.edublogs.org/2015/01/16/the-best-resources-about-inductive-learning-teaching/) .

## Attribution

Portions of this section originally appeared in our book, *The ESL/ELL Teacher's Survival Guide* (Ferlazzo & Sypnieski, 2012, p. 41–43, 53, and 58).

Emily F. Calhoun (1999) is credited with developing the picture word inductive model in her book *Teaching Beginning Reading and Writing with the Picture Word Inductive Model.*

## Figures

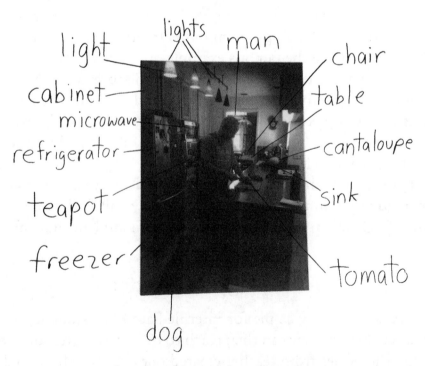

**Figure 11.1**    A Man in the Kitchen

1. The refrigerator is _____.

closed              soft              tiny              open

2. The _____ is on the _____.

tomato              man              stove              teapot

3. The _____ is above the stove.

refrigerator        sink              microwave         dog

4. The _____ is behind the cantaloupe.

man                 dog               refrigerator      sink

5. The dog is looking at the _____.

refrigerator        table             man               light

6. There are _____ above the _____ and microwave.

freezer             refrigerator      dishes            cabinets

**Figure 11.2** Kitchen Picture Cloze Sentences

7. The freezer is below the _____.

floor                    dog                    refrigerator              chair

8. The _____ is cutting a tomato.

dog                      man                    chair                    teapot

**Figure 11.2** (*Continued*)

**Categories:** Food, Names of New Year, Times of New Year, How New Year Is Celebrated

1. Many cultures celebrate New Year's Day on January 1st.
2. The Chinese New Year is also called the Lunar New Year.
3. There is always a big celebration in Times Square in New York City on New Year's Eve.
4. The Persian New Year is called Nauruz.
5. Khabse are cookies that are only made on Losar, the Tibetan New Year.
6. Rosh Hashanah is the name of the Jewish New Year.
7. Losar is the name of the Tibetan New Year.
8. Seven foods starting with the letter *s* are served on the Persian New Year.
9. Apples and honey are served on Rosh Hashanah.
10. The Vietnamese New Year is usually on the same day as the Chinese New Year.
11. The Islamic New Year is also known as the Hijri New Year.
12. In Vietnam the new year usually begins in February.
13. A shofar (ram's horn) is blown during Rosh Hashanah.

**Figure 11.3** International New Year's Traditions Data Set (for Intermediates)

**Categories:** Family, Accomplishments, and Challenges

1. John F. Kennedy was president of the United States from 1961 to 1963.

2. Kennedy was married to Jacqueline Kennedy and had three children. One died shortly after birth.

3. His ship was sunk in World War II and he almost died.

4. He was a United States senator from 1953 to 1961.

5. He was the first Catholic to become president. Some voters did not support him because of his faith.

6. He was assassinated by Lee Harvey Oswald on November 22, 1963.

7. Kennedy supported exploring space and promised that the United States would put a person on the moon.

8. He was the youngest person ever to be elected president.

9. He was the youngest president to die.

10. Kennedy wrote a book, *Profiles In Courage,* which won many awards.

11. He challenged the Soviet Union when that country put nuclear missiles in Cuba.

12. His father was the US ambassador to England, and his two brothers became US senators.

**Figure 11.4**  John F. Kennedy Data Set (for Intermediates)

**Categories:** Summer, Fall, Winter, and Spring

1. Students start going to school.
2. It's cold.
3. It rains or snows a lot.
4. It's very hot.
5. The leaves change color.
6. Christmas takes place during this season.
7. School ends when this season begins.
8. Cinco de Mayo takes place during this season.
9. Flowers bloom.
10. Most students don't go to school.

**Figure 11.5** Seasons of the Year Data Set (for Beginners)

1. Choose a topic and pick at least four categories about that topic.
2. Create a document named *Data Set Answer Key* and type the names of your categories there.
3. Look for information on one category.
4. Choose at least three passages of no more than five sentences each that relate to that category.
5. Copy and paste those three passages on that document under the name of that category on the Data Set Answer Key.
6. Repeat this process with your other three categories.
7. Now, create a new document and title it *Data Set for Students*. Type the names of your four categories under the title.
8. Now copy and paste all 12 passages on to this document so they are mixed up. In other words, passages from the same category are not next to each other. Once they are mixed up, number each passage.
9. Print out one copy of the Data Set Answer Key and four copies of the Data Set for Students document. You are now ready to be a teacher!

**Figure 11.6** Data Set Instructions

**Sounds Easy!** _____

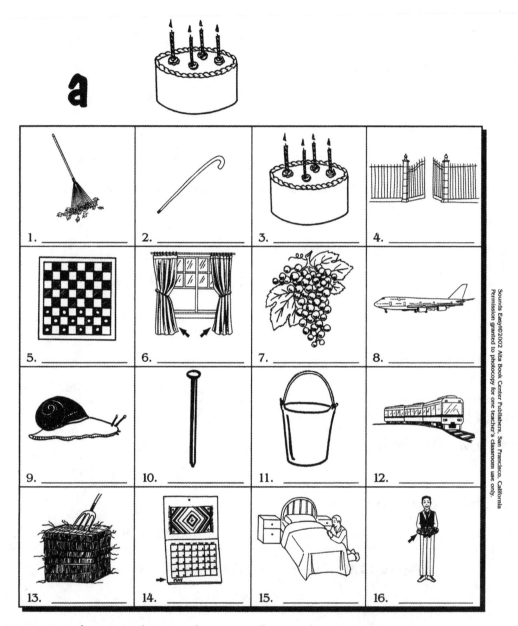

**Figure 11.7** Page from *Sounds Easy! Phonics, Spelling, and Pronunciation Practice*
*Source:* Reproduced by permission of S. Bassano. Palm Springs, California USA. Copyright 2002
ALTA English Publishers.

| Yes | No |
|---|---|
| He has a brown shirt. | |
| | She has a t-shirt pink. |
| She has a small dog. | |
| | The eagle has eyes big. |
| She has blue eyes. | |
| | He has hair black. |

**Figure 11.8** Concept Attainment Example on Adjectives and Periods

| Yes | No |
|---|---|
| She has shoes. | |
| | She have a small house. |
| She has a black shirt. | |
| | He have two cars. |
| He has blue eyes. | |
| They have a big house. | |
| | They has a dog. |
| John and Ana have a dog. | |
| | Carlos, Ava, and Leo has a cat. |

**Figure 11.9** Concept Attainment Example on *Has* and *Have*

## STRATEGY 12

# Concept Attainment—Plus!

### What Is It?

Concept attainment—plus! is a strategy we developed building on the popular concept attainment inductive learning concept (see Strategy 11: Inductive Learning). In it, student writing can be used (though teacher-created models are fine, too) to help students identify mistakes and immediately apply what they learn from them through a series of exercises.

### Why We Like It

Whereas concept attainment can be very effective in helping students gain a grasp of key concepts, this plus version challenges them to apply that understanding to a broader context.

### Supporting Research

Though there is no research specifically on this variation (because we recently invented it!), we believe it is safe to say the studies cited for inductive learning have equal relevance because the same methodology is used.

### Common Core Connections

This strategy can be used to support the writing of arguments, informative or explanatory texts, or narratives. It also specifically supports student planning, organizing, and editing their writing. This strategy can result in publication of student work online, as suggested in the Writing Standards, if the ideas mentioned in Technology Connections are used.

# Application

This strategy has several steps and can take an entire class period. The examples used here are designed for intermediate ELLs, but the strategy can be modified for higher- or lower-level English-proficient students. Depending on text complexity, it can take 30 minutes to 1 hour of teacher preparation time.

1. The teacher chooses an example of student writing (typically done in a response to a prompt) that illustrates one type of writing mistake and asks the student for permission to use it in teaching the class (with a commitment to not connect his or her name to the essay). In our experience, students are eager to have it used and often announce to the class that it is their writing being featured in the lesson. The teacher can also write his or her own example to model a particular mistake. The one in Figure 12.1: Student Example and Correction was written in response to the question "Is it important to know more than one language?" and was part of a unit on argument.

   In this figure, the student version is under one column labeled *No*. The teacher version has corrected student errors and is in the column titled *Yes*.

2. The teacher gives each student a copy of Figure 12.1 and reads the correct passage to the class. Then, students have to compare the two passages, identify the errors in the student's writing, and explain why they are mistakes (see Figure 12.2: Student Annotation of Mistakes). After students have completed their review, the teacher calls individual students up to the overhead individually to identify one mistake at a time. In this example, run-on sentences are highlighted as the primary issue.

3. The teacher then distributes a second sheet to students (see Figure 12.3: Teacher Mimic Write of Student Mistakes). It contains a short humorous passage in the *No* column that he or she has written and that mimics the errors in the first student passage (of course, humor is not required, but it is always helpful). Students have to identify the mistakes and rewrite it correctly on the left under the *Yes* column (see Figure 12.4: Teacher Mimic Write with Student Corrections). Students are called to the overhead to correct passages.

4. Next, the teacher gives students a simple and engaging prompt (see Figure 12.5: Student Writing Prompt and Response) where they need to write a passage demonstrating their understanding of the writing feature they have learned in the first two sheets. Ideally, the prompt is somewhat similar to the initial one, but it can also be different. Students can complete it as homework if there is not enough time left in the period.

## Student Handouts and Examples

Figure 12.1: Student Example and Correction

Figure 12.2: Student Annotation of Mistakes

Figure 12.3: Teacher Mimic Write of Student Mistakes

Figure 12.4: Teacher Mimic Write with Student Corrections

Figure 12.5: Student Writing Prompt and Response

## What Could Go Wrong?

Don't overdo it! Keep the passage short, and focus on *one* writing mistake. It's fine to also include one or two other minor mistakes that students can easily identify. Don't turn this exercise into a lengthy, tedious process that can reduce engagement and learning.

## Technology Connections

Research, and our own experience, shows that students tend to be more motivated to write when they know that others besides their teacher or a classmate are going to read it. There are many places on the web where students can find an audience for their writing, and you can find many options at The Best Places Where Students Can Write for an "Authentic Audience" (http://larryferlazzo.edublogs.org/2009/04/01/the-best-places-where-students-can-write-for-an-authentic-audience/). Research on the importance of authentic audiences can also be found there.

We've found an easy way to create this kind of audience is through hosting a class blog, having students publish their work there, and then creating time for multiple students to read and comment on it. Parents can easily access their child's work, too. You can read more about this process at The Best Sources for Advice on Student Blogging (http://larryferlazzo.edublogs.org/2008/12/26/the-best-sources-for-advice-on-student-blogging/) and see Larry's class blog (www.sacschoolblogs.org/larryferlazzo/). It is important to be aware of student online privacy issues, though, so be sure to read more at The Best Teacher Resources for Online Student Safety & Legal Issues (http://larryferlazzo.edublogs.org/2009/08/10/the-best-teacher-resources-for-online-student-safety-legal-issues/).

# Figures

## YES

This is important because it is good to know another language today. Many people speak two languages and many people speak English and Spanish. In the United States many people speak English. It is good to know English because in the United States in the shops the people speak only English. In the schools people only speak English and teachers only speak English.

## NO

This is important because it is good to know another language today many people speak two language and many people speak English and Spanish and in United State many people speak English it is good to know English because in United State in the shops the people speak only English in the schools people only speak English and teachers also only speak English.

**Instructions:** Mark mistakes with a colored pencil and explain why they are mistakes below (use the back of the paper if you need space):

**Figure 12.1** Student Example and Correction

# YES | # NO

**YES**

This is important because it is good to know another language today. Many people speak two languages and many people speck English and Spanish. In the United States many people speak English. It is good to know English because in the United States in the shops the people speak only English. In the schools people only speak English and teachers only speak English.

**NO**

This is important because it is good to know another language Today many people speak two language and many people speak English and Spanish, and In United StateS many people speak English. It is good to know English because in United State's in the shops the people speak only English, In the schools people only speak English and teachers also only speak English.

**Instructions:** Mark mistakes with a colored pencil and explain why they are mistakes below (use the back of the paper if you need space):

*1. The sentences is too longer. New sentences begin with a capital letter.*

*2. The sentence need period at last of the sentences.*

*3. He need know when the sentences need period or not and where.*

*4. He need put capital letter in each sentences.*

*5. He need to put the letter s after State*

**Figure 12.2** Student Annotation of Mistakes

# YES

# NO

**Instructions:** Mark mistakes in this text with a colored pencil and write a corrected version in the left column:

It is important to work hard in class because if you do not study you will not learn English Mr. Ferlazzo will cry because he will be very sad if he is sad his wife will never bake cookies to give to students he may not give students a passing grade Felipe and Carlos will be happy if they fail because they get to spend another year with Mr. Ferlazzo in English class. Sonia and Jackie will be very sad because they do not want to spend another year with him this is a joke because all of Mr. Ferlazzo's students think he is the best teacher in the world they want to spend the rest of their lives with him.

**Figure 12.3** Teacher Mimic Write of Student Mistakes

# YES | NO

**YES**

It is important to work hard in class because if you do not study you will not learn English. Mr. Ferlazzo will cry because he will be very sad. If he is sad his wife will never bake cookies to give to students. He may not give students a passing grade. Felipe and Carlos will be happy if they fail because they get to spend another year with Mr. Ferlazzo in English class. Sonia and Jackie will be very sad because they do not want to spend another year with him. This is a joke because all of Mr. Ferlazzo's students think he is the best teacher in the world. They want to spend the rest of their lives with him.

**NO**

**Instructions:** Mark mistakes in this text with a colored pencil and write a corrected version in the left column:

It is important to work hard in class because if you do not study you will not learn English Mr. Ferlazzo will cry because he will be very sad if he is sad his wife will never bake cookies to give to students he may not give students a passing grade Felipe and Carlos will be happy if they fail because they get to spend another year with Mr. Ferlazzo in English class. Sonia and Jackie will be very sad because they do not want to spend another year with him this is a joke because all of Mr. Ferlazzo's students think he is the best teacher in the world they want to spend the rest of their lives with him.

**Figure 12.4**   Teacher Mimic Write with Student Corrections

Name _____

Date _____

Mr. Ferlazzo says that it is important to spend at least 30 minutes each night reading, writing, or speaking English, or listening to English. Do you agree with what he says? Write at least seven sentences using what you learned in the Yes-No exercise we just did supporting your position with your own experience, your observations of others, and your readings.

*I agree that it is important to spent 30 minutes each night learning English. I read books English and I understand better. I play games on class blog when I home. I learn new words. American movies help learn English. I say it important because in my observation my uncle speak three languages and he study hard. I want be like my uncle.*

**Figure 12.5** Student Writing Prompt and Response

# Sentence Navigators and Sentence Builders

## What Is It?

Sentence navigators, also called *sentence builders,* are puzzle-like structures that challenge students to choose words and put them in order to construct a sentence. They must "navigate" through a grid of multiple words in order to pick the correct ones. Sentence navigators were created by Jason Renshaw, a former English teacher, who has given us permission to discuss and reproduce them here.

## Why We Like It

We like sentence navigators because they are versatile, low-prep tools that can reinforce vocabulary and sentence structure in an engaging way. We are especially attracted—and believe other teachers will feel the same—by the fact that students themselves can easily create navigators for use by their classmates.

## Supporting Research

Extensive research has shown the effectiveness of game-like activities in teaching and learning English (Martin, 2006). Sentence navigators easily can be seen as puzzles and, as we discussed in Strategy 6: Sequencing, completing puzzles encourages participants to move into a status of flow, which is the highest form of intrinsic motivation.

## Common Core Connections

Sentence navigators support many of the Language Standards. They particularly encourage students to understand and apply language conventions and acquire and reinforce vocabulary.

## Application

Teachers can create sentence navigators by first determining the vocabulary (e.g., family-related words) and sentence structure (e.g., answering a question) they want to reinforce. They then write the words that make up the correct sentence in different columns on the grid, followed by filling the rest of the squares with words of their choice to hide the correct words. See Figure 13.1: Model Sentence Navigator Answering Questions for an example of a sentence navigator designed to respond correctly to questions. Figure 13.2: Blank Sentence Navigator Answering Questions is a similar blank sheet, and Figure 13.3: Blank Sentence Navigator for Any Sentence is a blank sentence navigator sheet designed for sentences of any kind.

Teachers can create several of the navigators and pass copies out to students. During the first several times implementing this strategy, the teacher should model completing one on the overhead while thinking aloud (e.g., "The noun has more than one person or thing, so that means the verb doesn't have an *s* at the end of it."). He or she should then use a pencil and make a mistake. Next, the teacher can ask the class if they think he or she has it correct and make the appropriate revisions suggested by students. Drawing an appropriately ugly image in the box on the left representing the sentence so it can elicit laughter can also be a nice teacher move.

After modeling how it's done (you can never do too much modeling, and we're not talking about walking down the runway!), students can work on their sheets quietly and by themselves. The teacher circulates around the room and gives feedback to individual students (e.g., putting light check marks over the columns where the correct words were chosen and an *x* where the incorrect ones were picked so that students can revise their work). After several minutes (depending on the number of navigators they have to complete), the teacher can ask students to share their work in pairs. Next, the teacher can review them with the entire class by asking different students to come to the overhead and complete different ones.

After students become familiar with the navigators, they can be challenged to create their own. The teacher can model how he or she creates them by first writing the correct words down and filling in the other squares with additional words. Students can make their own (they don't need to be original at first—they can copy them out of their textbook or other texts the class has used) and challenge individual classmates to complete them. They can also turn them in to the teacher, who can make copies for everyone. If students want to use sentences with fewer words than the number of boxes on the grid, just tell them to cross out the boxes. If they want to make longer sentences, encourage them to make their own grids!

Jason has developed more sentence navigator versions than you can shake a stick at. See the Technology Connections section for information on where they can be downloaded for free.

## Student Handouts and Examples

Figure 13.1: Model Sentence Navigator Answering Questions
Figure 13.2: Blank Sentence Navigator Answering Questions
Figure 13.3: Blank Sentence Navigator For Any Sentence

## What Could Go Wrong?

We love sentence navigators, and there is not too much you can do to mess them up. Don't give too many at once (a page or two at one time would be our recommended maximum) and don't forget to model—again and again. When it comes to students creating their own, be sure to insist that they start by copying sentences from other texts and that they first get their original sentences approved by you—having incorrectly written sentence navigators is not helpful to anyone's English acquisition.

## Technology Connection

You can download—for free—many different versions of sentence navigators from Jason, as well as read and view videos about different ways to use them, at http:// larryferlazzo.edublogs.org/2014/04/19/sentence-navigator-is-jason-renshaws-gift-to-esleflell-teachers-everywhere/.

## Attribution

Thanks, Jason!

# Figures

 SENTENCE NAVIGATOR 1

 C. Find the Way

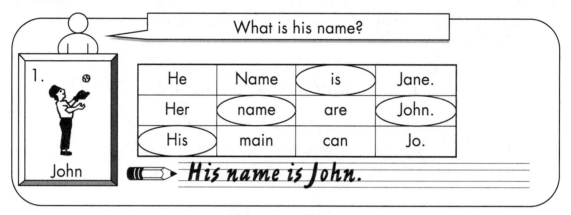

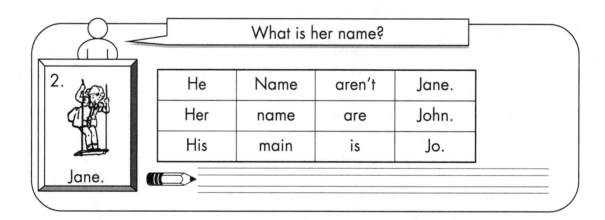

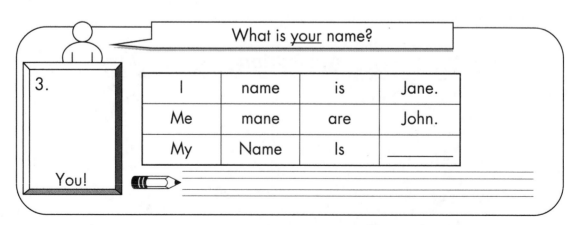

**Figure 13.1** Model Sentence Navigator Answering Questions *Source:* Reproduced with permission of Jason Renshaw.

SENTENCE NAVIGATOR 1

C. Find the Way

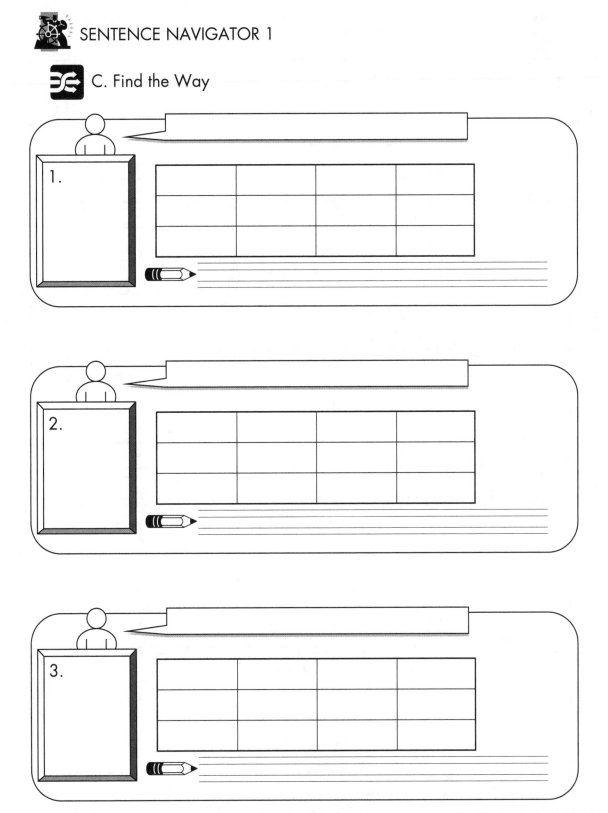

**Figure 13.2** Blank Sentence Navigator Answering Questions *Source:* Reproduced with permission of Jason Renshaw.

SENTENCE NAVIGATOR 1

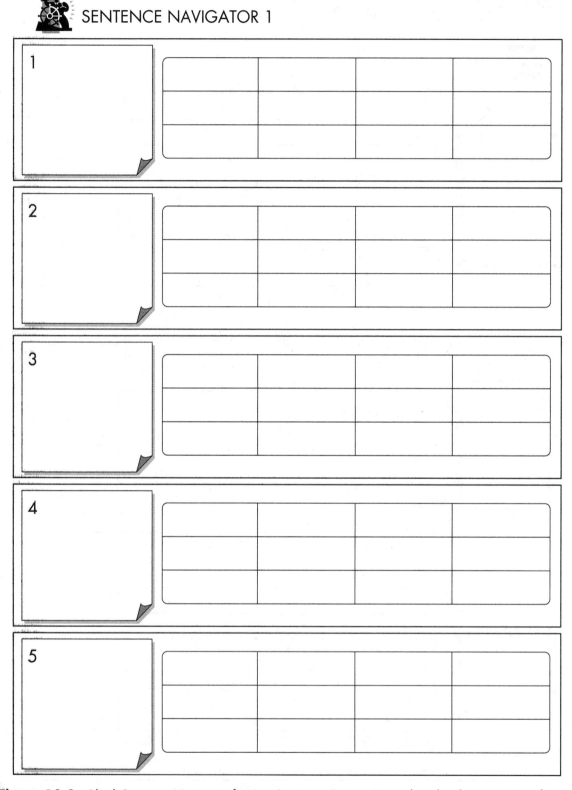

**Figure 13.3**    Blank Sentence Navigator for Any Sentence *Source:* Reproduced with permission of Jason Renshaw.

# Writing Frames and Writing Structures

## What Is It?

Writing frames are commonly described as templates that include sentence starters, connecting words, and an overall structure that provides extensive scaffolding to a student responding to a question or prompt (Warwick et al., 2010, p. 4). Writing structures is the term sometimes used to describe a "series of instructional prompts" designed to support students creating sentences themselves in responding to a question or prompt (Carthew & Scitt, 2015, p. 3).

These definitions are not necessarily formally recognized universally by educators or researchers. We tend to view writing frames and writing structures as a continuum. Both are steps along the way where students can use their experience to apply the writing strategies they have gained to writing situations in which no teacher scaffolds are available to them.

Individual sentence starters can perform similar functions in response to simple questions (you'll find an example in Strategy 4: Vocabulary and in other portions of this book) and are at the very beginning of the continuum. Here, though, we are concentrating on assisting ELLs to write lengthier pieces of writing.

## Why We Like It

Writing frames and writing structures hold many benefits for English language learners:

- Providing models for how words and phrases look within a logical context
- Allowing teachers and students to focus on the key target language that is the emphasis of that current lesson

- Reducing student stress levels—as second-language learners ourselves (Spanish), we know it can be intimidating to be given a question or a task, along with a blank piece of paper

- Building on the Zeigarnik effect, which says we tend to want to finish something that we have started (Dean, n.d.b); sentence starters can have the effect of calling out to students that they want to be completed

## Supporting Research

Writing frames and writing structures have been found to support greater writing fluency among English-proficient students (Carthew & Scitt, 2015; Warwick et al., 2010). In addition, they have also been shown to be effective when used with English language learners (George, 2011; Reyes, 2015).

## Common Core Connections

No surprises here—writing frames and writing structures fit in with most of the Writing Standards. If you use ideas in the Technology Connections section, you can hit them all!

## Application

As we mentioned when we first described this strategy, we view it as part of a continuum—beginning with simple single-sentence starters (also called *stems*); then moving on to writing frames that are basically fill-in-the-blank sentences; followed by writing structures in which scaffolding is provided but sentences are student-created; and, finally, to students using all their past experience and present skills to write without teacher-generated scaffolds.

### WRITING FRAMES

Figure 14.1: George Washington Writing Frame is an example of a fill-in-the-blank writing frame. These writing frames differ from clozes because the blanks can require more than one word.

Figure 14.1 was given to beginning ELL students after we did a teacher read aloud and watched a simple animated video (with English subtitles) on George Washington. Students were asked to write a response to the question, "Why is it important to know about George Washington?" We were trying to teach the concept of topic sentences and supporting details. We read the writing frame aloud before students were given a few minutes to write on their own. They then shared what they wrote with a partner—orally and by showing them. Next, they were given a minute to make changes based on feedback from their partner. We then reviewed topic sentences and supporting details in a visual way by holding up our wooden stool and explaining that the top was like a topic sentence and the legs were the supporting details.

Figure 14.2: Mexico Writing Frame is an example of a more-complex writing frame for intermediate ELLs. After studying a text data set (see Strategy 11: Inductive Learning), students were given this writing frame, called an *ABC model* (*a*nswer the question; *b*ack it up with a quotation; make a *c*omment or *c*onnection).

After students completed it, we then used a pair-share process. While that sharing was going on, we were circulating around the room looking for student examples that we could show to the class (with student permission)—particularly ones that had a good paraphrase of the quotation they used. Paraphrasing well is not easy for ELLs, which is why we have a separate strategy on it (see Strategy 15: Quoting, Summarizing, and Paraphrasing).

After students shared with a partner, they had a chance to make revisions, and we then highlighted examples of finished student work on the overhead.

## WRITING STRUCTURES

As we have previously explained, writing structures do not usually contain sentence starters or connectors. Instead, questions or additional prompts are provided by the teacher. For example:

Figure 14.3: Mexico Writing Structure illustrates one way to turn the Mexico Writing Frame into a writing structure using the ABC format. It turns the sentence starters into questions.

Figure 14.4: ABC Writing Structure is a writing structure from our colleague Jen Adkins that also uses the ABC format but contains less scaffolding.

Figure 14.5: PEE Writing Structure is a writing structure from our colleague Antoine Germany and uses the PEE format: *p*oint, *e*vidence, *e*xplain. Obviously this acronym, if used in younger learners, may elicit some giggling.

Figure 14.6: RACE Writing Structure contains several graphics from teacher Meghan Everette illustrating the RACE writing structure (*r*estate, *a*nswer, *c*ite the source, *e*xplain/examples).

Figure 14.7: AREE! Writing Structure is our final writing structure graphic. It's from our colleague Mary Osteen, who calls it AREE (she enjoys pronouncing it like a pirate *ARRRR!*). It stands for *a*ssertion, *r*eason, *e*vidence, *e*xplanation. What makes it even more effective is the grid puzzle she uses with students to teach its elements. That grid can be found in Figure 14.8: AREE! Writing Structure Teaching Grid.

Perhaps the most popular writing structures in many schools are the ones found in the well-known book, *They Say, I Say: The Moves That Matter in Academic Writing*

(Graff & Birkenstein, 2015). We use those resources with our more-advanced ELLs. See a link in the Technology Connections section for online resources.

When applying any of these writing structures, we often use a follow-up process similar to what we do with writing frames—pair-share, circulate around the room to identify exemplars, then give students time to revise. In addition, we will often use examples of student writing to prepare concept attainment lessons highlighting specific conventions (see Strategy 11: Inductive Learning).

One more example worth sharing: Kernel essays, introduced to us by experienced educator Gretchen Bernabei, are a sister strategy to writing structures. They familiarize students with the text structures of various writing genres, including expository, argument, and narrative, and assist them in developing kernel ideas that can later be developed into longer writing pieces.

The kernel essay process involves students using a text structure (divided into sections or boxes with a prompt or question for each box) in order to write one-sentence responses for each prompt. This series of sentences is called a *kernel essay*. Students then read their kernel essays aloud to other students in order to see whether that structure works for their topic and whether it is worth developing into a longer piece of writing. For example, the teacher could show students this memory text structure:

**A Memory**

| Where You Were | Moment It Started | Next Moment | Final Moment | What You Thought |
|---|---|---|---|---|

Next, he or she could give the following questions one at a time with students writing one sentence answers for each:

1. Where were you and what were you doing?
2. What happened first?
3. What happened next?
4. What happened last?
5. What did you learn or realize?

For more explanation on this strategy, multiple examples of text structures, and its applications in content area writing, see a link to Gretchen's website in the Technology Connections section.

## Student Handouts and Examples

## What Could Go Wrong?

A critique of writing frames and writing structures is that they can restrict students to formulaic writing methods. Because of that potential issue, it is important for teachers to constantly remind ourselves that the goal is to help students progress to the point where teacher-provided writing scaffolds are no longer needed. We want to move students forward on a continuum from the most heavily scaffolded to the least scaffolded through practice, peer-to-peer collaboration, and teacher feedback. After students become proficient with writing structures, we remind them that they are just guides—they should feel free to experiment and even create their own writing structures to share!

You also don't want to teach *all* the writing structures we've included in this strategy. You can have too much of a good thing—teaching all of them can turn into alphabet soup in our students' minds. Pick one and try it out. If it's not a good fit for you or your students, forget about it. If it works well, use it several more times. Then, consider trying out another one. Plan on regularly using two or three different structures over the course of a year so that students acquire different models they can use in future situations when teacher scaffolding is not available.

As we discussed previously, writing can be a scary endeavor for ELLs and often results in an overreliance on Google Translate. It's a tricky balance—the app can be a great asset for communicating with students (not to mention with their parents!) with whom you don't share a language—but it also can become a crutch that hinders written language acquisition. Students can easily get into the habit of writing sentences and even entire essays in their home language and then copying and pasting the Google Translate English version.

We deal with this issue by facing it head-on and asking students to use Google Translate for words only and not entire sentences when they are writing (however, they can use it to translate larger portions of text when reading). Students understand that using it will not help them write (especially if we show the class a Google Translate version of a passage—one not necessarily written by a student—and point out its deficiencies), but that doesn't always stop them! Fear of mistakes and the siren call of ease can be hard to resist for all of us. We assist with regular gentle, but firm, reminders.

## Technology Connections

The writing structures we've shared here are just the tip of the iceberg. You can find many more at The Best Scaffolded Writing Frames for Students (http://larryferlazzo .edublogs.org/2016/12/01/the-best-scaffolded-writing-frames-for-students/).

As we've mentioned elsewhere in the book, having an audience beyond just the teacher can be very motivating for students. There are many places where their work can be published, and a number are shared at The Best Places Where Students Can Write for an "Authentic Audience" (http://larryferlazzo.edublogs.org/2009/04/01/ the-best-places-where-students-can-write-for-an-authentic-audience/).

Links to online "They Say, I Say" resources can be found at http://larryferlazzo .edublogs.org/2015/07/05/they-say-i-say-is-a-great-writing-resource/.

For more on the strategy of kernel essays see Gretchen Bernabei's website at http://trailofbreadcrumbs.net/writing-strategies/kernel-essays/.

## Attribution

Thanks to our colleagues Antoine Germany, Jen Adkins, and Mary Osteen for letting us reproduce their writing structure graphics.

Thanks to Meghan Everette and to Scholastic for letting us reproduce the RACE materials.

Thanks to Gretchen Bernabei for letting us share about her kernel essay ideas.

## Figures

There are many reasons why it is important to know about George Washington. He was _____. He was also _____ _____.

In addition, it is important to know about him because every February people in the United States celebrate _____ and we don't go to school.

**Figure 14.1** George Washington Writing Frame

Name_____Date_____

What is the most interesting thing you learned about Mexico from the data set?

## Planning to Write

Use the ABC outline to answer the question:

## Answer the Question

_____ is the most interesting thing about Mexico.

## Back It Up with Evidence to Support Your Answer

The author says that _____.

OR

The author says, "_____."

This means _____.

## Make a Comment and Connection

This is interesting because _____.

It reminds me of _____.

## Putting It All Together

Put all your sentences together in one paragraph and write it below—be sure to indent!

**Figure 14.2**  Mexico Writing Frame

Name _____

Date _____

*What is the most interesting thing you learned about Mexico from the data set?*

## Planning to Write

Use the ABC outline to answer the questions:

**A.** What is the most interesting thing you learned about Mexico?

**B.** What is a quotation from the data set that backs up or supports your answer? What does the quotation mean in your own words?

**C.** Why is it interesting? What does it remind you of?

## Putting It All Together

Please put all your sentences together in one paragraph:

**Figure 14.3** Mexico Writing Structure

ABC Literature Response Format
A–Answer the prompt/Make a point

 Back it up with evidence from the text

C–Comment with further opinion or personal connection


"ICE" your B!!

I–Identify who said the quote
C–Copy the direct quote
E–Explain: (1) What the quote means: what the author is saying
(2) How the quote helps to prove your point


**REMINDER: Each of these steps MAY take multiple
sentences.

**Figure 14.4** ABC Writing Structure *Source:* Reproduced with permission of Jen Adkins

**PEE**

PEE Stands for POINT EVIDENCE EXPLAIN

P-make your point (what are you trying to get at?)

For example: Mobile phones are better than landlines.

E-You need to support your point with some evidence.

For example: Mobile phones are better than landlines. I think this because mobiles (on average) cost less and you can do a lot more with them.

E- You need to explain your evidence in more detail and how it relates/proves your point.

For example: Mobile phones are better than landlines. I think this because mobiles (on average) cost less and you can do a lot more with them. This proves that mobiles are better than landlines and shows a couple of reasons why they are better. They are also a lot better because you are less restricted with mobile phones and can freely move without being controlled by connection problems.

Make Your Point: _____.

Support Your Point With Evidence: I know this because _____

_____.

Evidence Details and How It Proves Your Point: This shows

_____. In addition, we know _____

_____.

**Figure 14.5** PEE Writing Structure *Source:* Reprinted with permission of Antoine Germany.

RACE TO A GREAT ANSWER

**R**ESTATE

**A**NSWER

**C**ITE THE SOURCE

**E**XPLAIN / EXAMPLES

| R | **R** stands for *restate the question*. We want students to practice flipping the question into part of their answer. This avoids students starting with *because* or *yes* and sets them up to actually answer the question given. Often students who don't or can't restate the question are going to provide an incomplete or off-base answer. |
|---|---|
| A | **A** stands for *answer the question*. Here is where students give the simple or direct answer. **R** and **A** are usually contained in the same sentence. |
| C | **C** stands for *cite the source*. This is where students find the supporting evidence in the text for their answer. |
| E | **E** stands for *explain* or *examples*. Often, the evidence cited needs further explanation to tie back to the answer. Other times, just giving another example or extending the answer will suffice. |

| R | The lesson the reader should learn is |
|---|---|
| A | Never tell a lie. |
| C | In the story, the boy cries wolf three times. The first two times, the villagers come, but then they don't believe him when the wolf actually shows up. |
| E | The boy lied so he wasn't believable. That is why you shouldn't tell lies. |

**Figure 14.6** RACE Writing Structure *Source:* Reprinted by permission of Scholastic Inc. From blog by Meghan Everette https://www.scholastic.com/teachers/blog-posts/meghan-everette/responding-text-how-get-great-written-answers/ from Scholastic.com. Copyright by Scholastic Inc.

| R | The animals that rely on the cactus life cycle to survive include |
|---|---|
| A | bats, birds, and insects. |
| C | In the text it says the bats eat the fruit of the cactus in the mature stage. |
| E | The birds use a mature cactus as a home. Both birds and bats use the seed stage for food. When the cactus dies, insects use the body for nutrients. |

**Figure 14.6**  (Continued)

**Argument = AREE!**

**Assertion:** a claim or thesis

**Reason:** reasons why the claim is true

**Evidence:** proof, usually data or examples, quotations, statistics, etc.

**Explanation:** Explain/comment more about your evidence

**Figure 14.7**  AREE! Writing Structure *Source:* Reproduced with permission of Mary Osteen.

| | **Assertion** | **Reasoning** | **Evidence** |
|---|---|---|---|
| 1 | The minimum driving age should be raised to 18. | Raising the driving age will save lives by reducing accidents. | 16-year-old drivers have three times as many crashes as drivers aged 18 and 19. |
| 2 | Television is a bad influence. | Television shows too much violence. | |
| 3 | The United States should not have the death penalty. | | Since 1973, 108 people in 25 states have been released from death row because they were found innocent. |
| 4 | | Eating junk food is bad for your health. | Junk foods are high in fat and sugar. Too much fat and sugar puts you at risk for diabetes and heart disease. |
| 5 | | Allowing younger people to vote would increase their involvement in politics and society. | |
| 6 | | | Incidents of school violence have shown that students use their cellular phones to notify police and parents. |
| 7 | Schools should not use animal dissection in classes. | | |

**Figure 14.8**  AREE! Writing Structure Teaching Grid *Source:* Reproduced with permission of Mary Osteen.

# Quoting, Summarizing, and Paraphrasing

## What Is It?

We all know what quoting entails, and this is how we describe it to students: writing the exact words that someone else has said or written, putting these words within quotation marks, and attributing them to the original source.

Summarizing is saying or writing the main idea or ideas that someone else said or wrote and typically contains many fewer words than are found in the original text.

Paraphrasing is putting what someone said or wrote into your own words and is typically a similar length to the original passage.

Having students understand how to quote, summarize, and paraphrase are critical skills for academic writing success. This strategy in our book is more of a series of lessons done at different times to help students acquire those abilities. Once they are learned, quoting, summarizing, and paraphrasing become important strategies students can use to help them with their reading and writing. Teachers can use them as effective formative assessment tools.

## Why We Like It

We like using this strategy, of course, because it's critical to student academic success, and we believe it has a positive impact on language acquisition. More important, though, we think that summarizing and paraphrasing especially provide a superior opportunity to highlight the *assets* English language learners (and all students) bring to class instead of the supposed *deficits* they carry. By helping students learn these concepts through seeing that they already paraphrase and summarize frequently, we reinforce the reality that ELLs are as intelligent as any other student in our schools. It's not a question of intelligence—instead, it's a challenge of language. It's a reminder that we can be more effective educators by remembering to look at our students through this lens of assets and not deficits.

## Supporting Research

Research has found that paraphrasing skills have a positive impact on ELL student reading comprehension—they are able to better focus on the key ideas in the text. Subsequently, the quality of student writing improves because they are able to write better once they have clarity about what they want to communicate (Hans, n.d., p. 7). Similar results have been found when teaching summarization techniques (Khathayut & Karavi, 2011).

## Common Core Connections

Reading a text, analyzing it for main ideas, and identifying context clues to assist with comprehension all fall under the Language and Reading Standards. The writing required in paraphrasing and summarizing also fits into a number of the Writing Standards.

## Application

There are many different lessons out there about teaching quoting, summarizing, and paraphrasing to English language learners and English-proficient students. Many, if not most, teach all three at the same time in order to compare and contrast them. We think that this strategy can be overwhelming to students, and we take a different tack.

### QUOTING

We generally begin by introducing the idea of quotations and quotation marks in the context of having students write dialogue—whether it is imagining a conversation between two people in a photo used in the picture word inductive model (see Strategy 11: Inductive Learning) or in a story they are writing (see Strategy 3: Graphic Organizers) or in a simple autobiographical incident essay. We also, through simple ABC paragraphs (see Strategy 14: Writing Frames and Writing Structures), familiarize students with how to use quotations when working with text written by others.

We explain that quotation marks are used to represent exactly what someone says. Further, we explain that if you copy what someone else says or writes without quotation marks, then it's like stealing.

It typically does not take very long for students to gain an understanding of this concept. We also explain that copying other people's words can get them into trouble at school.

Nevertheless, many ELLs continue to be scared of making mistakes and may still copy work without providing attribution or quotation marks. We continually reinforce its importance, and writing frames and writing structures (see Strategy 14) provide excellent and regular opportunities to do so.

## SUMMARIZING

We look for a good opportunity to teach summarizing after we have taught quoting—the following week, month, quarter. Generally, we do it after we have read a story as a class and are going to watch a short animated adaptation of it (e.g., *The Story of Ferdinand* [Leaf, 1977]). We periodically stop the video and ask for summaries. This process tends to work well because students have already acquired much of the vocabulary and experience needed to comprehend the story.

The teacher begins this lesson by writing the word *summarize* on the board or overhead. With words and gestures, the teacher explains that when we summarize, we take many words and turn them into a few words. The teacher tells students that they may not realize it, but that they summarize all the time—when a friend asks them what happened in the movie they just saw, when their parents ask them what happened in school that day, and when a classmate asks them in January what they did during winter break. They don't spend hours explaining every single thing that happened! No, they summarize with a few words. And the summary is in their own words—they don't quote someone else (this could be a good time to remind students what a quotation is). Again, teachers can use their hands to illustrate going from a lot to going to a little. The teacher explains that learning to summarize in English will be something they can use to help them understand something they have read or watched.

After providing that mini-lesson, and before showing the video, a teacher can pass out a sheet such as Figure 15.1: Summarizing Examples (the humorous first example always generates student reaction!). The teacher reads the first example and the three options for a good summary. He or she explains why each option is either good or bad and circles the correct answer.

The teacher then reads the next example and the options and asks students to take a minute and silently circle the correct answer. The teacher then asks students to think about the reason why each one is either right or wrong and to explain the reasons to a partner. Afterwards, the teacher calls on students to share their responses and reasons. This same process is repeated with the last two examples.

Next, the teacher passes out mini-whiteboards to students and explains that they are going to watch a video of the story they recently read. He or she is going to stop the video every few minutes and then ask students to write down on their board a summary of the last few minutes of the video. The teacher explains that he or she will do it the first time, and then the students will do it during the rest of the video.

Each time the teacher stops the video, students can write quietly and show their boards when complete (newcomers can draw their summaries). The teacher can give feedback. Remember—we're not looking for perfect grammar or spelling here! The primary point of the exercise is teaching and assessing if students understand and can apply the concept of summarizing.

If the video is lengthy, there is no need to repeat this process during the entire time. Do it enough times to function as a formative assessment to determine who grasps and who doesn't grasp the concept. If it seems clear that the lesson was not effective, then model it one or two more times after stopping the video before letting students try again. In our experience, this usually does the trick for most, though teachers can note if some individual students might need extra support in the future. If it becomes clear that the lesson was effective, we don't see any problem with telling students to put their boards down and just enjoy the video for the remaining few minutes.

A subsequent reinforcing activity we've sometimes done is to ask students to make posters of their favorite (classroom-appropriate) movie, including a summary of the plot. Depending on the English-proficiency level of the students, we might provide a simple writing frame or writing structure as a scaffold. Once students acquire this summarizing skill, of course, we ask them to regularly summarize portions of a text (see Strategy 10: Reading Comprehension).

Note that our lessons for quotations and summarizing emphasize explicit instruction. Though we are big fans of assisted-discovery learning (e.g., inductive), we also think that explicit instruction is a key component of any classroom. Balance is the key!!

## PARAPHRASING

We believe that paraphrasing is difficult to teach and learn, and that is why we generally leave it to last. Contrasting paraphrasing with what it is not—quoting and summarizing—can be one more way to help students understand the concept.

The teacher can begin by writing the word *paraphrasing* on the class whiteboard or on the overhead. The teacher explains that *paraphrasing* means putting what someone else said or wrote in your own words. The teacher tells students that they do something like paraphrasing all the time when they don't know the exact word for something. For example, if you don't know the word for this (the teacher points to a microwave), you might call it "the thing that cooks fast." That is a type of paraphrasing—you are putting something in your own words and showing that you understand it.

The teacher writes the word *quotation* and asks students to take a minute and remember what that word means. After a minute, he or she asks students to share with a partner what they remember, and then the teacher calls on one or two students to share with the entire class.

Then the teacher explains that paraphrasing means taking a quotation and putting it in your own words. Paraphrasing helps you make sure you understand the quotation, and it show readers that you understand it, too. The teacher explains that students will use quotations and paraphrases when they write essays in school to support what they believe.

The teacher explains that he or she is going to show a number of good and bad examples of paraphrasing. Using the concept attainment strategy (see Strategy 11: Inductive Learning for instructions), the teacher will first put Figure 15.2: Concept Attainment Paraphrasing 1 on the overhead and use the process to elicit from students why some are *yeses* and others are *nos*.

There are too many *yeses* and *nos* about paraphrasing to teach in one concept attainment sheet, so the teacher will use two of them. The reason the first example is under the *no* category is that it is just a quotation. The reason for the second example is that it does not cite the source.

The reasons for the *yes* examples, which can be elicited from students when reviewing either this figure or the next one, are as follows:

- It is a similar length to the quotation.
- Some words are changed (synonyms).
- Key words are often kept.
- The order of words are changed.
- The source is cited.
- Complex words are simplified.
- The paraphrase is accurate.
- The student's opinion is not included within the paraphrase.

After having students, with teacher guidance, determine why the examples in the figure are *yes* and *no*, the teacher puts Figure 15.3: Concept Attainment Paraphrasing 2 on the overhead and uses the same process. The *no* reasons for Figure 15.3 are that the first example is a summary (the teacher might want to remind students about their previous lessons on summaries) and the second example is not an accurate paraphrase of the quote. If students don't identify all the reasons for the *yes* examples, the teacher can explicitly point them out.

The teacher should have student copies of both concept attainment sheets available to pass out *after* the process is complete. This will provide students with models as they complete the next activity, which is Figure 15.4: Paraphrase Sheet (note that some of the passages there are intentionally similar to ones found in the concept attainment sheets to function as an additional scaffold). The teacher will tell students that it's now their turn to write paraphrases of the quotations on the sheet. The teacher tells the students they will do one at time—after a few minutes, students will share with a partner, and then one or two examples will be shared with the entire class. Then students will proceed to the second quotation, where the process will be repeated. Finally, students complete the third quotation.

By that time, most—and, with luck, all—students will have a grasp of how to write paraphrases. They should be able to apply it to future writing and, as with summarizing, teachers can also ask them to do it periodically when annotating a text.

We are fully aware that our teaching suggestions for quoting, summarizing, and paraphrasing—and for other strategies in this book—might be viewed as somewhat simplified and not covering sophisticated nuances. We are making these choices intentionally and do not view it as dumbing down our teaching. We believe the strategies we use to teach our students support language acquisition, maximize higher-order thinking, meet Common Core Standards, and prepare them to be lifelong learners and have a long and successful academic career. As the authors of the Common Core Standards state:

> Teachers should recognize that it is possible to achieve the standards for reading and literature, writing & research, language development and speaking & listening without manifesting native-like control of conventions and vocabulary. (Council of Chief State Officers and the National Governors Association, n.d., p. 1)

## Student Handouts and Examples

Figure 15.1: Summarizing Examples

Figure 15.2: Concept Attainment Paraphrasing 1

Figure 15.3: Concept Attainment Paraphrasing 2

Figure 15.4: Paraphrase Sheet

## What Could Go Wrong?

In our experience, things generally go pretty well—including with beginning ELLs—when teaching quoting and summarizing. Paraphrasing, though, can be an entirely different kettle of fish. Intermediate ELLs often find it challenging, as do many of our mainstream English-proficient students. We suggest that it doesn't make sense to even try teaching paraphrasing until students reach the high-beginning stage at least. We'd also recommend having students continue to practice, including having them try the online exercises found in the Technology Connections section.

## Technology Connection

Additional suggestions for teaching about plagiarism *and* online interactives for students to reinforce the skill of paraphrasing can be found at The Best Online Resources to Teach About Plagiarism (http://larryferlazzo.edublogs.org/2009/09/21/the-best-online-resources-to-teach-about-plagiarism/).

# Figures

**1.** All the students in school love Mr. Ferlazzo. They want to be in his class because they know they will learn a lot from him. He is very smart and kind. He is never absent, is never angry, and gives treats to his students every day. The students in his class are very lucky!

Circle the summary:

**a.** All the students in school love Mr. Ferlazzo.

**b.** Students think Mr. Ferlazzo is a good teacher.

**c.** "He is very smart and kind."

**2.** One bite from the black mamba snake can kill a person within 20 minutes. They don't just bite once—they will keep on biting you! They are very fast so you cannot run away from them.

Circle the summary:

**a.** Snakes are fun!

**b.** "One bite from the black samba snake can kill a person"

**c.** Black mamba snakes are very dangerous and can kill you.

**3.** Over 300 million people live in the United States. It is a big country. It has a strong military. There is a lot of money in the United States. Many people visit the United States.

Circle the summary:

**a.** It is a big country.

**b.** The United States is a powerful country.

**c.** I live in the United States.

**4.** It was a sunny day. The woman walked her little dog down the street. As they were walking, they saw a man walking with a big dog across the street. The big dog started barking at the woman and the little dog. The little dog started crying and tried to run away from the big dog.

Circle the summary:

**a.** The big dog didn't like the little dog, and the little dog was afraid of the big dog.

**b.** The man didn't like the woman.

**c.** "It was a sunny day."

**Figure 15.1** Summarizing Examples

"Failure is success if we learn from it."

—Malcolm Forbes

### YES, This Is a Good Paraphrase

Malcolm Forbes said that we can still learn when things go badly.

Malcolm Forbes suggests that even if we fail, we can get something good out of it.

### NO, This Is Not a Good Paraphrase

"Failure is success if we learn from it."

Even if we fail, we can get something good out of it.

**Figure 15.2**  Concept Attainment Paraphrasing 1

"Elephants' brains are bigger than the brains of any other land animal, and the cortex has as many neurons as a human brain. The ability of elephants to learn is impressive, and they are also self-aware—they can actually recognize themselves in mirrors!" (http://healthypets.mercola.com/sites/healthypets/archive/2015/08/22/10-most-intelligent-animals.aspx)

| YES, This Is a Good Paraphrase | NO, This Is Not a Good Paraphrase |
| --- | --- |
| The Healthy Pets website says that elephants have big brains and have lots of connections inside them. The website also says the elephants know it's them when they look in a mirror and that they can learn a lot. | |
| | The Healthy Pets website says that elephants are smart. |
| The Healthy Pets website says elephants have the ability to learn many things and that they have big brains and lots of connections inside them. The website also states that elephants know it's them when they look in a mirror. | |
| | The Healthy Pets website says that elephants are very big, ugly, and smell bad. They also look in the mirror a lot. |

**Figure 15.3** Concept Attainment Paraphrasing 2

Name _____

Period _____

Paraphrase each of these quotations:

**1.** "Without education, you are not going anywhere in this world."—Malcolm X

_____

_____

_____

**2.** "Dolphins are considered some of the smartest animals on Earth . . . Dolphins have been shown to recognize themselves in mirrors, to create language-like personalized whistles, solve problems and even follow recipes." http://bigthink.com/paul-ratner/what-are-the-smartest-animals-on-the-planet

_____

_____

_____

**3.** "Mistakes are opportunities to learn. Students who are not afraid of making mistakes will do better in school."—Katie Hull Sypnieski

_____

_____

_____

**Figure 15.4** Paraphrase Sheet

# Cooperative Writing

## What Is It?

Cooperative writing can be any sort of group activity that requires more than one person to write a finished product. It is often called *collaborative writing* but, given our description of the distinctions between cooperative learning and collaborative learning in Strategy 9: Jigsaw, we are using the former word here. The activities we describe in this section are not designed to further the collaborative goals of helping an individual first work on his or her writing alone, get feedback from others to improve, and then revise it further.

Instead, some are plain old fun lessons with a focus on engaging students and getting reluctant writers to develop more self-confidence to write *something*. Others emphasize reinforcing writing skills that would have already been taught and create conditions in which students can do it as a team. In some instances, however, these activities can be labeled *collaborative* if the group is able to develop a product better than any individual member could develop on his or her own.

These kinds of small-group interactions also promote increased language acquisition, especially if the use of English is encouraged (and, often, it is the only common language students in the group might share).

## Why We Like It

It's not that hard to get close to 100% student participation 100% of the time while doing these cooperative writing activities. There is a great deal of student choice and autonomy involved, which are key elements behind intrinsic motivation (Ferlazzo, 2015, September 14). They are all fast-moving and accountability is high—your classmates are counting on you to complete your task so that they can build off of it.

## Supporting Research

Many studies support the benefits of different types of cooperative learning for English language learners, including its creation of opportunities for language use (Grundman, 2002). Other, more-limited research, suggests that students working together to create a text can result in a better writing product than if one student worked on it alone (Lin & Maarof, 2013; Mulligan & Garofalo, 2011).

## Common Core Connections

All of the activities in this section provide opportunities to practice different English conventions, including grammar and capitalization. Students can practice the elements of argument, narrative, and expository writing with some of the activities. If teachers have students read their writing aloud, then some Speaking and Listening Standards can be met. Students publishing their work online by using the sites discussed in the Technology Connections section can meet the tech-related Writing Standard.

## Application

The following four lesson ideas are the primary ways we incorporate cooperative writing in our classrooms.

### COOPERATIVE DRAWINGS

In cooperative drawing, students are each given an 8 1/2″ × 11″ paper, along with colored markers, and are told they have one minute, three minutes, or even just the length of a song the teacher is playing to draw whatever classroom appropriate image they want (another option is that the teacher can give students an initial idea to work from—you are in an airport, a monster is attacking the school, people are climbing a mountain, etc.). Then, when time is up, students pass their drawing to the next person who, in turn, will have the same amount of time to add to that drawing. Then, it's passed again, and so on. This process is continued for as much time as the teacher wants to devote to it. We usually announce during the last round that students should draw at least two people or animals in the final image if they aren't there already.

When the picture is done, then there are many different options of what to do next:

- Write a story about it.
- Label the objects, people, and animals in it with English words.

- Describe it to a partner.

- Write a dialogue or thought bubbles for the people and animals in the image.

- Create an art show by posting the pictures on the classroom walls and having students go around and write quick responses on sticky notes to questions the teacher poses about the pictures ("What do you think is happening in the picture?" "How does the picture make you feel when you look at it and why?" "What do you think the people or animals in the picture are thinking or saying?" "How would you describe the people or animals in the picture?" "Whom or what does the picture remind you of?").

Of course, the teacher would want to provide a model or example for any of these follow-up activities prior to having students do them on their own.

Another variation of this cooperative drawing activity could be to give students papers with four to eight boxes drawn on them like a comic strip. After the teacher shows the class an example, students could each have a few minutes to draw a comic strip in one of the boxes and fill in a speech bubble before passing it on to the next person.

**CHAIN STORIES**

In chain stories, students are given a piece of paper and the teacher dictates a title, opening line, or genre (ghost story, love story, monster story, etc.). Students then have one to four minutes to start writing a story and then, after the time is up, pass it on to the next student. Students can be given different colors or types of markers to help with easy accountability or are asked to put their initials near the text they write. The teacher can end the process whenever he or she wants, probably by announcing at the last round that students should write some kind of conclusion. Then, students can break into partners and read their stories to each other (after they edit them a bit!).

There could be several variations to this exercise:

- Students could have a very short amount of time to write just one sentence each (with a minimum word count, with an exception for newcomers).

- Partners could work on the chain stories—they would have a minute to talk about what they would want to write and draw and one student would do both on the paper. At the next turn, after deciding what to write and draw, it would be the other partner's turn to put them down on paper. Or, one partner could write the sentence while the other draws the picture.

- During any of the activities, the teacher could interject saying the next sentence has to begin with a certain word, such as *Suddenly* or *Help*.

**COOPERATIVE STORYTELLING**

This cooperative storytelling activity is a good way to review and reinforce the elements of whatever writing genre the class is doing at the time or has recently finished. We begin by giving each pair of students a piece of easel-size poster paper. We then explain that we are going to ask a series of questions. After each one, they will be given a short amount of time to discuss the question and then one person has to write the answer down while the other draws a picture next to the sentences. Afterwards, pairs develop a simple verbal presentation of their answers.

If the class is working on a story, which supports the Common Core Writing Standards for narrative writing, we ask these questions:

- What is the setting?
- Who is the protagonist?
- Who is the antagonist?
- Who are the other characters?
- What is the main problem or conflict?
- What happens first?
- What happens second?
- What happens third?
- What is a dialogue that happens?
- What is the conclusion?

If the class is writing or has written an argument essay, we ask these questions:

- What do you want?
- Who has the power to give it to you?
- Why do you want it?
- What is one reason why you should get it?
- What is another reason you should get it?
- What is an opposing argument?
- What is a counter argument?

If the class is writing or has written an expository text, we focus on an instructional task and ask these questions:

- What do you want to teach someone to do?
- Why would they want to know it?

- What do they do first?
- What do they do second?
- What do they do third?
- What do they do fourth?
- What is the final thing they do?

When students complete the activity, they can tell it to another small group or in front of the class. It's even more fun, though, if one person says it and the other acts it out!

**STICKY CHATS**

We learned about this neat sticky chat activity from English teacher Christian Schenk (2012). The activity basically involves creating a physical representation of a social media chat (albeit with no text acronyms and with appropriate classroom content) and is more appropriate for intermediate or advanced ELLs.

Multiple posters (perhaps four to eight) with one engaging question each written on them are posted in different parts of the room. Each student is given a pack or two of sticky notes and, ideally, a different color pen or type of marker (this helps for accountability purposes). The class is told they have to be silent for the next 20 minutes and during that time they can text each other with sticky notes—writing answers to the questions and respectfully responding to what others have written. The teacher explains that the purpose of this activity is not just to practice their writing but also to practice serious listening to what others have to say before responding to them. Listening does not always have to be done by our ears—we also listen by thoughtfully reading what others write.

The teacher assigns a group of three or four students at each question and tells them they will have three minutes to write and post their responses (including their initials on each one so their classmates know to whom they are responding) to the question.

Then, the whole class will rotate to another question and so on. The teacher can model responding to a question, along with providing examples of classroom-appropriate comments (reminding students that they should be writing more than a word or two).

Questions could include these:

- If you could have lunch with anyone who is living or dead now, who would it be and why?
- If you could be anyone else now, who would it be and why?

- If you could time travel, when and where would you go and why?
- Who is a celebrity you most admire and why?
- Who is a celebrity you least admire and why?
- If you could change one historical event, which one would it be and why?

Hundreds, if not thousands of others, can be found by searching *lists of fun questions* on the web. Students can also be invited to contribute questions for this activity.

Teacher review of sticky chats, as well as the final texts from cooperative drawing, chain stories, and cooperative storytelling, can provide a wealth of formative assessment information. Future lessons can be developed based on the common English strengths and weaknesses exhibited in them.

## What Could Go Wrong?

Students writing inappropriate comments in the sticky chats activity is an area of concern. We've found that students each being given different colors or types of markers reduces the odds of that problem arising, along with reminding students that we are teachers and learners and we want to support one another.

Having any one of these activities going too long is also a danger. It's always best to end it when the energy is still high—leave them wanting more and wanting to do it again!

It can be a challenge for newcomers to participate in some—though not all—of these activities. Pairing them up with a higher-level English-proficient classmate usually works well, even if everyone else is doing the activity on his or her own. Newcomers can also participate through drawing and through responding in their home language.

## Technology Connections

As we've discussed in several other places, including Strategy 12: Concept Attainment—Plus and Strategy 14: Writing Frames and Writing Structures, there are different ways students can publish their writing, including on class blogs. The same is true for the text generated by students as a result of the activities in this strategy—even images can be photographed and published on blogs (with appropriate online privacy and legal issues in mind—see The Best Teacher Resources for Online Student Safety & Legal Issues [http://larryferlazzo.edublogs.org/2009/08/10/the-best-teacher-resources-for-online-student-safety-legal-issues/]).

There are also many online sites where teachers can create private virtual rooms where students can do many of the activities listed in this strategy on the web. You can find these options at The Best Sites for Collaborative Storytelling (http://larryferlazzo.edublogs.org/2010/12/29/the-best-sites-for-collaborative-storytelling/), The Best Online Tools For Real-Time Collaboration (http://larryferlazzo.edublogs.org/2008/03/02/the-best-online-tools-for-real-time-collaboration/), and at The Best Online Tools for Collaboration—NOT in Real Time (http://larryferlazzo.edublogs.org/2008/04/10/the-best-online-tools-for-collaboration-not-in-real-time/).

## Attribution

Versions of some of these ideas appeared in our book, *Navigating the Common Core with English Language Learners* (Ferlazzo & Sypnieski, 2016, p. 180).

Modifications to the cooperative drawing activity were inspired by Jo Budden at the British Council (2008).

We learned about the sticky chat activity from Christian Schenk (2012).

# Using Photos or Other Images in Reading and Writing

## What Is It?

Who doesn't use photos or other images while teaching English language learners? The visual support that they provide is a tremendous aid to comprehension and communication.

There are a million ways to use photos and other images in the classroom. For reading and writing instruction (we share other ideas in the Speaking and Listening part of our book), however, there are three primary ways *we* use them. One is while teaching inductively with the Picture Word Inductive Model (PWIM) and with phonics (see Strategy 11: Inductive Learning). Another is through cooperative drawing (see Strategy 16: Cooperative Writing). The third is a simple process we use when we teach our ELL social studies classes, which is described in the Application section.

In addition to those three primary uses, we will share a number of other simple ways we periodically use photos and other images in our classes to support reading and writing.

## Why We Like It

When teaching ELLs (and anyone else, for that matter!), scaffolds such as photos and images only increase the odds of successful teaching and learning. They are a superior tool for differentiated instruction—newcomers can label objects, and advanced ELLs can answer more-complex questions and write a story about it. Plus, they're free and accessible, and teachers and students can easily make their own, to boot!

## Supporting Research

Many researchers have identified benefits of using visuals with ELLs in multiple contexts (Petrie, 2003, p. 141). Images can also serve as a catalyst (Petrie, 2003, p. 141) for improved ELL student writing.

## Common Core Connections

Common Core Standards highlight the importance of being able to close-read and analyze and evaluate diverse forms of visual media (Common Core State Standards Initiative, n.d.d). In fact, there is one Standard within the Reading Anchor Standards that focuses on this skill.

## Application

As we previously stated, the applications we discussed in inductive learning and in cooperative writing are two of the main ways we use visual images in the classroom. Here are a few others.

### SLIDESHOW ANNOTATION

After intermediate ELL students have spent time studying a unit (in geography, the unit might be Brazil; in world history, it might be World War II), we show a slideshow of related images. Students have all the materials we've used for that unit on their desks. When each new image is shown, students are asked to write a description of the image, along with connecting it to something they have previously learned (see Figure 17.1: Slideshow Notes). Every three slides we have partners share and then invite some comments to be shared with the entire class.

This activity reinforces what students have previously learned, creates opportunities for them to make multiple touches on different texts they have read as they search for connections, and lets them write and receive feedback on their commentary.

### CLOSE-READ PHOTOS AND OTHER IMAGES

When students close-read images they can apply many of the same strategies used to analyze written text (see Strategy 10: Reading Comprehension). One lesson we do is project an image on the board and have students answer a series of reading strategy-related questions about it (interspersed with pair-share and classroom discussion activities).

Figure 17.2: Examining an Image is a photo analysis sheet that we have ELL beginners use to analyze an image, and Figure 17.3: Examining an Image (for

Intermediates) is one we use with intermediates. In a mixed-level class, it's often possible to have students annotate different sheets at the same time while viewing the same photograph.

We sometimes use a variation of pair-share during this activity. We label each row of students as A or B. The Bs move to the desk in front of them after each question is answered. They then share with the student next to them. This gets students up and moving and talking with multiple students about their work during the course of a class period.

Another option, depending on time constraints, is to just write one to three of the questions on the board from the analysis sheets and have students respond to them.

Additional or alternative questions could include these:

- How do you think the person who took the photograph or image felt at the time and why?

- Imagine a conversation between two or more of the people in the photo or image—what would they be saying to each other?

- What do you think each of the people in the photo or image is thinking and why?

- If the image included areas outside of the frame, what else would you see?

- Does this image remind you of anything connected to your life?

## UNVEILING PARTS OF AN IMAGE

In one activity we've used the first step to show a screenshot of a small section of a painting or photo. Next, we ask students to write what they see and predict what they think will be in the full image. Then, we gradually show more and more of the image while periodically stopping to ask students the same question. If you don't want to take the time to make screenshots, just show a picture on a doc cam or overhead and cover it up with another piece of paper. Then, move the paper gradually to show larger portions of the image.

## WRITING CAPTIONS AND CLOZE CAPTIONS

After introducing students to the concept of photo captions (we explain them as "titles for pictures" and show several examples), we sometimes will project a funny photo on the class whiteboard and ask students to write a caption for it (searching *collections of funny photos* online will yield tons of classroom-appropriate and -inappropriate pictures, so don't search while the computer projector is on!).

There are also news sites with photo galleries that allow you to *not* show the captions to photos. We have shown an image from one of them with captions off, had students write their own, and then compare them with what appears after we click captions on. Another version that works particularly well for ELL beginners is for the teacher to retype the captions as a cloze with three potential words as answers that students can choose for the blank (teachers can also modify the captions to make them more accessible). Then the teacher can project the image on the screen with the typed cloze below it. Students can have mini-whiteboards where they write what they think is the correct word and why. There are also specific sites for ELLs where they can post their own captions. See the Technology Connections section for these resources.

If you're feeling ambitious, and we only felt that way one year, you can cut out a bunch of photos from the newspaper and then clip their captions. Students then have to match the captions with the picture and write about the clues they used to connect them. It's a great activity, and the photos and captions can be reused (at least until they get too beat up). Or, even better, laminate them.

**COMPARE AND CONTRAST**

There are two ways we use the idea of compare and contrast with images.

1. This first one is great for ELL beginners. If you search *spot the difference picture* or *find the difference pictures* online, you will find many examples of two very similar pictures that have a few, hard-to-spot differences between them. We will divide students into pairs, project one of the images onto the class whiteboard, and provide this sentence frame (or, if we are better prepared, print out sheets in advance with many of the same frames on it):

   In the top picture, _____, but in the bottom picture, _____.

   > After the teacher provides a model or example, we give students a certain period of time to identify as many differences as they can and write down the sentences describing them. Sometimes we make it a game or contest, and sometimes it's an activity minus the competitive aspect. Either way, students learn from it and have fun at the same time.
   > Because we're not very good at the game, we try to show pictures that come with an answer key!

2. The second way we use a compare-and-contrast activity is through projecting two pictures and having students create a Venn diagram. With beginning ELLs, we'll often stop at a completed Venn diagram (of course, we model one first). With high beginners, we may have them complete a writing frame compare-and-contrast essay, while having intermediates use a writing structure to complete an essay (see Strategy 14: Writing Frames and Writing Structures).

**PICTURE STORY**

This is a simple lesson that requires little teacher preparation and we've found that it's generated high student engagement and learning—so what's not to like?

The teacher displays any picture containing at least two people on the overhead or from the computer projector, ideally one that is connected in some way to the theme or unit the class is studying. Students are then divided into pairs and have to develop a simple story about the picture based on a series of teacher prompts:

What is her name?

What is his name?

How long have they known each other?

What are they talking about?

Where do they live?

What problems do they have?

What are they thinking?

What are they going to do later today?

What will they be doing ten years from now?

If you are teaching argument writing, you could tell students that one of the people in the picture is trying to convince the other of something—what is it? Then have them imagine the elements of an argument taking place between the people in the picture. You could follow the same model for expository text by telling students one of them is giving the other instructions—to do what? Or it could just be more of a fun exercise to practice language conventions such as punctuation and spelling.

## Student Handouts and Examples

Figure 17.1: Slideshow Notes

Figure 17.2: Examining an Image

Figure 17.3: Examining an Image (for Intermediates)

## What Could Go Wrong?

Our regular refrain is not to overdo it! Don't have students annotate a slideshow that has 20 slides and don't feel like every question in the photo analysis forms has to be assigned during a lesson.

Why do we harp on not making this mistake, you might ask? An excerpt from Larry's book, *Helping Students Motivate Themselves* (2011, p. 93), provides an answer:

Nobel Prize winner Daniel Kahneman tells about an experiment done in the 1990s when two groups of patients were given colonoscopies. One group "finished" when the procedure was completed. The other group stayed a while longer, believing the procedure was continuing when in fact it had ended, so the pain was gone or reduced dramatically. The second group described the procedure afterward as much less painful than the first group did, even though both groups had recorded similar levels of pain during the procedure except for the extra time provided the second group. Kahneman uses this example to explain that we have an "experiencing self" and a "remembering self."

The "remembering self" is composed of the one or two "peak" moments we have had in a situation combined with how it ends (this is known as the "Peak-End Rule"). It is the remembering self that tends to stick with us and the one we use to frame future decisions.

We want our students to leave our rooms having had peak moments and a good end. We want them to leave feeling like they want to learn more with us and enter our classroom the next day with the same frame of mind.

Are we able to succeed with every student every day of the year? Of course not. But it's not a bad thing to strive for, right?

## Technology Connections

There are many places on the web where the activities we listed in this strategy can be done by students online—whether as a change of pace or as a way to create content for a class blog so that others can view student work. In addition, we've collected, and continue to update, resources at the following links:

The Best Online Tools for Using Photos in Lessons (http://larryferlazzo .edublogs.org/2012/10/19/the-best-online-tools-for-using-photos-in-lessons/)

The Best Resources on Using "If This Animal or Image Could Talk" Lesson Idea in Class (http://larryferlazzo.edublogs.org/2015/08/01/the-best-resources-on-using-if-this-animal-or-image-could-talk-lesson-idea-in-class/)

The Best Resources on Close Reading Paintings, Photos & Videos (http://larryferlazzo.edublogs.org/2015/08/05/the-best-resources-on-close-reading-paintings-photos-videos/)

## Attribution

Versions of some of these ideas appeared in our book, *Navigating the Common Core* (Ferlazzo & Sypnieski, 2016, p. 177).

We were inspired by teacher Colette M. Bennett's blog post on using photo fragments (https://usedbooksinclass.com/2013/10/03/close-reading-constables-the-hay-wain-and-turners-the-fighting-temeraire/).

## Figures

| Student Name _____ | | |
|---|---|---|
| Date _____ | | |

| Slide Number and What It Is | Describe What You See ("I see _____ _____.") | Make a Connection to Something You Learned ("This makes me remember _____ because _____.") |
|---|---|---|
| | | |
| | | |
| | | |
| | | |
| | | |

**Figure 17.1**  Slideshow Notes

**1.** List the people, objects, and activities you see in the picture:

| People | Objects | Activities |
|--------|---------|------------|
|        |         |            |
|        |         |            |
|        |         |            |
|        |         |            |
|        |         |            |
|        |         |            |
|        |         |            |

**2.** Write three sentences about the image:

**3.** Write a title for the image:

**4.** What might the people in the image be thinking or feeling? Why?

**5.** Write one question you have about the image:

**Figure 17.2**  Examining an Image  *Source:* The National Archives Education Staff, Licensed under CC0 1.0 Universal license.

**1.** Describe the objects in the image.

**2.** Describe the people and/or animals in the image.

**3.** Describe the different activities you see happening in the image.

**4.** Describe the mood of the image. Is it happy, sad or something else? What evidence do you see that supports your answer?

**5.** Write a title for the image and explain why you chose that title.

**6.** What might the people in the image be thinking or feeling? Why?

**7.** If you could see outside the frame of the image, what things or people would be there? What do you think would be happening? Why?

**8.** What year do you think the image was taken or made? What evidence do you see that supports your answer?

**9.** What questions do you have about the image?

**Figure 17.3** Examining an Image (for Intermediates)

## STRATEGY 18

# Writer's Notebook

## What Is It?

In the classroom, writer's notebooks can serve as a safe place for students to experiment with new ideas and language while writing about meaningful topics. Some teachers also have their students keep a separate reader's notebook to track and respond to their reading. Others combine the two into a reader's-writer's notebook. In our ELL classroom, we use them for reading and writing (and as a place for students to put other resources they use on a regular basis), but we refer to them as *writer's notebooks* for simplicity's sake.

## Why We Like It

Just as our students are more motivated when given the opportunity to read whatever they want, they are also more motivated to write about topics that they are interested in or that connect to their lives. Writer's notebooks offer a place where students can write in English without the pressure of being graded or where they can write in their home language. They serve as a daily tool for students to gain valuable literacy practice while also acting as a physical record of the progress they are making.

Another reason we like this strategy is that it motivates *us* to write, too! We keep a writer's notebook along with our students, which makes it much easier to model activities and keeps everyone more organized! We often ask students to glue or staple certain activities into their notebooks. This seems to be more effective than keeping loose sheets of paper in a folder.

# Supporting Research

Journal writing can provide a safe space for ELLs to take risks in their writing and develop fluency. Specific research has found that journaling "greatly benefits English language learners as it motivates them to write more in length and richer in content" (Cole & Feng, 2015, p. 11). In addition, encouraging ELL students to write in their home language is recognized by many researchers as a best practice (Howard Research, 2009, p. 31) because research indicates that L1 writing skills are transferrable to L2 writing. Students writing in their L1 also helps them to see themselves as writers (Roberts, 1994).

# Common Core Connections

Writer's notebooks support students in regularly practicing their use of English grammar and conventions in writing. This strategy also supports students in developing their writing abilities through "planning, revising, editing, rewriting, or trying a new approach" (Common Core State Standards Initiative, n.d.b).

# Application

All our books contain ideas and lessons for teaching different types of writing, including argument, narrative, and on-demand writing, among others. Although the writer's notebook strategy presents students with the opportunity to practice these types of writing, it also provides them the time and space to write about *themselves* in more informal ways.

Many of our beginner ELL students are navigating the process of being a teenager while learning a new language and adjusting to a new culture. Our higher-proficiency adolescent ELLs are often maneuvering between two cultures and two or more languages. The writer's notebook can serve as a tool for expressing their feelings and grappling with these struggles. Students often feel empowered by finding the words in English to express their feelings or to tell a story. Other times, it brings them comfort to write in their home language (and, as we stated previously, research says this is a good thing!).

We have had success using writer's notebooks with students at all levels of English proficiency. We describe how we tailor them to meet the needs of our diverse learners in the following sections.

## GETTING STARTED

At the beginning of the school year (or when students first come into our class) we provide them with a notebook. Students then spend a day decorating the cover (we bring in a pile of magazines, stickers, colored duct tape, etc.). We encourage students to use decorations—photos, drawings, colors, pictures from magazines, and so on—to represent their interests, personality, culture, or anything else meaningful to them.

It is helpful to show students models from previous years and to decorate our teacher notebooks along with them. We don't make any rules about the cover, other than it must contain the student's name and all the decorations must be appropriate for school.

Most of our students really enjoy this process and take their time! For students who finish more quickly, we ask them to find a partner who is also finished and to take turns sharing three of the decorations on their cover and why they chose them. We have found this decorating process increases students' ownership of, and excitement about, their notebooks.

After their notebooks are decorated, students create two key sections they will use on a regular basis.

The first is a section where they can list the books they are reading. We have them record the book title, author, and how many pages they read. They often finish the book, but other times they may only get halfway through when they realize they have lost interest, it is too difficult, and so on. We should point out this list includes all the books students are reading—in class, at home, in English, in their home language, and online (some of our students include online books, especially if they are longer texts, but we leave it up to their discretion). Newcomers might include picture books on their list.

Having students keep track of what they are reading serves to reinforce a culture of literacy as their reading progress is celebrated. We make it clear, however, that it is not a race to see who finishes the most books; rather it is a recognition of what each individual student has accomplished and not what they have done in comparison to others. It also helps us to be more aware of students' interests and progress.

The second section in their writer's notebook is for generating possible topics for writing. We have tried many different ways of helping students brainstorm ideas for writing, but the two strategies we like best are developing a heart map and a list of writing territories.

There are many variations of heart maps (which can easily be found by searching online), but we use a simple version that we first model in our own writer's notebook. We show students how to draw a heart (or you can make copies of a heart shape that can be glued onto a page in their notebook) and fill it with things that are important in their lives—they may write or draw pictures (see Figure 18.1: Student Example of a Heart Map). Students can add to their heart maps throughout the year, and they serve as a valuable resource for new writing ideas.

Making a list of writing territories—originally coined by Nancie Atwell (2014) in her well-known book *In the Middle* and further modified by educator Kelly Gallagher (2006, p. 94)—is another way for students to generate topics for writing and is a great opportunity to teach the word *territory*. It involves students making a list of their territories (areas of their lives and experiences they know well) in order to generate possible writing topics. As with the heart map, beginners can access this strategy by drawing pictures to represent their territories or writing in their home language.

## HOW STUDENTS USE THEM

Our students write in their notebooks daily for multiple purposes. As we mentioned, our students use their writer's notebooks to keep track of what they're reading. They also use them as a place to respond to the books they are reading during independent reading time (see Strategy 1: Independent Reading). A couple of times a week, we give students the opportunity to respond to their reading. We have them glue Figure 18.2: Prompts for Responding to My Reading into their notebook so they can choose from a list of possible prompts. As the year goes on, we may cross some off the list and add new ones suggested by students. We also promote variety and keep interest high by offering students some of the creative response prompts we include in Strategy 2: Literary Conversations. Other times, instead of choosing a prompt to write about, we will have students choose one to talk about with a partner or in a small group. In Strategy 10: Reading Comprehension, we share other ways for students to interact with their reading and demonstrate comprehension.

Students can also write journal entries about topics from their heart maps or writing territories list. Once they've had time to freewrite about several different topics, we have students pick their favorite to develop into a longer piece of writing and participate in a variety of revision activities (see Strategy 20: Revision).

Beginners can use a picture from their heart map or writing territories to label with English words and then be given sentence frames to describe the picture using the words. They can also write in their home language and choose a few sentences or a paragraph to translate into English with help from the teacher, an aide, or a higher-proficiency student who shares their home language. If you are in a situation in which Google Translate is the only option, have students use it with teacher guidance so they can see its shortcomings (we discuss this issue in Strategy 14: Writing Frames and Writing Structures). Writing in any language promotes literacy and builds confidence. Being strategic about helping students convert small portions of their writing into English will further enhance language acquisition. Many studies point to the facilitative role of translation when taught in the context of meaningful communication activities (Mogahed, 2011).

Sometimes we ask students to glue or staple pieces of work into their notebooks. These can serve as prompts for further writing or speaking. For example, when our beginners are using the picture word inductive model (see Strategy 11: Inductive Learning) they glue the picture onto a page, label it, and eventually generate sentences and paragraphs about it. Our beginners also glue a series of speaking prompts into their notebooks, which they can easily reference and practice with each other. We also have students keep a personal dictionary or glossary of important words they are learning. However, we try to limit what we require students to glue into their notebooks because we want it to be as student-centered as possible.

**HOW TEACHERS USE THEM**

Writer's notebooks help us learn about our students' experiences, background knowledge, and academic strengths and weaknesses. We use them in this way as a tool for formative assessment. We sometimes give feedback on content, sentence structure, and spelling, especially when it is student-prompted. We take examples (keeping them anonymous) to use for concept attainment (see Strategy 11: Inductive Learning). What we *don't* do is take out a red pen and write all over students' notebooks pointing out every single mistake. This would defeat the purpose of their notebook being a safe, student-owned space for writing practice.

We periodically collect student notebooks, especially after they've written a response to their reading, and provide brief written feedback on sticky notes in the form of questions or encouragement. We have also had success writing quick notes to students praising them for a specific success we've observed, checking in with them about how they're feeling, or making a book recommendation. Interacting with students through their notebooks in a positive and helpful way can be another step teachers can take to build trusting, productive relationships with their students.

## Student Handouts and Examples

Figure 18.1: Student Example of a Heart Map
Figure 18.2: Prompts for Responding to My Reading

## What Could Go Wrong?

There are a few things to try and avoid if you want the writer's notebook strategy to really work for students. One, don't let them sit on a shelf collecting dust—they should be living, breathing tools that students access daily. Also, it is important that they truly belong to the students, not the teacher. This means most of the writing generated by students is rooted in their experiences and interests. Teachers can support students in their writing *process* but shouldn't always assign what writing *products* appear in the notebooks. Finally, please don't collect their notebooks and correct their grammatical errors! Read them, interact with them, and use them to inform you about what type of instruction is needed by your students. And use them to learn more about your students' lives, interests, and goals.

## Technology Connection

Students can take pieces they've written in their writer's notebooks and further develop or publish them online in a variety of ways. For a list of resources see The Best Places Where Students Can Write Online (http://larryferlazzo.edublogs.org/2008/10/19/the-best-places-where-students-can-write-online/).

## Attribution

Writing and reading workshop pioneer Nancie Atwell introduced us to the concept of writing territories in her book *Lessons That Change Writers* (2017), and educator and author Kelly Gallagher presented us with further ideas on the strategy in his book *Teaching Adolescent Writers* (2006).

## Figures

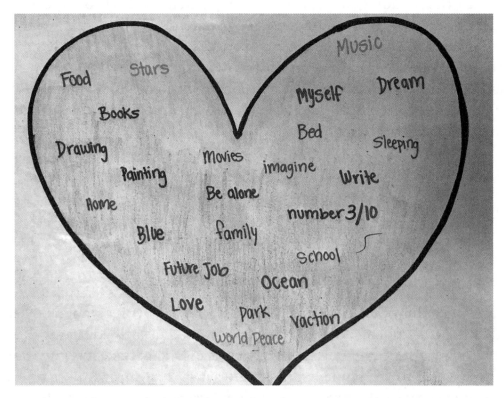

**Figure 18.1** Student Example of a Heart Map *Note:* Used with permission.

1. Choose a sentence or short passage from your reading today and copy it on the left side of your paper. On the right side, write your ideas about this sentence—what it means, why you like it, or a question you are wondering about it.

2. Choose a character from your book and write a quick letter or text message to him or her—you could offer advice, ask questions, or share how you are alike or different.

3. Draw a picture of a something you read today, label it, and then use the words to write a few sentences describing it.

4. If you started a new book today, explain why you chose this book. What predictions can you make after reading the first few pages?

5. If you finished a book today, how would you rate this book (5 stars to 1 star, A to F)? Give two specific reasons why you would give it this rating.

6. Explain how your reading today connects to you or your life. You can use the sentence starter: This character, part, idea reminds me of _____because_____.

7. Explain how your reading today connects to something else you've read, watched, or observed. You can use the sentence starter: This character, part, idea reminds me of _____because_____ _____.

8. Choose a new word you learned today during your reading. Write down *what* it means, explain *how* you learned what it means, and draw a picture to *show* what it means.

9. Add your own:

10. Add your own:

**Figure 18.2** Prompts for Responding to My Reading

## STRATEGY 19

# Error Correction Strategies

### What Is It?

This strategy is really a series of different steps we take to deal with the very tricky issue of error correction. When it comes to reading and writing (as well as speaking), our ELLs make plenty of them.

The question is: How can we best assist our students to learn from their mistakes and at the same time not have our corrections be de-motivators?

Don't believe anyone who tells you they *know* the best way to handle this critical component of language instruction. This is one of those areas in which there is definitely no best answer. However, we can share with you what seems to work for us and our students and what research guides us in our practices.

### Why We Like It

As we discuss in the next section, research is mixed on the best ways to provide student error correction. Given that murkiness, and given the uniformly strong evidence in favor of the effectiveness of the inductive process and games (see Strategy 11: Inductive Learning and Strategy 23: Learning Games for Reading and Writing), we emphasize error correction through these two methods in our classroom practice. In addition, we also apply *one* method of feedback that has been found to be somewhat effective for student writing—pointing to an incorrect word as a prompt for student self-correction. Finally, research suggests that encouraging a growth mind-set among students—the idea that mistakes are just opportunities to learn and not obstacles to be avoided—can have a positive impact on overall academic performance (Ferlazzo, 2012, October 13).

## Supporting Research

Here is what we wrote about error correction in *Navigating the Common Core with English Language Learners* (Ferlazzo & Sypnieski, 2016, p. 254):

> A number of studies (Goldenberg, 2013, p. 5) suggest that correction—either through prompts that point out the error to a student and require an immediate attempt at a "repair" or through "recasts" when teachers rephrase correctly what the student said—can be a useful tool to assist language acquisition.
>
> Other research, however, suggests the opposite—that overt grammar correction can actually be harmful to the English Language Learner. Some researchers (Truscott, 2005, p. 17) suggest that oral grammar correction interrupts communicative activities and can generate a negative reaction from students.
>
> These studies also point to similar hindrances resulting from correcting written grammatical errors, saying that it contributes to stress that inhibits language learning (Truscott, 1996).
>
> These two points of view partially rely on varying perspectives on the difference between language "acquisition" and language "learning." To "acquire" language, according to researcher/educator Stephen Krashen and many others who question the use of error correction, it is important to place a greater emphasis on communication rather than on the correct form. Professor Krashen would suggest that "learning" a language in schools can, instead, focus too much on the correct forms through grammar instruction and worksheets and not result in students actually being able to communicate effectively in the real world (Krashen, 1981).

Since we wrote those words, it appears that there might be a little more clarity from research, but it is still murky. It seems that there *may* be a bit more positive evidence about the effectiveness of error correction for incorrect spoken English (AnthonyTeacher.com, n.d.b). There does appear to be much more evidence demonstrating the ineffectiveness of the typical ways teachers provide feedback on written work, such as marking a student's paper (Conti, 2015, May 7; 2017).

One practice that seems to have some evidence of success in feedback on writing, however, is pointing to an incorrect word as a prompt for student self-correction (Conti, 2015, May 20).

## Common Core Connections

Really, what Common Core Standard does not apply to students learning from their mistakes and developing the resilience to recover from them?

# Application

These are the four primary error-correction strategies we use in our classrooms.

### CONCEPT ATTAINMENT AND CONCEPT ATTAINMENT PLUS

In Strategy 11: Inductive Learning and in Strategy 12: Concept Attainment—Plus, we explain in detail how we take student writing mistakes and create the conditions for them to identify what is wrong and correct it.

### GAMES

Here are our versions of two games incorporating student mistakes:

### Buy a Mistake

This is our version of a popular game among ELL teachers called *Grammar Auction*. We type up a list of sentences containing written student mistakes (either actual student-written sentences or ones we create) and put an amount next to each one (e.g., $10 if we think it's a particularly tricky one, $5 if we think it's medium hard, and $1 if we think they'll pick up on it right away). We divide students into teams, with each group having a mini-whiteboard. We'll show one sentence and give students a minute to write the correct version on their board. If it's right, they get the dollar amount. If it's wrong, in our version they don't lose anything. The team with the most money at the end of the game wins.

### Correct a Sentence

Here, we again type up a list of sentences containing student mistakes. In this game, though, after we divide students into teams, we give each team a sheet containing all the sentences, and they have to race through to correct them all in a certain period of time. At the end of that time (depending on the number of sentences—it could be 5 to 15 minutes), the team who has accurately corrected the greatest number of sentences is the winner. The first team to finish all of them correctly receives bonus points.

## ENCOURAGE A GROWTH MIND-SET

In our book *Navigating the Common Core with ELLs,* we share a lesson plan designed to help students not be hesitant to take risks and make mistakes (Ferlazzo & Sypnieski, 2016, p. 82). Its essence is first to have students make a list of the times they spoke or wrote English incorrectly over the previous few months and what they learned from each experience. Afterwards, we all reflect on the long list of things students would not have learned if they had not been willing to take risks using their new language. This lesson plan can be downloaded for free at our book's website. See the Technology Connections section for the link.

## GIVING INDIVIDUAL FEEDBACK

Of course, providing individual feedback can be a key error correction tool. How we use this tool is guided by a number of considerations:

- What type of relationship do we have with this student? Is he or she brand-new to the class and to this country? Has he or she been with us for several months and what do we know about him or her? The better relationship we have, the more candid the error feedback can be.

- Is it an error or a mistake? In linguistic terms, a *mistake* is doing something wrong that you have already been taught or should have known. An *error* is doing something incorrectly that you haven't yet been taught (Error, n.d.). Individual feedback on mistakes might be worth doing carefully. Generally, we hold off on doing feedback on errors and, instead, use them for class mini-lessons. This distinction between students doing something incorrectly that they have already been taught and their doing something incorrectly without having any prior knowledge of the concept *is* an important instructional consideration. Whether you call it a mistake or an error *is not* very important because the vast majority of people in the world, including us, do not care.

- When there are written mistakes, we point to it—whether it be a word or a punctuation issue. Students are typically then able to correct it then and there.

- We give very minimal feedback on oral mistakes—unless we are asked—as long as they do not seem to affect the primary message that the students want to communicate. We want to encourage them to talk and are thrilled when they are willing to do just that!

- If we have a solid relationship with a student, and if he or she appears to be highly motivated, we will have a conversation with him or her explaining how we handle providing feedback on incorrectly used language. We then ask if that is what he or she would like us to do, or if he or she would prefer more intensive individual correction. Invariably, these students choose the latter and appear to benefit from it.

## What Could Go Wrong?

Each one of our students is an individual and it is easy to miscalculate the fine line between what is the appropriate amount of correction and what amount will result in de-motivation. Many of our students come from highly vulnerable personal situations, which affects their learning outlook. Be aware and be flexible!

## Technology Connections

Practicing writing at online sites that provide immediate feedback is a great way to reinforce language acquisition and practice weak areas. There, the only one who knows when you make a mistake is the computer. There are lots of great sites at The Best Sites for Grammar Practice (http://larryferlazzo.edublogs.org/2008/12/07/the-best-sites-for-grammar-practice/).

Risk-taking is essential in learning a new language. Encouraging students not to shy away from taking them is important, and you can get many ideas on how to do that in the classroom from these sources:

The Best Ways to Use Mistakes When Teaching Writing (http://larryferlazzo .edublogs.org/2013/11/07/the-best-ways-to-use-mistakes-when-teaching-writing/)

The Best Posts, Articles & Videos About Learning from Mistakes and Failures (http://larryferlazzo.edublogs.org/2011/07/28/the-best-posts-articles-videos-about-learning-from-mistakes-failures/)

The Best Resources on Helping Our Students Develop a Growth Mindset (http://larryferlazzo.edublogs.org/2012/10/13/the-best-resources-on-helping-our-students-develop-a-growth-mindset/)

You can download our growth mind-set–related resilience lesson plan at our *Navigating the Common Core with English Language Learners* website (www.wiley .com/WileyCDA/WileyTitle/productCd-1119023009.html).

## Attribution

Versions of some of these ideas appeared in our book, *Navigating the Common Core with English Language Learners* (Ferlazzo & Sypnieski, 2016, p. 82, 254).

# STRATEGY 20

# Revision

## What Is It?

In the United States, the word *revision* is generally used to describe the act of reviewing a piece of writing and making improvements to it. In the United Kingdom and Commonwealth countries, it's more often used to describe the act of studying and preparing for exams (American English..., n.d.). We are using the former definition as we talk about the strategy, which is a series of steps we use to help ELL students improve their writing.

## Why We Like It

We like doing revision for two reasons—it seems to help our ELLs improve their writing and they also usually don't object to it! We find much more resistance to revision in our classes with English-proficient students. A perfect example of this perspective is shown in a video we wrote about in our last book (*Navigating the Common Core with English Language Learners*, 2016, p. 171). In the video:

> President Obama is being interviewed by a middle school student (https://www.youtube.com/watch?v=e7C8vEDhhVQ). As the president is explaining the importance of students revising their writing, the student interviewer cuts him off saying, "Yeah, I think you've pretty much covered everything about that question." We think that reaction "pretty much" sums up how many of our [English-proficient] students feel about the revision process—they'd rather just move on!

Our experience with ELLs seems to be shared by many other educators—ELL students are generally open to revising more often (Kietlinska, n.d., p. 70). This *might* be attributable to the fact that researchers have found many ELLs believe that their learning is based more on effort than natural-born intelligence (Byers-Heinlein & Garcia, 2015). In other words, it appears that ELLs might be more prone to having a growth mind-set and to see mistakes as opportunities to learn (Decades of Scientific Research . . . , n.d.).

This doesn't mean that ELLs are not afraid of making mistakes or never get frustrated. However, every day they are likely to be in a situation in which they see an immediate gain in understanding and communicating based on their efforts. This success can be experienced in being better able to understand ordering in a restaurant, watching an English-language TV show, comprehending a text, communicating in writing, or socializing more easily with English-speaking friends.

## Supporting Research

There does not seem to be clarity among researchers about the best ways to assist ELLs in revising their writing, but they all seem to agree that one of the best things teachers can do is to give ELLs more time—more time to write, more time to think, more time to revise (Kietlinska, n.d., p. 70). This need is one of the major reasons why many researchers recommend including an opportunity for peer review and feedback (Decades of Scientific Research, n.d., p. 8; Kietlinska, n.d., p. 80)—this process provides more time, as well as social support. Individual tutoring is generally considered the most-effective way to provide feedback for revision (Kietlinska, n.d., p. 85), and we discuss some ways to do that in Strategy 37: Peer Teaching and Learning. Finally, researchers typically suggest that the feedback process should focus on the content first and grammar later (Kietlinska, n.d., p. 75).

## Common Core Connections

Revision of student writing can assist in meeting several of the Standards, including one Writing Standard that is specifically *about* revision: "Develop and strengthen writing as needed by planning, revising, editing, rewriting, or trying a new approach." Remember, however, as we mentioned previously, that the Common Core authors have made it very clear that ELLs can meet the Standards without exhibiting "native-like" skills in all areas. We don't need to be the grammar police!

## Application

We typically use the following multistep process in assisting our students with revision (you can read about revision strategies we use more occasionally in our book, *Navigating the Common Core with English Language Learners*, 2016, p. 173). Please note that we used the word *typically* and not *always*. Sometimes, because of time constraints or because our access to technology is limited (we're not going to demand our students write entire essays by hand three or four times), we'll work on revising just a portion of an essay and not the entire piece:

1. After pre-planning their essay with a graphic organizer (see Strategy 3: Graphic Organizers), students write out their first draft with pen on paper. We'd be fine having students do this electronically if we had more access to technology.

2. We review a hard copy of their essay with each student, primarily focusing on key issues such as these: Is it basically communicating what they want it to say? Is the content corresponding with the essay's purpose? Does it have an introduction, topic sentences, and so on? We generally don't cover grammar issues at this time, though we *might* point out one or two of them.

3. Students will then type out their essay on computers. Though our access to technology is limited, we usually can arrange to get computers for a day or two. In addition to incorporating our feedback, students can use the grammar and spelling corrections provided by Google Docs or Microsoft Word.

4. Students will work with a partner using a peer reviewing process. Each student prints out two copies of his or her essay—one is for the peer reviewer. Each student also gets one copy of Figure 20.1: Peer Review Sheet.

   The first student who gets his or her essay reviewed reads the essay aloud and the reviewer follows along on his or her copy. During this time, the writer and the reviewer make notes about mistakes and improvements, primarily targeting grammar and sentence construction issues. After the writer is done reading, the writer and the reviewer discuss the points they both noted. Then, the reviewer goes through the peer review sheet one section at a time taking a minute or so to silently read that section of the essay and noting suggestions on the sheet. After he or she is done with each section, the reviewer shares comments with the writer, who makes notes on his or her copy of the essay. This process is repeated until the entire sheet is completed, and then the roles are reversed.

   Note that teachers will probably want to modify the peer review sheet to reflect the essay their students are writing.

5. We'll then quickly review this marked-up version of the essay with the student and, depending on his or her English proficiency and overall confidence level, may give specific feedback on one or two grammar issues by pointing at the mistake and having students identify the correction. More important, we'll note to ourselves what specific skills we need to cover in future lessons.

6. Students will next return to the electronic version of the essay they saved. Then they will make the revisions identified in the peer review process and in the follow-up conversation we had with them.

7. Students will print out two copies of their essay—one for us to keep in a file where we can track student progress and one they can glue into their writer's notebook (see Strategy 18: Writer's Notebook).

8. Students can then copy and paste their essay onto our class blog. Classmates will read them and leave comments using appropriate sentence starters such as "I like your essay because" and "Your essay makes me remember."

9. Sometimes we'll give students another opportunity to review and revise their essay by having them turn it into a narrated book or slideshow presentation, which they will post on our class blog. We then show it to the entire class. Students love it! Not only does this extra step provide more time for ELLs to revise (remember in the research section that's what everyone agrees they need) but also it is an excellent opportunity for pronunciation practice. You can see a link to the free tools we use in the Technology Connections section. That list also includes many student examples.

Then, it's time to move on to the next essay or project!

## Student Handout and Example

Figure 20.1: Peer Review Sheet

## What Could Go Wrong?

Don't feel like you have to follow our nine-step process every time you have students write an essay! You won't have time and even your ELLs, though they are likely to be less resistant to revision than other students, may get burnt out. We're generally able to use this entire process once every quarter.

## Technology Connections

Not all our ELL students are thrilled with revision. Good, student-friendly videos and images that show its importance can be found at The Best Resources for Getting Student Writers to "Buy-Into" Revision (http://larryferlazzo.edublogs.org/2015/07/23/the-best-resources-on-getting-student-writers-to-buy-into-revision-help-me-find-more/).

Students can use many tools to turn their essays into narrated books. You can see the links to the online tools we use, along with student examples, at The "All-Time" Best Web 2.0 Tools for Beginning English Language Learners (http://larryferlazzo.edublogs.org/2015/04/16/the-all-time-best-2–0-tools-for-beginning-english-language-learners/).

There are quite a few online tools that will analyze writing and provide feedback. We're not big fans and don't use them with students because we think the feedback they provide can be overwhelming and not prioritized. There are a few, however, that *might* have potential in the future that can be accessed at The Best Online Tools That Can Help Students Write an Essay (http://larryferlazzo.edublogs.org/2015/06/29/am-i-missing-something-or-are-there-very-few-online-tools-than-can-help-students-write-an-essay/).

We've discussed here and in other sections how we use classroom blogs. You can access all of Larry's professional and class blogs at Resources from All My Blogs (http://larryferlazzo.edublogs.org/2017/03/06/resources-from-all-my-blogs-10/). ELL teachers might be particularly interested in his ELD class blog (www.sacschoolblogs.org/larryferlazzo/).

For additional information on creating blogs, visit The Best Sources of Advice for Teachers (and Others!) on How to Be Better Bloggers (http://larryferlazzo.edublogs.org/2009/06/03/the-best-sources-of-advice-for-teachers-and-others-on-how-to-be-better-bloggers/) and The Best Sources of Advice on Student Blogging (http://larryferlazzo.edublogs.org/2008/12/26/the-best-sources-for-advice-on-student-blogging/).

# Figure

This sheet should be stapled on top of your essay

Name of Writer _____

Name of Reviewer _____

**First,** have the writer read his or her essay to you while you are looking at his or her essay. Mark down any grammar issues you find. After your partner is done reading, share your comments.

## Essay Check List

**1.** Does it have a title related to the topic?

## First Paragraph

**1.** Does it have a good hook?

**2.** Does it have a thesis statement communicating the main idea of the essay?

**3.** Does it have a sentence listing major topics the essay will cover?

## Body Paragraphs

**1.** Does it have a topic sentence?

**2.** Does it have good supporting details?

## Conclusion

**1.** Does it summarize the content that was covered in the essay?

**2.** Does it say why the essay topic is important?

**Figure 20.1**   Peer Review Sheet *Source:* Modified from Exhibit 4.2 in *Navigating the Common Core with English Language Learners* (Ferlazzo & Sypnieski, 2016, p. 175).

*STRATEGY 21*

# Problem-Posing

## What Is It?

Problem-posing is an element of the critical pedagogy concept developed by Brazilian educator Paolo Freire. The idea is to draw from students the issues and concerns they have about their lives and help them identify actions they can take to effectively respond to them. The Peace Corps, drawing on the work of Nina Wallerstein (Crawford-Lange, 1983), developed a multistep instructional strategy to also use this process as a language-learning opportunity (Schleppegrell & Bowman, 1995, p. 298).

## Why We Like It

As we've said elsewhere and repeatedly in this book, looking at our students through the lens of assets, and not deficits, is a central element of our teaching beliefs. Problem-posing is a classic example of how students can use their own life experiences to learn and grow in an academic environment. In addition, it can assist them to use what they learn in our classrooms to improve their lives outside of school.

Last, it's a versatile strategy that can be used in just about any thematic unit. Unfortunately, all of us have problems and challenges!

## Supporting Research

There appears to be limited research available specifically on this kind of problem-posing instructional strategy with its roots in Freirian critical pedagogy. However, this strategy has many similarities to culturally responsive pedagogy, and research finds that it can have a positive impact on student achievement (Liebtag, n.d.). Also see Strategy 36: Culturally Responsive Teaching.

## Common Core Connections

The writing involved in this strategy connects to the Language Standards of acquiring and applying language conventions, as well as to the Standard of argument writing. In addition, depending on how much time the teacher wants to devote to the lesson, it can also support student Speaking and Listening Standards. Finally, the process of problem-posing is really a form of close-reading an image or dialogue (see Strategy 10: Reading Comprehension and Strategy 17: Using Photos or Other Images in Reading and Writing for more on close reading). This makes the strategy very relevant to several of the Reading Standards.

## Application

There are eight (and sometimes nine) primary steps to our modified version of this instructional strategy:

1. Select a picture or short video clip portraying a national or international problem directly affecting students or a common challenge students and their families face (a photo of a long line of people wanting to apply for a job, a movie scene in which someone is a victim of crime, a photo of a child being bullied on a playground, an image of damage caused by a hate crime). Another option for high ELL beginners or intermediates is to have the teacher write a dialogue demonstrating the problem.

   Of course, a prerequisite of being able to use this strategy is having a *relationship* with your students and knowing their hopes, dreams, and concerns. Does this mean you have to spend hours asking them questions? Of course not. However, it does mean you can do the following:

   - Have all students do a simple introductory poster and small-group presentation sharing their likes, worries, dreams for the future, favorite songs, and so on.

   - Follow up that assignment with brief individual conversations about what they said. Just take a minute or two when they're working on computers or quietly reading a book.

   - Make arrangements with the classroom teacher they have during your prep period to pull each student out to have what our principal Jim Peterson calls a *walk-and-talk*. This is just a 15-minute walking conversation when you can check in with your student and learn more about him or her.

   - Visit the home of your student. Our local teachers union was one of the founders of the national Parent-Teacher Home Visit Project. See the Technology Connections section for more details.

**2.** Show the image or video clip, or a student and the teacher can act out the dialogue.

Make sure you turn on the video's English captions—if available.

If you are using a dialogue, be sure to arrange a brief practice time with the student or students.

**3.** Next, ask students to share what they believe is happening. What is the problem they think is being portrayed?

Ask students to first describe what they see with simple prompting questions such as "Who is in the picture or video?" "Where are they?" "What is happening?" "What else do you see?" "How do you think the person is feeling?" Give students a minute to think about their responses before calling on them.

Write student answers to the questions on the overhead and recast any errors. *Recasting* means writing and saying in correct English if something is said incorrectly (Student: "Boy in picture." Teacher: "There is a boy in the picture."). Students can copy what you write in the first question in Figure 21.1: Problem-Posing Graphic Organizer.

Then, ask students what they think is the problem in the picture. Depending on the English proficiency level of the students, the teacher might have to teach what the word *problem* means (e.g., "It means something bad" and play-act being thirsty: "No water is a problem."). Write the response on the overhead and have students copy it down. Students could say more than one type of problem. If that's the case, as long as they make sense, write them down and have students copy the words in the second section of the graphic organizer.

**4.** This is followed by asking students if they, members of their family, or friends have ever experienced a similar problem now or in the past.

The teacher can probably begin by saying that he or she has either experienced it or has known former students or others who have experienced it and share that example. The teacher can write a simple sentence about it on the overhead. This can serve as an ice-breaker. Students should not copy the sentence, but it can serve as a model.

The teacher then asks students to share if they, their family, or friends are experiencing this problem now or have experienced it in the past. If some students say yes, the teacher can ask simple questions ("Are you having the problem?" "Is your family having this problem?" "When did you have this problem?" "Where are you having the problem?" "How does it make you feel?") and compose simple sentences on the overhead for students to copy in the second section in the graphic organizer. As always, after asking a question the teacher should ask students to think about it for 30 seconds or a minute prior to calling on someone to share.

If they have no experience with the problem, they can just circle that answer on the graphic organizer.

5. Ask students what they think caused the problem.

The teacher first might have to define the world *cause* through doing some physical examples (e.g., putting a book on the floor and pretending to trip over it and asking, "Why did I stumble?" or telling students he or she is hungry and asking them why they think that is the case).

The teacher can then ask students what they think caused the problem and write down what they say on the overhead. Students can copy down all or some of the causes listed. They don't have to copy down any causes with which they don't agree.

6. Next, students can share potential solutions to the problem, including any ones they might have already tried.

The teacher may need to teach the meaning of the word *solution* (he or she can refer back to the play-acting about needing water as being a problem. Then, go around play-acting asking students for water to see who will give it. Not only will it teach the world *solution* but also it will be fun to see who refuses to help!).

If the process has been going on for a while, we sometimes will end it for the day at this point and ask students to think about potential solutions for homework. Other times, we will continue on to finish this multistep process on the same day.

After giving students a minute to think about it, and then to share with a partner, the teacher asks students what they think are solutions to the problem that they have either tried in the past or think would work in the future. The teacher writes them down on the overhead and asks students to copy them on the graphic organizer.

7. Then, students are asked to choose which solution they think would be the best one.

Students write their answer on the graphic organizer. Ideally, they can also explain in English why they think one is the best solution. However, that is not always possible for ELL beginners. In those situations, students can answer in their home language.

8. Finally, students are asked what they could do to help solve the problem.

The graphic organizer provides a space for students to write down what they could do individually and what they could do with others.

Students can make a simple illustrated poster with their responses to each of the steps and practice reading them in small groups. We've also recorded their presentations and posted them online—with permission from them and their family (see the Technology Connections section).

9. In some cases, the final step is to have students decide if they want to take action to try to solve the problem. We use this multistep process several times during the school year, but it's not feasible to move to the action stage every time due to time constraints. However, when student energy is obvious, it makes sense to move forward.

Actions can be simple or more complicated. In our classes over the years, actions have ranged from students making posters about the importance of picking up trash on school grounds to organizing a neighborhood-wide jobs fair with 20 job-training providers and 300 people in attendance. Other student actions have included organizing neighborhood campaigns to complete US Census forms, creating and distributing flyers with accurate information on the SARS virus, organizing a forum on the rights of immigrants, and writing letters to public officials about government immigration policy.

## Student Handout and Example

Figure 21.1: Problem-Posing Graphic Organizer

## What Could Go Wrong?

Don't feel like you have to complete this lesson in one day! The originator of the expression "Always leave them wanting more" is in dispute, but the advice is not! This strategy easily lends itself to being taught in chunks on different days.

Be politically savvy when it comes to the class deciding on student action steps. Don't put you or your students in the middle of a firestorm with administrators and parents. Don't encourage students to take actions that could make them or you politically vulnerable. Don't get involved in partisan politics.

Do encourage students to take fact-based actions such as the ones we described in Step 9 and, before anything is done, make sure you have support from your school administrators. This may be the first time any of your students have taken a step toward participating in public life, a step that may very well have put their lives in danger in their home countries. This makes it doubly important that teachers make sure that any action has the support of the school and parents.

## Technology Connections

To learn more about making home visits to help build relationships with students and their families, visit The Best Resources for Learning About Teacher Home Visits (http://engagingparentsinschool.edublogs.org/2011/10/10/the-best-resources-for-learning-about-teacher-home-visits/).

We have recorded students presenting their problem-posing posters and posted it online. There are many tools for this kind of recording. See Using Freire & Fotobabble with English Language Learners (http://larryferlazzo.edublogs.org/2013/11/01/using-freire-fotobabble-with-english-language-learners-2/).

We mentioned various action projects our students took, including informing their neighborhood about the advantages of completing Census forms. You can read more about it, and see their posters, at Combining an "Assets" Perspective with an Authentic Audience (http://larryferlazzo.edublogs.org/2016/09/21/a-look-back-combining-an-assets-perspective-with-an-authentic-audience/).

## Attribution

Versions of some of these ideas appeared in our book, *The ESL/ELL Teacher's Survival Guide* (Ferlazzo & Sypnieski, 2012, p. 45) and in our book, *Navigating the Common Core with English Language Learners* (Ferlazzo & Sypnieski, 2016, p. 201).

# Figure

Name _____

**1.** What do you see in the picture/video/dialogue?

_____

_____

_____

**2.** What is the problem?

The problem is _____.

**3.** Do you, your family or your friends have this problem now, or have you had it in the past?

Yes, I/we/they have this problem now when _____

_____.

Yes, I/we/they had this problem in the past when _____

_____.

OR

No, I/we/they do not have this problem now and have not had it in the past.

**4.** What do you think is the cause of that problem?

I think _____

is/are the cause/causes of the problem.

**5.** What are solutions to that problem?

One solution is _____.

Another solution is _____.

**6.** What is the best solution to that problem?

The best solution to that problem is _____

because _____

_____.

**7.** What is one thing you can do to help solve the problem?

One thing I can do alone to help solve the problem is _____

_____. One thing I can do with others is to _____

_____.

**Figure 21.1** Problem-Posing Graphic Organizer

## Student Handouts and Examples

Figure 22.1: Micro-Progression—Claim and Evidence

Figure 22.2: Micro-Progression—Predictions

## What Could Go Wrong?

Micro-progressions are not visual tools that can just be thrown up on the overhead and digested by students without any scaffolding. This strategy needs to be carefully planned so it doesn't overwhelm students or the teacher! It helps to do each box step-by-step and to have the students actively engaged in the process—prompting them to write on their own copy or to talk to a partner. Be strategic about what you include on the page—too much text can turn students off and especially overwhelm English language learners.

Making these micro-progressions can take up a lot of your time. Don't make one for *every* skill and, before you create them, look online for ones you can use or modify. You don't have to reinvent the wheel!

## Attribution

Our thanks to Kate Roberts and Maggie Beattie Roberts for allowing us to share this versatile strategy from their book *DIY Literacy: Teaching Tools for Differentiation, Rigor, and Independence* (2016). See Kate and Maggie's videos for helpful suggestions on micro-progressions and other teaching strategies: www.kateandmaggie.com/videos-diy-literacy/.

# Figures

| High school should start at 10:00 in the morning. | High school should start at 10:00 in the morning because teens will learn more if they get more sleep. | High school should start at 10:00 in the morning because teens will learn more if they get more sleep. For example, it is easier for me to pay attention in my third-period class that starts at 10:00 than my first-period class that starts at 8:00. |
|---|---|---|
| • Make a <u>claim</u><br><br>• Use the word *should* in my claim<br><br>★ | • Make a <u>claim</u> and explain <u>why</u> I think this.<br><br>• Use the word *should* and *because* in my claim.<br><br>★★ | • Make a <u>claim</u> and explain <u>why</u> I think this.<br><br>• Give an <u>example</u> to support my thinking.<br>• Use the phrase *for example.*<br><br>★★★ |

**Figure 22.1**    Micro-Progression—Claim and Evidence

| I predict that Ferdinand will not fight the Matador. | I predict that Ferdinand will not fight the Matador because he doesn't like to fight. | I predict that Ferdinand will not fight the Matador because he doesn't like to fight. For example, when all the young bulls would fight each other all day, Ferdinand liked to sit quietly under the cork tree and smell the flowers. |
|---|---|---|
| • *Make a prediction*<br><br>**OKAY** | **BETTER** | **BEST** |

**Figure 22.2**    Micro-Progression—Predictions

# STRATEGY 23

# Learning Games for Reading and Writing

## What Is It?

This strategy lists our 14 favorite games to reinforce reading and writing with English language learners. We've previously shared five of them in our first two books, and nine of them are new.

## Why We Like It

There are countless games that teachers have used while teaching English language learners. Many, however, don't meet our criteria:

- They require very minimal teacher preparation time.
- The financial cost is nothing or next to nothing.
- Students enjoy them, but there is an emphasis on learning as much as there is on playing.
- After teacher modeling, students can lead the game or create game materials as a way of doubling language-learning opportunities.
- All students participate (or, at least, are *supposed* to participate) all the time—there are no opportunities to be eliminated from the game.

These games, similar to all the strategies in the book, are ones we periodically use in the classroom and, along with the ones later in the book, specifically reinforce speaking and listening (our decisions on which section to put each game were sometimes arbitrary because most of them support all four domains). They provide an adequate repertoire for our teaching—we don't play any often enough for students to get tired of them and we're able to easily modify all of them to teach anything we happen to be focusing on at the time.

And did we mention teacher prep time?☺ We don't know about you, but with everything else on our plate, we don't need to find another 15 minutes to an hour to prepare materials for a game!

## Supporting Research

Plenty of research shows that strategic use of games promotes language learning in several ways, including by increasing motivation and creating opportunities for low-anxiety communication in the target language (Martin, 2016; Mubaslat, 2011/2012). Education researcher Robert Marzano's examination of multiple studies has also found that games can have a relatively strong positive impact on student achievement (Marzano, 2010).

Research specifically targeting technology-based games (see the Technology Connections section) has also found that it promotes academic achievement (Shapiro, 2014). Studies conducted with language learners have found similar results (Ashraf et al., 2014; Yip & Kwan, 2006).

## Common Core Connections

Specific Common Core connections would depend, of course, on the game and the target language it is reinforcing at the time. Most, if not all, of the games almost certainly support the Language Standards, including acquiring vocabulary, learning conventions, and demonstrating "knowledge of word relationships."

## Application

Here are our 14 favorite reading and writing games.

### NINE BOX GRID

We use this simple game, which we learned and modified from English teacher Katie Toppel (2017) *a lot*. As you can see from Figure 23.1: Nine Box Grid with Health Care Words Example and Figure 23.2: Nine Box Grid Template, it's just a matter of putting nine words (or, when we teach phonics, letters) on a numbered three-by-three grid (for a total of nine boxes or spaces) on the class whiteboard.

Then, we give students mini-whiteboards (sometimes they play with a partner and sometimes individually), markers, and erasers or cloths (if you haven't invested in a class set of mini-whiteboards, we'd strongly advise you do so—either buying them from a store or making your own—search *make mini-whiteboards* online for instructions).

Next, we take out two huge foam dice we bought online for a few dollars. One student rolls the dice and then everyone gets one minute to write a sentence on their board using the chosen word or writing a word using the letter. If they roll an 11 or 12, they must use their choice of two words or letters on the grid. Students are told to hold up their boards at the end of a minute and the teacher gives some quick feedback.

Then, another student rolls the dice and the game continues. Unlike some of our other games, we don't keep score in this one and students enjoy it just the same.

After a few turns, we'll ask the rollers of the dice to change a word or letter on the grid. This move promotes more student engagement and ownership (though it can get a bit loud each time the dice roller is lobbied by the rest of the class when he or she is at the board!).

We talk more about how we use Katie Toppel's game to promote speaking in Strategy 33: Learning Games for Speaking and Listening.

**PHONIC DARTS**

Years ago we were able to purchase a game called *Phonicball*. It's a series of Velcro dart boards with letters (one with consonants, another with vowels, and a third with phonic blends) instead of numbers. We have one student throw a Velcro ball at the board, and then, depending on the English proficiency level of the students, he or she can have a certain amount of time to write as many words down on the whiteboard that start with that letter or, in the case of vowels, use the vowel that is selected. After students get their points for the words the wrote, they can practice saying the words in small groups.

Unfortunately, the company that made those Velcro boards went out of business years ago. But there are plenty of pictures of their products available if you search the web, and you can create your own versions. Searching for *Velcro ball dartboard* will lead you to instructions to make your own. Alternatives include drawing one on a poster board or projecting an image of it on the board, and having students throw a beanbag. Laying the poster on the floor and tossing a beanbag on it might, however, reduce the number of arguments you have about which letter the beanbag lands on.

**FILL-IN-THE-BLANK**

This simple game also requires mini-whiteboards—one per group. We usually have students divide into pairs and give each partner group a number. We then put the number on the board and give them points when they make a correct answer.

In this game, the teacher writes and reads or just says a cloze or gap-fill sentence ("Mr. Ferlazzo is a _____"; "I am going to _____ over the weekend.").

Students must fill in the blank and write a complete sentence on their board. They will get one point for every word they add if the sentence is correct—this feature encourages students to avoid the easiest answers. However, if there is an error in their more-complex sentence, they do not get any points—no matter how many other words they use. In this game, as in all of the games, the teacher is the ultimate decider!

However, even though the teacher is the final judge, students can also take turns being the leader and giving the class their own clozes.

### FLYSWATTER GAME (WITH OR WITHOUT FLYSWATTERS)

In this game, students will be running up to the class whiteboard and swatting words. You can buy several flyswatters for a few dollars, or you can just have students use a rolled-up a piece of paper, instead.

First, ask three or four students to go up to the classroom whiteboard. Then ask them to write—in large letters and scattered all over the board (it's even better if you have boards on two classroom walls so the words can be very spread out)—20 or so words recently studied by the class. Ideally, there is a vocabulary list they can quickly divide up among themselves.

Divide the class, or have them divide themselves, into three to six teams (the more the better), with each team having a number. Each team sends one member to the front with his or her back to the board (they can stand diagonally if the words are on two boards).

The teacher will either call out the word itself (the easiest version), a cloze or gap-fill sentence using one of the words, an antonym or a synonym (making it clear if it's one or the other), or make a related gesture. As soon as the word or clue is given, the students with the flyswatter can turn around and start swatting. The first person who swats the correct answer gets a point for his or her group and the second person gets one-half point. Group members cannot leave their seats, but they can help by shouting out directions or suggestions (if your classroom has thick walls). Each group rotates the person doing the swatting.

In this game, and in most of our games where students earn points, we let groups decide on how many they will bet on the last question in order to generate more suspense and enthusiasm, though it's not like there's a shortage of the latter by that time. Students can take turns leading the game, too.

You can do a less-noisy and more-sane version of this game by dividing the class into groups of four. Then have the four in each group write the same list of vocabulary words on index cards or small sheets of paper. Next, have them combine their desks so they are all facing each other and spread out the words between them. When the teacher calls out the word or clue, the first person in each group who slaps the correct word with his or her hand gets a point. You'll have multiple groups of four (expanding it to six is an option with desks at each end) playing and keeping score on their own. When we play this version, before the game begins we ask each group to choose a scorekeeper they trust.

## NAME IT

This game has a few similarities to the flyswatter game. As in that game, the teacher will either call out a word itself (the easiest version), a cloze or gap-fill sentence using one of the words ("I will drive my _____ to work"), an antonym or a synonym (making it clear if it's one or the other), or make a related gesture. However, in this game students are divided into pairs with one mini-whiteboard per group and are given 60 seconds (as in all of these games, the time limit can be adjusted based on the English proficiency level of the students) to write down the words—they are not written on the classroom whiteboard. Remember, though, that teacher clues could result in more than one answer making sense, so flexibility about the correct response is required.

An easy modification of this game could be the teacher just saying sentences and having students write them correctly on their boards.

## ROUND-AND-ROUND SHE GOES

This game incorporates one of the most versatile free sites on the web, ClassTools (www.classtools.net/), which has a huge number of easily usable online tools. Round-and-Round She Goes uses the *Random Name Picker* (n.d.) feature. It is basically a roulette wheel that lets you write anything you want in the different sections and then spin it with a click of your mouse. You can save your wheel for repeated use or make up new ones with different wording. It's also easy for students to create their own wheels that teachers can use during a classroom game.

In the game, a teacher or student clicks the wheel for a spin and then student teams of two or three (again with one mini-whiteboard per group) have a time period to perform the task that is picked. The wheel could include vocabulary words that students have to use correctly in a sentence, irregular verbs that they have to write in the correct past tense, three words starting a sentence that they have to complete, a story topic that they have to write about—the possibilities are endless!

## WRITING BINGO

This game is designed for high-beginner or intermediate ELLs. First, students write briefly about a topic of their own choosing. Then, they share their title and other students predict what words they think might be used in the short writing piece. They earn a point for every accurate prediction.

To start, the teacher writes a model short story or essay about a simple topic (favorite sport, favorite teacher, food he or she likes, least-favorite food, etc.). Ideally, it would be related to a theme the class has recently studied.

The teacher announces the topic of his or her essay and explains that he or she is going to read it to the class. Prior to reading it, though, students will be given a few minutes to write down words they believe will be used in the story. They will receive a point for every correct prediction.

After students have written down their predictions, they are told to put away their pens or pencils and are given a colored pencil (this reduces the chances of students cheating by writing down new words as they hear them). Every time they hear one of their words, they should cross it off the list. After the teacher reads his or her essay, students count their points and a winner is declared. Obviously, the teacher should double-check the winner's sheet.

Next, students are given five or ten minutes to write a story or essay on a topic of their choice. The teacher can list ideas on the board to help students who have trouble thinking of a subject on their own. Students can be divided into groups of four (including a group leader) and the same process can take place with each group declaring a winner.

We were inspired to use this game by English teacher Sandy Millin (2013). We modified her original idea, so you might want to read how she uses the game.

**SENTENCE SCRAMBLES**

Sentence scrambles are words and punctuation in one sentence that are scrambled out of order. Students then have to put them in the correct sequence.

A lot of preparation is required for this game, and it is mostly student work. Students are given paper clips and many index cards or sheets of paper that they can cut into the size of index cards. They are asked to choose 10 or 15 sentences from their textbook or from the books they are reading. They write each word and punctuation mark in the sentence on a separate card. They must be copied down exactly, and even a period has to have its own card. If a sentence has five words and a period, then the student would need to prepare six cards.

Students are not creating original sentences (the needed checking for errors would not make this feasible). After they have completed one sentence, they mix up the order and clip them together. It's important to note that they do not mix sentences together—only the words from the same sentence. Trust us, teacher modeling of these instructions is critical to ensure that students clearly understand the required steps. In addition, we suggest that the first two sentence scrambles created by each student be checked by the teacher to ensure that these directions are followed—it's obviously easy for an ELL to copy a sentence incorrectly.

After all the sentence scrambles are done, one or two students are asked to shuffle them to ensure that the 10 or 15 scrambles done by each student are not together. They are shuffling the completed scrambles, not mixing up the words within a sentence. In other words, not all the sentence scrambles created by Juan are grouped together—they are mixed in with the scrambles from all the other students. Once mixed, the scrambles are all put into a box.

The next day, students are divided into teams of four or five students each and asked to put their desks together. The teacher gives each group 30 (this number may vary based on the English proficiency of the class) of the sentence scrambles, and the first group that completes them all correctly is the winner (it's always nice to have a prize for second place, too). As students place the words in what they believe is the correct order, the teacher can circulate and tell them if they are right or not. After they are checked by the teacher, the group paper clips them together and puts them on a tray or on another desk. Obviously, the teacher needs to be working quickly, too. If you have a large class, you probably want to make the groups larger and increase the number of sentence scrambles so you have to move around less often. But we've found that we can handle four or five groups at one time if we are fast on our feet. In the best of all worlds, teachers can draft English-proficient students from other classes for this short period to help evaluate the scrambles.

The sentence scrambles can be kept for future games or for practice as part of another lesson.

## ACADEMIC LANGUAGE SENTENCES

We explicitly teach academic language, and we use this game to reinforce those words. However, this same game can also be used to review vocabulary words learned in a specific unit.

Students are in groups of two or three and have one mini-whiteboard per group. All students have access to their materials that list the academic language they have learned or their unit vocabulary.

Each group is given 90 seconds to write one sentence correctly using as many of the targeted vocabulary words as possible. Their group will gain one point for every word used correctly. At the end of that time, one person from each group stands up and reads the sentence (this step is optional). The teacher determines how many points the group should be given. Sentences cannot be reused exactly, but students can model sentences they write after ones that others have said. (Teachers don't have to worry about remembering all the sentences—students are the first to accuse others of copying their sentences!) To reduce copying, we usually keep this game short—only four rounds or so—and we tell students they can write two sentences during that last round to gain as many points as possible.

## PICTIONARY

Everybody reading this book probably is already familiar with Pictionary. The teacher or a student draws an object, living being, or action on the front board or document camera, and then students (again with whiteboards) are given a minute to write down what they think is being drawn. We want to encourage full-class participation, so in our version people don't shout out their answer and students don't get points for being first. Everyone who has the correct answer written down 30 seconds after the drawing is completed receives a point and can bet it all prior to the last drawing.

## TEAM-WRITING SENTENCES

In this game, students are divided into groups of four or five each with one whiteboard per group. One representative from each group stands in front of the classroom with the mini-whiteboard, and his or her group is seated in front of him or her.

The teacher, or a student, says a sentence, and the students standing in front have to write it out correctly. Though members of their group cannot get out of their seats, they can shout encouragement and suggestions. The first person who writes out the sentence correctly, including capital letters and punctuation, gets a point for their team.

All group members rotate to have a turn standing in front with the whiteboards.

## HANGMAN

We play this game without the illustration of the hanged man and challenge students to determine not one word but all the words in a sentence. First, the teacher thinks of a sentence and draws short lines on the class whiteboard representing each letter of each word in the sentence (we use a different color marker for each word and leave a space between them).

Next, students are divided into small groups with one mini-whiteboard. Each group takes turns guessing letters (with luck, after some kind of analysis). If the letters are included in the words, the teacher writes them in their appropriate spot. If not, they are written at the bottom of the board.

The first group to write the entire sentence correctly is the winner. Any group can write what they think is the correct sentence and yell it out at any time. However, if they guess incorrectly, they cannot guess again until it is their turn to suggest a letter.

**CATEGORIES**

We use this game primarily for vocabulary review. Students are divided into pairs and, as usual, each group is given one mini-whiteboard. The teacher calls out names of categories (home, animals, things that move, things made of metal, things that people do for fun, etc.). Students are given one minute to write down as many (classroom-appropriate) items as they can on their whiteboard. They get a point for each one that is correct. This game can also create opportunities for speaking practice when there is a dispute about an answer—students had to convince us once that *fighting* qualified under "things that people do for fun."

The category could also be "words that start with the letter *b*." And, if you are teaching a more-advanced ELL class, you can even make it more challenging by combining two categories (e.g., "words that start with *t* and are in a home").

You can do this occasionally in reverse and throw in a question in which *you* give the words and *they* have to write the name of the category.

**WHAT DOESN'T BELONG?**

As usual, students are divided into small teams with each group having a small whiteboard. In this game, the teacher writes down three or four words. He or she shows and says the words to the class. One of the words in the group does not belong to the same category as the others (e.g., dog, cat, lion). Sentences could also be used (e.g., "I like you"; "I love this picture" "I'm hungry"). Students have 30 seconds or a minute to write down the word that doesn't belong *and* write an explanation for their choice. Teams get one-half point if they choose the correct word and one-half point if they give the correct explanation. Also, as usual, students can bet a large amount prior to the last question.

After students become familiar with the game, they could create several posters. Each poster could be divided into three or four sections with one word or one sentence that doesn't belong. In addition to text, students could illustrate each word or sentence. Teachers can use them along with their own examples for the game. You can keep the best for future years, too.

## Student Handouts and Examples

Figure 23.1: Nine Box Grid with Health Care Words Example
Figure 23.2: Nine Box Grid Template

## What Could Go Wrong?

No surprise here—the primary potential problem is student cheating and the tensions created by it. We deal with that issue by beginning each game with a short explanation of the rules. Then, we ask everyone who agrees with following these rules to raise their hands. We've found that spending a minute doing this exercise reduces, though may not eliminate, the problem. If it still happens, we remind the student of the agreement he or she made. In a worst-case scenario, a repeat offender is told he or she cannot continue to play and a one-on-one conversation takes place after class.

The next big problem can be high noise levels for some of the games. Again, we cover this issue when we discuss the rules prior to the game, but generally still have to repeatedly remind students. Luckily, our classroom neighbors are patient and we periodically send them candy bars.

Prizes are another issue to consider. Many times the bell rings signaling the end of class and the end of the game, and no one really cares about a prize. Even when the games end in the middle of class time, it's clear that the games generate intrinsic motivation and students are not in it for the reward. Nevertheless, we always have on hand small and inexpensive packages of dried fruit or trail mix we purchase at warehouse stores or a couple of graham crackers. These are usually sufficient for the winners. Another option is to use Katie's one-liner: "You all have extra credit in my heart!"—though we cannot guarantee positive student reactions to that comment.

## Technology Connections

There are many, and we mean *many*, online games geared toward English language learners. To narrow down the list a bit, you can visit these two lists:

"All-Time" Best Web Tools for English Language Learners (www.teachingenglish .org.uk/blogs/larry-ferlazzo/larry-ferlazzo-online-tools)

The Best Beginner, Intermediate & Advanced English Language Learner Sites (http://larryferlazzo.edublogs.org/2011/09/19/the-best-beginner-intermediate-advanced-english-language-learner-sites/)

Online learning games come-and-go, but we'd rate Duolingo (www.duolingo .com/) and LingoHut (http://lingohut.com/) as two of the best. They also look like they'll be around for a while. Plus, they're free! Duolingo has the added benefit of allowing teachers to create virtual classrooms to monitor student progress.

In addition, one of our all-time-favorite online games for beginning ELLs is called Draw a Stickman (www.drawastickman.com/). We hope it never goes off-line! It provides instructions to draw figures and objects that the game uses to participate in actions that move the story along.

All these online games are fun and educational, but one thing they lack is promoting collaborative learning. We've found one way to combine tech with students working together: through the use of online video games and walkthroughs. These walkthroughs are freely available step-by-step instructions for players on how to proceed through the game. Printing out these instructions, having two students share one computer in an attempt to follow those steps, and competing to see which groups would be the first three to finish promotes collaboration and language acquisition. Though the process is as straightforward as we have just described, you can read an article Larry wrote about it (http://larryferlazzo.com/videogamearticle .html) and access a list of games and their walkthroughs that we use in our classes (www.sacschoolblogs.org/larryferlazzo/category/games/).

Students can also create online learning games for their classmates to play. The Best Websites for Creating Online Learning Games (http://larryferlazzo.edublogs .org/2008/04/21/the-best-websites-for-creating-online-learning-games/) has a lengthy list of sites where they can easily make them. Teachers can also do the same, but with so many premade games out there on countless subjects, is that really how you want to spend your time?

ClassTools (www.classtools.net/) is one of the most versatile free sites on the web. It has a huge number of easily usable online tools including the Random Name Picker feature used in Round-and-Round She Goes.

The last, but not least, way we use tech and games for learning English is through the use of sites like Kahoot! (https://kahoot.com/), Quizalize (www.quizalize.com/), and Quizizz (quizizz.com/), which provide countless games (and teachers and students can create their own). Students compete against each other on these sites using their own electronic devices (we usually play these when we visit the computer lab). After a teacher chooses a game, students sign on with a code and can see their standings or how their teams are doing in the competition as they play. At the time of this book's publication, Quizizz is our favorite. However, they are all adding new features frequently and new similar gaming apps are coming online all the time, so we'd encourage you to explore them all to figure out which works best for you and your students.

Two final notes:

> The 14 non-tech classroom games we listed here and the ones in the Speaking and Listening section of this book are just a drop in the bucket of the games teachers have developed for the ELL classroom. If you are interested in more, you might want to explore The Best Ideas for Using Games in the ESL/EFL/ELL Classroom (http://larryferlazzo.edublogs.org/2013/10/27/ the-best-ideas-for-using-games-in-the-esleflell-classroom/).

> And if you want to really find out about more online learning games, explore to your heart's content at A Collection of "The Best . . ." Lists on Learning Games (http://larryferlazzo.edublogs.org/2010/08/28/a-collection-of-the-best-lists-on-games/).

## Attribution

Portions of this section originally appeared in our book, *The ESL/ELL Teacher's Survival Guide* (Ferlazzo & Sypnieski, 2012, p. 239).

Thanks to Katie Toppel for the nine box grid (https://twitter.com/Toppel_ELD/status/852598723779493892).

Thanks to Carissa Peck (2012) for suggestions to modify the Flyswatter game (http://eslcarissa.blogspot.com/2012/09/flyswatter.html).

Thanks to Cristina Cabal (2016) for ideas on the Round-and-Round-She-Goes game (www.cristinacabal.com/?p=5269).

Thanks to Sandy Millin for inspiring us with her idea of writing bingo (https://sandymillin.wordpress.com/2013/10/15/writing-bingo/).

## Figures

| 2. sick | 3. doctor | 4. nurse |
|---|---|---|
| 5. hospital | 6. cough | 7. appointment |
| 8. medicine | 9. broken | 10. help |

**Figure 23.1** Nine Box Grid with Health Care Words Example *Source:* Reproduced with permission of Katie Toppel.

| 2. | 3. | 4. |
|---|---|---|
| 5. | 6. | 7. |
| 8. | 9. | 10. |

**Figure 23.2**  Nine Box Grid Template *Source:* Reproduced with permission of Katie Toppel.

# PART II

# Speaking and Listening

# Dictation

## What Is It?

There are many different types of dictation activities in an ELL classroom (see the Application section). They all share the common qualities of a teacher or student (or, in the case of tools shared in the Technology section, a recorded voice on the computer) saying or reading something while a listener is writing it down. This action is followed by a check for accuracy.

## Why We Like It

Dictation is a very versatile strategy—it can be used for demonstrating comprehension, practicing listening and spelling, and assisting in pronunciation. Teachers can also use the text strategically to reinforce or clarify grammar issues facing students. It's also the kind of activity that can be easily adjusted to the amount of time available—you can use it for 20 minutes or during the final few minutes of class if you finish your primary lesson early.

## Supporting Research

Studies have found that dictation activities can assist with grammar instruction (Kidd, 1992, p. 50; Tedick, 2001), listening comprehension (Kiany & Shiramiry, 2002, p. 61), spelling and punctuation (Alkire, 2002), and can increase student engagement (Kit, 2004).

## Common Core Connections

Surprisingly enough, dictation activities do not appear to meet any of the Anchor Standards under Speaking and Listening. However, they do fall under a number of the Language Standards, including learning the "conventions of capitalization, punctuation and spelling when writing" and to "comprehend more fully when . . . listening." Don't ask *us* why that last one is not under the Speaking and Listening Standards!

# Application

The following dictation methods are listed in the order of frequency that we use them in our classes.

## PAIRED DICTATION

We've previously mentioned this method in several reading and writing strategies. It's a simple and effective one that we typically use after reading a few pages of a short and accessible text. We show the text on the document camera and make sure all students have copies (see the Technology Connections section about where to obtain free copies of accessible texts).

We then divide students into groups of two or three and give them mini-whiteboards, markers, and erasers. Each student takes turns reading a sentence from the text while the other one or two are writing down what he or she says. Ideally, the students doing the writing don't need to look at their copies of the text, but they can if necessary. The reader then checks for accuracy and gives corrective feedback in a supportive way.

This kind of supportive feedback needs to be modeled (e.g., "Oops! You forgot to capitalize the letter *T*.") in order to avoid inappropriate corrections (e.g., "You're dumb! You forgot a capital letter!").

A variation of this activity (especially for more-advanced ELL students) is for the reader to leave a blank in the sentence that is being dictated. This functions as a challenge for the listeners to remember or use their language knowledge to determine what word belongs in that space without having to resort to looking at the text. As in all clozes (see Strategy 7: Clozes), students can say or write a word that makes sense in the context even if it differs from the exact one found in the original text.

## DICTOGLOSS (AND VARIATIONS)

Dictogloss is the word often used to describe this next dictation activity and it, too, has multiple variations. One option is to first select a short passage—perhaps a paragraph—from a familiar text (from the textbook, a story we've just read, etc.). We ask students to draw a line across their paper roughly one-third of the way down and then to draw one two-thirds down.

Next, we ask students to put their pencils down and carefully listen as we read the text at a regular pace. Prior to beginning to read, we tell students they are going to have to reconstruct what we say after hearing it a few times. Students do not write anything down after our first reading.

Next, we tell students we are going to read it again a little slower and they can write notes on the top third of their paper *after* we are done—we explain we want them to focus only on listening. After we finish reading a second time and students have had five minutes to silently write down notes, we give them a few minutes to compare with a partner and both can improve their notes.

Then, we ask them to put down their pencils and we read it again at the same pace as our second reading. Once we're done, students can either write additional notes in the second section of their paper or edit what they previously wrote down. They then can review their notes with a new partner and work toward writing a final text reconstruction on the bottom third of their page.

We also explain that their final version doesn't have to be a perfect copy of what we said, but the meaning should be the same, the grammar should be correct, and it should be as close as possible to what we read.

We then show the original passage on the overhead and ask students to reflect on how well they did. We have already done our own assessments while circulating during the activity and looking at student work in progress. We do not grade this exercise, as long as it appears that students are trying their best.

With beginning ELLs, ways to make dictogloss more accessible could be by doing the following:

- Providing them with a cloze of the text so they could view the words while they are being read. This way, they have to pay particular attention to fewer words.

- Asking students to number their paper leaving two blank lines for each dictated sentence. Then, instead of dictating an entire paragraph, just go through the same process of note-taking, pair-share, and reconstruction one sentence at a time.

- Writing a very simple text for students using vocabulary that they know, previewing any new words, and also providing photo support during the dictation activity.

Another dictogloss option is to either write or duplicate a short text that contains conventions or grammar issues that you have identified as particularly challenging for students. Hearing and writing down challenging grammar patterns can assist students in internalizing and acquiring them (Kidd, 1992, p. 51). For example, we've used this strategy to reinforce subject-verb agreement. We follow up the text reconstruction process with a class discussion of the targeted grammar concept.

An additional twist that we've used occasionally with intermediate ELLs is to pick a few words from the text we are using and replace them with a "mmmmmm" sound when we are reading it—basically turning it into an oral cloze. Then, when they have to reconstruct the text, they also have to determine which words they think belong in the blanks. When we use this version, we've typically deleted only the same types of words (only articles, only verbs, etc.), but don't feel obligated to use the same method. The key is that you have *some* kind of strategy for the deletions.

## PICTURE DICTATION

In a picture dictation lesson, a teacher can draw an image—generally, though not always, reflective of the theme the class is studying. Then, without showing students the image, the teacher dictates what it looks like while students attempt to draw it based on the verbal description ("There is a big tree to the right of the house"; "The sun is in the sky on the left"; etc.). Inviting anyone to the document camera who is willing to share their masterpiece is always a fun way to end the activity. Larry, who has no artistic ability whatsoever, generally compares each drawing with one of his and asks for a class vote on which they think is the better image. He has not yet won—and it's been 14 years!

After the teacher leads this lesson once, future versions can have students drawing their own pictures and taking turns dictating their description in English to a partner. After checking for accuracy, the roles are reversed.

## INFORMATION GAP

Information gap activities are often used in language-learning classrooms. Their basic definition is that students have to complete a task together, but neither student has all the information necessary to do it. They must communicate with each other to fill that gap. These activities often, though not always, fall under the umbrella of dictation.

To be truthful, despite their popularity, we haven't used the more-traditional text-based types of information gap lessons in our classrooms very often. Neither students nor we have been particularly engaged by them. Nevertheless, you'll find a link to a huge collection of them in the Technology Connections section if they work for you and you want printable copies or if you just want to give them a try.

However, there is one activity that falls under the information gap umbrella that we regularly use and that we'd like to share here.

**Running Dictation**

Running dictation, also known as messenger-and-scribe, is a staple of many ELL classrooms. We tape four to six sentences in different sections of the room and divide the class into pairs. One of them (the messenger) has the job of running to the different texts, reading them, and running back to his or her partner. Then, the student has to tell the writer (scribe), who writes it down. Partners can alternate roles, if desired.

Newcomers can be part of a three-person group including two students with a higher English-proficiency level. We often play it as a game, with the first three pairs to write down all the sentences perfectly, including punctuation and capitalization, being declared the winners.

Students love the game, but it can get quite rowdy. We caution students about our neighboring classrooms and the need to keep the noise in check. In addition, our students cheat at this activity more than any other, so we make it very clear that photos of text cannot be taken by cell phones, no one can tear the text off the wall and bring it to their partner, students can't stand by the text and read it loudly to their partner across the room, and the messenger cannot grab the pen from the scribe and write the text—it must be verbally communicated. If you don't think your students will do any of these things, then we also have a bridge that we'd like to sell to you!

To mix things up, we sometimes put pictures instead of text on the walls. Students then have to run back and forth and describe the image to their partner. Next, the scribe can either draw it or write down the description that the messenger is saying to them (we announce ahead of time if the scribe will be drawing or writing sentences). We then call a halt to the activity (usually after 10 minutes or so) and share the original images and the scribes' version of them on the document camera (often to great laughter). Students vote on who drew the most-accurate images (they cannot vote for themselves).

# What Could Go Wrong?

Don't pick a text for dictation that's too long or that has too many new words for your students. Other than those points, along with our cautions about noise and student cheating during running dictation, it's hard to mess up dictation activities.

Be thoughtful about student partners prior to organizing a running dictation activity. Don't create opportunities for frustration by pairing up two less-proficient ELLs. Instead, consider grouping higher-level students with others newer to the language.

# Technology Connections

There are several excellent free online sites that provide dictations at different levels of English proficiency—ranging from simple one-word versions to complex paragraphs. Once users type what they believe they heard onto the site, their accuracy is automatically graded by its software. We have our students use them when we have access to technology at school, and they're great for home use, too. You can find them at The Best Sites for ELLs to Practice Online Dictation (http://larryferlazzo.edublogs.org/2017/07/15/the-best-sites-for-ells-to-practice-online-dictation/).

We briefly discussed traditional information gap activities in the language-learning classroom. You can find many different examples, including scores of free printable versions, at The Best Online Resources for "Information Gap" Activities (http://larryferlazzo.edublogs.org/2011/09/06/the-best-online-resources-for-information-gap-activities/).

You can obtain free copies of accessible texts for dictation and for other purposes at The Best Sources for Free & Accessible Printable Books (http://larryferlazzo.edublogs.org/2009/07/31/the-best-sources-for-free-accessible-printable-books/) and at The Best Places to Get the "Same" Text Written for "Different" Levels (http://larryferlazzo.edublogs.org/2014/11/16/the-best-places-to-get-the-same-text-written-for-different-levels/).

# Attribution

Versions of some of these ideas appeared in our book, *The ESL/ELL Teacher's Survival Guide* (Ferlazzo & Sypnieski, 2012, p. 51) and in our book, *Navigating the Common Core with English Language Learners* (Ferlazzo & Sypnieski, 2016, p. 241).

# *STRATEGY 25*

# Conversation Practice

## What Is It?

This strategy is really a series of activities that we use to help our students develop competence and confidence in oral communication.

## Why We Like It

We want our students to be able to *communicate* with others in English. In order to make that happen, they will need to overcome anxiety, know the necessary language, and have a desire to apply it. We think the activities we use in our classroom and list here effectively assist students to achieve that trifecta.

## Supporting Research

Communicative opportunities, such as dialogues, have been found to be one effective way to promote speaking skills (Dewi, 2011). Anxiety, self-confidence, and motivation are three factors often identified by researchers as issues holding back ELLs from speaking English (Tuan & Mai, 2015, p. 8). Studies have found that speaking anxiety for ELLs can be reduced by providing planning time prior to a conversational activity (Bashir, 2014, p. 220), which we do with many of the speaking activities discussed in the Application section. This planning time also can help increase confidence in learners that they can perform the task.

This sense of confidence and competence (feeling like you have the skills to perform the task) is one of four key elements researchers have found to be critical for developing intrinsic motivation. Autonomy (having some level of control over the work you have to do), relatedness (working with people you like and respect), and relevance (the work will help you achieve your goals or is something of interest) (Ferlazzo, 2015, September 14) are the other three critical factors. All the activities listed under the Application section and, in fact, in most of the Application sections in this book, are designed to build on these four pillars of motivation.

## Common Core Connections

The first Standard under Speaking and Listening says, "Prepare for and participate effectively in a range of conversations . . ." If we were more wordy, that sentence could effectively serve as the name for this strategy instead of *conversation practice*. The last Standard in that section begins, "Adapt speech to a variety of contexts and communicative tasks . . ." That phrase also aptly describes all the activities we describe here.

## Application

These are the five activities we use the most in our classroom to promote conversational skills.

### DIALOGUES

We use dialogues in multiple ways. One way is for the teacher to create short, simple, and funny dialogues related to the theme that is being studied. This means most dialogues in textbooks are out because they tend to be pretty boring. Figure 25.1: Holiday Dialogue is an example of one we use with high beginners—it's short, provides space for student choice, and injects a little humor into it all. The teacher first models it and then strategically creates student pairs. They practice for a while and then perform.

Another activity we do is to have the class select videos of their choice from Brainpop, Jr. (n.d.), show it to the entire class (with closed captions), and then have students complete the easy quiz feature in pairs with mini-whiteboards. Next, we have students work in pairs and use a simple word-play activity offered by the site. It lists several key words from the video and provides a form where students write a super-short skit about one of the words they just learned and act it out (you have to pay for Brainpop, but the cost is minimal if you buy the feature that allows only three log-ins at any one time). We ask students to use at least two words and offer extra credit if they include all four of them. Again, students practice and then perform them.

Of course, you don't need a Brainpop movie to do this activity. You can show any short video and identify the words on your own for students to use in a dialogue. In fact, sometimes we don't even preface this task with a video. For example, if we've been studying the theme of feelings, we'll just ask students to create a simple dialogue of, let's say, ten lines using at least four words from the theme we've been studying.

In Strategy 6: Sequencing, we discussed ways to scramble sentences and then have students put them back in order. This kind of activity can work well with dialogues, too. Teachers can create dialogues and give a scramble such as the one we use in Figure 25.2 when studying health care (Figure 25.3 is the teacher answer key). After students cut and glue them in the correct order (being sure to highlight or underline the clues they used to figure it out), they can practice and perform the dialogue. Students can also create their own dialogue scrambles to challenge their classmates.

Sometimes, especially for beginners, speaking anxiety decreases if they can pretend it's not actually them engaging in the dialogue. Puppets can work as a good substitute. Also, having students imagine a conversation (supported by imagery) between animals or inanimate objects such as fruits and vegetables can create fun *and* confidence. Links to resources for these kinds of substitutions can be found in the Technology Connections section.

### 3-2-1

We described this activity in *The ESL/ELL Teacher's Survival Guide* (Ferlazzo & Sypnieski, 2012, p. 66) and still use it regularly. This is a modification of an exercise developed by Paul Nation (2007) called the *4–3-2 fluency activity*. In his original activity plan, students line up (standing or sitting) facing each other. Each one must be prepared to speak on something that they are already quite familiar with. First, they speak to their partner for four minutes about the topic.

Then, they move down the line, and say the same thing for three minutes to a new partner. Next, they move again and speak for two minutes. Then, the students on the other side do the same thing.

We developed a modification of this which could be called *3–2-1* or, for beginners, even *2–1.5-1*. In it, students are told to pick any topic they know a lot about, and that they will be asked to talk about it to a partner for three minutes (or two minutes, depending on the English level of the students), and then for two and then for one. But first, they should write down notes about what they might want to say.

Next, if possible, students are taken to a computer lab where they practice speaking by recording all or part of what they want to say (or, if all students have smartphones, those could be used instead). Afterwards, students are told they have two minutes to review their notes before they have to be put away. Next, the teacher models questions that students who are listening could ask the speaker if they appear to get stuck. It is also useful to model characteristics of being a good listener (eye contact, not talking to another student, etc.). Then, students begin the speaking and switching process described previously.

## ASK-ANSWER-ADD

Neil T. Millington from Dreamreader, an excellent online site with free ELL lesson plans, and Todd Beuckens from Ello, a site filled with interactive listening activities, shared an activity they call *ask-answer-add* (Millington, n.d.). We've used it successfully with high-beginning ELLs and intermediates and share parts of their instructions with permission.

First, students are lined up facing one another. If the classroom is not big enough to accommodate two long lines (like ours), students can be seated across from each other in a snake-like series of rows. We often use this kind of set-up to facilitate speed-dating for students to share their work. One row is designated *A* and the other is *B*.

We put a series of questions on the board related to the theme we are studying. For example, if we are studying food, the questions might be as follows:

- What is your favorite food?
- What is a popular meal in your home country?
- What is your favorite dessert?
- What did you eat for breakfast this morning?
- What did you eat for lunch yesterday?
- What did you eat for dinner last night?
- What did you eat the last time you went to a restaurant?

We then announce to the class that everyone in row A is going to ask the student across from them in row B the first question. Everyone in row B is given a minute to plan their answer.

After a minute, it might go something like this:

> **Ask**—A: "What is your favorite food?"
> **Answer**—B: "My favorite food are pupusas" or "I love papaya salad."

Then, it's time for Student B, the one who answered, to *add* something more. The teacher can provide a model or example, along with 30 seconds for Student B to plan his or her add. The conversation could now look something like this:

> **Ask**—A: "What is your favorite food?"
> **Answer**—B: "My favorite food are pupusas." **Add**—"My mother makes them on holidays."

Then it's time for Student B to ask the next question on the board to Student A and repeat the same process. After they've done ask, answer, add, then everyone in row A can move down one person and start with the third question on the list.

Hold on, though! That's the process we use for mid-beginner students. For high-beginners and intermediates, we make it more challenging. After the first ask, answer, add we *don't* switch partners.

Instead, we give 30 seconds to Student A so he or she can formulate another question based on Student B's response and repeat the sequence one more time before we start all over again with a new partner.

As students become more confident and skilled, ask-answer-add can continue with the same partners repeating the sequence for several minutes.

### CONVERSATION CHEAT SHEETS

In *The ESL/ELL Teacher's Survival Guide* (Ferlazzo & Sypnieski, 2012), we included a multipage conversation cheat sheet containing over 60 simple question or answer frames beginning students can practice ("What time is it? It is _____."; "How are you? I am _____."). You can download them for free at that book's website. You can find the URL address in the Technology Connections section.

### SELF-ASSESSMENT

We discussed the progress principle in Strategy 3: Graphic Organizers. As we explained, researchers have found a key factor in building intrinsic motivation is people seeing themselves making progress.

An easy way to help students see the progress they are making in speaking is through having them record themselves speaking various dialogues over the course of the year and saving it on the class blog. We've found that it's very energizing for students to listen to prior recordings as the year goes on—their speaking improvement is very obvious to them. Links to recording tools can be found in the Technology section. In addition, English Central, partially funded by Google, allows students to watch videos, repeat the audio they hear and read, and then be graded by the site's software on the accuracy of their pronunciation. Students love it, especially seeing their grades go up!

## Student Handouts and Examples

Figure 25.1: Holiday Dialogue
Figure 25.2: Dialogue Scramble
Figure 25.3: Dialogue Scramble (Teacher Answer Key)

# What Could Go Wrong?

Make sure you give students time to prepare! Our students don't need to be set up for failure by us. We're not talking about a huge amount of prep time. Often, 30 seconds is sufficient.

In addition, as we've often said in other strategies throughout this book—don't let any of these activities go on too long! There's no shortage of ways for students to learn English. Know when it's time to move on.

# Technology Connections

There are plenty of practice and recording sites for ELLs, and you can find links to the best of them at The Best Sites to Practice Speaking English (http://larryferlazzo .edublogs.org/2008/03/17/the-best-sites-to-practice-speaking-english/). You'll also find links to great apps where students can take photos of illustrated dialogues they have created (e.g., talking heads). They can then provide audio narration and post them on a class blog.

Other useful online sites for speaking practice can be found at The Best Sites for Developing English Conversational Skills (http://larryferlazzo.edublogs.org/2008/ 04/05/the-best-sites-for-developing-english-conversational-skills/) and The Best Websites for Learning English Pronunciation (http://larryferlazzo.edublogs.org/ 2008/03/31/the-best-websites-for-learning-english-pronunciation/).

For puppet ideas, check out The Best Resources for Using Puppets in Class (http://larryferlazzo.edublogs.org/2009/10/07/the-best-resources-for-using-puppets-in-class/).

You can download our conversation cheat sheets at *The ESL/ELL Teacher's Survival Guide* website (www.wiley.com/WileyCDA/WileyTitle/productCd-1118095677 .html). It's Exhibit 4.3.

# Attribution

Versions of some of these ideas appeared in our book, *The ESL/ELL Teacher's Survival Guide* (Ferlazzo & Sypnieski, 2012, p. 66).

Thanks to Neil T. Millington from Dreamreader (http://dreamreader.net/), an excellent online site with free ELL lesson plans and Todd Beuckens from Elllo (www .elllo.org/), a site filled with interactive listening activities, for the ask- answer-add activity.

# Figures

| | |
|---|---|
| A | What is your favorite holiday? |
| B | My favorite holiday is _____. |
| A | What does your family do on _____? |
| B | We _____. |
| A | You should bring food from that day to Mr. Ferlazzo. He is a good person. |
| B | Yes/No I will/will not. I like him/I don't like him. |

**Figure 25.1** Holiday Dialogue

| | |
|---|---|
| A | Okay, I will throw up now instead! Bleeeeaaaahhh! |
| A | But they tasted so good! And I was so hungry! |
| A | I have a stomachache! |
| B | Okay, I will take you to the doctor. Please don't throw up in my car! |
| B | But you don't feel so good, do you? You deserve to feel bad. |
| A | I feel better now. You don't have to take me to the doctor. |
| B | You should not have eaten ten bags of Hot Cheetos! |
| B | Eeeewww, that's disgusting! |
| A | Please don't be angry. Help me. I need a ride to the doctor. |

**Figure 25.2** Dialogue Scramble

A    I have a stomachache!

B    You should not have eaten ten bags of Hot Cheetos!

A    But they tasted so good! And I was so hungry!

B    But you don't feel so good, do you? You deserve to feel bad.

A    Please don't be angry. Help me. I need a ride to the doctor.

B    Okay, I will take you to the doctor. Please don't throw up in my car!

A    Okay, I will throw up now instead! Bleeeeaaaahhh!

B    Eeeewww, that's disgusting!

A    I feel better now. You don't have to take me to the doctor.

**Figure 25.3**    Dialogue Scramble (Teacher Answer Key)

# Total Physical Response (TPR)

## What Is It?

Total physical response (TPR) is a popular activity in language-learning classrooms where students learn vocabulary by physically acting out actions typically performed and commanded by the teacher. It is primarily done with beginners and usually for a period no longer than 10 to 15 minutes during a day. TPR was originally developed by professor James J. Asher.

## Why We Like It

TPR is a great way to get students moving, help ELLs gain confidence by learning new vocabulary easily, and get students to review previously learned words in a fun way.

## Supporting Research

TPR has been found to be effective in teaching vocabulary (Howard Research, 2009, p. 34) and increasing student engagement with ELLs (Qiu, 2016). There is substantial research on the advantages of using movement when learning anything, including a new language (Ferlazzo, 2011, June 2).

## Common Core Connections

TPR helps meet several Standards, including in Language where we are assisting students "to comprehend more fully when reading or listening" and in Speaking and Listening, where they must "adapt speech to a variety of contexts and communicative tasks."

# Application

The following describes the TPR process we use with our beginning ELLs. First, we decide on five or six new words we want to teach that day. The Technology Connections section has links to sites that provide extensive lists of words that easily lend themselves to being taught through TPR, and they generally begin with the basics—*stand, sit, walk, point,* and so on.

Next, we ask two students to come up to the front and stand on either side of us. We then model the command (e.g., "sit") two times, and then we ask the two students in the front to do it afterwards. We think that students find it more helpful and interesting to have classmates modeling instead of always just the teacher. Our welcoming classroom environment and our own regular practice of making fun of ourselves seems to minimize student resistance toward coming to the front.

Then, the two students return to their seats, we write the word on the class whiteboard, and then command the entire class to do the action—we don't physically model it this time.

After we repeat this sequence for that day's new words, we move on to the next step in the process. This time, without student or teacher modeling, we begin combining those new commands with previously learned ones (e.g., "Walk to your right and point to a student.") and students act them out. We also create funny combinations (e.g., "Hop on one leg and put your finger in your ear.").

Sometimes, we even try to trick students by saying a command and doing a different action to emphasize the importance of listening. As we mentioned, the positive atmosphere of TPR and our classroom tends to ensure that students find it funny and not embarrassing when they make a mistake.

We use TPR as a constant formative assessment activity and keep our eyes out for words that seem to be more difficult for our students. We reinforce those words with more practice and more modeling by us. This entire TPR process is less a map and more of a compass, so be flexible!

In addition, students can take turns teaching the class, and, best of all (in students' eyes, at least), periodically students can command the teacher to do whatever they want!

After 10 or 15 minutes of these activities, students add the new words on the board to their writer's notebook (see Strategy 18: Writer's Notebook) and we move on to a different activity.

## TPR EXTENSION ACTIVITY

After students begin developing a higher English proficiency, we begin to move TPR sessions more into story-like sequences. For example, we model our morning routine ("go into the bathroom"; "wash your face"; "put toothpaste on your toothbrush";

"rinse your mouth"; "spit the water out," etc.) and have students act it out. Then, individual students could plan out their individual routine and teach their version using TPR.

Other routines we've used include these:

- Making breakfast
- Getting ready for bed
- Getting into a car
- Washing dishes
- Riding a bike to school and locking it up
- Taking care of a pet
- Going to a doctor's office and being examined
- Making lunch
- Preparing dinner
- Cleaning the kitchen
- Changing diapers

We usually, though not exclusively, use these routines in parallel to the themes we are emphasizing during other parts of the class (e.g. home, school, food, etc.). In addition, we invite students to make their own suggestions (that's where the "changing diapers" sequence came from).

## What Could Go Wrong?

Don't try to teach too many new words at one time, and don't let TPR go longer than 15 minutes (we've actually found ten minutes works best most of the time).

## Technology Connections

You can access downloadable word lists and short videos of the TPR strategy in action at The Best Resources for Learning About Total Physical Response (TPR) (http://larryferlazzo.edublogs.org/2016/09/10/the-best-resources-for-learning-about-total-physical-response-tpr/).

There are some online tools that mimic real-life TPR. Teacher Henny Jellema's site (n.d.) shows many images, and students have to choose the matching audio-recorded commands. Try it out at *For English as a Second Language: TPR Exercises* (http://static.digischool.nl/oefenen/hennyjellema/engels/tpr/voorbladtpr.htm).

There are several sites that allow users to either type in or say commands and then the online characters will act them out. You can explore those sites at The Best "When I Say Jump" Online Sites for Practicing English (http://larryferlazzo.edublogs.org/2010/07/03/the-best-when-i-say-jump-online-sites-for-practicing-english/).

# Attribution

Versions of some of these ideas appeared in our book, *The ESL/ELL Teacher's Survival Guide* (Ferlazzo & Sypnieski, 2012, p. 61).

# STRATEGY 27

# Music

## What Is It?

Music can assist ELLs to develop their reading, writing, listening, and speaking skills. Though we'll list all the ways we use it in in our classroom, we will specifically describe activities that maximize listening and speaking.

## Why We Like It

Most students like music, and it's always an opportunity if we can leverage something they already like to help them learn English! In addition, anything we can do to get our ELLs speaking is a plus—and choral singing or chanting counts!

## Supporting Research

As we shared in *The ESL/ELL Teacher's Survival Guide* (Ferlazzo & Sypnieski, 2012, p. 63):

> Extensive research has shown that using songs is an effective language-development strategy with English Language Learners (Schoepp, 2001). They are often accessible because popular songs tend to use the vocabulary of an eleven-year-old, the rhythm and beat helps students speak in phrases or sentences instead of words, and the word repetition assists retention (Li & Brand, 2009, p. 74). Neuroscience has also found that music can increase dopamine release in the brain and generates positive emotions. This kind of emotional learning reinforces long-term memory (Jensen, 2001).

In addition to this research specifically on songs, there have also been studies showing that jazz chants, a rhythmic activity originated by Carolyn Graham, have positive effects on student engagement (Kung, 2013, p. 16) and English prosody (Felix, 2013, p. 15).

# Common Core Connections

Our focus here is on the speaking and listening aspects of using music in the ELL classroom, so these activities certainly help students "prepare for and participate effectively in a range of conversations" (Common Core State Standards Initiative, n.d.c) and "adapt speech to a variety of contexts and communicative tasks, demonstrating command of formal English when indicated or appropriate" (Common Core State Standards Initiative, n.d.c). In addition, these lessons enhance listening comprehension. The other music-related ideas we mention also meet several other Language, Writing, and Reading Standards.

# Application

**TYPICAL SEQUENCE**

This is a typical process we use with songs, though we don't use *all* steps *all* of the time.

**Choosing the Song**

We generally play songs that fit into the theme (home, school, feelings, etc.) or writing genre (narrative, argument, problem-solution) we're teaching at the time. However, we also choose songs for other reasons, including if we feel the song's messages might resonate with our students. Larry loves the musical *Hamilton*[1] and has used songs from the show with ELLs. We talk about those lessons later in this section. The *Hamilton* songs illustrate another important criterion that we use when choosing music for our classes—they must have simple choruses that don't require being sung too quickly. Our students may not be able to sing most of the words to a song, but focusing on the chorus reduces the difficulty, maximizes the fun, and creates lots of opportunities for repetition.

We also look for songs that can incorporate movement. There are old favorites, such as "Heads, Shoulders, Knees, and Toes," but also more mature songs, such as

---

[1] *Hamilton: An American Musical* (written and created by Lin-Manuel Miranda, who, incidentally, is a former seventh-grade English teacher) has been a huge hit in the United States. Its songs celebrate history and immigrants through the story of founding father Alexander Hamilton and is popular among the young and old alike.

Bob Marley's "Get Up, Stand Up," in which it's easy to improvise our own moves. Substantial research documents that gestures and movement can support language acquisition (Ferlazzo, 2011, June 2).

So, our baseball-inspired equations for songs that we use in our classroom are as follows:

Relevance + Accessible chorus + Movement = Home run

Relevance + Accessible chorus = Triple

### Pre-Listening

We preview a song in similar ways we might preview a book. We might tell students the title of the song and ask them to predict what it might be about. Or, before we teach "I Just Called To Say I Love You," we might ask students what they think love is and to share with classmates whom they love and who loves them (if they feel comfortable doing so).

### Free Listening

We then play the music and ask students to just listen to it—they don't see the lyrics and have no assignment except for listening to the song.

Sometimes, we'll play the song twice and, prior to the second time, ask students to make notes of the words they recognize. Afterwards, we'll ask them to draw simple pictures of the words they know—without labeling them. After they've drawn a few images, students can share them in small groups to see if other students can identify the words represented by the picture. This process is called *song pictures,* and we learned it from English teacher Nico Lorenzutti (2014).

### Listening and Reading

We'll then distribute the lyrics to the song and encourage students to read along (particularly the chorus). Ideally, we show a lyrics video of the song at the same time. These are videos that scroll the lyrics as the song is being played. Just search *lyrics video* plus the name of the song and it is very likely you'll find one online (Ferlazzo, 2013, September 25). If a video is not available, the students just read lyrics that we have distributed to the class.

### Saying and Singing

After listening to the song two or three times, we tell students that it's time to lip-sync—again, not necessarily all the words (though that would be great). We ask them to lip-sync the chorus, at least. This exercise helps them become comfortable with the words and rhythm of the song without having to take the risk of actually saying the words.

Some classes are filled with students who relish singing, some are filled with students who are all scared at the thought of singing, and some are half and half. We teachers play with the hand we're dealt, and if you're not confident that your students will sing you've got nothing to worry about—tell your students that, next, we are all going to say the words and not sing them. When it's time for the chorus, just lead the class in saying the words. It accomplishes the same goal of having students speak and, if they say it enough times, you might be surprised how easily some will slip into singing. Play the song two or three more times as students are saying or singing the words.

The teacher has to be up in the front lip-syncing and saying or singing in an exaggerated manner along with students. If we aren't willing to model taking that kind of risk, why should we expect students to do so?

### Comprehension Activities

Following those pre-listening, listening, and singing activities, we might have students complete a cloze exercise as a follow-up exercise (probably on a different day). It's easy to print out lyrics, white out the words you want students to replace, and then make copies (sometimes we have a word bank at the bottom and sometimes we don't). We typically have students complete these clozes while we are repeatedly playing the song.

We might also do a sequencing activity in which we have copied and pasted the lyrics out of order. Students then have to cut them out and put them in the correct order while listening to the song a few times.

### Extension Activities

There are multiple options for extension activities:

- Ask students to substitute words, write their own chorus, and sing it for the class. For example, if we've just learned "Hello, Goodbye," then students can change the words to *big* and *small*.
- Have students sing a chorus or an entire song together, record it on their phones, and post it on our class blog. Often times, students love to hear themselves sing.

- English teacher Nati Gonzalez Brandi gave us the idea of "drawing a song" (ELT Brewery, 2016). After students learn a song, she has them draw a representation of it with some words and some pictures, which they then present to the class. You can see links to examples in the Technology Connections section.

**TOPICAL PROJECTS**

Trending popular music and music videos often offer opportunities for creative language-learning lessons. Here are two examples we've recently done with our ELL classes. You may or may not want to use these activities with your students. We offer them here more as inspirational examples so teachers can be on the lookout for upcoming popular music trends and be thinking if and how they might be used in the classroom.

**Mannequin Challenge**

Many teachers might be familiar with the use of a frozen tableau, when students design and act out a frozen scene from a text. And if you're not familiar with the frozen tableau, you might very well know (depending on what year you read this book!) about the mannequin challenge, which was a brief viral sensation of groups remaining motionless for a short video scene, accompanied by music.

We worked with Mary Stokke (then a talented student teacher and now a teacher on her own) to use this fad in connection with writing a problem-solution essay. Students worked in small groups to identify a problem and a solution and create a four-frame storyboard illustrating them. The first three frames were photos they took with written captions. The fourth was a mannequin challenge in which they created with a song of their choice. The Technology Connections section contains a link to related resources and examples.

**Hamilton**

As mentioned previously, Larry is a big fan of this Broadway musical. "My Shot" is one of his favorite songs from the show, though, similar to most of the songs, it's sung too rapidly for many English language learners. It does, however, have an accessible chorus. It emphasizes Hamilton's grit and ambition through repeating the line, "I am not throwing away my shot." After explaining what it means, having the class listen to the song, and then singing the chorus several times, Larry gave his students this sentence frame to respond to the question "How can you apply this idea to your own life?":

"I'm not throwing away my shot because _____." Things I will do to not
   throw away my shot are _____, _____, and _____.

Larry did something similar with another *Hamilton* song, including "I wrote my way out" in the chorus.

In both instances, he took advantage of a very fast-moving and popular song that had accessible lyrics to help ELLs find nuances of the language and support social emotional learning skills at the same time.

Again, the point of these examples is not to encourage you to use the mannequin challenge or these *Hamilton* songs in your class (though you're welcome to do so). Rather, we offer them here as encouragement to get your creative juices flowing as you become aware of each year's popular hits.

## PERSONALIZED SONG LESSONS

*Personalized learning* is a buzzword in education circles these days and often refers to using technology to fit lessons that are more personalized to a student's interests, strengths, and challenges. We're not using much tech in these two examples of personalized song lessons, but in each case we are building on each student's unique musical interest to leverage motivation for language learning.

### My Favorite Song

Alma Avalos, a talented educator who worked with us in our classrooms, developed this two-part high-interest lesson. In Part 1, choose any song that you are confident will engage your students and meets the Relevance + Accessible Chorus + Movement equation we shared previously in this strategy. Then go through some of the Pre-Listening through Comprehension activities listed previously. Next, have students complete Figure 27.1: Song Lyric Analysis Sheet. Last, ask students to use an online tool that lets them easily write and illustrate their favorite lyrics to present to the class (doing it by hand is fine if tech is not available). See the Technology Connections section for resources.

After having completed Part 1, students then use their work as a model for Part 2. Each student chooses his or her own favorite song—whether it is in the home language or in English—and completes a similar form (see Figure 27.2), creates a visual representation of his or her favorite lyrics, and then presents them to the class, as well as playing the song.

It's easy to modify the number of lyrics and questions on the forms. Our students have always loved this exercise, and there has been very little resistance—if any—to making full-class presentations.

### Personal Theme Song

We use this activity after students have learned the concept of theme in our narrative (story) writing unit (see Figure 3.8 in Strategy 3: Graphic Organizers). We ask students to think about a theme for their lives and often rewrite the list of themes we discussed when we first taught the concept, while clarifying that their personal theme doesn't have to be from the list. If students are high-beginner or intermediate ELLs, we sometimes have students take online quizzes designed to help people choose their theme song (just search online for *quiz to pick personal theme song* and you'll find many options), though we also point out that they don't have to agree with the results. We then give students a copy of Figure 27.2: My Favorite Song with minor changes—we replace the word *favorite* that appears two times with the word *theme*. Students then follow a process similar to Part 2 in the my favorite song exercise, including making a class presentation. We borrowed this idea from English teacher Shelly Terrell (2012).

## CHANTS

The idea of using jazz chants, which are short, rhythmic lines that support vocabulary and grammar development to help in language acquisition, was developed by Carolyn Graham. Graham encourages teachers to create their own chants using a pattern of three syllables, two syllables, and one syllable, though we and many other teachers do not feel bound by that pattern. Figure 27.3: Information Chants is an example of one we use with our students to help learn the months and days of the week. After practicing saying the words in a non-chant way, we and students then tap on their desks and chant in a unified beat. We sometimes have students record their chanting and post it on our class blog.

A link to many more resources on chants can be found in the Technology Connections section.

## Student Handouts and Examples

Figure 27.1: Song Lyric Analysis Sheet
Figure 27.2: My Favorite Song
Figure 27.3: Information Chants

## What Could Go Wrong?

As we already mentioned, sometimes students don't want to sing. If that's the case, don't worry about it—just have them say the words. Forcing students to sing will not lead to a positive classroom environment for learning.

Some students can get into loud pounding instead of light tapping when doing chants. As in all things, model desired behavior prior to doing the activity. This usually preempts disruptions.

# Technology Connections

If you are looking for ideas of songs to use in the ELL classroom, you won't have to look further than The Best Music Websites for Learning English (http://larryferlazzo.edublogs.org/2008/01/30/the-best-music-websites-for-learning-english/). That list also contains links to free sites that show music videos and accompany them with clozes that students complete online. Unfortunately, many of the videos are blocked by school district content filters, but the site can still be used by students at home and teachers can get specific clips unblocked and use them as an all-class activity.

Karaoke sites can also provide fun singing opportunities; explore The Best Online Karaoke Sites for English Language Learners (http://larryferlazzo.edublogs.org/2008/10/15/the-best-online-karaoke-sites-for-english-language-learners/).

You can see an example of how our students handled the mannequin challenge at The Mannequin Challenges, ELLS & a Frozen Tableau (http://larryferlazzo.edublogs.org/2016/11/18/the-mannequin-challenge-ells-a-frozen-tableau/).

For student examples of the my favorite song activity, visit Here's a Successful Music Lesson We Did with Beginning ELLs (http://larryferlazzo.edublogs.org/2015/05/10/heres-a-successful-music-lesson-we-did-with-beginning-ells-handouts-student-examples-included/). And for online tools to use with that lesson, go to The Best Tools for Creating Visually Attractive Quotations for Online Display (http://larryferlazzo.edublogs.org/2013/02/23/the-best-tools-for-creating-visually-attractive-quotations-for-online-display/).

Finally, you can watch lots of chant examples at The Best Sites (& Videos) for Learning About Jazz Chants (http://larryferlazzo.edublogs.org/2011/07/28/the-best-sites-videos-for-learning-about-jazz-chants/).

# Attribution

Versions of some of these ideas appeared in our book, *The ESL/ELL Teacher's Survival Guide* (Ferlazzo & Sypnieski, 2012, p. 62–63).

Thanks to Nati Gonzalez Brandi for her drawing a song idea (https://myeltbrewery.wordpress.com/2016/10/17/beyond-gap-fills-using-songs-to-learn-a-language-why-how-and-which/).

Thanks to English teacher Nico Lorenzutti for the song pictures activity (https://americanenglish.state.gov/files/ae/resource_files/52_1_4_lorenzutti.pdf).

Thanks to Shelly Terrell for the personal theme song lesson (http://blog.esllibrary.com/2012/03/05/20-tips-language-through-song-lyrics/).

# Figures

*Directions:* Choose lyrics that you liked from the song and copy them onto this paper. You must choose five different lines or more. Please write neatly.

**Name of Song:**_____

My favorite lyrics:_____
_____
_____

When done copying the lyrics, *translate* them in your own language. (Use Google translate if you need help.)

**1.** Lyric:

My translation:

**2.** Lyric:

My translation:

**3.** Lyric:

My translation:

**4.** Lyric:

My translation:

**5.** Lyric:

My translation:

**Figure 27.1** Song Lyric Analysis Sheet

Answer the following questions about two of your favorite lyrics:

**A.** Why did you choose these lyrics?

I chose lyric number _____ because

_____.

I chose lyric number _____ because

_____.

**B.** What are some new words you learned in these lyrics? What does each word mean in English?

_____ means _____.

_____ means _____.

_____ means _____.

**C.** How do these lyrics make you feel and why?

Lyric number _____ makes me feel _____ because

_____.

Lyric number _____ makes me feel _____ because

_____.

**Figure 27.1** (*Continued*)

**1.** What is the name of your favorite song?

The name of my favorite song is _____.

**2.** Who is the artist?

The recording artist is _____.

**3.** What is the genre of the song?

_____ is the genre of the song.

**4.** Why did you choose this song?

I chose this song because _____.

Choose five lyrics or more from your favorite song.

Please copy them below. (If your lyrics are in your home language, please also write the English translated version. If the lyrics are in English, then also write them in your language.)

**1.** Lyric:

My translation:

**2.** Lyric:

My translation:

**3.** Lyric:

My translation:

**4.** Lyric:

My translation:

**5.** Lyric:

My translation:

**Figure 27.2** My Favorite Song

Answer the following questions about two of your favorite lyrics:

**A.** Why did you choose these lyrics?

I chose lyric number _____ because

_____.

I chose lyric number _____ because

_____.

**B.** What are some new words you learned in these lyrics? What does each word mean in English?

_____ means _____.

_____ means _____.

_____ means _____.

**C.** How do these lyrics make you feel and why?

Lyric number _____ makes me feel _____ because

_____.

Lyric number _____ makes me feel _____ because

_____.

**Figure 27.2** (Continued)

January is the Winter.

February is the Winter.

March is the Spring.

March is the Spring.


April is the Spring.

May is the Spring.

June is the Summer.

June is the Summer.


July is the Summer.

August is the Summer.

September is the Fall.

September is the Fall.


October is the Fall.

November is the Winter.

December is the Winter.

December is the Winter.


Monday starts the week.

Monday starts the week.

Then comes Tuesday.

Then comes Tuesday.

**Figure 27.3** Information Chants

Wednesday comes next.

Wednesday comes next.

Then comes Thursday.

Then comes Thursday.


School ends Friday.

School ends Friday.

Next comes the weekend.

Next comes the weekend.


The weekend starts with Saturday.

The weekend starts with Saturday.

The weekend ends with Sunday.

The weekend ends with Sunday.

**Figure 27.3** (*Continued*)

# STRATEGY 28

# Using Photos or Other Images in Speaking and Listening

### What Is It?

Photos and other images can be used to promote reading and writing, as we shared in Strategy 17: Using Photos or Other Images in Reading and Writing. Though many of the ideas we shared in that strategy have speaking and listening components, the three activities we share in this section use images primarily to promote speaking and listening.

### Why We Like It

We've found that these three applications have been successful in encouraging students to listen with intention and to speak. It is not often an easy job to get our teen ELLs to do either, and we kissed a lot of frogs before we found these three effective activities.

### Supporting Research

Previously cited studies in Strategy 17: Using Photos or Other Images in Reading and Writing clearly support the use of visuals in ELL classes. In addition, there is specific research that suggests using images can enhance student motivation to engage in speaking activities (Trang, n.d., p. 4).

## Common Core Connections

All the activities listed here support the Language Standards of developing the ability to apply English conventions and to become a skilled listener. The Speaking and Listening Standard saying that students must "prepare for and participate effectively in a range of conversations and collaborations with diverse partners, building on others' ideas and expressing their own clearly and persuasively" is also a slam dunk!

# Application

In Strategy 17, we discussed numerous ways to use photos or other images in reading and writing activities. Many of those lessons can be easily extended to the speaking and listening domains. Here are three photo activities that lend themselves particularly to speaking and listening.

### PHOTO COLLAGES

Photo collages are great tools to use in class for listening and speaking practice. News organizations, especially the *New York Times,* publish online photo collages in grid form about specific topics (summertime, pigeons, dog show winners, etc.). We project them on our class whiteboard before class and write a visible number on each image in the grid. We give students mini-whiteboards and explain, "I'm going to describe one of the images and ask you which number I'm talking about." For example, a teacher describing the pigeon images could, after teaching any specialized vocabulary needed, say, "Two eyes are showing and its beak is pressed down to its chest." Once students understand how the strategy works, we sometimes change the collage and pair students up to continue on their own.

There are plenty of online tools that let you easily create your own collages from photos on the web or pictures you take. Not only can teachers make ones to project for the class but also students can make collages. See the Technology Connections section for links to ready-made collages and do-it-yourself tools.

### BACK AND FORTH

We build on the idea of using photo collages by reproducing pages from the book *Back & Forth: Photocopiable Cooperative Pair Activities for Language Development* (Rodgers et al., 1985). An example of one of its pages can be found in Figure 28.1. They are basically a series of image strips that are very similar to one another. After quickly teaching any needed vocabulary, we divide the class into partners. Then, we have one student describe the image he or she has in mind ("The man and dog are walking to the right.") and the other has to point to the correct one. After students become familiar with the exercise, we sometimes have them create their own similar picture strips.

### IF ANIMALS OR INANIMATE OBJECTS COULD TALK

As we discuss in Strategy 25: Conversation Practice, sometimes ELLs, particularly beginners, have less anxiety about speaking if they do it through other objects—such as puppets. In those cases, it can feel like the object is doing the talking (as well as making any mistakes) and not the student.

The same idea is at work with this activity. We often show funny images of animals, and students then have to write and say what they believe the animal is thinking at the moment the photo was taken. It can be a short and fun exercise for students. You can find links to lots of examples, as well as to many usable images, in the Technology Connections section.

## Student Handout and Example

Figure 28.1: Back-and-Forth Page

## What Could Go Wrong?

Be sure to give students time to prep! Don't put a collage up on the board and give students five seconds to answer your questions. Don't give students just a few seconds to write down what they think the funny-looking duck is thinking! Provide sentence starters to newcomers or give them a list of answers to choose from.

## Technology Connections

Find links to photo collages made by news organizations and online tools to create your own at The Best Ideas for Using Photos in Lessons (http://larryferlazzo .edublogs.org/2010/06/27/the-best-ways-to-use-photos-in-lessons/).

Find links to fun examples of animals "thinking" and images your students can use at The Best Resources for Using "If This Animal or Image Could Talk" Lesson Idea in Class (http://larryferlazzo.edublogs.org/2015/08/01/the-best-resources-on-using-if-this-animal-or-image-could-talk-lesson-idea-in-class/).

Instead of potentially feeling overwhelmed by looking for photos on a certain theme using a search engine, consider going to ELTPics (www.eltpics.com/) and their free categorized photo sets (www.flickr.com/photos/eltpics/albums) and take advantage of the work that other ELL teachers have done (you can also contribute your own photos there).

## Attribution

Thanks to Alta Book Center Publishers for letting us reprint a page from *Back and Forth* (https://altaenglishpublishers.com/product/back-forth-photocopiable-cooperative-pair-activities-for-language-development/).

# Figure

# Exercise 2.6

PARTNER

**Instructions:** Describe the indicated pictures ( • ) to your partner, and listen as your partner describes other pictures to you. Mark (X) the picture described. Do not look at your partner's page while you are doing this exercise!

1. Describe.

2. Listen and mark.

3. Describe.

4. Listen and mark.

5. Describe.

6. Listen and mark.

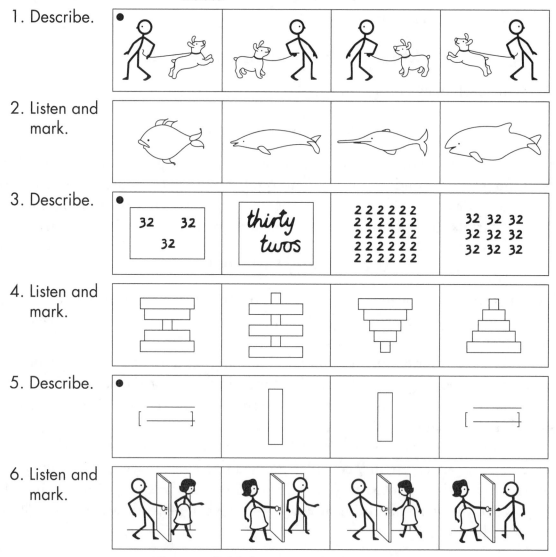

**When you finish** this exercise, show your page to your partner and compare your answers. Are they all the same? Which ones did you miss? If there is time, do the exercise again, but choose different pictures to describe and make different marks on your page.

**Figure 28.1** Back-and-Forth Page *Source:* Reproduced by permission. Palm Springs, California USA. Copyright 2014 ALTA English Publishers.

# STRATEGY 29

# Video

## What Is It?

Using video in the ELL classroom is a great way to boost language skills and motivation. Videos can play a range of roles in learning—students can watch them to build listening skills and comprehension or practice speaking by creating their own.

In Strategy 21: Problem-Posing, we discuss the use of video as a way to help students develop critical thinking and writing skills. We also explain the use of a video activity to build students' summarizing skills in Strategy 15: Quoting, Summarizing, and Paraphrasing. And, we describe students using videos to create dialogues and practice pronunciation in Strategy 25: Conversation Practice.

Here, we will share some ways to use video as an instructional strategy to specifically increase students' speaking and listening abilities.

## Why We Like It

Who doesn't enjoy watching engaging videos? It's something many of us do on a regular basis, and many students do it daily and sometimes hourly! We can build on this interest by bringing some of the videos they are already watching at home or sharing with their friends into the classroom, as well as introducing new ones to them. Videos are excellent tools for language study because students can *listen* to English being spoken; *see* facial expressions, gestures, and body language among other visual cues; and *read* the English subtitles all at the same time. In addition, they can be re-watched as many times as needed. Students are also highly motivated to create their own videos (something many of them already do) and share them with authentic audiences online.

# Supporting Research

Research shows the use of video in ELL instruction can benefit learners' comprehension, language skills, and motivation (Almurashi, 2016; Morat, Shaari, & Abidin, 2016). Specifically having students watch videos with same language subtitles (e.g., watching a video in English with English subtitles) can result in better word recognition and comprehension skills (Brady-Myerov, 2015).

# Common Core Connections

Using videos for listening and speaking practice can support many of the Speaking and Listening Standards. One of them is being able to "integrate and evaluate information presented in diverse media and formats, including visually, quantitatively, and orally."

# Application

This section contains general guidelines for using videos, a typical sequence we follow when showing clips, and five additional ways we use them in class.

### GUIDELINES

We keep the following considerations in mind when we use videos to build speaking and listening skills (and for any other reason):

- **Video length:** Short clips (usually one to five minutes) work best at keeping students engaged while offering enough context and language for study. Another option is to use a longer video divided into shorter chunks with activities and discussion. Recent research on video length and student engagement reveals the optimal length to be six minutes or less, and we prefer the less (Guo et al., 2014).

- **Purpose:** Video clips that directly relate to the topic of study are helpful in deepening understanding while building language skills. Selecting relevant and engaging video clips can increase student participation and language-learning opportunities.

- **Accessible vocabulary:** Students don't need to know all the words in a video in order for it to be effective. However, between the visual support and the subtitles contained in the video, students should be able to get the gist—the overall meaning or main idea. It can be helpful to keep the idea of *comprehensible input* in mind when selecting a video (or a text) to use with ELLs.

Linguist Stephen Krashen, along with many other researchers, proposes that learners can make more progress and acquire a language more naturally when some of the language input they are receiving is slightly above their current English proficiency level (Krashen & Terrell, 1983; Wong & Van Patten, 2003, p. 418). In other words, they can use their present English skills to acquire new vocabulary and language structures. In terms of video, this means that students can understand the gist of the video without initially knowing all the words. The speed of the words being spoken in a video and accent also enters into this accessibility equation.

- **Video and audio quality:** When viewing videos, ELLs are navigating new content in a new language. We don't want to make this process even more difficult by using video clips that have poor visual or audio quality. This can be distracting and frustrating for everyone!

- **Subtitles:** As we discuss in the Supporting Research section, turning on the closed captioning feature can boost students' literacy skills. Of course, there may be times when we want students to do a specific activity without using the subtitles (e.g., watching a brief conversation with the sound off and having students write what they think the people might be saying), but, most of the time, we find it helpful to turn on this feature.

- **Active, not passive viewing:** We've all experienced turning our students and ourselves into zombies when a video clip goes too long! To avoid this, we break longer videos into shorter clips and provide opportunities for students to be active while viewing—by asking them oral or written questions, having them take notes, or working with a partner to discuss the video, and so on.

  New research has pointed specifically to the effectiveness of giving students questions *before* viewing a video in order to enhance learning and focus. Researchers found that students who were provided these pre-questions were better able to learn and recall not only the answers to those questions but also material from other parts of the video (Carpenter & Toftness, 2017; Willingham, 2017).

- **Access to video:** School district content filters may block certain videos, especially ones from YouTube, even though they are educationally appropriate. See the Technology Connections section for a link to a search engine that accesses nearly 50 non-YouTube video collections.

## TYPICAL SEQUENCE

We use the following general process when incorporating videos into lessons with ELLs. It is similar to the one we describe in Strategy 27: Music. Again, we may not follow *all* the steps *all* of the time.

### Choosing the Video

As we stated, we choose videos that are short (typically one to five minutes) or if they are longer, we break them into shorter clips. We also select video clips that are related to a topic of study and are engaging and accessible to our students. Then, we make sure the video is unblocked by our school district. Finally, we turn on the subtitles.

### Before Watching

Before showing a video, we often tell students the title and its type (an advertisement, a movie clip, etc.) and ask them to make one or two predictions to share with a partner. Sometimes these predictions can turn into pre-questions for students to investigate while viewing the video. Other times we create a few pre-questions and write them on the board for students to reference while they are watching the video (e.g., "What is the penguin trying to do? Is he successful? Why or why not?").

### While Watching

When using a video clip, we often show it to students one time without stopping and assign no task other than to watch it. Then, we show it again with a task in mind—giving students a couple of pre-questions and having them share the answers or pausing a few times to have students make predictions, ask questions, or summarize what is happening.

### After Watching

After watching a video clip, we often ask students to revisit their initial predictions and revise them. We also check for understanding by providing students with a few questions to answer. Sharing these responses in small groups can provide speaking and listening practice. Some examples of questions we give to students can be found in Figure 29.1: Video Thinking Sheet. This sheet can be used with almost any video and contains questions and answer stems for students to complete before and after watching a clip.

Another option is for each student to come up with a few questions based on the video and invite a partner to answer them. We have also had students use their answers to create a mini-poster about the video, which contains the video title, two to three sentences about it based on their question responses (e.g., their favorite part or two things they learned), and an illustration representing a key idea in the video. Students can then informally present their mini-posters in small groups or to the class.

Along with the typical sequence we just described, here are five video activities that we use to specifically help students develop their speaking and listening skills.

**BACK TO THE SCREEN**

Back to the screen, also called *back-to-back* by some educators, is a popular video activity in our classroom. We were introduced to it by Laurel Pollard and Natalie Hess in their book *Zero Prep: Ready-to-Go Activities for the Language Classroom.*

In this activity, the teacher chooses a short clip (movie clips with a lot of action work best) and divides the class into pairs. One group turns their desks so they face the screen and the other students have their backs to it. The teacher starts to show the clip with the sound off and the person who can see the screen describes in English what is happening to their partner. The teacher then pauses the video, students switch places, and the teacher hits play and the roles are reversed. Depending on the length of the clip, this switch can happen three or four times (we usually change every two minutes or so). The pairs then work together to write a chronological sequence of the events in the clip. They can share with another group and then with the class. The activity concludes with the class watching the whole clip with the sound turned on (if extra support is needed, the whole clip can be shown to the class *prior* to creating the chronological sequence).

We described this activity in our first book *The ESL/ELL Teacher's Survival Guide* (Ferlazzo & Sypnieski, 2012, p. 67) but have since improved it in a few ways. We've found it helpful to scaffold the activity for beginners by writing key words from the clip on the board. If any are new words, we quickly provide the definition or ask students to translate them into their home language. Students can then access these words when they are talking to their partners and writing their chronologies. If we have newcomers in class, we often have them pair up with a more-proficient student so they can watch the clip and listen to what their partner is saying to the other partner. We've also paired up newcomers who speak the same home language to do the activity in that language.

Then, they can write the chronology in their home language and work to translate it, or parts of it, with assistance from the teacher, a student with higher English proficiency, or Google Translate.

**SEQUENCING**

In this activity, students are given sentence strips containing different events in the video clip and they have to put them in order after watching it. As we explained in Strategy 6: Sequencing, we print out the strips on one sheet in mixed-up order. Then, students can cut them out before doing the sequencing activity. Once students put the strips in an order, they can compare with a partner, and then the class can come to agreement about the correct sequence. Here's where the speaking practice comes in—students can get into pairs and re-watch the video clip with the volume off while taking turns narrating the events as they happen. Newcomers can participate in a similar activity using flashcards with just a word or short phrase on them. They can also work to put the flashcards in the correct sequence and then practice narrating the video by saying the words aloud in order.

As an extension, the teacher can show another video, but this time the students can create the sentence strips (or flashcards) describing the main events in the clip. Then students can practice narrating the video using their sentence strips. This can be done in small groups or as a class, and students can note the similarities and differences between their narrations.

**TRUE OR FALSE**

This is a quick and easy activity to keep students active during a video and to encourage speaking and listening practice. The teacher shows part of a video clip and pauses to ask students a true or false question based on what they just watched. Students can respond by writing their response on a piece of paper or on a mini-whiteboard. To increase the challenge students can be asked to also write a reason why they think a statement is false. Then they can share their response with a partner and the teacher can select a few pairs to share with the class. The teacher can continue the video and repeat the process a couple more times.

**PAUSE AND PREDICT**

The pause and predict activity is exactly that—the teacher pauses a video so students can predict what is coming next. Students can write their predictions down or simply share them aloud with a partner. They can be encouraged to share the thinking behind their predictions with the simple sentence frame, "I predict because." Students can revisit their predictions after viewing the whole video clip and share (by writing or speaking) how and why they were correct or not.

Figure 29.2: Pause and Predict Sheet is a simple form we've used to scaffold this activity for intermediate students. The sentence frames contained in this figure could also just be written on the board for student use. The teacher can divide a video clip into four sections. After showing the first section, the teacher can pause the video and ask students to make a prediction about what is coming next and why they think that is the case. Each student can write his or her prediction in sentence frame number 1 on the pause and predict sheet. The teacher can have students share these or just move on and have them share at the end. Then the teacher shows the second section of the clip and students write new predictions in sentence frame number 2. The teacher can use the same process after showing section 3 and then show the last section to students. Then, students can watch the whole video again without any stops. They can revisit the predictions they made by completing the bottom half of the pause and predict sheet and share their new learnings in pairs or small groups.

**HOW-TO VIDEOS**

Showing students how-to videos, also called *tutorials,* is another way to build speaking and listening skills. We start by showing students several simple how-to videos that only have five or six steps. Before watching, we encourage students to pay attention to the different steps. After watching the video, we give students time (either in pairs or individually) to write down the steps in order. We then play the video again and students can make any necessary changes. This activity can reinforce ordinal numbers by asking students to use them when writing the steps (e.g., first, second, third, etc.). Students can study the steps and then practice saying them in order with a partner.

We have also had our students make their own how-to videos by thinking of something they know how to do and writing down the steps using ordinal numbers. Then, they practice saying each step while also demonstrating it. Demonstrations could include fun pantomimes and pictures as stand-ins for real objects, animals, or people. We use our phones to record the students' demonstrations, show them to the class, and, with permission, post them on our class blog. Some examples from past years include how to tie a tie, how to make papaya salad, and how to brush a cat. See the Technology Connections section for more resources on creating online tutorials.

## Student Handouts and Examples

Figure 29.1: Video Thinking Sheet
Figure 29.2: Pause and Predict Sheet

## What Could Go Wrong?

Having access to millions of free videos online can be a double-edged sword. It is wonderful to be able to search for videos containing specific features or on certain topics, but the results can be overwhelming. See the Technology Connections section for links to many videos that are specifically effective with ELLs.

## Technology Connections

For links to numerous movie and video clips and ideas for using them with ELLs see these sites:

The Best Popular Movies/TV Shows for ESL/EFL (& How to Use Them) (http://larryferlazzo.edublogs.org/2008/04/26/the-best-popular-moviestv-shows-for-eslefl/)

The Best Fun Videos for English Language Learners in 2017—So Far (http://larryferlazzo.edublogs.org/2017/05/21/the-best-fun-videos-for-english-language-learners-in-2017-so-far/)

The Best Movie Scenes to Use for English-Language Development (http://larryferlazzo.edublogs.org/2010/02/01/the-best-movie-scenes-to-use-for-english-language-development/)

For more resources on helping students create their own videos, see The "All-Time" Best Ways to Create Online Content Easily & Quickly (http://larryferlazzo.edublogs.org/2014/02/23/the-all-time-ways-to-create-online-content-easily-quickly/). This list includes a link to the site Tildee (www.tildee.com/). This is not a video site, but it does contain a feature for students to create their own online tutorials.

Also, see The Best Ways for Students to Create Online Videos (Using Someone Else's Content) (http://larryferlazzo.edublogs.org/2008/05/14/the-best-ways-for-students-to-create-online-videos-using-someone-else%E2%80%99s-content/) and A Potpourri of the Best & Most Useful Video Sites (http://larryferlazzo.edublogs.org/2012/11/06/a-potpourri-of-the-best-most-useful-video-sites/).

For multiple examples of how-to instructional videos, see The Best Online Instructional Video Sites (http://larryferlazzo.edublogs.org/2008/07/24/the-best-online-instructional-video-sites/).

For ideas on how to use Instagram to make student-created videos, see The Best Resources for Learning to Use the Video Apps "Vine" & Instagram (http://larryferlazzo.edublogs.org/2013/02/18/the-best-resources-for-learning-to-use-the-video-app-twine/).

If you are having trouble accessing videos from your school computer, see If You Don't Have Teacher Access to YouTube at Your School, Then This Search Engine Is a "Must" (http://larryferlazzo.edublogs.org/2013/08/13/if-you-dont-have-teacher-access-to-youtube-at-your-school-then-this-search-engine-is-a-must/) and The Best Ways To Deal With YouTube's Awful Safety Mode (http://larryferlazzo.edublogs.org/2015/10/16/the-best-ways-to-deal-with-youtubes-awful-safety-mode/).

If you're feeling really adventurous and want to be on the cutting edge, try virtual reality! Our students used Google Cardboard to view a variety of virtual reality videos and write about them. Then some of our students made their own virtual reality videos. For resources, including student-made examples, see A Beginning List of the Best Resources on Virtual Reality in Education (http://larryferlazzo.edublogs.org/2017/02/27/a-beginning-list-of-the-best-resources-on-virtual-reality-in-education/).

## Attribution

Versions of some of these ideas appeared in our book, *The ESL/ELL Teacher's Survival Guide* (Ferlazzo & Sypnieski, 2012, p. 67).

Thank you to Laurel Pollard, Natalie Hess, and Jan Herron for their great activity back to the screen, which is just one of many excellent lesson ideas in their book *Zero Prep: Ready-to-Go Activities for the Language Classroom* (https://altaenglishpublishers.com/product/zero-prep-activities-for-all-levels-activities-for-the-language-classroom/).

## Figures

---

*Before watching:*

What is the title of the video?
Based on the title, what do you predict it might be about?
Write three words that you think you might hear in this video.

*After watching:*

Were your predictions correct? Why or why not? Did you hear any of the words?

Write two important things you noticed in the video:

Write a question you have about the video:

Write the part of the video that you liked most:

Write how this video made you feel:

If you had to use only five words to describe this video, what would they be?

If you could give this video a new title, what would it be and why?

---

**Figure 29.1**  Video Thinking Sheet

## Making Predictions

1. I predict _____

   because _____.

2. I predict _____

   because _____.

3. I predict _____

   because _____.

## Revising My Predictions

1. My first prediction was _____ (right/wrong) because_____

   _____.

2. My second prediction was _____ (right/wrong) because_____

   _____.

3. My third prediction was _____ (right/wrong) because_____

   _____.

**Figure 29.2**  Pause and Predict Sheet

# STRATEGY 30

# Oral Presentations

## What Is It?

Oral presentations can take many different forms in the ELL classroom—ranging from students briefly presenting their learning in small groups to creating a multi-slide presentation for the whole class.

## Why We Like It

Having the confidence to speak in front of others is challenging for most people. For ELLs, this anxiety can be heightened because they are also speaking in a new language. We've found several benefits to incorporating opportunities for students to present to their peers in a positive and safe classroom environment. It helps them focus on pronunciation and clarity and also boosts their confidence. This type of practice is useful because students will surely have to make presentations in other classes, college, and in their future jobs. However, what may be even more valuable is giving students the chance to take these risks in a collaborative, supportive environment.

Presentations also offer students the opportunity to become the teacher— something we welcome and they enjoy! They can further provide valuable listening practice for the rest of the class, especially when students are given a task to focus their listening.

## Supporting Research

Research confirms that in order for ELLs to acquire English they must engage in oral language practice and be given the opportunity to use language in meaningful ways for social and academic purposes (Williams & Roberts, 2011).

Teaching students to design effective oral presentations has also been found to support thinking development because "the quality of presentation actually improves the quality of thought, and vice versa" (Živković, 2014, p. 474).

## Common Core Connections

The Speaking and Listening Standards specifically focus on oral presentations. These Standards call for students to make effective and well-organized presentations and to use technology to enhance understanding of them.

# Application

In this section, we give some general guidelines for oral presentations with ELLs. We then share ideas for helping students develop their presentation skills and describe specific ways we scaffold short and long oral presentations.

### GUIDELINES

We keep the following guidelines in mind when incorporating oral presentations into ELL instruction:

- **Topic:** It can be easier and more motivating for students speaking a new language to deliver presentations on topics they find meaningful and interesting. We try to give students opportunities to select their own topics as much as possible or to choose from a list of topics. It is also helpful for student presentations to be connected to a current unit of study. This enables them to apply new vocabulary, demonstrate their learning, and feel more confident in their knowledge.

- **Length:** We have students develop and deliver short presentations (usually two to four minutes) on a regular basis so they can practice their presentation skills with smaller, less-overwhelming tasks. These presentations are often to another student or a small group. Once or twice a semester, students do a longer presentation (usually five to eight minutes), many times with a partner or in a small group.

- **Novelty:** Mixing up how students present (in small groups, in pairs, and individually) and what they use to present (a poster, a paper placed under the document camera, props, a slide presentation, etc.) can increase engagement for students and the teacher!

- **Whole-class processing:** We want to avoid students tuning out during oral presentations. Not only can it be frustrating for the speakers but also students miss out on valuable listening practice. During oral presentations, and in any activity, we want to maximize the probability that *all* students are thinking and learning *all* the time. Jim Peterson and Ted Appel, administrators with whom we've worked closely, call this *whole-class processing* (Ferlazzo, 2011, August 16) and it is also known as *active participation*. All students can be encouraged to actively participate in oral presentations by being given a listening task—taking notes on a graphic organizer, providing written feedback to the speaker, using a checklist to evaluate presenters, and so on.

- **Language support:** It is critical to provide ELLs, especially at the lower levels of English proficiency, with language support for oral presentations, in other words, thinking about what vocabulary, language features, and organizational structures they may need and then providing students with scaffolding such as speaking frames and graphic organizers. Oral presentations can also provide an opportunity for students to practice their summarizing skills (see Strategy 15: Quoting, Summarizing, and Paraphrasing).

  When students are presenting information on a topic they have researched, we remind them to summarize using their own words and to give credit when using someone else's words.

- **Technology support:** It can't be assumed that students have experience using technology tools in presentations. We find it most helpful using simple tools that are easy for students to learn (such as PowerPoint without all the bells and whistles or Google Slides). We also emphasize to students that digital media should be used to help the audience understand what they are saying and not just to make a presentation flashy or pretty. We also share with our students what is known as *the picture superiority effect*—a body of research showing that people are better able to learn and recall information presented as pictures as opposed to just being presented with words (Kagan, 2013).

- **Groups:** Giving ELLs the opportunity to work and present in small groups is helpful in several ways. Presenting as a group (as opposed to by yourself) can help students feel less anxious. It also offers language-building opportunities as students communicate to develop and practice their presentations. Creating new knowledge as a group promotes collaboration and language acquisition—an ideal equation for a successful ELL classroom!

- **Teacher feedback–student evaluation:** The focus of oral presentations with ELL students should be on the practice and skills they are gaining, not on the grade or score they are earning. Teachers can give out a simple rubric before students create their presentations. Then students can keep these expectations in mind as they develop and practice their presentations.

The teacher or classmates can then use the rubric to offer feedback to the speaker. We also often ask students to reflect on their own presentation and complete the rubric as a form of self-assessment. Figure 30.1: Presentation Peer Evaluation Rubric, developed by talented student teacher Kevin Inlay (who is now a teacher in his own classroom), is a simple rubric we used to improve group presentations in our ELL world history class.

## TEACHING PRESENTATION SKILLS

We use the following two lesson ideas to explicitly teach how to develop effective presentation skills.

### Speaking and Listening Dos and Don'ts

We help our students understand and practice general presentation skills through an activity we call *speaking and listening dos and don'ts*. We usually spread this lesson out among two class periods.

We first ask students to create a simple T-chart by folding a piece of paper in half and labeling one side *Do* and the other side *Don't*. We then post Figure 30.2: Speaking Dos and Don'ts on the document camera and display the first statement (the rest we cover with a blank sheet of paper).

We read the first statement "Make eye contact with the audience" and ask students if this is something they want to *do* when they are giving a presentation or if it is something they *don't* want to do. Students write the statement where they think it belongs—under the *Do* column or *Don't* Column. Students then share their answer with a partner and discuss *why* they put it in that column. After calling on a few pairs to share with the class, we move down the list repeating the same process of categorizing each statement as a do or a don't. Students write it on their chart and discuss why it should be placed there.

After categorizing the statements for speaking, we give students Figure 30.3: Listening Dos and Don'ts. We tell students to work in pairs to categorize the statements as something they *do* or something they *don't* want to do when listening to a student presentation. This time, we ask students to make a quick poster with the headings *Dos* and *Don'ts* for listening. Under each heading students must list the corresponding statements—the teacher can circulate to check for accuracy. Students are asked to talk about why each statement belongs in each category and should be prepared to share their reasoning with the class. Students must also choose one *do* statement and one *don't* statement to illustrate on their poster. Students can present their posters in small groups or with the whole class. This serves as a great opportunity to apply the speaking and listening *dos* they just reviewed and heightens their awareness of the *don'ts*!

A fun twist, which also serves as a good review on a subsequent day, is to ask groups of students to pick two or three *dos* and *don'ts* from speaking and listening to act out in front of the class.

**Slide Presentations Concept Attainment**

We periodically ask students to make slide presentations using PowerPoint or Google Slides to give them practice with developing visual aids (see the home culture activity later in this section). We show students how to make better slides along with giving students the language support they may need in the form of an outline or sentence starters. An easy and effective way to do this is through concept attainment.

As we described in Strategy 11: Inductive Learning, concept attainment involves the teacher identifying good and bad examples of the intended learning objective. In this case, we use a PowerPoint containing three good slides and three bad ones (see the Technology Connections section for how to access this PowerPoint).

We start by showing students the first example of a good or *yes* slide (containing very little text and two images) and saying, "This is a *yes*." However, we don't explain why it is a *yes*. Then we show a bad or *no* example of a slide (containing multiple images randomly placed with a very busy background), saying, "This is a *no*" without explaining why. Students are then asked to think about them and share with a partner why they think one is a *yes* and one is a *no*.

At this point, we make a quick chart on a large sheet of paper (students can make individual charts on a piece of paper) and ask students to list the good and bad qualities they have observed so far. For example, under the *Good/Yes* column it might say "Has fewer words and the background is simple" and under the *Bad/No* column "Has too many pictures and the background is distracting."

We then show the second *yes* example (containing one image with a short amount of text in a clear font) and the *no* example (containing way too much text and using a less-clear font style). Students repeat the think-pair-share process and then the class again discusses what students are noticing about the *yes* and *no* examples. Then they add these observations to their chart.

Students repeat the whole process a final time with the third examples. The third *yes* example slide contains one image, minimal text, and one bullet point. The third *no* example, however, contains multiple bullet points.

To reinforce this lesson at a later date, the teacher could show students more examples or students could look for more *yes* and *no* examples online. They could continue to add more qualities of good and bad slides to their chart. See the Technology Connections section for links to good and bad PowerPoint examples, including the PowerPoint we use for this concept attainment lesson.

**SHORT PRESENTATIONS**

As we stated, most of the time we have students make short presentations to a group or a partner because it is more practical, time efficient, and energizing for students. Here are some ways we have students practice making short presentations.

**Speed Dating**

Speed dating is a quick way for students to present their work to classmates while gaining speaking and listening practice. The teacher divides students into two rows facing each other (students can be standing or seated in desks). One row is assigned as the *movers*. The teacher tells students the amount of time each partner will have to speak (this depends on the length of what they are sharing). When time is up, the teacher says "switch" and the mover row stands and moves to the right. This can be done several times so that students can present to multiple partners. Students can share their work in different ways (e.g., by sharing specific parts of a mini-poster or explaining something they've written). To boost listening skills, we often require students to ask a question after their partner presents (sometimes providing question and answer frames).

The previous paragraph describes individual presentations. An easy way to do speed dating after students have worked in groups to prepare presentations is to assign half the groups to different parts or corners of the room (they become the stationary groups). Each remaining group (who will be the movers) is assigned to start with a stationary group partner. After each group presents to each other, the mover rotates and the process repeats itself.

**Talking Points Presentations**

This activity is a fun way for students to practice the presentation skill of speaking from their notes, not reading from them.

In this activity, the teacher first asks students to generate a quick list of topics they know a lot about or students can consult their heart maps or writing territories discussed in Strategy 18: Writer's Notebook for ideas. Students then choose one topic to write about for several minutes—writing anything they know or that comes to mind. The teacher can model the same process on the document camera with a topic of his or her choice.

After writing, the teacher shows students how they can use this quickwrite to create several talking points or categories by looking for ideas that they can expand from their original writing. For example, if they wrote about Disneyland then the categories might include "my favorite rides," "my best memory at Disneyland," "my worst memory at Disneyland," or "my favorite Disney character."

Students then choose three of their categories and draw a quick picture representing each one. For the Disneyland example, Katie modeled drawing a picture of the submarine ride, a picture of her throwing up after going on Star Tours, and a sketch of Minnie Mouse!

The teacher then gives students a simple outline and models using it as an assist while speaking for a brief amount of time (no more than two minutes). See Figure 30.4: Talking Points Presentation Model and Outline for the teacher model and outline we used for this activity.

The teacher reinforces the difference between reading the talking points (a *don't*) and speaking from the talking points (a *do*). Students are then given time to practice presenting using the outline as a guide—an opening, talking about each picture (using the talking points as cues), and a closing.

Students can give their presentations in small groups or in pairs (preferably with different students than they practiced with). Depending on their English proficiency level and the amount of practice they've had, students may or may not need to look at their outline. Listeners can be tasked with thinking of a relevant question to ask the speaker at the end of their presentation.

**Top Five Presentations**

This activity involves students working in groups to develop a top five list based on their interests and preparing a short presentation to share with the class. We were introduced to the idea by ELT specialist Clare Lavery (n.d.) in her British Council post "Short Projects to Get Them Talking."

In our version of the activity, we put students in groups of three and give them a few minutes to come up with three to four topics they all find interesting. Sometimes students need a few ideas to get them started so we list some examples on the board (animals, sports, music, fashion, etc.). Then, we tell students to select one of the topics—preferably the one they know the most about—and to develop a top five list for this topic. Some examples might be top five animals, top five sports cars, top five musical artists, or top five movies. Students then receive Figure 30.5: Top Five Outline (depending on the proficiency level of students, the teacher can choose to include or not to include the sentence frames).

Students use the outline to develop their presentation ideas—to list their choices for the top five in their topic and to explain why they believe each one belongs in the top five. We've found it is also helpful and enjoyable for students to create a visual aid to further communicate their points. In the past, students have created top five posters and five to seven slide PowerPoints. Students have also incorporated songs and movie clips into their presentations. We usually give groups a speaking time limit of three minutes with the requirement that each person in the group must speak during the presentation.

Students are then given time to practice their presentations (again, it might be necessary for the class to review the dos and don'ts for speaking and listening). The presentations can be done in front of the whole class or small groups can be paired up and present to each other. Listeners can be asked to provide feedback on a sticky note (writing something they liked about the presentation or a question they had).

**PechaKucha Book Talks**

PechaKucha ("chit-chat" in Japanese) is a popular presentation format in which 20 slides are shown for 20 seconds each (20 × 20). The slides, which usually contain one to two images and minimal text, are programmed to advance automatically as the speaker talks along with them. In other words, each slide is used as a background or visual cue as the speakers progress through their presentation. Many language teachers use the PechaKucha presentation format because they can be easily modified and they have several advantages for ELLs—they are short, structured, highly visual, and informal.

Students can use the PechaKucha format to develop presentations on basically any topic. Teachers can adjust the time format if they want to give students more time on each slide or have students present fewer slides (e.g., 10 slides × 30 seconds).

One variation of Pecha Kucha we've used in our classes was introduced to us by educator Anthony Schmidt (AnthonyTeacher.com, n.d.a) in his helpful blogpost "The Power of PechaKucha." His modified version involves students creating a short PechaKucha presentation on a book they've read. We often have students do book talks with a partner (see Strategy 2: Literary Conversations) and this is a great way to give those a different spin. Here is the outline Anthony used with his intermediate students:

**Five Slide PechaKucha (2:40)**

- Slide 1—10 seconds: Introduction, title of book
- Slide 2—60s: Plot, summary
- Slide 3—30s: Favorite scene, character, part
- Slide 4—60s: Evaluation and recommendation
- Slide 5—0s: Thank you

We provided our students with this outline. Students then created their slide presentations about their books. They selected online images based on a key idea for each slide (e.g., one student chose an image of the cover of his book for Slide 1 and an image of a gold medal for Slide 4). Because we had beginners and intermediates, we gave students the option of using sentence frames to write their notes for each slide and posted them on the front board (e.g., "The title of my book is." "I recommend this book because." ). Students then printed out a copy of their PowerPoint to use for practice and sent them to us. We had one or two students present their PechaKucha book talks each day over the course of a few weeks.

**Additional Ideas for Short Presentations**

Here are a few other ideas about how students can briefly present to classmates in low-stakes but high-interest ways. A popular strategy in our classroom is known as 3–2–1 and was introduced to us by Ekuwah Moses (2015) in her online piece "3–2–1 and the Common Core Writing Book." It can be modified in various ways, but we use it mainly as a way for students to summarize a text and then present their findings. After reading a text (or a section of a longer text), students are asked to identify three important words, two phrases, and one full quote that summarizes the text. Students work in pairs or small groups to make a quick poster containing these elements to present either in small groups or to the class. See the Technology Connections section for other versions of these 3–2–1 presentations.

We describe in Strategy 9: Jigsaw how we use this versatile strategy to scaffold complex literacy tasks. It is also an excellent strategy for making presentations less overwhelming and more successful for ELLs. Students can be given different sections of one text or different short texts and then assigned to expert groups—everyone with Section 1 or Text 1 becomes Expert Group 1, everyone with Section 2 or Text 2 becomes Expert Group 2, and so on. After reading the text and completing any annotating or graphic organizers, students meet with their expert groups to share their learnings and prepare short presentations they will give in small, mixed groups. Teachers can provide written directions, such as "Each presenter must make a small poster containing a summary (one to two sentences) of the text, a key word with its definition and why it's important, a question, and a drawing to represent one of the key ideas in the text." Once students have practiced, they move into their mixed teaching groups (composed of one member of each expert group) and take turns presenting. The listeners can record key ideas from each presentation on a student- or teacher-created graphic organizer.

A final type of short presentation we do with students involves having them report their learnings after working in small groups. We call them *one-minute reports*. After students have completed a group activity (e.g., sharing their individual answers to a question and working together to determine the best answer), we give them a few minutes to prepare a one-minute report. This report should summarize what they learned or created during the group activity (e.g., explaining the group's best answer and why they feel it is the best) and should not be longer than one minute. Everyone must practice the report because we randomly call on someone from each group to be the reporter. Although the reporter from each group is presenting, the rest of the class should be actively listening. This can be encouraged by having students take notes on each report or by the teacher telling students he or she will be calling on a few students after each report to share something they learned.

## LONG PRESENTATIONS

Short presentations help us meet our goals of teaching students to develop and deliver effective oral presentations, providing them with lots of practice, and enabling them to feel empowered, not overwhelmed, by the experience. Longer presentations, however, can be more challenging for teachers and for students. They can't be done as often because they are more time intensive. Even more important, beginning- and intermediate-level students often feel intimidated by the idea of speaking in English for several minutes alone in front of the class. For this reason, when we do have students prepare longer presentations, we allow them to work in pairs or small groups. This doesn't mean, however, that if a student is ready and eager to do a solo presentation, we would say no. We would encourage it!

The following project describes how we typically facilitate longer oral presentations with our ELL students.

### Home Culture Presentations

Asking students to give presentations on their home countries is a fairly typical assignment in many ELL classes. However, it can get pretty old for ELLs who are not newcomers to do it every year. In our ELL geography class we have students create and deliver similar presentations, though we try to make the assignment a little different from what they've done in the past. These home culture presentations support students in building their speaking and listening skills while they teach and learn from their classmates.

We start this project with a lesson on culture—we discuss what culture is and what would be included as its primary components in any country. After we make an initial list (usually including ideas such as language, food, music, traditions, and clothing), we view a simple slide presentation and a video on the seven elements of culture (you will find a link to it and other similar presentations in the Technology Connections section): social organization, customs and traditions, language, arts and literature, religion, forms of government, and economic systems. We then add these additional ideas to our class list on culture.

We explain to students that they will be creating a slideshow highlighting those elements (and any other ones of their choice that we might have brainstormed) from their home country. We give students the option of working with a partner who shares their home culture. To further ease any anxiety, we explain that once students are ready to present their slideshows, they have the option of presenting to the class or presenting one-on-one to the teacher at lunch or after school. However, once students have practiced multiple times with their classmates, they rarely choose the second option.

Students receive Figure 30.6: Home Culture Planning Sheet and are given two basic guidelines for their slideshow: It should contain eight to ten good slides (we review the *good* vs. *bad* slide qualities list) and the total time should be between four to seven minutes. Students usually don't need a lot of further explanation—they are eager to begin thinking and sharing the different elements of their home cultures.

Students create a paper draft of their slideshow after completing their planning sheets. We pass out legal size paper and have students fold it into eight to ten boxes where they can note what key points and type of image they want to share on each slide. Students then use this draft to guide them while they are making their slideshows. We have our students use PowerPoint or Google Slides and, on the days they are in the computer lab making their slides, we try to borrow a couple of technology-proficient students from another class to assist us. We also have students print out copies of each slide to make practicing in the classroom an easier process (students can flip through the paper copies of their slides instead of having to use a computer).

Once their slideshows are finished, we give students a lot of practice time. We model and discuss different ways students can use to help them talk about their slides instead of reading them. Some students like to create bullet points on index cards for each slide, and others just use the slides as a visual cue to speak from. For beginners, we provide a list of sentence stems (see Figure 30.7: Sentence Stems for Oral Presentations), which they can use to write on index cards for each slide. During the years when we did not have access to technology, students created their home culture presentations on large poster boards using a similar presentation process. This non-tech version worked very well, too.

Presenting their home culture slideshows takes several class periods. To keep everyone focused and engaged, we first review the speaking and listening dos and don'ts as a reminder of what effective presenting and listening should look and sound like. We also provide students with Figure 30.8: Oral Presentation Feedback Form and have students fill one out for each presenter during and immediately after the presentation. When each presentation is finished, we call on one or two students to share a question from the form and the presenters have time to answer them. While students are finishing up their feedback forms and the next group is getting ready, we quickly offer our feedback to the group (focusing on one or two positive elements and one area needing improvement).

Once all the presentations are completed, we give students time to review the feedback forms they received from their classmates, and they respond to the following questions:

- What did your classmates like about your presentation? What did you like the most about it?
- What was easiest about this project and what was most challenging?
- What will you do differently next time? Why?

## Student Handouts and Examples

Figure 30.1: Presentation Peer Evaluation Rubric

Figure 30.2: Speaking Dos and Don'ts

Figure 30.3: Listening Dos and Don'ts

Figure 30.4: Talking Points Presentation Model and Outline

Figure 30.5: Top Five Outline

Figure 30.6: Home Culture Planning Sheet

Figure 30.7: Sentence Stems for Oral Presentations

Figure 30.8: Oral Presentation Feedback Form

## What Could Go Wrong?

Don't correct students while they are presenting! Be mindful of what types of feedback you offer to students, when, and how you give it to them. We often provide brief oral feedback privately while the next group is setting up for their presentation. If teachers have built strong relationships with students, they will be more open to receiving constructive feedback. It can also be helpful to ask students if they want to work on any specific areas of their speaking prior to their presentations. Based on their answers, the teacher then can focus on providing feedback in those areas. We find the creed "Do no harm" always steers us in the right direction!

## Technology Connections

For additional ideas on the 3–2–1 activity, see The Best Ways to Use "3–2–1" as an Instructional Strategy (http://larryferlazzo.edublogs.org/2015/09/19/the-best-ways-to-use-3–2–1-as-an-instructional-strategy/).

For links to examples of good and bad PowerPoint slides, and to access the PowerPoint we used for our concept attainment lesson on this topic, see The Best Resources for Teaching Students the Differences Between a Good & Bad Slide (http://larryferlazzo.edublogs.org/2017/08/01/the-best-resources-for-teaching-students-the-differences-between-a-good-bad-slide/).

For a plethora of resources on making good presentations, see The Best Sources of Advice for Making Good Presentations (http://larryferlazzo.edublogs.org/2009/05/25/the-best-sources-of-advice-for-making-good-presentations/).

You can find examples of our students' home culture presentations, along with the resources we used during this project, at Larry's blogpost "Home Culture Presentations with English Language Learners" (http://larryferlazzo.edublogs.org/2014/01/20/home-culture-presentations-with-english-language-learners/).

# Attribution

Portions of this section are adapted from our books, *The ESL/ELL Teacher's Survival Guide* (Ferlazzo & Sypnieski, 2012, p. 147) and *Navigating the Common Core with English Language Learners* (Ferlazzo & Sypnieski, 2016, p. 123, 243–245).

Thank you to Kevin Inlay for his excellent presentation peer evaluation rubric.

Thank you to Clare Lavery for the great ideas in her British Council post "Short Projects to Get Them Talking" (www.teachingenglish.org.uk/article/short-projects-get-them-talking?utm_source=facebook&utm_medium=social&utm_campaign=bc-teachingenglish).

Thank you to Anthony Schmidt for his helpful blogpost "The Power of PechaKucha" and his PechaKucha. For more teaching ideas see Anthony's blog at www.anthonyteacher.com/.

Thank you to Ekuwah Moses for her online piece "3–2–1 and the Common Core Writing Book" (http://ekuwah.blogspot.com/2015/01/3-2-1-and-common-core-writing-book.html).

# Figures

| | 1—Needs Improvement | 2—Fair | 3—Good | 4—Excellent |
|---|---|---|---|---|
| **Names of group members:** _____ | | | | |
| **Directions**: Circle the score you think the group performed at for each category. | | | | |

**Names of group members:** _____

**Directions**: Circle the score you think the group performed at for each category.

| | 1—Needs Improvement | 2—Fair | 3—Good | 4—Excellent |
|---|---|---|---|---|
| **Eye Contact** | Group members **mostly did not** hold eye contact with the audience. | Group members **sometimes** held eye contact with the audience. | Group members **mostly** held eye contact with the audience. | Group members **always** held eye contact with the audience. |
| **Speaking Role** | **Not all** group members had a speaking role. | X | X | **All** group members had a speaking role. |
| **Voice Volume** | Group members **mostly did not** speak loud enough to be heard clearly. | Group members **sometimes** spoke loud enough to be heard clearly. | Group members **mostly** spoke loud enough to be heard clearly. | Group members spoke loud enough to **always** be heard clearly. |
| **Facing Forward** | Group members **mostly did not** face forward. | Group members **sometimes** faced forward. | Group members **mostly** faced forward. | Group members **always** faced forward. |

**Total:** _____/16

**Comments:**

_____

_____

**Figure 30.1** Presentation Peer Evaluation Rubric *Source:* Reproduced with permission from Kevin Inlay.

- Make eye contact with the audience.
- Mumble or whisper so only the people in the front can hear.
- Apologize for making mistakes.
- Look down at the floor or look at the ceiling.
- Speak loud enough to be heard clearly by everyone in the room.
- Read my notes to the audience.
- Stand up straight and face my audience.
- Chew gum.
- Speak to the audience, looking at my notes only when needed.
- Turn my back to the audience.
- Relax and remember everyone makes mistakes when they are learning.
- Speak very quickly.

**Figure 30.2** Speaking Dos and Don'ts

- Look at the speaker and lean in.
- Look down at my phone or put my head down.
- Wait until the speaker is finished to ask questions.
- Laugh when the speaker makes a mistake.
- Interrupt the speaker to share a comment or ask a question.
- Turn my body toward the speaker.
- Talk to other students while the speaker is presenting.
- Let the speaker know I am understanding their words by nodding my head.

**Figure 30.3** Listening Dos and Don'ts

# Teacher Model

*Opening:* "Good morning (afternoon), I would like to tell you about Disneyland."

Picture 1 or Talking Point 1:

- My favorite ride is the submarine.
- Explain the old submarine ride versus new Finding Nemo ride.
- Explain why the old ride was better.

Picture 2 or Talking Point 2:

- My worst memory was throwing up after Star Tours.
- Explain why it happened and how I felt.

Picture 3 or Talking Point 3:

- Minnie Mouse is my favorite character.
- In cartoons she is smarter than Mickey.
- This is my favorite Minnie souvenir.

*Closing:* "Thank you for listening. Do you have any questions?"

**Figure 30.4**  Talking Points Presentation Model and Outline

# Outline

Opening: "Good morning/afternoon, I would like to tell you about _____."

Picture 1/Talking Point 1:

Picture 2/Talking Point 2:

Picture 3/Talking Point 3:

Closing: "Thank you for listening. Do you have any questions?"

**Figure 30.4** *(Continued)*

Opening and introduction of topic:


Good morning/afternoon, today we will be presenting our top five
_____.

Explanation of topic:

Number 5 is_____because_____.

Number 4 is_____because_____.

Number 3 is_____because_____.

Number 2 is is_____because_____.

And our number 1_____ is_____!

It is our number 1 choice because _____.

Closing:

*Thank you for listening. Does anyone have any questions?*

**Figure 30.5**  Top Five Outline

You will be preparing a slideshow on the culture of your home country. Your slideshow must have eight to ten slides and be five to eight minutes long. Include the following elements (feel free to add other ones, too):

## Language

- Spoken and written
- Gestures

## Social Organization

- Who are the most important people in a community and why?
- What are the most important groups in a community and why?

## Traditions

Food:



Arts:



Religion:



Form of government:

**Figure 30.6**  Home Culture Planning Sheet

## Opening My Presentation

Good morning/afternoon
My name is . . . and I will be talking about . . .
My project is about . . .
Today I will be sharing . . .
The purpose of my presentation today is to . . .

## Body of My Presentation

First, I will talk about . . .
I would like to begin by . . .
This image represents . . .
Next . . .
Now let's move on to . . .
As you can see . . .
My next point is about . . .
Finally . . .
Last but not least . . .

## Concluding My Presentation

To sum up . . .
In conclusion . . .
Thank you for listening . . .
Does anyone have any questions?

**Figure 30.7**  Sentence Stems for Oral Presentations

Presenter's name_____

Listener's name _____

Two things I really liked about your presentation are:

**1.**

**2.**

One question I have about your presentation is:

**1.**

**Figure 30.8** Oral Presentation Feedback Form

# *STRATEGY 31*

# Listening

## What Is It?

Active listening, inside and outside the classroom, means to actively focus on understanding what you are *listening* to as opposed to *hearing* language being used around you. It's similar to the difference between listening to instructions and hearing music playing in the background. Common activities in ELL classrooms involve students listening to something (a text, a dialogue, a song, a video clip, etc.) and completing a task that requires them to listen for certain language or content. Although this is certainly a helpful practice, we also want our students to know *why* listening skills are important and *how* they can improve these skills. The activities in this section support those goals.

## Why We Like It

Listening can often be a hidden skill that gets less attention in the classroom. We try to make it more visible to students because it is so critical to the development of skills in every domain! Good listening skills can obviously increase language learning and content knowledge. Active listening also has many benefits in life in general, especially in the workplace and in our personal relationships. We like to make our students aware of these benefits because it helps create further motivation to practice these skills.

Students often need this extra support because listening to authentic speech in a new language can be a frustrating and overwhelming task. Helping them see the immediate and long-term impacts of active listening can help them stay motivated to apply this skill in and out of the classroom.

# Supporting Research

Research has found a significant positive relationship between ELLs' metacognitive awareness and listening performance and thus supports a process-oriented approach to listening instruction (Goh, 2014, p. 15; Vandergrift & Goh, 2011, p. 65). A process approach assists students in learning listening strategies and becoming aware of which ones work best, and least best, for them.

# Common Core Connections

As in Strategy 24: Dictation, specific listening activities hit more of the Language Standards than the Speaking and Listening ones. They specifically meet the Language Standard that requires students to "apply knowledge of language to understand how language functions in different contexts... and to comprehend more fully when reading or listening."

# Application

This book includes many ideas that support students in building their listening skills. Strategy 24: Dictation, Strategy 27: Music, Strategy 29: Video, and Strategy 33: Learning Games for Speaking and Listening all contain specific listening activities and resources. These types of lessons help students develop their listening comprehension skills in English as they progress in other domains. Another key element of listening instruction, however, involves making students aware of the value of these skills and how to improve them.

## THE WHY AND THE HOW: LISTENING BENEFITS AND METACOGNITIVE LISTENING

We help students become more aware of the benefits of listening in their lives. We explore this idea by asking students to think and write about how *active listening* (fully concentrating in order to understand, remember, and respond to what is being said) can benefit them right now. Students usually come up with answers such as being able to help their families, to learn English more quickly, and to have better relationships with friends. We also have students think about how active listening might be important in their future. We share research that shows that listening is seen as one of the most important traits in leaders and among colleagues in the workplace (Nowogrodski, 2015; Rodriguez, 2012).

After students consider the value of listening skills in their lives, they are often more motivated to learn, use, and evaluate different listening strategies. Research supports this type of strategy instruction—ELLs can make more progress if they are aware of how listening processes work and apply them in their own listening (Vandergrift, n.d.). Helping students understand metacognition (being aware of how and when to use different learning processes) can improve their listening skills in English and in their home language.

We described one way of doing this in our book *Navigating the Common Core with English Language Learners* (Ferlazzo & Sypnieski, 2016, p. 237). We give students Figure 31.1: Listening Practice Sheet before starting a listening practice activity using any of a variety of texts—a video, podcast, news report, dialogue, TED Talk, and so on. We write the title and type of text on the board (e.g., a radio news report titled "Earthquake in Greece and Turkey"). Then we ask students to write anything they know about the topic and the type of text in the first section of Figure 31.1. Students share with a partner and work together to generate more ideas. Students then write a few predictions based on this knowledge. We model how to make predictions about the content (e.g., "I predict the news report will give information about how big the earthquake was and if it caused any damage.") and how the content will be delivered (e.g., "I predict the news report will contain audio interviews with people who lost their homes and will describe the damage to the area."). Students write their predictions in the first section labeled "Before Listening" in Figure 31.1 and share them with each other, adding any new ideas from their partner.

Students then move to the second section of the listening practice sheet and are asked to list strategies they think might be helpful in understanding this particular text. We guide students to remember the different strategies they use while reading and explain that they can apply many of those when listening to texts—including activating prior knowledge, making predictions, visualizing, asking questions, summarizing, using context clues to determine word meanings, and so on. During this listening task, it is important for the teacher to pause and replay the listening text several times so students can use these strategies. Taking students to the computer lab with headphones is also helpful so they can pause on their own and re-listen when needed. See the Technology Connections section for links to sources of good, free audio recordings accessible to ELLs.

Once they've finished the listening task, we ask students to reflect on which strategies were most helpful to their understanding and what was difficult, so they can set goals for improvement. Students write these reflections in the third section of Figure 31.1 and then share them in a class discussion.

We want to restate that the point of this listening exercise is *not to give a comprehension quiz on content*. Rather, its purpose is to challenge students to see for themselves (with our assistance) what strategies they can use to become better listeners in English and in their home language.

Helping students practice these types of listening strategies and metacognition (thinking about which strategies to use, when to use them, and why they help) is easier to do in a classroom environment where students or the teacher can pause the task at any time. It is much more difficult to employ these processes to listening situations out in the world—students can't hit pause when someone strikes up a conversation or when the pharmacist is explaining a medication to them. However, we can help make these processes more automatic by providing this type of practice in the classroom and encouraging them to try it on their own. We can also give them the language to improve their understanding in these situations. The next section contains ideas on how to provide this kind of support.

### LISTENING LANGUAGE FRAMES

Teaching students the words and language structures they can use to improve their understanding provides an opportunity for growth in listening, communication, and confidence. Students need to know what to do when they don't understand something and when they think they do understand it but want to confirm that it is correct. When someone says something an ELL doesn't understand, they need to know different ways that they can ask for clarification in English. (e.g., Teacher: "Everyone take out your outline." Student: "Excuse me, what does *outline* mean?"). ELLs also need to be able to paraphrase what they've heard as a comprehension check when they are not 100% sure of their understanding (Teacher: "Everyone take out your outline." Student: "Just to be clear, the *outline* is the paper with the boxes, right?") We use Figure 31.2: Listening Frames to have students practice these skills.

We provide copies to each student and have a large version posted on the wall. Students can then practice using these questions as they participate in small-group discussions. The teacher can also provide dialogues containing these language frames that students can practice and then perform (see Figure 31.3: Sample Dialogue).

Students can be asked to underline the phrases in the dialogue that demonstrate active listening. Students could also write their own dialogues for other listening situations (e.g., talking with a teacher, making a phone call to get information, talking to a neighbor about a problem, or anything else relevant to their experiences).

### MORE LISTENING IDEAS

All of our books include a variety of ways to specifically support students' listening skills. Here are a few more ideas we've either come across or made better since our last two books were published.

### Back-to-Back

Back-to-back is a listening activity frequently used for team-building and to improve communication skills. In our classroom, we use it as a modified dictation activity with a challenging twist. Because students are seated back-to-back, they have to listen carefully to their partner without the visual support of lip reading, facial expressions, body language, or gestures.

Students can do various tasks while seated back-to-back. One option is to give Partner 1 a mini-whiteboard and Partner 2 a picture. Partner 2 must describe the picture as Partner 1 listens and draws. This option always elicits laughter when the real picture is compared to the student-drawn one! Another way to do back-to-back is to give Partner 1 the name of an animal written on a piece of paper. He or she must describe the animal and give clues without saying the animal's name. Partner 2 listens and tries to guess the animal. The same process could be used with one partner describing a place or a famous person for the other partner to guess. Students can also take turns dictating from a text they've recently read while the other person writes what they are hearing on a mini-whiteboard.

Back-to-back provides a great opportunity for students to use the listening language frames in Figure 31.2 because they frequently need to ask for clarification during this activity!

**Different or Same?**

This is a listening activity that encourages students to listen closely to each other and to interact in a meaningful way. We were introduced to it by teacher trainer and writer Adrian Tennant (n.d.) in his blogpost "Listening Matters: Active Listening."

The teacher writes a student- or teacher-generated topic on the board (e.g., "What I did over the weekend"; "What I like about our school"; "What I don't like about learning English"). Students take a few minutes to write or make notes about the topic. Then the teacher puts students into pairs and tells them they will have three minutes to have a conversation about the topic, and—here's where the *conversation* and *active listening* parts happen—they must identify two things that are the same and two things that are different as they discuss the topic. Once time is up, the teacher can call on pairs to share any similarities or differences they found.

**Choose Your Own Adventure**

These stories, also called *action mazes,* are always a hit with students. Students are periodically given choices of what they want characters to do, and then they participate in the construction of the story itself. There are numerous choose your own adventure stories on the web that are accessible to ELLs (see the Technology Connections section for a list of links to the best ones). Our students enjoy reading these stories online and writing their own in small groups or using online sites to create them (also listed in Technology Connections). However, we also do a low-tech version of choose your own adventure that specifically targets listening practice.

We begin by telling students they will be listening to a story and making choices about what happens next—in other words, choosing their own adventure. We also say that they need to listen carefully without taking any notes because they will be reconstructing the story with a partner when we are done reading it. We sometimes choose an online story (from one of the recommended sites we list) and read it from our tablet or laptop.

Other times, if we are feeling ambitious, we create the story on our own or on the fly. When it comes time for students to make a choice (e.g., which door a character should go through), they vote by show of hands and the winning choice is announced and made. The same process is continued until the best ending to the story is chosen.

Then it is time for students to get into pairs or groups of three and retell the story. Students write down everything they remember and then meet with another pair or group to compare notes and make any changes. We end the activity by asking for volunteers to read their reconstructions of the story to the class.

Some technologically adventurous teachers have been exploring ways to use electronic personal assistants such as the Amazon Echo or Google Home in the classroom. If you are one of those teachers, unlike us, you may want to check out the audio-only choose your own adventures that both of those tools are making available to users. You can find them at the Amazon Alexa Skills Store and at the Google Home Store.

## Student Handouts and Examples

Figure 31.1: Listening Practice Sheet
Figure 31.2: Listening Frames
Figure 31.3: Sample Dialogue

## What Could Go Wrong?

It is safe to say that many teachers, not just those of ELLs, underestimate the importance of explicit instruction in listening skills. For ELL students, listening in English can be one of the most-challenging skills to practice and is often one area in which they lack confidence. Teachers can help students boost their confidence over time by providing fun, meaningful listening practice. Don't do it once and check it off your list!

## Technology Connections

For more ideas on helping ELLs improve their listening skills and for tons of links to accessible listening sites, see The Best Ideas to Help Students Become Better Listeners (http://larryferlazzo.edublogs.org/2012/07/23/the-best-ideas-to-help-students-become-better-listeners-contribute-more/) and The Best Listening Sites for English Language Learners (http://larryferlazzo.edublogs.org/2008/05/28/the-best-listening-sites-for-english-language-learners/).

For more resources on choose your own adventure stories, including places students and can read them and write them online, see The Best Places to Read & Write "Choose Your Own Adventure Stories" (http://larryferlazzo.edublogs.org/2009/05/02/the-best-places-to-read-write-choose-your-own-adventure-stories/).

For further information on metacognition, see The Best Posts on Metacognition (http://larryferlazzo.edublogs.org/2012/05/13/my-best-posts-on-metacognition/).

## Attribution

Portions of this section are adapted from our book *Navigating the Common Core with English Language Learners* (Ferlazzo & Sypnieski, 2016, p. 235–238).

Thank you to Adrian Tennant for the great ideas in his blogpost "Listening Matters: Active Listening" (www.onestopenglish.com/skills/listening/teaching-tips/listening-matters/listening-matters-active-listening/554465.article).

## Figures

Title of listening text:_____

Type of text: _____

1. Before listening: "What do I already know? What predictions can I make?"

2. While listening: "What strategies can I use to help me understand what I'm listening to?"

3. After listening: "Which strategies helped me the most? What will I do next time?"

**Figure 31.1** Listening Practice Sheet *Source: Navigating the Common Core with English Language Learners: Practical Strategies to Develop Higher-Order Thinking Skills* (Ferlazzo & Sypnieski, 2016, p. 237).

## Asking for Clarification

Could you repeat that, please?
What do you mean by _____?
Could you explain that more?
What does the word _____ mean?
Can you give me an example of _____?
I'm confused when you say_____. Can you explain it to me?

## Checking for Understanding

So, what you're saying is . . .
You said _____. Does that mean _____?
If I understand you correctly, . . .
You mean _____, yes?
So, an example of _____ is _____, right?
Just to be clear, you mean _____, right?

**Figure 31.2** Listening Frames

Doctor:     How are you feeling?

Patient:    Not good in my throat.

Doctor:     Tell me about your symptoms and when they started.

Patient:    Could you repeat that, please?

Doctor:     Yes, I asked what are your symptoms and how long you've beenexperiencing them?

Patient:    What does the word *symptoms* mean?

Doctor:     Oh, that means where does your throat hurt and is anything elsewrong?

Patient:    My throat hurts right here and my head feels bad since Saturday.

Doctor:     Well, you don't have a fever so I think you just have a cold. Drink alot of fluids, take some aspirin, and get some rest.

Patient:    What are *fluids*? Can you give me an example?

Doctor:     Fluids are liquids like water or juice.

Patient:    Oh okay. So Gatorade is a fluid, right?

Doctor:     Yes, you can drink some Gatorade along with your medicine.

Patient:    So I need to take some aspirin, go home to rest, and drink somefluids, yes?

Doctor:     You got it! Hope you feel better soon!

Patient:    Thank you so much.

**Figure 31.3**  Sample Dialogue

# Debate

## What Is It?

Typical classroom debates involve dividing students into two teams representing the different (for and against) sides of a controversial topic, giving them time to research and prepare their arguments, and then having students follow a traditional debate structure of presenting arguments and rebuttals using formal language. There is a moderator (the teacher or a student) who enforces time limits for each side, and usually one team is declared the winner based on a vote by the audience or a small group of student judges. In our classroom, we focus less on the result—who wins the debate—and more on the process—the speaking, listening, and critical thinking skills students are developing while doing the activity.

## Why We Like It

Debates can be used in the classroom to instantly engage students and to get them thinking, talking, and working together. It is a popular activity for adolescents in particular—they are more than willing to share with others how *their* beliefs are right!

Debates can also help students expand and solidify their thinking about an issue they are going to be writing about in an argument essay. Or they can participate in a debate *after* writing an argument piece or in place of writing an essay as a culminating task. Debates also offer meaningful practice with the concepts and language structures of argumentation.

## Supporting Research

Research has shown that debating has several positive effects in the classroom. It facilitates active learning, improves students' listening and speaking skills, increases knowledge acquisition by reinforcing previously taught content, promotes critical thinking and creativity, and helps students develop empathy (Shen, n.d.).

## Common Core Connections

Debate, similar to many of the speaking and listening activities we've discussed, meets a number of the Language Standards. It also meets the Speaking and Listening Standard of helping students "prepare and participate effectively in a range of conversations and collaborations with diverse partners, building on others' ideas and expressing their own clearly and persuasively." Debate further supports the Standards focused on argument in the Writing Standards.

## Application

Having students do an assignment that requires multiple days of research in order to build their arguments and participate in an intricate multistep debate just isn't going to work in our classroom. It is too overwhelming for students and for us. However, that doesn't mean we're throwing the baby out with the bath water! Students can practice their argumentation skills in highly engaging and less time-intensive ways.

In this section, we will be describing the main debate activity we use in our intermediate classes that students enjoy. We begin by determining a topic. Sometimes we use one that students are currently studying as a way to expand their thinking and vocabulary in preparation for writing an essay. Other times we might address a current issue—identified by students—at our school (should cell phones be allowed in class) or in the community (should the light rail train operate at night). And some days we keep it light and debate who is a better superhero, Superman or Batman!

We write the topic (phrased as a claim: "Students should be allowed to use cell phones in class.") on the board and students are given a few minutes to write down their thoughts. We explain they can write to what extent they agree or disagree with the statement, reasons for their opinion, and any questions they have (sometimes we include sentence starters such as "I strongly agree because . . ." "I'm wondering . . ."). We also emphasize it is okay if they are unsure about their opinion because they are confused or need more information.

Two large pieces of poster paper are posted on either side of the classroom. One is labeled *Agree* and the other *Disagree*. Another piece of poster paper is placed on a desk in the middle of the room and is labeled *Unsure*. We instruct students to take their writing with them and to go to the section of the room that best represents their opinion (*Agree, Disagree,* or *Unsure*).

We also tell them that they will be sharing their writing with each other and developing a list of reasons to support their position. They will need to write the reasons down on the poster paper and be prepared to share them with the class. For the students who are in the *Unsure* group, they will also share their writing and come up with a list of any questions or comments explaining why they are unsure. If we have a particularly large class and depending on how many students choose a certain position, we break students into two or three mini-groups representing the same position and give each group their own poster paper.

We then pass out copies of Figure 32.1: Debate Language and have it posted on the document camera. If this is the first time we are doing the activity, we give it to students at an earlier time (the previous day). Students would then spend time practicing the phrases and, if needed, translating them into their home languages. We remind students that one of our goals in a debate is to practice using these phrases as we discuss ideas in small groups and share them with the whole class. Many other examples of debate language can be found online (by searching *debate sentence frames* or *debate language examples*) and can be modified to meet the needs of different English proficiency levels.

We usually give students about 10 to 20 minutes to discuss and prepare their posters. They also determine who is going to say what because we require each person to speak during the debate. We circulate during this time to offer assistance, push student thinking, and encourage and praise examples of debate language use.

When groups are ready to share we start with the *Agree* side and ask that group to share their reasons with the class. Then the *Disagree* side shares their reasons, followed by the *Unsure* group. If we have multiple groups, we ask them to go to different parts of the room to share their posters. In other words, two or three larger gatherings of an *Agree* group, a *Disagree* group, and an *Unsure* group meet in different sections of the classroom. The teacher then circulates among them.

Once the groups have finished sharing their posters, we tell them they will now have five minutes to develop a rebuttal. We explain this means they will need to respond to what the other side has said. If they disagree with the reasons provided by the other side, they must explain why they disagree. At this time, we ask the *Unsure* group if they have heard any reasons that convince them enough to move to the *Agree* or *Disagree* side. If not, they can work to develop questions they have for each side. We also explain that *any* student can switch sides if their views have changed—keeping your same position or changing your mind are equally valid actions to take in an informed democracy. Students can write these rebuttal statements and questions on the other side of their poster paper or can be given another piece of paper.

Student groups then share their rebuttals and questions in the same order (*Agree, Disagree, Unsure*). All students are given a final opportunity to move to either side and can be asked to share aloud or in writing why they did or did not move.

We usually end the activity not by declaring a winner but by having students reflect on the process by answering the following questions:

- Did you enjoy this activity? Why or why not? How could it be better next time?
- What skills did you practice by doing this activity?
- What did you do well? What was challenging for you? What will you work on to improve next time and how will you do that?

## Student Handout and Example

Figure 32.1: Debate Language

## What Could Go Wrong?

Debate doesn't have to be done in a formal way for students to practice the basic elements of argumentation. In fact, it can be more engaging to do it informally and more often.

Any time strong opinions are shared, strong language can also follow and often times in negative ways. Before doing a debate activity, it is always a good idea to review with students the dos and don'ts of speaking and listening (see Strategy 30: Oral Presentations)—with a special reminder about how to respectfully disagree with one another. We also think carefully about debate topics and don't choose ones that might incite hurtful conflict based on cultural or religious beliefs.

## Technology Connection

There are several debate sites designed for informed conversation on controversial issues. As a follow-up writing activity, students can write for an authentic audience on any of the sites listed at The Best Sites for Students to Create & Participate in Online Debates (http://larryferlazzo.edublogs.org/2009/10/24/the-best-sites-for-students-to-create-participate-in-online-debates/).

# Figure

## Expressing Your Opinion

In my opinion . . .
I strongly believe that . . .
In my view . . .
I think . . .
I am convinced that . . .

## Agreeing

I agree with _____because _____.
I like the idea that . . .
You make a good point when you say . . .
You are right about . . .

## Disagreeing

I disagree with _____because_____.
I see it differently because _____.
I hear what you're saying, but . . .
I understand your point about _____, but I want to add/disagree
_____.

## Unsure

I am confused about . . .
I have a question about . . .
What if . . .
I am not convinced that . . .

**Figure 32.1**  Debate Language

# STRATEGY 33

# Learning Games for Speaking and Listening

## What Is It?

This strategy lists our seven favorite games to reinforce speaking and listening with English language learners. We've briefly shared two of them in our previous books.

## Why We Like It

We like these games for the same reasons we like the ones listed in Strategy 23: Learning Games for Reading and Writing. Students enjoy them and learn from participating in the activity. Plus, they all require minimal teacher prep time!

## Supporting Research

Again, the same research we cite for the reading and writing games holds true for these speaking and listening ones. This book is long enough, so we don't think it's necessary to reprint those citations here. However, there is one piece of additional research we'd like to share: Many of us who try to learn a new language feel very anxious when prompted to speak in that language. Researchers have found the same issue with ELLs (Bashir, 2014, p. 217; Boonkit, 2010, p. 1305; Savaşçı, 2014, p. 5). Games can provide a low-risk and positive atmosphere that can lower student anxiety.

Literacy researcher Stephen Krashen has identified anxiety as one of the elements of the "affective filter" that influences language acquisition. The higher the affective filter, which also includes motivation challenges and low self-confidence, the more difficult it is to learn a new language. The lower the affective filter, the easier it is to learn a new language (Du, 2009). Games are just one tool that teachers can use to lower the affective filter for our students. Other ways include creating a supportive and welcoming classroom environment, developing positive teacher-student and student-student relationships, and making lessons relevant and engaging to students.

# Common Core Connections

These activities will assist students to meet several Language Standards. They include using conventions and grammar in speaking and enhancing comprehension when listening.

# Application

Many of the games in the Reading and Writing section have obvious connections to speaking and listening as well. The following seven games are particularly effective in building speaking and listening skills with ELLs.

### NINE BOX GRID

You might remember Katie Toppel's Nine Box Grid game that we shared in Strategy 23: Learning Games for Reading and Writing. In that version, we drew a grid on the class whiteboard. In this case, students are assigned a partner, each group gets its own pair of dice, and each student gets a sheet like the one in Figure 33.1. Students take turns rolling the dice and have to use the word that they roll in a sentence. If they roll an 11 or 12, they must use their choice of two words on the grid. The other students provide feedback using the sentence starters in the image. If students are not sure if the word was used correctly, they call the teacher over to judge. On occasion, we give students a grid sheet where we've typed the words. Most of the time, however, we have students create their own template using their choice of nine words from the theme or picture word inductive model (see Strategy 11: Inductive Learning) we've been studying that week.

As in the reading and writing version, this activity has game-like qualities but we don't keep score.

### ANSWER—QUESTION

In this game, students are asked to make a list of six things (it could be less or more). We got the idea for this game (which we slightly modified) from English teacher Larissa Albano (2017), and the example she uses is to have students make a list of six things they did the previous day. Students then get into groups of three with two mini-whiteboards. One student says the first answer, and then the other two are given 30 seconds to come up with a corresponding question. They have to write it down on their board without the other seeing it. When time is up, they hold up their board and say what they wrote. If the student who shared the answer approves of the question, then the questioner gets a point (as always, the teacher can be consulted as needed).

Here's Larissa's example:

The answer is "I ate fish and chips."
Question by Maria: "What did you eat for lunch yesterday?" Question by
   Francesco: "What did you eat for dinner yesterday?"

Here are other topics we've used for this game, including an example of an answer and a corresponding question:

- Six actions you want to take in the future ("be a doctor"—"What kind of job do you want?")

- Six favorite things or people ("soccer"—"What is your favorite sport?")

- Six things in your house ("television"—"What is in your living room?")

- Six things you don't like ("beets"—"What kind of food don't you like?")

- Six physical problems ("my head hurts"—"Do you have a headache?" or "How does your head feel?")

- Six feelings (student acts out a feeling—"Are you angry?" or "What are you angry about?")

**LETTER SCAVENGER HUNT**

There are many variations of this game (search *letter sounds scavenger hunt* or *letter scavenger hunt* online). In the version we play, students are divided into groups of three with one mini-whiteboard for each group. The teacher then calls out a letter or says a letter sound (e.g., "buh" for *b*). Each group then has about a minute to find one object in the classroom that begins with that letter or sound and bring it back to their group. Then, the group has to write down the name of that object *and* come up with a another word that also begins with the same letter or sound. At the end of that time limit, the teacher calls on one of the students in the group to stand and say the name of the object he or she found and the word he or she wrote (this is to make sure they all know how to say it because they don't know who the teacher is going to choose to speak). Each group gets a point for every word they say correctly and can bet all their points on the last round.

We read about a neat twist on this game at FluentU (Genesisd, n.d.). Instead of saying the letter or letter sound, we sometimes say a word and tell students they have to find an object that begins with the same letter or letter sound (or even one that *ends* with the same letter or letter sound). This change makes it slightly more challenging for students.

## SOUND EFFECTS

Students are divided into pairs and each group receives one mini-whiteboard. The teacher goes to an online sound effects site and plays a sound. Students have 20 seconds to describe the sound that is being played.

We usually play this game during a thematic unit and have found it works best when learning about animals, home, and transportation. We share links to sound-effect sites and other ways to use sound in the Technology Connections section, including for creative story prompts.

## GUESS THE WORD

This is probably one of the oldest games used in language classes and the model has been exploited in more than one commercial game. We divide the class into pairs and give each group a whiteboard. First, each pair has to choose a word and then develop a series of clues in words or phrases that would help the class guess their word (shape, color, what you do with it, where it can be found, noun or verb, living or thing, etc.). The clues cannot use the word itself or any other forms of the word. Students then share all their clues and the class is given 30 seconds to write a guess on their board. Correct answers are worth one point.

Cambridge University Press has developed an excellent website on which English students from around the world can videotape themselves presenting their clues. Not only can the videos be shown in your class but also your students can create their own to be used by an authentic audience of students in many countries. See the Guess What site in the Technology Connections section for more information.

## TELEPHONE

Telephone is a tried-and-true game that has been used for years in language-learning classrooms. We use it by first dividing the class into halves or thirds. We then ask the students seated at the front of each group to come up so that we can whisper a sentence in their ear. They each then go back and whisper it in the next student's ear and so on. The winner is the group that has whispered the message to everyone and the last person comes up to the teacher and correctly repeats the original sentence.

This seldom occurs the first time around. Then the teacher re-whispers the sentence to the student in front and they do it all over again.

There are online games that let students do versions of this telephone game, and teachers can create private virtual rooms so they are playing only with classmates. See the Technology Connections section for information.

**RUNNING DICTATION**

We described running dictation in Strategy 24: Dictation and felt we needed to mention it again here because it is one of our (and our students') favorite games!

## Student Handout and Example

Figure 33.1: Nine Box Grid

## What Could Go Wrong?

The same concerns we share in Strategy 23: Learning Games for Reading and Writing hold true for the ones here—student cheating, noise levels, and prizes. These concerns can all be managed, however—just check out the "What Could Go Wrong" section in Strategy 23 for our suggestions on how to do it.

## Technology Connections

Students can find many online sites, including speaking and listening games, at The Best Sites to Practice Speaking English (http://larryferlazzo.edublogs.org/2008/03/17/the-best-sites-to-practice-speaking-english/).

Sites for sound effects and ideas on how to use them in class can be found at The Best Resources & Ideas for Using Sound Effects in ELL Lessons (http://larryferlazzo.edublogs.org/2017/07/20/the-best-resources-ideas-for-using-sound-effects-in-ell-lessons/).

Learn how your students can create guess-a-word videos and access others at "Guess What" Is a Great "New" Game—Plus ELLs Can Create a Video for an Authentic Audience (http://larryferlazzo.edublogs.org/2016/07/12/guess-what-is-a-great-new-game-plus-ells-can-create-a-video-for-an-authentic-audience/).

Online versions of the telephone game seem to come and go. Drawception (n.d.) (https://drawception.com/) is one that combines the concept with a drawing feature. As new ones come online, we'll be posting them at The Best Online Games Students Can Play in Private Virtual "Rooms" (http://larryferlazzo.edublogs.org/2009/02/10/the-best-online-games-students-can-play-in-private-virtual-rooms/).

## Attribution

Versions of some of these ideas appeared in our book, *The ESL/ELL Teacher's Survival Guide* (Ferlazzo & Sypnieski, 2012, p. 242).

Thanks again to Katie Toppel for the nine box grid game idea.

Thanks to Larissa Albano for her great game, which we call *Question-Answer* (http://larissaslanguages.blogspot.com.es/2017/04/the-dice-game-fun-low-prep-speaking-game.html).

Thanks to Genesis Davies at FluentU (www.fluentu.com/blog/educator-english/esl-listening-games/) for the scavenger hunt idea.

## Figure

| | | |
|---|---|---|
| prey 10 | message 2 | attack 3 |
| predator 4 | recognize 5 | shelter 6 |
| feature 7 | attract 8 | repel 9 |

Partner responses:

Nice job using the word _____ in a sentence.

I don't think you used the word _____ correctly. Try again.

**Figure 33.1** Nine Box Grid *Source:* Reproduced with permission of Katie Toppel.

# PART III

# Additional Key Strategies

## STRATEGY 34

# Differentiation for ELLs in Mainstream Classes

## What Is It?

Many schools are not able to have classes exclusively for ELL students. In those cases, ELLs are in mainstream classes—with or without an ELL co-teacher (see Strategy 38: Co-Teaching). We think most, if not all, of the strategies in this book are useful in mainstream classes and, in fact, use them in *all* of the classes we teach. Good teaching for ELLs is good teaching for all students. In fact, Larry coauthored an article with Ted Appel, our former principal, talking about how our school wanted to get as many ELLs as possible to enroll because their presence challenged our teachers to improve their craft. As they wrote:

> All of our teachers have had to learn how to effectively teach English Language Learners simply because all of our classes have significant numbers of ELLs in them. Graphic organizers, visual supports, cooperative learning, modeling, and accessing prior knowledge are just a few of the instructional strategies that are used school-wide.
>
> Of course, all of these teaching methods are effective with any type of struggling student, whether they are struggling because of language or because of some other challenge.
>
> Our large number of English Language Learners pushed our school and faculty to invest in professional development so that our teachers would learn and refine these skills. Time and resources have been made for extensive in-service training and peer- to-peer support, including observations and weekly "study teams" where groups of teachers meet to enhance their professional practice. (Appel & Ferlazzo)

In our previous books, we have separate chapters devoted to specific strategies English, math, art, social studies, and science teachers can use to make their content more accessible to ELLs. The strategy here is designed to provide a few general suggestions to mainstream teachers who have one or more ELLs placed in their classes.

## Why We Like It

It's a safe bet to say that most English language learner students are *not* in classes exclusively for them most of the time. Given that fact, it's important for those of us who are primarily ELL teachers to be able to offer practical advice to mainstream content teachers. As a graphic we saw in Carol Salva and Anna Matis's book, *Boosting Achievement,* explains, content teachers tend to be trained to use language to teach concepts, whereas ELL teachers use concepts to teach language (p. 58). By combining our expertise, everybody wins!

## Supporting Research

The recommendations we share in the Application section are consistent with extensive research done on differentiation for ELLs in content classes (Baecher, 2011; Dahlman, Hoffman, & Brauhn, n.d.; Ford, n.d.).

## Common Core Connections

The suggestions in this strategy can be used by all content teachers to help their students—ELLs and non-ELLs alike—achieve the Standards they are teaching in each lesson.

## Application

We've divided this section into two parts. In the first dos and don'ts list, we've modified and revised two sections from *The ESL/ELL Teacher's Survival Guide* (Ferlazzo & Sypnieski, 2012, p. 10, 210) to provide a quick summary of the key points we think content teachers should keep in mind when they have ELLs of various levels in their classes.

In the second part, we discuss how mainstream content teachers can handle an unfortunately all-too-common experience—a newcomer with zero or next-to-zero English proficiency being placed in their class.

### DOS AND DON'TS

Here are a few basic best practices that might help teachers respond to the needs of these students. We also feel it is important to include a few worst practices in the hope that they will not be repeated!

**Use Proactive Strategies to Activate and Build Prior Knowledge**

**Do** use the many ways to activate and build prior knowledge we discuss in Strategy 5: Activating Prior Knowledge. These include accessing huge amounts of online resources for many content areas that are available in students' home languages as well as sites that offer multiple versions of the same text provided at different lexile levels. See the Technology Connections section in Strategy 5 and here for links to them.

**Don't** erroneously think that all you have to do to teach ELLs is to speak louder. We understand that all of us are very busy carrying our regular teacher load. However, remember that good ELL teaching is good teaching for everybody. All your students will benefit from your increased attention to the scaffolding required by ELL students.

**Recognize the Many Assets ELL Students Bring to the Table**

**Do** remember all the assets that ELL students bring to the table—they are as intelligent as any other student in your class. ELLs just have a temporary challenge of learning a new language. In addition, they have demonstrated grit and perseverance in their lives, important qualities for success. Look for opportunities when they can model those characteristics to the class as well times their international experiences can contribute to classroom topics.

**Don't** look at ELLs through a lens of deficits. For example, if they come from a country where certain numbers and some mathematical equations are written differently, view it as an opportunity for them to teach your class something new about the world. Don't just view it as a mistake that needs to be corrected.

**Modeling**

**Do** model for students what they are expected to do or produce. This is especially important for new skills or activities. This can be done by explaining and demonstrating the learning actions, sharing your thinking processes aloud, and showing good teacher and student work samples. Modeling promotes learning and motivation as well as increasing student self-confidence—they will have a stronger belief that they can accomplish the learning task if they follow steps that were demonstrated.

**Don't** just tell students what to do and expect them to do it.

**Rate of Speech and Wait Time**

**Do** speak slowly and clearly and provide students with enough time to formulate their responses, whether in speaking or in writing. Remember, they are thinking and producing in two or more languages! After asking a question, wait for a few seconds before calling on someone to respond. This wait time provides all students with an opportunity to think and process and especially gives ELLs a needed period to formulate a response.

**Don't** speak too fast, and if a student tells you he or she didn't understand what you said, never, ever repeat the same thing in a louder voice!

### Use of Nonlinguistic Cues

**Do** use visuals (such as pictures), sketches, gestures, intonation, and other nonverbal cues to make language and content more accessible to students. Teaching with visual representations of concepts can be hugely helpful to ELLs. Use word charts such as the ones recommended in Strategy 4: Vocabulary.

**Don't** stand in front of the class and lecture or rely on a textbook as your only visual aid.

### Giving Instructions

**Do** give verbal *and* written instructions—this practice can help all learners, especially ELLs. In addition, it is far easier for a teacher to point to the board in response to the inevitable repeated question, "What are we supposed to do?"

**Don't** act surprised if students are lost when you haven't clearly written and explained step-by-step directions.

### Check for Understanding

**Do** regularly check that students are understanding the lesson. After an explanation or lesson, a teacher could say, "Please put thumbs up, thumbs down, or sideways to let me know if this is clear, *and it's perfectly fine if you don't understand or are unsure—I just need to know.*" This last phrase is essential if you want students to respond honestly.

Teachers can also have students write answers to specific comprehension questions on a sticky note that they place on their desks or on mini-whiteboards. The teacher can then quickly circulate to check responses.

When teachers regularly check for understanding in the classroom, students become increasingly aware of monitoring their own understanding, which serves as a model of good study skills. It also helps ensure that students are learning, thinking, understanding, comprehending, and processing at high levels.

**Don't** simply ask, "Are there any questions?" This is not an effective way to gauge what all your students are thinking. Waiting until the end of class for students to do a written reflection is not going to provide timely feedback. Also, don't assume that students are understanding because they are smiling and nodding their heads—sometimes they are just being polite!

### Encourage Development of Home Language

**Do** encourage students to use their home language (L1) to support learning in your classroom. Research has found that learning to read in a home language can transfer to increased English acquisition (Ferlazzo, 2017, April 10). These transfers may include phonological awareness, comprehension skills, and background knowledge.

Identify the home languages of your ELL students, make sure you have the appropriate bilingual dictionaries in your classroom, and allow students to access their smartphones to use for translation. Google Translate also lets students takes pictures of, and then translate, writing on the board and textbook pages.

Although the research on transfer of L1 skills to L2 cannot be denied, it doesn't mean that we should not encourage the use of English in class and out of the classroom.

**Don't** ban students from using their home language in the classroom. Forbidding students from using their primary languages does not promote a positive learning environment where students feel safe to take risks and make mistakes. This practice can be harmful to the relationships between teachers and students, especially if teachers act more like language police than language coaches.

### Provide Graphic Organizers and Sentence-Starters

**Do** use the strategies and resources we provide in Strategy 3: Graphic Organizers, Strategy 4: Vocabulary, and Strategy 14: Writing Frames and Writing Structures. Graphic organizers can help all students, and particularly ELLs, organize what they are learning and help them make connections between new and prior knowledge. Sentence starters can help ELLs communicate what they already know.

**Don't** think your secondary students should have already outgrown these kinds of scaffolds and don't think of them as a form of cheating. Scaffolds can be temporary and even Michelangelo needed them in order to paint the Sistine Chapel. View scaffolds as a helpful hand up and not an unjustified handout.

### Note-Taking Strategies

**Do** explicitly teach note-taking strategies. For ELLs in content classes, academic listening is a critical skill that places the heaviest processing demands on students. Providing note-taking scaffolds is a key accommodation teachers can use with their ELLs to help students process new vocabulary. A note-taking scaffold can look similar to a cloze passage and include the most important content with blanks for students to fill in as they listen throughout the lesson. For example, a social studies scaffold sheet might have several lines similar to "was the primary cause of the Civil War." As students gain more experience with academic listening and note-taking, teachers can gradually remove the scaffold or adjust it to include only a few key words.

**Don't** assume that students, including ELLs, know how to take notes during a lesson, when you are talking, or when they are watching a video. And don't assume that they see value in doing so.

### Cooperative and Collaborative Learning Opportunities

**Do** create opportunities for cooperative and collaborative learning. Many of your English-proficient students may be more than willing to provide additional support to ELL students. ELLs may also be more open to asking for help from their classmates.

**Don't** lecture. It's not good for ELLs or for your other students. See the Technology Connections section for links to research documenting its ineffectiveness.

### Videos Showing These Strategies in Action

**Do** take a few minutes and look at a collection of short videos we've put together that demonstrate these instructional strategies and modifications in action. You can find the link in the Technology Connections section.

**Don't** assume you know all the ways to implement these strategies by reading about them in this book and in others.

### NEWCOMER IN CLASS

Although we don't have any hard data on this, we hear enough anecdotes to suspect that this is a very common issue for teachers across the United States: A newcomer with minimal or no English skills is parachuted into a mainstream class and the teacher is just told to integrate the student into his or her instruction—with little support.

Here are some suggestions for how you or your colleagues can help students in this situation.

### Provide Emotional Support

Learn their story—why their family came here, what their interests are, goals they might have for their life. If you cannot speak their home language or can't find another staff person or student who can, using Google Translate is a very viable option. Using the audio translation mode will automatically provide verbal interpretation.

**Provide Academic Support**

Provide access to a computer or tablet (we often will let a student use our teacher computer). If a student has zero or next-to-zero English, the best help any teacher—no matter what subject he or she is teaching—can provide is to support students in developing basic English communication skills. Duolingo, LingoHut, USA Learns, and English Central are the four best online tools for that kind of support (find links to those and other sites in the Technology Connections section). Doing this—for a short time at least—can help these students begin to develop self-confidence, get them familiar with online tools they can also use at home (if they have Internet access there), and give you some time to develop a longer-term plan on how you are going to teach them your content matter and pull together needed resources.

If the newcomer is literate in his or her home language, you can also provide access to online materials in that language that are comparable to what you are teaching in English. Links to many such resources can be found in the Technology Connections section.

If you are fortunate enough to speak your newcomer's language, using the preview, view, and review method is an option (preview the lesson in the home language, then give the main lesson in English, and then review it in the home language). We've also used the bilingual resources listed in the previous suggestion in the same way—previewing and reviewing with those materials.

There are many sites that provide similar high-quality materials on multiple subjects using different levels of English text (some also provide Spanish versions). For example, an article on the electoral college might be edited for three or four different reading levels. Using a high-English-level version of one for most of your students and a simplified version for your newcomer is a fairly easy way to make content accessible. In fact, there are tools that let you do the same for any text you copy and paste into them. You can find links to all these options in the Technology Connections section.

There are a number of content-specific books that are designed to be particularly accessible to ELLs. You can see a link to a few of them that we use in our social studies and English classes in the Technology Connections section as well as where they—and accessible textbooks for other content areas—can be purchased. Providing these textbook alternatives, which likely cover similar subjects to the ones you use with the majority of your students, could be a useful scaffold.

At the very least, make sure you have a bilingual dictionary in your newcomer's home language or let them use one on a smartphone. Google Translate also lets users translate photos by looking at textbook pages or writing on whiteboards.

At our school, seniors often get a class period when they are TAs (teaching assistants) or peer tutors. With support and minimal training from us, a student who doesn't even speak the newcomer's home language can provide invaluable support to him or her. In addition, having the title *peer tutor* can look better on a senior's transcript when applying to college. You can learn more in Strategy 37: Peer Teaching and Learning.

Inductive teaching emphasizes pattern-seeking, which is a skill found to be particularly important to those learning a new language (and it's important for everybody else, too!). If you presently employ inductive methods in your instruction, creating simpler versions of data sets for your newcomer should be fairly easy, though would take a little extra time. If you are not using inductive teaching now, we'd encourage you to consider experimenting with it. Also see Strategy 11: Inductive Learning.

If your newcomer does not have Internet access at home (or even if he or she does), providing him or her with accessible books that can be read at home can be a big help—plenty of research documents the importance of home libraries (Ferlazzo, 2010, May 17b). Our local friends of the library have provided thousands of free books for our newcomer students, and you can also print out many free books available online (see the Technology Connections section for useful sites).

If your school has a specialized class where newcomers learn English, regularly talk with the teacher to learn more about the students and brainstorm how you can both support them in classes. If this teacher is available to co-teach with you, please see Strategy 38: Co-Teaching.

Also, don't forget to turn on the English subtitles feature when watching any videos in class.

### Provide Social Support

Provide a peer mentor to your newcomer—ideally, someone who speaks his or her home language. At our school, peer mentors leave one of their classes for 15 minutes each week to chat with their mentee. You can read more about it in Strategy 37: Peer Teaching and Learning.

Ask individual students who have previously demonstrated empathy to reach out to your newcomer. Perhaps share stories with them of how other students have done the same (see the Technology Connections section for links).

# What Could Go Wrong?

The main answers to this question can be found in the list of don'ts in the Application section. In addition, not everything do you try is going to be wildly effective. When that happens, don't get frustrated and try to keep this story from Larry in mind: Many years ago, he met a man who worked with Mahatma Gandhi in the campaign for Indian independence. The key to Gandhi's success, the man told Larry, "was that he looked at every problem as an opportunity, not as a pain in the butt." We hope that you will look at the challenge of teaching ELLs in the same way—as an opportunity to become a better teacher for all your students.

# Technology Connections

To see short videos of some of these differentiation strategies in action, go to The Best Videos for Content Teachers with ELLs in the Classroom (http://larryferlazzo.edublogs.org/2017/07/14/the-best-videos-for-content-teachers-with-ells-in-their-classes-please-suggest-more/).

Even more ideas on how to help content teachers support ELLs can be found at The Best Sites for Learning Strategies to Teach ELLs in Content Classes (http://larryferlazzo.edublogs.org/2011/09/07/the-best-sites-for-learning-strategies-to-teach-ells-in-content-classes/).

For specific math support, go to The Best Resources for Teaching Common Core Math to English Language Learners (http://larryferlazzo.edublogs.org/2014/11/22/the-best-resources-for-teaching-common-core-math-to-english-language-learners/) and for specific science support, go to The Best Resources for Teaching the Next Generation Science Standards to English Language Learners (http://larryferlazzo.edublogs.org/2014/11/22/the-best-resources-for-teaching-the-next-generation-science-standards-to-english-language-learners/).

Multilingual sites with materials for math, social studies, and science are at The Best Multilingual & Bilingual Sites for Math, Social Studies, & Science (http://larryferlazzo.edublogs.org/2008/10/03/the-best-multilingual-bilingual-sites-for-math-social-studies-science/).

The same text written at different lexile levels is available at a number of sites. Those links can be accessed at The Best Places to Get the "Same" Text Written for Different Levels (http://larryferlazzo.edublogs.org/2014/11/16/the-best-places-to-get-the-same-text-written-for-different-levels/).

Free printable books can be found at The Best Sources for Free & Accessible Printable Books (http://larryferlazzo.edublogs.org/2009/07/31/the-best-sources-for-free-accessible-printable-books/).

Content subject books that are specifically designed to be accessible to ELLs can be found at The Best Places to Buy ESL/EFL Books, Software & Multimedia (http://larryferlazzo.edublogs.org/2009/02/09/the-best-places-to-buy-eslefl-books-software-multimedia/), and our book recommendations for content and ELL classes are at The Best Books for Teaching & Learning ESL/EFL (http://larryferlazzo.edublogs.org/2008/04/19/the-best-books-for-teaching-learning-eslefl/).

Support for students to learn note-taking strategies is at The Best Resources on Effective Note-Taking Strategies (http://larryferlazzo.edublogs.org/2015/06/23/the-best-resources-on-effective-note-taking-strategies-help-me-find-more/).

If you're wondering why we're not big fans of lectures, check out The Best Research Demonstrating That Lectures Are Not the Best Instructional Strategy (http://larryferlazzo.edublogs.org/2014/06/14/the-best-research-demonstrating-that-lectures-are-not-the-best-instructional-strategy/).

For links to help students with little or no English skills that have been placed in a mainstream class, please visit Ways a Mainstream Teacher Can Support an ELL Newcomer in Class (http://larryferlazzo.edublogs.org/2016/11/24/ways-a-mainstream-teacher-can-support-an-ell-newcomer-in-class/).

Links to the sites we recommend for newcomer students can be found at *Larry Ferlazzo—Online Tools* (www.teachingenglish.org.uk/blogs/larry-ferlazzo/larry-ferlazzo-online-tools).

And, if you're still looking for more scaffolding suggestions, go to The Best Resources on Providing Scaffolds to Students (http://larryferlazzo.edublogs.org/2017/01/05/the-best-resources-on-providing-scaffolds-to-students/).

## Attribution

Versions of some of these ideas appeared in our book, *The ESL/ELL Teacher's Survival Guide* (Ferlazzo & Sypnieski, 2012, p. 10, 210).

# *STRATEGY 35*

# Supporting ELL Students with Interrupted Formal Education (SIFEs)

## What Is It?

Students with interrupted formal education (SIFEs), also called *students with limited or interrupted formal education (SLIFEs),* are ELLs who may have very little formal schooling, may not be literate in their home language, or may come from a pre-literate culture (one that does not have a written language or has only recently developed one). This term is also sometimes used to describe students who, though they may face challenges related to missing months or years of schooling, do not necessarily face the more severe issues of the first group.

This strategy will focus on that first group. We are not trying to minimize the challenges faced by this second group of students. Some ways to help them can be found in Strategy 34: Differentiation for ELLs in Mainstream Classes. Those activities, as well as ones discussed in Strategy 36: Culturally Responsive Teaching and Strategy 39: Working with Parents and Guardians, can also be particularly helpful to all SIFEs.

The number of SIFEs entering the United States can come in waves and may vary by location. For example, in 2004 many Hmong came to California and Minnesota when their main refugee camp in Thailand closed. However, the wave of unaccompanied minors who fled gangs in Central America in 2014–2015 went to more geographically dispersed areas. SIFEs, however, are not limited to these groups or time periods—they come from all over the world and continue to arrive here.

## Why We Like It

Even experienced ELL teachers can feel at a loss when working with SIFEs for the first time. We still remember years ago on the first day Larry taught his class of Hmong refugee students. He came to Katie's room after the first period in a panic telling her, "I don't know how to teach students to hold a pencil!" Larry and his students persevered that day and beyond using the strategies here and in other portions of this book. His time with them became the most memorable of his teaching career (his students might or might not characterize them the same way!).

The suggestions in the Application section of this strategy, and in Strategy 34: Differentiation for ELLs in Mainstream Classes, Strategy 36: Culturally Responsive Teaching, and Strategy 39: Working with Parents and Guardians, should provide a good start for teachers who are working with SIFEs for the first time (and may even have some good ideas for more experienced educators, too!).

## Supporting Research

The activities listed here and in Strategies 34, 36, and 39 are consistent with the kind of support researchers have identified that best assist SIFEs in making a successful transition to US schooling (Robertson & Lafond, n.d.) and "SLIFE: Students with Limited or Interrupted Formal Education" (WIDA Consortium, 2015).

## Common Core Connections

We're talking here about assisting adolescents who have minimal or no experience with schooling and who often have had an extensive periods filled with traumatic experiences. We think it's a little ridiculous to talk about meeting Common Core Standards in this situation—these activities are designed to assist our students to get to the point where they can begin to do some of the other activities in this book, which do address the Standards. It's less about building connections to Common Core Standards and more about building connections to basic literacy and an academic mind-set.

## Application

Here are four important ways that we support SIFE students.

### ONLINE SUPPORT

Many of the bilingual and multilingual sites accessible to most English language learners are not usable by many SIFEs because they show a word in a home language and then show it and say it in English. That's not very helpful if you can't read your home language. There are a few learning sites that provide audio and text in English and Spanish. Others show images of actions and objects along with short audio descriptions in English. In addition, there are some sites designed for young English speakers who are just beginning to read that provide limited support to non-literate students. You can find links to these free sites in the Technology Connections section. In addition, there are helpful sites that can assist students as they begin to acquire handwriting skills, and you can find those links in the same place.

## PHONICS INSTRUCTION

We shared in Strategy 11: Inductive Learning how we teach phonics inductively. We think this instructional strategy works for all ages but especially for adolescents because it requires higher-order thinking as they seek, find, and expand patterns. It minimizes the chances of secondary students feeling like they are being treated as young children.

In addition to doing those lessons with SIFEs and others, we also have students do follow-up phonemic awareness activities, particularly onset-rime (writing a word on the board such as *cat* and then changing the first letter so that it turns into different words that students can sound out—*fat, sat, bat,* etc.). Onset-rime is easy for teachers to do, easy for students to understand, and can easily be incorporated into all sorts of reading and writing activities. It can literally just take a few seconds.

We have links in the Technology Connections section to instructions for many phonemic awareness activities and to online exercises students can do to reinforce phonics knowledge.

## HOME LANGUAGE INSTRUCTION

We've previously discussed in Strategy 1: Independent Reading how use of a home language can assist a student's acquisition of a new one. With Spanish-speaking students who are not literate in their home language, we've worked with our supportive Spanish teachers to provide peer tutors to help them gain reading and writing skills in their home language. There are also some, but not many, online sites that can support nonliterate Spanish speakers in learning basic Spanish literacy (see the Technology Connections section). In addition, we have also recruited ELLs and English-proficient students who are fluent in other languages to be peer tutors to SIFEs in their home language.

## ENCOURAGEMENT, PATIENCE, AND SUPPORT

We want to make it very clear that our track record with SIFEs is decidedly mixed. Larry likes to illustrate his effectiveness with SIFEs by retelling a relatively recent story about a heart-to-heart talk he had with Jose at the end of one school year. Jose, who was an unaccompanied minor refugee from Central America, had experienced many challenges in his first year of schooling. As Larry walked with him on his prep period, Jose shared his goals for the following year. "I want to show teachers more respect," he emphasized, "and I want to be more serious about learning." Larry was thrilled and supportive as they walked back to Jose's class. Jose entered and Larry began to walk away. Five seconds later, his teacher walked out with Jose in tow, "Mr. Ferlazzo," she said, "can you talk with Jose? He just walked in and yelled "Hello, b-t-hes, I'm back!"

Unfortunately, Jose dropped out of school shortly afterwards.

His decision is reflective of the high drop-out rate for SIFES in general (WIDA Consortium, 2015, p. 2). Support, including counseling and legal assistance to deal with immigration issues, is critical to helping SIFEs not feel overwhelmed by the many challenges they face.

Fortunately, the legislature in our state of California voted to provide Medi-Cal (the state's name for Medicaid) to all children under the age of 18—whether they are documented or not (Ferlazzo, 2016, April 30). These benefits include mental health services, which are important for many of our SIFEs who suffer from PTSD (post-traumatic stress disorder). So, assuming our school's support staff members can find counselors who speak the home language of our SIFEs, and assuming that they accept Medi-Cal reimbursement (two big assumptions), our students can receive some support through that avenue.

We're also lucky to have nearby law schools with immigration clinics that, depending on how overwhelmed they are at the time, can relieve some additional stress on our students by providing legal representation in immigration courts.

With all of these pressures and the resulting stress, our SIFEs need all the patience and compassion that we teachers have to give. Admittedly, we sometimes fall short—the challenges facing some SIFEs (who may have a very difficult time adjusting to the standards of conduct and the academic mind-set required in schools) may just be too much for them and for us. But the ideas we share here, and the strategies we offer in the rest of the book, increase the odds of success for all of us.

## What Could Go Wrong?

Sometimes the challenges facing SIFEs can seem overwhelming to teachers and students alike. Certainly, our track record with SIFEs is nothing to brag about. However, the recommendations we make in this strategy, remembering the assets these students bring, *and* reminding them of these assets have all helped us and them.

## Technology Connections

For links to language-learning sites accessible to SIFEs (including sites to help non-literate Spanish speakers learn Spanish vocabulary) and for more ways to support them, visit The Best Online Resources for Teachers of Pre-Literate ELL's & Those Not Literate in Their Home Language (http://larryferlazzo.edublogs.org/2008/12/06/the-best-online-resources-for-teachers-of-pre-literate-ells/).

You can find links to step-by-step instructions for teaching phonemic-awareness activities and to online exercises for phonics reinforcement at The Best Articles & Sites for Teachers and Students to Learn About Phonics (http://larryferlazzo.edublogs.org/2011/03/01/the-best-articles-sites-for-teachers-students-to-learn-about-phonics/).

# STRATEGY 36

# Culturally Responsive Teaching

## What Is It?

Although the majority of students in US schools are students of color from linguistically and culturally diverse backgrounds (National Center for Education Statistics, 2017), the vast majority of educators who teach them are white (Rich, 2015). Two of the most-common philosophies guiding how teachers of all races can be better teachers to students of color are *culturally responsive teaching (CRT)* and *culturally sustaining pedagogy*.

CRT, also known as *culturally relevant teaching*, was initially popularized by Gloria Ladson-Billings (1995). CRT isn't a strategy or even a set of strategies; rather, it is a mind-set that underlies and guides everyday classroom practices. Its focus is on validating the cultural learning tools that diverse learners bring to the classroom and leveraging them to effect positive learning outcomes for all students.

Culturally sustaining pedagogy (CSP) is an emerging perspective that builds on the tenets of culturally responsive teaching. This educational stance was first proposed by professor Django Paris (2012),who defines it as a pedagogy that "seeks to perpetuate and foster—to sustain—linguistic, literate, and cultural pluralism as part of the democratic project of schooling." In other words, this concept makes sure our educational practices not only *respond* to the diversity of languages and cultures in our classroom but also that they aim to *sustain* these elements at the center of teaching and learning.

We hope you agree that many of the practices included in this book embody these philosophies.

## Why We Like It

As we've stated many times, looking at ELLs through the lens of assets and not deficits guides what we do in the classroom and the choices we make about how to do it. Instruction that is culturally responsive and sustaining explicitly challenges the deficit perspective. Rather, students are viewed as possessing valuable linguistic, cultural, and literacy tools. Recognizing, validating, and using these tools—in our experience—ultimately provides the best learning environment for our students and ourselves!

## Supporting Research

Much research points to links between culturally responsive teaching and positive learning outcomes for all students (Gay, 2002; Krasnoff, 2016). In addition, recent research has found culturally responsive teaching to be vitally important to educating ELLs with disabilities (University of Kansas, 2017).

## Common Core Connections

Although the focus of culturally responsive teaching isn't on meeting certain Standards, it is on leveraging students' cultural and linguistic tools in order for them to learn at high levels. This learning can meet any number of Standards.

## Application

So what does culturally responsive teaching look like in the ELL classroom? For us, it is an awareness that we try to bring to everything we do. It is a process we are constantly working on as we learn from our students and their experiences. Have we made mistakes along the way? Many. However, like we tell our students, mistakes are opportunities for learning, and we try our best to model this mind-set.

The following section contains several critical questions we ask ourselves when considering how our work with ELLs can be more culturally responsive and sustaining. Although these questions don't cover every aspect of culturally responsive teaching, they do represent foundational best practices we use in our classroom.

### HOW WELL DO I KNOW MY STUDENTS?

In order to build on the rich linguistic and cultural experiences of our students, we must get to know them! This doesn't mean doing interrogations on the first day of school, however. It means building positive relationships with our students so they feel safe sharing their experiences with us. It involves daily interactions with students to learn about their struggles, their joys, and their goals.

It means taking the time to gather information that the school may possess about our students—their English proficiency levels, assessment results, home language surveys, health information, transcripts from previous schooling, and so on. It can also be making time to learn about students' home countries, the conflicts that may be going on there, the cities or towns they come from, and the languages they speak.

Of course, a key factor in knowing our students is getting to know their families as well. See Strategy 39: Working with Parents and Guardians for resources on building connections between home and school.

### DO MY WORDS REFLECT A CULTURALLY RESPONSIVE MIND-SET WHEN I AM TALKING TO STUDENTS AND ABOUT STUDENTS?

One of the simplest ways to honor students' cultural backgrounds and identities is to correctly pronounce their names. Mispronouncing a student's name and not making any attempt to get it right can cause them to feel embarrassed and can heighten their anxiety. Correctly pronouncing a student's name signals respect and a validation of who they are. It is a critical first step in building strong, trusting relationships with students. For more information and research on the value of correctly pronouncing students' names see the Technology Connections section.

As teachers, we also need to be mindful of the words we are using when discussing cultural experiences with students. Characterizing our students' beliefs as "right" or "wrong" through our words or our facial expressions may not only be inaccurate but also removes students from the center of the teaching and learning process. We want students to feel comfortable sharing with each other in order to build a community of learners in which all experiences are valued. As teachers, we can be far more effective in raising questions than in making judgments. At the same time, it is also our job to teach US cultural norms and laws (e.g., equal treatment of women and LGBTQ individuals) and create a classroom environment where everyone feels safe and respected. We can do this by teaching in a way that is cognizant of our students' home cultures, which may or may not promote different perspectives.

For those of us who work in schools located in high-poverty areas, we can often be asked questions by well-meaning people, such as, "How do you do it?" "Aren't you afraid working in that neighborhood?" "How can the students learn when their lives are so crazy?" In these situations, one can feel any number of emotions including anger, frustration, or hopelessness. It can be tempting to tell the stories of our students (the challenges or trauma they have faced) in an attempt to demonstrate their resilience.

Unfortunately, sharing these details can often do more to perpetuate stereotypes than to shatter them. Instead, we can promote culturally sustaining pedagogy by sharing with others the rich cultural and linguistic contributions our students make to our school and to the community.

We must be intentional with our words and in the actions that we discuss in other portions of this Application section. In addition, we must educate ourselves so we truly believe in what we are saying and doing. If we don't, students will see right through us, and we speak from direct experience.

### HOW ARE MY INSTRUCTIONAL PRACTICES CULTURALLY RESPONSIVE?

Many of us have tried to engage our students by dropping a cultural reference into a lesson (mentioning an important person or event from our student's culture). Although it usually gets students' attention, it isn't an instructional practice that can maximize student learning, and it isn't a culturally responsive instructional practice.

Educators, however, *can* increase learning outcomes by teaching in ways that build on the cultural and linguistic experiences of their students. These methods, in turn, lead to increased engagement. Zaretta Hammond, educator and author of the book *Culturally Responsive Teaching and the Brain* (2015), explains this when she states:

> The most common cultural tools for processing information utilize the brain's memory systems—music, repetition, metaphor, recitation, physical manipulation of content, and ritual. The teacher is "responsive" when she is able to mirror these ways of learning in her instruction, using similar strategies to scaffold learning. (Aguilar, 2015)

We can illustrate this point with several simple examples from our classroom. We know that many of our ELL students come from cultural backgrounds that particularly value and practice working together to accomplish tasks (Krasnoff, 2016, p. 13). We mirror this in our instruction by providing daily opportunities for our students to work collaboratively in small groups.

A more-specific example comes from our experience working with Hmong refugees. While in refugee camps, many Hmong women created "story cloths" (embroidery that told stories about their lives). In a series of lessons, our Hmong students created their own hand-drawn versions of story cloths and helped the non-Hmong students to do the same. We then used their creations as springboards to learn the English words needed to talk and write about these stories. Students were more engaged in this language-learning activity because it mirrored, valued, and respected an important part of their home culture.

We have used the process of building on cultural experiences to create language-learning opportunities in many other lessons. These include ones in which students have made presentations about their home cultures (see Strategy 30: Class Presentations) and have done language-learning activities related to their favorite contemporary music (see Strategy 27: Music) and ancient cultural music. In addition, when learning about the elements of feudalism students questioned the textbook authors' claim that it ended hundreds of years ago when, in fact, their families recently experienced it in their own lives. This connection led to high-interest studying of the socioeconomic conditions of various countries as well as direct student communication with textbook authors.

Culturally responsive instruction is ultimately student-centered. It requires the teacher to help students build on their prior knowledge and cultural and linguistic experiences as they are challenged to read, write, speak, and think at high levels. For ELLs, in particular, it requires using best practices, such as modeling, instructional scaffolding, and collaborative learning, just to name a few, to build the language, academic, and critical thinking skills they need to be successful lifelong learners.

See the Technology Connections section for more resources on what culturally responsive instruction looks like in the classroom.

## HOW IS THE CURRICULUM I AM USING CULTURALLY RESPONSIVE?

We, like most teachers, want to have an idea of what we will be teaching before we actually start teaching it! However, culturally responsive teachers must be flexible with their curriculum and allow for modifications based on student interests and experiences. Curriculum that is culturally responsive doesn't mean having to incorporate texts and information about every student's culture into every lesson. It also doesn't mean having a token "multicultural day" once a year to "celebrate" different cultures.

In our experience, culturally responsive curriculum involves the following:

- Trying our best to choose materials that represent diverse cultures and perspectives
- Encouraging students to share their cultural and linguistic knowledge with each other
- Allowing students to choose books they want to read from a diverse classroom library
- Valuing literacy in the home language and English (see Strategy 1: Independent Reading and Strategy 34: Differentiation for ELLs in Mainstream Classes for more on home language use)
- Inviting family and community members to the classroom to share cultural knowledge (see Strategy 39: Working with Parents and Guardians for ideas)
- Using digital content to instantly connect students to cultural and linguistic resources

- Creating lessons on issues directly affecting students' lives, including ones related to current political dynamics that might affect their immigration status or the situation in their home countries (see the Technology Connections section for more information)
- Facilitating open classroom dialogue about the role of race, racism, and religious prejudice (e.g., Islamophobia) in our students' daily lives, including at school (see the Technology Connections section for resources on having these types of conversations with students)

**How Does My Physical Classroom Reflect Diversity?**

When students enter our classrooms each day they receive critical messages about the learning environment and their place in it. Students feel more safe, supported, and valued when they see themselves reflected in the classroom: Do the posters on the walls reflect multiple cultures and languages? Is student work displayed? Are the books in the classroom library written by diverse authors? Do students have access to bilingual dictionaries and books in their home languages? How are the seats arranged? Can students easily move into groups? Considering these questions and others is an important step toward creating a learning environment that values student diversity.

# What Could Go Wrong?

We are not martyrs, nor are we saviors. If you think you are, perhaps you should consider seeking a different profession. We still remember the time one of our former colleagues who lived in a predominantly white, middle-class suburb of Sacramento spoke to students at a school pep rally. He exhorted the students to work hard in class. He continued, "People ask me why I drive all the way down from Roseville to this neighborhood to teach you. It's because I want to help you!" This is not a culturally responsive mind-set. However, it is a mind-set that we have probably had during different times of our career. The important thing is to be aware of our biases, work toward overcoming them, and be open to having them pointed out to us.

There is nothing wrong with wanting to help our students; that's why we are teachers. What *is* wrong is when we educators believe that students need to be fixed and that only we can fix them because *we* are already fixed.

# Technology Connections

For links to many resources on culturally responsive and sustaining pedagogy, see The Best Resources About "Culturally Responsive Teaching" & "Culturally

Sustaining Pedagogy" (http://larryferlazzo.edublogs.org/2016/06/10/the-best-resources-about-culturally-responsive-teaching-culturally-sustaining-pedagogy-please-share-more/).

More resources on the value of correctly pronouncing student names can be found at The Best Resources on the Importance of Correctly Pronouncing Student Names (http://larryferlazzo.edublogs.org/2016/06/11/the-best-resources-on-the-importance-of-correctly-pronouncing-student-names/).

For additional advice on talking with students about race, religious prejudice, and other challenges, see A Collection of Advice on Talking to Students About Race, Police & Racism (http://larryferlazzo.edublogs.org/2016/07/14/a-collection-of-advice-on-talking-to-students-about-race-police-racism/), A Beginning List of the Best Resources for Fighting Islamophobia in Schools (http://larryferlazzo.edublogs.org/2017/03/22/a-beginning-list-of-the-best-resources-for-fighting-islamophobia-in-schools/), and The Best Practical Resources for Helping Teachers, Students & Families Respond to Immigration Challenges (http://larryferlazzo.edublogs.org/2017/02/26/the-best-practical-resources-for-helping-teachers-students-families-respond-to-immigration-challenges/).

# Peer Teaching and Learning

## What Is It?

Our students have a great many abilities, and those can include assisting their classmates acquire language, academic and life-skills knowledge. In several previous strategies, we've included activities in which students have prepared materials and lessons to teach their classmates. This strategy highlights five additional ways we've encouraged our ELL students to act as teachers.

## Why We Like It

We like this strategy for so many reasons! It puts into action the value of looking at our students through the lens of assets instead of deficits; it heightens levels of student engagement; and, as we discuss in the next section, it is exceptionally effective in facilitating learning for the teacher and the student.

## Supporting Research

Researchers have found that knowing you will be teaching others enhances your own learning ability (Washington University, St. Louis, 2014). The results of other studies reinforce this conclusion and suggest that peer tutoring helps the academics of the tutor and the student receiving the assistance. In addition, researchers found that the tutor didn't have to be an academic star in order to be effective (Sparks, 2015).

## Common Core Connections

The Standards being met in this strategy depend on which activity students are doing at the time. All five of the exercises described here meet multiple Standards in all four domains.

# Application

Here are five ways we have facilitated peer teaching and learning with English language learners.

## EMPATHY PROJECT

Luther Burbank High School, where Larry teaches and where Katie formerly taught (she now works at a nearby middle school), has a heavy emphasis on restorative practices and social emotional learning. School administrators made *empathy* a focus of one month and asked Pam Buric, a talented colleague, if she would have her intermediate ELLs write short vignettes about their immigrant experiences (see the Technology Connections section for links to access them). Though they didn't use a graphic organizer to plan their writing, they later used Figure 37.1: Personal Story Outline to teach ELL beginners. This figure represents the same outline used in the intermediate students' stories. After the intermediates completed writing their stories, Pam reserved the library for several periods each day over the course of a week and invited other teachers to sign up for a one-period visit to listen and learn from some of our school's ELLs. The response was overwhelming, and there wasn't enough space or time to accommodate all the interested classes.

Prior to coming to the library, teachers from the visiting classes used the lesson plan in Figure 37.2: Story Sharing and had their students complete the prompt in Figure 37.3: Writing Prompt: Building Empathy. They arrived at the library to find the ELL students seated on one side of various tables. Each student from the listening class arrived with copies of Figure 37.4: Story-Sharing Listening Chart and took a seat across from the ELL students. The students began to tell their stories as the listeners took notes. Every several minutes, the teachers would announce it was time to move, and the listening students moved down a seat in a sort of speed-dating progression. This process took the entire class period. The following day, the ELL class debriefed about the previous day's experience while waiting for a new class to arrive at the library. The listening students also reflected in their own classroom at the same time.

It was universally hailed as a powerful experience by students and faculty members alike and will become a regular occurrence at the school. However, it didn't stop there.

The week after the ELL intermediates completed this exercise at the library, they went into Larry's beginners class. There, using the graphic organizer in Figure 37.1, the intermediates worked one-on-one with the beginner students to help *them* write their own stories (you can find those at a link in the Technology Connections section). Then, while spread between two different classrooms, the beginners did a speed-dating process with the intermediates and told them their stories.

As mentioned previously, the school has made a decision to do this activity annually. However, we are making one change—in the future, the non-ELL students will also be writing their own personal stories (about a challenge that they have faced that may or may not be a story of immigration), which they will share with the ELL students. We feel that making it a reciprocal process will further strengthen our school's sense of community.

## PEER TUTORING

Luther Burbank High School supports juniors and seniors who might ordinarily have a period as a teacher's assistant to consider, instead, becoming a peer tutor (it's an official class on their transcript). Some of these peer tutors are advanced ELLs, others are proficient bilinguals, and others are English-only students. Peer tutors don't necessarily have to speak the home language of our ELL beginning and intermediate students. One thing they all share, however, is a desire to help ELLs.

Sometimes this help means circulating around the class as we are teaching and stepping in to assist students who are experiencing challenges with the lesson. Other times it's working intensively one-to-one with a new arrival to the school. Or, they might assist students in an after-school course designed to provide additional support to ELLs.

All these situations begin with the peer tutors watching a brief video created by English teacher Carol Salva sharing suggestions on how volunteers can assist ELLs (a link to it can be found in the Technology Connections section). We also take a few seconds at the beginning of each class to brief them on the upcoming lesson and quickly debrief after class, with periodic instructions in between.

During times when they are working with ELLs more independently, the peer tutors are given more specific instructions and debriefings are more complete. In those cases, they do some combination of these tasks:

- Following-up with projects being done in the class that they have not completed
- Practicing English conversations (see Strategy 25: Conversation Practice)
- Playing games (see Strategy 23: Learning Games for Reading and Writing and Strategy 33: Learning Games for Speaking and Listening)
- Having students complete worksheets reinforcing what we are doing in class (see the Technology Connections section for sources of free—and high-quality—ELL worksheets)

Sometimes, we're lucky enough to get a peer tutor who exceeds expectations and who has a special talent for the job. For example, one of our former peer tutors is presently in a teacher credential program, and her abilities were obvious even when she was in high school. In those cases, when the peer tutor is extremely enthusiastic and wants to try out some of his or her own ideas, we're very open to it. We want ELL students to be excited about learning English, and few things can be more effective at doing that than having a talented peer tutor who is excited about teaching them!

## PEER MENTORING

Having peer mentors, especially for ELL newcomers, enhances student-to-student relationships and provides needed support. Peer *mentors* are distinguished from peer *tutors* by the fact that their job is not to assist with daily academic tasks. Instead, mentors are there to provide overall school and life counsel. Older (though that is not always the case) trained student mentors who are ELL intermediates or mainstream students meet weekly with their mentees to build relationships, discover problems (at school and at home), offer advice, and regularly strategize with teachers on how they can best be helpful.

See Figure 37.5: Peer Mentor Guidelines for an example of the kind of training these mentors receive from us. The mentor and mentee are excused from one of their classes for at least 15 minutes each week to take a walk around the school campus and chat about their experiences. Ideally, mentors also meet all together with teachers once every two weeks during lunch to share their experiences.

## SISTER CLASSES

Dialogue journals are a well-known practice in ELL classrooms (VanderMolen, 2011) in which students typically write letters to their teachers in notebooks, and teachers then respond back, often by including some recast sentences (ones that were originally written by their students with mistakes and are now rewritten correctly by the teacher in their response). They can be a very effective learning tool. However, we can't imagine how any secondary teacher can find the time to do them.

But that doesn't mean we can't modify the idea and use it in our classrooms. We periodically use dialogue journals with the difference being that we arrange with the teacher of a mainstream class to have his or her students agree to be journal partners with our ELLs. In these cases, the mainstream teacher recognizes the benefits that his or her students gain from being teachers and recasting sentences as well as the opportunity to learn about the lives of ELL students.

We've found that this kind of activity works best when all students write using pseudonyms for the first few weeks, each writing in the dialogue journal once each week. This anonymity creates an air of suspense and mystery that culminates in a joint social gathering with food that occurs either during class time or during a special lunch when identities are unveiled. Dialogue journals continue for a few more weeks afterwards, but we end it while enthusiasm is still high—we would recommend a two-month period of time at most. However, the relationships that students gain during the process often continue through the rest of the school year and beyond.

These kinds of sister classes don't have to be restricted to the physical location of your school. Larry's ELL geography classes often connect with English classes in the regions of the world they are studying. Typically, after learning about a country, Larry's students will videotape themselves asking questions about the country they are studying and post them on their class blog. Then, an English class in that country will videotape themselves responding to those questions and posing their own questions about life in the United States. Larry's students respond, and then this short and sweet project is done. You can find links in the Technology Connections section for ways to find classes around the world who might be interested in doing this kind of activity with your school.

## EVERYONE IS A TEACHER

We regularly emphasize that our class is a learning community and that we all need to help each other learn. One day, however, we made this idea more of a central focus to our lesson. We explained to our students that English is hard to learn (no surprise to them!), they only had a few years of high school left, and that it was going to take more than one or two teachers to help everybody learn. So, we all had to be teachers. We shared some ideas to illustrate the concept ("I'm a teacher when I speak English because I'm an example"; "I'm a teacher when I come to school because I'm a model for others") and then invited students to contribute other ideas. They came fast and furious, and students made posters such as the one in Figure 37.6: Everyone Is a Teacher Poster.

Students took it seriously on different levels, but there was clearly one huge benefit—it was far more energizing to students and to us if we said to an off-task student "Everyone is a teacher!" instead of saying "Angela, please get back to work."

We also created a simple form listing the actions the class had determined they could do as teachers and had them glue it in their writer's notebook (see Figure 37.7: Everyone Is a Teacher Goal-Setting Chart). Each Friday, students graded themselves on how they had done in that area during the previous week, but we didn't look at it. We had students share their grades with a partner of their choice and also identify one—just one—area they wanted to improve on in the coming week. They then shared that goal with the entire class.

Though we made it clear that the grades were for their own personal assessments, we found that many students made a point of showing it to us—they were proud of their honesty in the self-assessment. See Figure 37.8: Example of Student-Completed Goal Chart for an example.

We've tried lots of goal-setting strategies over the years, but this appears to be among the most effective, if not *the* most effective.

## Student Handouts and Examples

Figure 37.1: Personal Story Outline

Figure 37.2: Story Sharing

Figure 37.3: Writing Prompt: Building Empathy

Figure 37.4: Story-Sharing Listening Chart

Figure 37.5: Peer Mentor Guidelines

Figure 37.6: Everyone Is a Teacher Poster

Figure 37.7: Everyone Is a Teacher Goal-Setting Chart

Figure 37.8: Student Example of Goal-Setting Chart

## What Could Go Wrong?

Peer tutors are not teachers, no matter how competent they may appear to be at times. Don't dump too much responsibility on them. And keep them happy—encouraging words and special treats now and then can't hurt (we also always pay their way when we go on field trips)! Remember, they are not getting paid to be tutors.

## Technology Connections

To learn more about the empathy project and to read our students' stories—which you can feel free to use as models with your students—visit What ELLs Taught Our School in a Week-Long Empathy Project (http://larryferlazzo.edublogs.org/2017/04/21/guest-post-what-ells-taught-our-school-in-a-week-long-empathy-project/).

See the video created by Carol Salva that we show our peer tutors about how they can best assist ELLs at This Is a Must-Watch Video for Any Volunteer Or Peer Tutor Working with ELLs (http://larryferlazzo.edublogs.org/2017/06/17/this-is-a-must-watch-video-for-any-volunteer-or-peer-tutor-working-with-ells/).

To find free—and good—worksheets peer tutors can use with ELLs, go to The Best Sites for Free ESL/EFL Hand-Outs & Worksheets (http://larryferlazzo.edublogs.org/2009/02/18/the-best-sites-for-free-eslefl-hand-outs-worksheets/).

See how Larry's ELL geography classes work with sister classes around the world at Links to the Joint Projects My ELL Geography Class Did with Classes Around the World—Want to Join Us This Year? (http://larryferlazzo.edublogs.org/2015/08/01/links-to-the-joint-projects-my-ell-geography-class-did-with-classes-around-the-world-want-to-join-us-this-year/).

If you'd like to connect with classes in different countries and do similar projects, check out The Best Ways to Find Other Classes for Joint Online Projects (http://larryferlazzo.edublogs.org/2009/05/30/the-best-ways-to-find-other-classes-for-joint-online-projects/).

There are many other ways students can help their classmates learn, and you can find them at The Best Posts on Helping Students Teach Their Classmates (http://larryferlazzo.edublogs.org/2012/04/22/the-best-posts-on-helping-students-teach-their-classmates-help-me-find-more/).

# Attribution

Thanks to our colleague Nichole Scrivner for letting us reprint her materials and to Pam Buric for letting us tell her story.

Thanks to Carol Salva for creating the video we show our peer tutors about how they can assist ELLs to best learn English.

# Figures

Name: _____

Summary of Event:

Emotions Involved:

When:

Who Else Was Involved:

Where:

What Happened:

First:

Second:

Third:

Fourth:

Conclusion (Includes What I Learned):

**Figure 37.1**    Personal Story Outline

## Message to the Visiting Teacher

Thank you for bringing your classes to visit our students. Please prepare your student listeners on the following *before* their visit:

- Instruct them to use active listening—being a respectful and engaged audience; using eye contact, leaning in, nodding and responding, and so on.

- For each student they visit, they will take notes in one of the boxes on their graphic organizer (please remind them to bring a pen or pencil).

- After the student is done telling his or her story, the visiting listener should ask one or two questions. A list of possible conversation starters is provided on the graphic organizer. The idea is to engage in conversation and build relationships. Please review the graphic organizer's layout and preread the possible prompts with your students so that they are prepared for these interactions.

- **Discussion About Empathy.** The students sharing their stories are taking a huge risk. Discuss being empathetic about language and speech issues, as well as about the content of the shared story. (Prewriting activity for building empathy follows in Figure 33.3.)

**Figure 37.2** Story Sharing *Source:* Reproduced with permission of Nichole Scrivner.

(To be done *pre*-visit. Have students journal write and then discuss as class.)

Imagine yourself suddenly and unexpectedly in a new country. You've left your home, friends, and some members of your family behind. Everyone around you speaks a brand-new language, celebrates different cultural holidays, and practices different customs.

Now imagine being in that situation and then being asked to share a sensitive story about your past to a total stranger in your new school.

- How might you feel in this situation?
- How would your ideal listener behave while listening to your story? What might he or she do or say? How might he or she respond?
- What would help you feel comfortable and safe?

**Figure 37.3** Writing Prompt: Building Empathy *Source:* Reproduced with permission of Nichole Scrivner.

**Listener's Name**:_____

Conversation Starters:

- How do you feel about . . . (ask something related to the story you heard or anything else that comes to mind)?
- What are your favorite . . . (hobbies, interests, musical tastes, sports, classes, books, etc.)?
- Can you share something about your home country (culture, music, food, sports, customs, etc.)?
- How does the current political climate make you feel? What about your family?
- Do you feel safe and comfortable at [name of school]? If so, why? If not, what could be done to make you feel more comfortable?

| Name of storyteller: |
| :--- |
| One thing I found interesting . . . |
| Notes on our conversation: |

| Name of storyteller: |
| :--- |
| One thing I found interesting . . . |
| Notes on our conversation: |

**Figure 37.4** Story-Sharing Listening Chart *Source:* Reproduced with permission of Nichole Scrivner.

1. Meet with your mentee at least one time each week for at least 15 minutes. Talk with Mr. Ferlazzo about the best time to meet with her or him, and Mr. Ferlazzo will make arrangements with teachers.

2. First, get to know your mentee—ask about his or her lives, families, interests, goals. Share your own stories him or her, too. It's especially important for them to hear from you about your challenges (especially if you have moved to a new school or country) and what has helped you overcome them.

3. Some questions to regularly ask your mentee could include these:

   • What have been the best things that have happened to you this week—in and out of school?

   • What have been the biggest challenges or problems you've face this week—in and out of school?

   • What classes are you doing well in, and what classes are you having problems in? What are some things you can do to help deal with those problems?

   • Do you feel like anyone is bullying you or making fun of you?

   • Are there any questions you have about the school or life in the United States?

4. Check in with Mr. Ferlazzo each week so he can let you know if he has suggestions about topics to discuss with your mentee—for example, if your mentee has done something particularly well in class or if he or she seems to having some specific challenges. You can also let Mr. Ferlazzo know if you learned anything helpful from your mentee—for example, if he or she feels like a class is too difficult for him or her or if your mentee has a suggestion about how Mr. Ferlazzo or another teacher can do something different that would help.

5. If your mentee shares something that makes you feel worried or uncomfortable (e.g., if you feel like your mentee might be in danger), please notify Mr. Ferlazzo or another teacher immediately.

**Figure 37.5**  *Peer Mentor Guidelines*

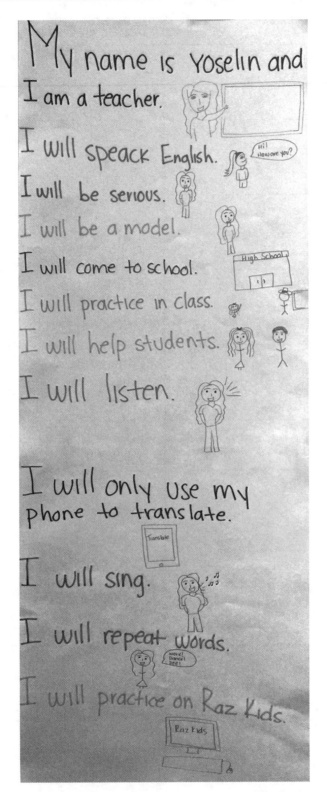

**Figure 37.6**  Everyone Is a Teacher Poster

| | Date: | Date: | Date: | Date: |
|---|---|---|---|---|
| I will speak English. | | | | |
| I will be serious. | | | | |
| I will be a model. | | | | |
| I will come to school. | | | | |
| I will practice in class. | | | | |
| I will help students. | | | | |
| I will listen. | | | | |
| I will only use my phone to translate. | | | | |
| I will sing. | | | | |
| I will repeat words. | | | | |
| I will practice Raz-Kids. | | | | |

**Figure 37.7** Everyone Is a Teacher Goal-Setting Chart

March 24

| I will speak English. | B | |
| I will be serious. | D | |
| I will be a model. | f | |
| I will come to school. | D | |
| I will practice in class. | A | |
| I will help students. | B | |
| I will listen. | C | |
| I will only use my phone to translate. | A | |
| I will sing. | B | |
| I will repeat words. | A | |
| I will practice Raz-Kids. | C | |
| | | |
| | | |
| | | |

**Figure 37.8** Student Example of Goal-Setting Chart

*STRATEGY 38*

# Co-Teaching

## What Is It?

Many ELL teachers are in situations in which they either go into a class to support students when a content teacher is teaching or pull ELLs out to support content instruction. This practice is often done when a school doesn't have enough beginning and intermediate ELLs to financially justify having courses exclusively for them or when schools believe that this form of instruction is best for their students.

## Why We Like It

We have actually applied every other strategy in this book multiple times in our own classrooms. The only times, however, when we have co-taught classes were when we did it with each other. Having two veteran ELL educators co-teach exclusively ELL classes is rare, and our experience is unlikely to be similar to what most ELL teachers face.

Unlike some who write on education issues, we do not feel comfortable writing about situations we know little about. So we have invited veteran ELL co-teacher Carlota Holder to share some of her experiences. You can also find links to additional co-teaching resources in the Technology Connections section.

## Supporting Research

Substantial research supports the recommendations included in this strategy. There are many different kinds of co-teaching models, and all have their own advantages and disadvantages (Burgess, 2011; Hendrickson, 2011; Honigsfeld & Dove, 2008).

## Common Core Connections

When an ELL educator is co-teaching in content classes, he or she is responsible for working with his or her colleague in supporting ELL students to access the Standards in that content area.

# Application

This section was written by Carlota Holder. Carlota is an English language learner coordinator and master teacher for Enlace Academy on the west side of Indianapolis. She just began her second year in this role and her tenth year of experience with English language learners. Her grade-level experience ranges from kindergarten to eighth grade with English language and Spanish instruction. Her roles have ranged from ELL assistant, ELL teacher, sheltered instruction observation protocol (SIOP) co-teacher, ELL coach, and Spanish teacher.

### CO-TEACHING DON'TS AND DOS

Having finally graduated from my ELL courses in grad school, I never knew that I'd be going into a field in which most of my instruction would be taking place with a co-teacher. Who would have thought? I began working with ELL students as an instructional assistant pushing into classrooms, and I was lucky enough to have mentors let me assist and observe their ELL classes. Then I became a teacher who was responsible for ELL students in a completely different environment—a co-teaching one. No one taught me how to co-teach. Here's what I have learned:

- Don't assume that the teachers with whom you're co-teaching have background knowledge on second language acquisition.
- Do help them learn through trial and error. This will help them build their background knowledge and shows that you trust them and their content.

  I have wanted to tell teachers how to teach their materials to *our* students many times, but I learned the hard way that this was not the most-effective communication strategy. Instead, let teachers achieve successes and make mistakes. Jump in and say, "I like how you did . . . , maybe next time we could do . . ." Then, add second-language acquisition data to support your suggestion. I would often take what they had developed back to my classroom and play with it. I would remake it with the suggestions I gave them and attach it in a follow-up e-mail. This practice also showed my co-teacher that I was willing to put in hard work to improve instruction for everyone.

- Don't refer to students as *my* students when talking with your co-teachers.

- Do refer to students as *our* students when talking with your co-teachers.

How many times do we refer to our students as *my* students? However, it is important that you refer to students as *our* students when you're in a co-teaching situation. In a co-teaching situation you are working toward the same goal: to improve the language and content knowledge of *all* students. You are both responsible for their education. This action acknowledges that you're working as a team.

- Don't avoid planning and collaboration.

- Do take time to plan and collaborate.

Complaints I sometimes hear from co-teachers include "My school doesn't give me time to plan and collaborate with my co-teachers" or "I don't have time to plan and collaborate with my co-teachers." A supportive school would give you time, but we live in the real world. Try to eat lunch with your co-teacher and collaborate. Stay an extra half-hour after school to make plans together or offer to visit them on their prep. You could even collaborate off campus with some margaritas. (You'll be surprised how much you can get done!) Planning and collaboration can begin to happen digitally after you have broken the ice in person. You can then start sharing your plans and assignments electronically. Google Drive is the best collaborative resource to ever exist! If planning and collaboration can't happen physically, be sure to use whatever you can digitally and continue to be persistent and patient.

- Don't allow one teacher to take all the responsibilities for instruction.

- Do share responsibilities for instruction.

Your co-teacher is an expert in his or her content area and you are an expert in language acquisition. Together, you can make a phenomenal team. Share responsibilities with each other. Offer to do some grading. Offer to make assignments for certain groups of students. My favorite is offering to make visual supports for my teachers. I tell them my ideas and then ask for their advice on the content portion, because I am not the content expert. I want my supports to be valuable, not only to our students but also to my co-teacher. This way we can build our resources and continue to use them year after year.

- Don't undermine the other teacher's authority or question the teacher in front of students.

- Do treat each other as equals in the classroom.

We want to model respectful relationships in front of our students. I had a co-teacher once who was very set in her ways. We had 100-minute English language arts blocks and she refused to let any student go to the bathroom for any reason. I did not agree with that policy—if a student needs to go, then a student needs to go. One day I decided to let one of our students use the bathroom. On her return I was reprimanded in front of the *entire class,* as if I were a student. Thankfully, this co-teaching "relationship" only lasted a year.

- Don't force it.
- Do keep trying!

If you have the power to choose your co-teacher, find someone who is willing to *learn* and keep trying. Not everything you do will work. It's a fail-and-learn process.

Thankfully, there's a book with seven different co-teaching styles that you can try and has a plethora of resources: *Collaboration and Co-Teaching* by Andrea Honigsfeld and Maria G. Dove (2010). There are also many ELL teachers to connect with on Twitter on other social media platforms. *Together* we can meet and exceed the high expectations we set for our English language learners.

## Technology Connection

You can find lots of additional information at The Best Resources on Co-Teaching with ELLs (http://larryferlazzo.edublogs.org/2017/07/07/the-best-resources-on-co-teaching-with-ells-please-suggest-more/).

## Attribution

Thanks to Carlota Holder for contributing her recommendations! A version of her don'ts and dos originally appeared at Co-Teaching Dos and Don'ts (2017, August 1b, http://larryferlazzo.edublogs.org/2017/08/01/guest-post-co-teaching-dos-and-donts/).

# STRATEGY 39

# Working with Parents and Guardians

## What Is It?

Parents or guardians can be critical partners in supporting ELLs. Unfortunately, it's not unusual for ELL family members to be working multiple jobs. This kind of schedule and economic pressure can be a barrier to traditional family involvement in a school's physical location, but it does not diminish a family's commitment to supporting their children in academic success. In addition, the prior school experience of the parents or guardians, including how schools and teachers were viewed in their home countries, can provide further obstacles to effective engagement. As a result of this experience, some parents of ELLs might feel reticent to ask questions or make suggestions about their child's academic work (Smith, 2005).

Another potential issue is that sometimes our students are not living with their parents. Instead, they may be living with an older sibling or an aunt or uncle who does not necessarily have the same kind of parental relationship with them. When we use the word *parent* in this strategy, we are including this broader definition.

The recommendations we share in the Application section take all of these challenges into account.

## Why We Like It

In our work with families, we always try to keep in mind the difference between *parent involvement* and *parent engagement*.

Simply put, parent involvement is often more of a *doing to* and engagement is a *doing with*. When emphasizing involvement, schools tend to lead with their *mouths*—generally telling parents what they should be doing. Engagement, however, has schools leading with their *ears*. By listening to parents' ideas, and by eliciting from them what they have found works best with their children, school staff members can develop more genuine partnerships that are helpful to young people. We have gained great insight over the years by asking parents a simple question: "Can you please tell me about the times in your child's life that he or she has seemed to be learning the most and working hard in school, and what you think his or her teacher was doing at that time to encourage it?"

Another example of parent involvement is a school's focus on *communication*, which is often one-way. Schools across the country emphasize sending sheets of information home (which often do not arrive or, if they do, can be in a language that parents don't understand) and using automated phone calls. Engagement tries to use two-way *conversation*, through efforts such as making home visits and phone calls that don't necessarily happen only when there's a problem with a child.

During Larry's 19-year community-organizing career, he often talked about the difference between irritation and agitation—we irritate people when we challenge them to do something about what *we* are interested in, and we agitate people when we challenge them to act on *their* interests. Involvement often leans toward irritation—schools might have a predetermined and limited list of ways they want parents to help, such as making copies, organizing bake sales, and so on. Engagement, instead, looks through the lens of agitation and emphasizes discovering the parents' interests and goals. See the story of Burbank High School's home computer project in the Application section to get an idea of results that can come from agitation.

Another important difference is that there is a tendency with involvement to focus solely on improving what goes on within the four walls of the school whereas, in engagement, there is recognition that the school must be participating as an institution in neighborhood-wide improvement efforts. This kind of engagement acknowledges the fact that many of the elements affecting student academic achievement have their roots outside of the classroom.

All the suggestions in the Application section fall under the engagement category.

## Supporting Research

Years of research have demonstrated the importance of family engagement to student academic achievement (Ferlazzo, 2011, October 30). This kind of engagement can mean parents participating in activities on the school site and supporting their children's school work at home. This same research highlights the benefits of *engagement* over *involvement*.

## Common Core Connections

Looked at in one way, parent engagement has no specific connection to any Common Core Standards. Looked at in a different way, it can be critical to every one of them. We'll leave it up to you and your administrator to look at the research, reflect on your experience, and decide which of those perspectives you should take.

# Application

Our parent engagement efforts have fallen into three primary categories over the years: communicating with parents, supporting them in the challenges they face, and inviting them to participate in our classroom learning.

### COMMUNICATING WITH PARENTS

Communicating with parents of our students is a key element of family engagement. This can be a particular challenge for teachers of ELLs who do not speak the home language of their students.

Schools are required by federal law (Mathewson, 2016; US Department of Justice and US Department of Education, 2015) to communicate "essential information" effectively with immigrant parents, so schools must bring in bilingual staff members or contracted interpreters for critical meetings such as ones related to a child's future (discipline issues, evaluation for special needs, etc.), as well as having important documents professionally translated into the parents' home language. Depending on your school district's policies, "essential information" may or may not include the kind of regular communication many teachers want to have with the parents of their students.

There are several ways we try to work around this obstacle. One way is to use Google Translate or one of the many other tools that are available to assist schools in communicating with parents who speak languages other than English. See the Technology Connections section for links to those resources.

Even if we do not fluently speak the home language of our students' parents, we can certainly learn a few words. Being able to say "hello," "We love having your child in our class," and "good-bye" in what is likely to be a poorly accented and garbled version of their language can go a long way toward beginning to build a trusting relationship.

Home visits to the parents of ELL students (with an interpreter if the teacher doesn't speak their home language) are another excellent way to build communication and relationships. Our local teachers union helped begin the national Parent-Teacher Home Visit Project, which you can learn more about through links in the Technology Connections section.

During one home visit Larry made to an immigrant family, the father spoke at length about how thrilled he was at our use of the Internet at school to help his daughter learn English. He explained how he wished he could afford a computer and web connection at his house so the entire family could learn, too. Instead of just listening politely and leaving (and forgetting), or going back to see if our school could organize such a program for parents, Larry asked him if he knew other parents who felt the same and if he would be willing to organize a meeting of them to see if there might be something we could do together. He agreed, and then parents worked with our school to develop a project that provided free home computers and Internet service to immigrant families. It was later named one of the most effective uses of technology to teach reading in the world by the International Literacy Association. See the Technology Connections section for more information on this project.

Even if your district does not have a large number of materials available for parents in their home languages, there are many other sources of these kinds of important resources. See the Technology Connections section for links to multilingual explanations of the Common Core Standards, requirements that districts have to meet to provide resources to English language learners (including those with special needs), and videos and written materials about how their children can further pursue their academic career beyond high school.

Finally, parents who do not speak English may have questions about how they can best support their children's academic work. A message we consistently give to parents is that asking their children questions about what they are doing in school, making sure they have time and a place to study at home, regularly encouraging them to have big dreams for their future, and discussing the issues going on in the world around them are all extraordinarily effective actions that parents can take—whether they speak English or not.

## SUPPORTING PARENTS

Many parents of ELLs are experiencing challenges in their lives. Here are a few ways we try to support them.

Parent academies are increasing in popularity across the country. This is when schools organize classes for parents where they are taught about how schools work. At schools where involvement takes the lead (remember our discussion of *involvement* versus *engagement*), the curriculum for these classes is often predetermined by the school, and classes are led and taught by school staff members. Compare that to the multilingual parent academy at Burbank High School, which regularly attracts 100 participants.

Families work with the parent coordinator to identify topics that should be covered—which might or might not be focused on the school (e.g., the citizenship process was one recent topic)—run the meetings, and own the entire project. You can learn more through the Technology Connections section.

Of course, it's not that uncommon for schools to sponsor adult English classes for parents of their students. Because schools are often in the neighborhoods where their ELL students live, having an accessible location for these educational opportunities can be very convenient for their parents.

Last, the changing political climate can create pressures and stresses for ELL families. Schools and districts can help in different ways. For example, our Sacramento City Unified School District launched a Safe Haven program to support undocumented students and their families. This effort includes informing them of their rights and publicizing the contributions they have made and are making to our community (Ferlazzo, 2017, March 8).

### INVITING FAMILIES TO PARTICIPATE IN CLASSROOM LEARNING

We always seek way to involve families in our classroom learning. One year, we invited a father who created Hmong flutes to show our class how he made them. When we are studying the US Civil War, we often have students interview family members about civil wars in their home countries. In addition, we ask students to interview their family as part of participating in the StoryCorps program that stores the recordings in the Library of Congress.

The Technology Connections section contains links to scores of other ideas on how teachers can encourage students to leverage the funds of knowledge held by their families for learning in the classroom.

## What Could Go Wrong?

It's not easy for overworked teachers to find time to communicate with families. We've got our hands full with everything we have to do in the classroom! We will be the first to admit that family engagement sometimes falls off the radar for us, too. All we can do is fit it in when we can, and we always find the benefits outweigh the time costs.

It can be easy for teachers to rely on students to carry the burden of translation for their parents. Do everything within your power to resist that choice and, instead, push your school to provide professional assistance. On occasion, however, absent that professional support, we *might* ask a student to help interpret informal *positive* feedback from us about his or her work to the parent (e.g., "Xeng worked very hard on his presentation and it showed. It was excellent!"). We would *never* use a student to communicate behavior or academic concerns or official school information or policy.

## Technology Connections

For many related resources, including suggested apps teachers can use to communicate with immigrant parents, visit The Best Parent Engagement Resources for Immigrant Families (http://larryferlazzo.edublogs.org/2017/08/06/the-best-parent-engagement-resources-for-immigrant-families/).

To learn more about teachers making home visits, and to learn about the home computer project that came out of our visits, check out The Best Resources for Learning About Teacher Home Visits (http://engagingparentsinschool.edublogs.org/2011/10/10/the-best-resources-for-learning-about-teacher-home-visits/) and The Best Resources for Learning About Schools Providing Home Computers & Internet Access to Students (http://larryferlazzo.edublogs.org/2011/03/19/the-best-resources-for-learning-about-schools-providing-home-computers-internet-access-to-students/).

Multilingual resources accessible to immigrant parents can be found at The Best Multilingual Resources for Parents (http://engagingparentsinschool.edublogs.org/2013/05/16/the-best-multilingual-resources-for-parents/).

Information on effective parent academies is at My Best Posts on Parent "Academies" & "Universities" (http://engagingparentsinschool.edublogs.org/2013/02/23/my-best-posts-on-parent-academies-universities/).

For additional resources on ways schools can support immigrant families, visit The Best Practical Resources for Helping Teachers, Students & Families Respond to Immigration Challenges (http://larryferlazzo.edublogs.org/2017/02/26/the-best-practical-resources-for-helping-teachers-students-families-respond-to-immigration-challenges/).

You can find lots of suggestions on how to involve families in student homework at The Best Places Where Students—and/or Their Families—Can Tell Their Immigration Story (http://larryferlazzo.edublogs.org/2016/10/12/the-best-places-where-students-can-tell-their-andor-their-families-immigration-story/) and at The Best Student Projects That Need Family Engagement (http://engagingparentsinschool.edublogs.org/2014/02/09/the-best-student-projects-that-need-family-engagement-contribute-your-lessons/).

## Attribution

Portions of this section originally appeared in "The Difference Between Parent 'Involvement' & Parent 'Engagement,'" *Education Week* (http://blogs.edweek.org/teachers/classroom_qa_with_larry_ferlazzo/2012/03/response_the_difference_between_parent_involvement_parent_engagement.html).

*STRATEGY 40*

# Learning Stations

## What Is It?

Learning stations, also called *interactive stations,* usually involve small groups of students rotating through several areas in different parts of the classroom and completing various activities at each one.

## Why We Like It

Whenever we can incorporate movement, variety, and student collaboration into our lesson, we see positive results. Learning stations accomplish these three goals along with many others. They can be used in a variety of ways—to practice targeted language skills, deepen content knowledge, apply new vocabulary, review and reinforce previously taught concepts and language, assess student understanding, and so on.

## Supporting Research

Learning stations can promote student motivation and the development of reading comprehension, language, and writing skills (Just Read, Florida!, n.d.). By allowing for differentiation (either multilevel tasks at each station or different stations for different students), learning stations can be an effective instructional tool (Movitz & Holmes, 2007).

## Common Core Connections

Learning stations can be designed to support any number of Standards in all four domains.

# Application

We use learning stations for two main reasons. One reason is to get students moving and working together in order to spice things up. Another reason is to provide small-group instruction—stations enable us to work with a small group while everyone else is engaged at the other stations.

For both purposes, we ask ourselves the following questions to guide our planning:

- Do we have classroom management strategies in place so we can even attempt this strategy (e.g., Does this class have a good track record of working independently and following directions? Do most of the students listen to us most of the time?)?

- What is the purpose for each station? What will students be practicing (e.g., speaking a dialogue, reading a text and doing a graphic organizer, playing a word game, doing listening practice on the computer)?

- How will students be grouped (e.g., mixed levels of English proficiency, how many students per group)? How many stations will we have?

- How long will students need at each station (usually anywhere from 5 to 15 minutes)?

- What materials will be needed at each station (e.g., handouts, electronic devices, texts, art materials, bilingual dictionaries, highlighters)?

- How will we provide instructions (e.g., whole-group, written steps at each station, teacher modeling of the activities at each station, peer tutor facilitators at some stations)?

- What will students produce at each station and how will we assess their progress (e.g., written responses on paper, audio recording, online content, group posters, short presentations)?

After answering these questions, we've also found it helpful to sketch out each station on a piece of paper and make a map for ourselves. For each station, we write the activity, the time limit, the materials needed, and which students will be starting at each station. Because one of the stations usually involves computer time, we have to schedule our station day when we have access to our school's laptops. If you only have one computer, students at that station could watch a short, closed-captioned instructional video at a reduced volume and complete a follow-up activity together.

The first few times we do stations, we might also have students draw a similar map to familiarize them with the process the day before the stations activity. We model the activities students will be doing and assign them to their initial stations. Then, when students enter the next day, desks can be grouped into stations and numbered (we use a large sticky note posted on each desk), and students know where to go and how to get started.

If we feel like we have classroom management under control and students are familiar with the stations process, we are then able to turn one of the stations into small-group instruction with the teacher. This gives us a chance to work on any number of things with just a few students at a time. Sometimes we do explicit instruction on a concept or reinforce language skills that we've observed students need more practice with. Other times, we may focus on student writing and helping students with revision. We may even play a quick game with students to build language and motivation (see Strategy 23: Learning Games for Reading and Writing and Strategy 33: Learning Games for Speaking and Listening for game ideas).

Learning stations are one of the most versatile ways to engage students in any number of learning activities. They can be directly based on students' needs and interests. They can involve independent and group work. They can promote collaboration when students first work independently and then share their work with students at their station in order to receive feedback and make improvements. Students can also be involved in planning learning stations. After we do a stations day, we ask students to reflect on what went well, what could be improved, and what types of activities they would like to see included the next time.

This strategy doesn't always require extensive planning. Sometimes we might quickly print out four to five copies each of several different worksheets and divide students into stations where they are given a few minutes to complete as much of the worksheet as they can and then rotate to complete another worksheet and so on. This can work as a game (students turn in their group's worksheets, correct answers for each group are tallied, and the group with the most correct answers is declared the winner). Other times, when we sense that students need to move and we need to increase engagement, we may quickly divide the class into stations where they can choose from a list of activities they have already practiced and know how to do, such as picture dictation (see Strategy 24: Dictation), a language-learning game (see Strategies 23 and 33), partner reading (see Strategy 2: Literary Conversations), online computer activities, and so on. Of course, we would only do these less-structured station activities once students have already successfully participated in structured ones.

## What Could Go Wrong?

Trying to do a stations activity on the fly with a class who is not experienced in the process can result in chaos, and we speak from experience! Stations should be thoroughly modeled and practiced in order to maximize learning opportunities.

## Technology Connection

For more learning station ideas visit The Best Resources for Planning "Learning Stations" (http://larryferlazzo.edublogs.org/2017/08/14/the-best-resources-for-planning-learning-stations-please-add-more/).

# STRATEGY 41

# Beginning the School Year

## What Is It?

Teachers must consider many factors at the beginning of the school year. These include how to build relationships with students, what content they will be teaching, the instructional strategies they will use, how they will manage behavior, what resources they will need, how their classroom will be physically organized, and many others.

Teachers of ELLs must also consider these questions in relation to their students' cultural, linguistic, and academic experiences.

## Why We Like It

We know that the choices and causes we make at the beginning of the school year can have many effects as we progress through the rest of the year—and we want these effects to be positive! In our experience, focusing on two elements at the beginning of the year—building positive relationships with students and their families and creating a safe, effective learning environment—lay a strong foundation on which to build throughout the school year. We will share ideas for cultivating these elements in the Application section.

## Supporting Research

Extensive research shows that students who have positive, supportive relationships with teachers tend to be more engaged in learning, have fewer behavior issues, and experience higher levels of social and academic development (Rimm-Kaufman & Sandilos, n.d.). Supportive school-based relationships have been found to play an especially important role in engagement and academic performance for immigrant students (Suarez-Orozco et al., 2009).

## Common Core Connections

The relationship and community building activities in this section can support some of the Standards in each domain. Although they may not hit every Standard, these activities are absolutely necessary to create the conditions in which students feel safe and supported as they work toward meeting them.

# Application

Building strong relationships and creating a positive, safe learning environment can't be accomplished the first day or week of school. It also doesn't involve checking off certain activities on a to-do list. It is a dynamic process that starts on the first day of school (or even before) and needs to be continually nurtured and modified *every day* as the school year progresses. Some of the activities we share in this section can be used for introductory lessons and ones throughout the year to maintain positive relationships and foster an effective learning environment. This is by no means an exhaustive list. It does contain new activities not discussed in our first two books, along with a few that we have improved since then. All of the activities can be easily adapted to meet the needs of students at various English proficiency levels. In addition, building relationships with parents is also an important piece of community building at the start of the year. See Strategy 39: Working with Parents and Guardians for resources on building connections between home and school.

### GREETING STUDENTS

Greeting students at the classroom door on the first day of school is an easy way to make them feel welcome and to assure them that they are in the right class. Establishing this practice as part of a teacher's *daily* routine can be more challenging but, in our experience, well worth the effort.

We try to greet all of our students at the door every day with a smile and a handshake, a fist bump, a verbal welcome, or any other greeting students are comfortable with. Even though this interaction only lasts a few seconds, it lets them know we see them and are glad they are there. Many times, students will use this greeting time to quickly let us know how they are feeling that day—sick, excited, tired, mad, and so on. Once students are engaged in their warm-up activity, we can then check in with these students. Some days are harder than others to get ourselves stationed at the door before each period. If we just can't get there and don't greet each student individually, we then make sure to greet the class as a whole. Once this practice is established students are quick to remind us when we forget!

## STUDENT NAMES

Making it a priority to learn students' names and how to correctly pronounce them by the end of the first week is another way to develop positive relationships in the classroom. As we discuss in Strategy 36: Culturally Responsive Teaching, making sure we are correctly pronouncing students' names signals respect and a validation of who they are. This respect also includes asking students if they want to be called a name other than the one printed on the roster. We find that writing down the phonetic spellings of students' names on our seating chart is a good way to learn them. We also have students make quick name plates by folding a piece of paper into a triangle and writing their name on it using a colored marker. They then place it on top of their desk during the first week of school and can fold it up each day and keep it in their folder. This helps students to learn each other's names as well.

## COURSE EXPECTATIONS ACTIVITY

During the first week of school (usually the second day), we give students Figure 41.1: Course Expectations, which contains general information about the class in simple language. We quickly go over each section and have beginning students translate the headings (materials, grading, class rules, etc.) into their home language. Then, we make it an interactive lesson by allowing students to work in partners or small groups to complete Figure 41.2: Course Expectations Questions. We may first demonstrate how to do Question 5 by writing the first rule "Be on time" and drawing a clock with the starting time for the class. We also might model how to quickly sketch the classroom for Question 6. Students then work together to reread Figure 41.1 in order to answer all of the questions in Figure 41.2. They get to walk around and tour the classroom so they can draw a map for Question 6. We circulate during the process to check for comprehension and to offer assistance.

As an extension, the class can be divided into groups and given a poster paper. Each group can create a poster for one of the class rules containing the rule in English, the translation in any home languages, and a picture showing what the rule means. These can then be hung on the wall for daily reference.

## LETTER EXCHANGE

This activity comes from our first book, *The ESL/ELL Teacher's Survival Guide* (Ferlazzo & Sypnieski, 2012, p. 21) that shares basic information about us—our teaching experience, family, interests outside of school, and so on. We read the letter to students and then ask students to write a letter back. Depending on the level of the class, our letter can be simplified and we may provide sentence frames for students to use (e.g., "My name is. I am _____ years old. I was born in. My favorite thing about school is _____.") This activity is a great way for us to learn about students and to get a quick sample of student's writing. Students and teachers can also exchange letters at different points during the year. We've found it particularly helpful to do at the end of a quarter to reflect on growth and highs and lows of those months.

## PARTNER INTRODUCTIONS

ELLs may feel anxious being asked to introduce themselves on the first day. It can be much more comfortable for them to talk about someone else. One way to do this is by dividing students into pairs and providing them with a short list of simple questions to use to interview each other. The teacher can provide a sheet with the questions and space for students to write the answers or they can fill in the answers if using sentence frames. See Figure 41.3: Partner Introductions for a sheet we use with beginners. Students can practice the questions first by listening to the teacher say the question and then repeating it. Then, after students ask each other the questions and write down the answers, they can practice introducing each other using the answers or sentence frames as a guide. This rehearsal can be followed by asking students to introduce their partners to the whole class or in small groups.

### "I Learn Best When . . ." Cards

This activity was introduced to us by educator and author Rick Wormeli (2016). It involves giving students an index card and asking them to list all the things that help them learn best. We structure this activity for intermediate ELLs by using the sentence stem "I learn best when . . ." and providing students with a few models (e.g., "I learn best when the teacher shows pictures"; "I learn best when I work with other students"; "I learn best when I can see an example first"). After students have had a few minutes to write, we ask them to share their ideas in small groups in order to see if any of the ideas that help their classmates learn best could also apply to themselves. We then create a class list of "I learn best when..." ideas that can be posted on the wall and added to throughout the year. We collect the students' index cards and periodically hand them back out to students (usually at the beginning of a new quarter) so students can reflect on how they learn best and make any modifications or additions to their list.

### "I Am" Project

There are many variations of *I am* activities—students can create a poem, a poster, a slideshow, a brief oral presentation, a collage, and so on (you can find many examples by searching *"Who am I?" activities* online). This activity encourages students to describe themselves in a creative format. At the beginning of the year, it serves as a way for teachers and students to learn about each other's experiences and interests. We change the format up from year to year, but we always provide sentence frames along with a model about ourselves. We also give the option for students to add illustrations. The sentence frames we shared in The ESL/ELL Teacher's Survival Guide:

I love because _____.

I wonder _____.

I am happy when _____.

I am scared when _____.

I worry about because _____.

I hope to _____.

I am sad when _____.

In the future, I will _____.

We modify the activity for newcomers by encouraging them to complete it in their native language. Students can also add drawings or pictures cut from magazines to visually represent their feelings, interests, and goals. We then have students share their projects in small groups of three to four and ask them to look for two similarities and two differences. Each group then shares their observations with the whole class.

**Two Truths and a Lie—Plus**

Two truths and a lie is a fun first-week activity that encourages writing and speaking. The teacher first models writing down three statements about himself or herself on an index card. He or she explains that two of the statements are true and one is a lie.

Students can then talk in pairs or small groups and guess which of the teacher's statements is a lie. We keep this part brief (we want the focus to be on the students and don't want to take up a lot of time talking about our lives). Students are then instructed to do the same process by writing their own statements (two truths, one lie) on an index card.

The teacher can circulate and suggest sentence frames for students who seem to need support ("I like _____"; "I don't like _____"; "I'm from _____"). Beginners can write the statements in their home language if desired and can be paired with another student who shares the same language (if there isn't anyone who shares their home language, the teacher can assist the student in using Google Translate to compose simple sentences in English). Students then get into small groups and take turns guessing each other's lies.

This activity can be extended into a version we call *two truths and a lie—plus*. For the plus version, we give students a piece of legal-size paper and explain they will be making a mini-poster called *My Truths, No Lies!* We model taking our two true statements from the first activity and writing three more so that we have five true statements total. We tell students they will do the same and that they will be writing them on the mini-poster and adding illustrations or symbols to visually represent the statements. Students work on their posters while the teacher offers assistance. Then, students get into pairs or small groups and share their mini-posters. These discussions facilitate student–student relationships as they learn about each other, discovering similarities and differences, which the teacher can ask each group to share with the whole class. Hanging these mini-posters on the wall instantly makes the classroom feel more welcoming because it reflects the truths of all the students.

**Candy Introductions**

A popular way to facilitate student introductions at the beginning of the year is called *candy introductions*. This activity is very popular because it is the only time during the year that we give out candy (graham crackers, granola bars, and fruit snacks are the snacks that we typically provide during the year). In this activity, students choose several different colored pieces of candy from the bag or a bowl and are told not to eat them. Students are then divided into small groups where they can choose from a list of color-coded topics. Students can take turns choosing a color to talk about and when finished can eat the piece of candy! Here is one way we've structured the topics at the beginning of the year:

- **Red:** What is one thing you like about school?
- **Blue:** What is one thing you don't like about school?
- **Green:** If you could be any animal, what would you be and why?
- **Orange:** Where is your favorite place?
- **Yellow:** What is something you want to do in the future?

Not only is this activity instantly engaging (candy!) but also it allows students to choose which topics they feel most comfortable talking about. This activity can be used at any time during the year to liven things up and get students talking about any number of topics. We've used it to structure discussions about a topic we are studying in class (e.g., "Give an example of figurative language" or "Explain what a topic sentence is in your own words") and as a way for students to share their reflections on their progress in English (e.g., "What is one area you are improving in and how do you know this?" or "What is something you want to get better at and what steps can you take to do this?").

**My Summer Cloze Activity**

When returning to school in the fall, many students get asked to write or talk about what they did over the summer. Although we may want to know what students did while they weren't in school, we also want to be sensitive to the fact that not all our students have positive summer vacation experiences, especially if they were moving. We can give them the opportunity to express their feelings, positive and negative, by writing about the summer in an honest way. We model this by writing a couple of quick sentences about our own summer sharing something positive that happened and something challenging.

Figure 41.4: My Summer is a cloze activity we used with our returning high-beginner and low-intermediate students during the first week of school to scaffold the process of writing and talking about their summer experiences. We first read it aloud to students and clarify any new vocabulary. Then students work independently to fill in the blanks. When finished, students can work in pairs or small groups and take turns reading parts or all of their completed *my summer* activity.

## Student Handouts and Examples

Figure 41.1: Course Expectations

Figure 41.2: Course Expectations Questions

Figure 41.3: Partner Introductions

Figure 41.4: My Summer

## What Could Go Wrong?

As Rick Wormeli (2016) wisely states, "The most urgent questions students ask as they begin a new school year are, 'Am I safe?' and 'Do I belong?'" We want our words and actions to represent a *yes* answer to these critical questions. Teachers who spend a large amount of time going over the rules and projecting a "this is how *I* do things" attitude may have the intention of creating a safe environment for students, but these actions don't cultivate a sense of belonging, where student input is sought and valued. Similarly, the classroom can feel like it belongs to the teacher when educators overshare and talk all about their interests or what they did over the summer. Instead, we want our students to feel safe, supported, and that they are the stars of the show. Once they feel this, real learning can happen!

## Technology Connections

For additional ideas and resources on building community in the classroom, see The Best Resources on Developing a Sense of Community in the Classroom (http://

larryferlazzo.edublogs.org/2017/07/18/the-best-resources-on-developing-a-sense-of-community-in-the-classroom/).

Further resources for the beginning of the school year can be found at The Best Resources for Planning the First Days of School (http://larryferlazzo.edublogs.org/2011/08/08/the-best-resources-for-planning-the-first-day-of-school/).

## Attribution

Versions of some of these ideas appeared in our book *The ESL/ELL Teacher's Survival Guide* (Ferlazzo & Sypnieski, 2012, p. 21–23).

Thank you to Rick Wormeli (2016) for the great ideas contained in his article "What to Do in Week One?" (www.ascd.org/publications/educational-leadership/sept16/vol74/num01/What-to-Do-in-Week-One%C2%A2.aspx).

## Figures

---

**Welcome to English Language Development!**

In this class, we will be working on our English listening, speaking, reading, and writing skills.

**Listening and speaking:** You will practice saying English words and sounds every day.

**Reading:** You will read English books together as a class and by yourself every day. You will learn new words through your reading. You will learn reading strategies that will help you in your other classes.

**Writing:** You will do a lot of writing in English every day. You will practice using new words in your writing. You will learn writing strategies that will help you in your other classes.

**Thinking:** You will be thinking a lot! You will practice thinking skills every day.

---

**Figure 41.1** Course Expectations

## Materials

Students need to bring the following every day:

- #2 pencil
- Blue or black pen
- A book for independent reading (students may check out books from the classroom, school library, or public library)

## Grading

Student grades will be based on three areas:
- Product (quality of student work)
- Process (how students do their work)
- Progress (evidence that students are progressing)

Students will earn points for class assignments and homework. Students are expected to come to class every day, participate in class activities, and demonstrate their growth as readers, writers, and speakers of English.

## Class Rules

Along with the expectations listed in the student handbook, here are five class rules that students are expected to follow:

1. Be on time (in your seat when the bell rings).
2. Be prepared. Bring a pen or pencil, paper, and your book every day.
3. *Show respect* for yourself, your classmates, the class materials and the teacher.
4. Follow classroom procedures and stay on task.
5. Work hard and make mistakes (that's how you learn!)

I am happy you are here! Let's have fun and learn a lot!

**Figure 41.1** (*Continued*)

**1.** My teacher for this class is _____.

**2.** Which English skills will we be practicing in this class?

_____

_____

_____

**3.** What materials do you need to bring to class with you every day?

_____

_____

**4.** What do you need to do to be successful in this class?

_____

_____

**5.** Write down the five class rules. Then draw a picture next to each one to show that you understand what it means.

- _____

- _____

- _____

- _____

- _____

**6.** Take a minute to look or walk around the classroom. Draw a map of our classroom below. Label the following things: bookshelves, dictionaries, classroom supplies (pencils, class folders, paper, notebooks), garbage cans, pencil sharpener, TV, computers, and anything else you think is important.

**7.** Please write down two questions you have about this class, this classroom, this school, or your teacher.

_____

_____

**Figure 41.2** Course Expectations Questions

Ask your partner the following questions and write down his or her answers.

Question: What is your name?
Answer: His or her name is _____.

Question: How old are you?
Answer: He or she is _____ years old.

Question: Where are you from?
Answer: He or she is from _____.

Question: What languages do you speak?
Answer: He or she speaks _____.

Question: What is your favorite food?
Answer: His or her favorite food is _____.

Now, write your partner's answers in this paragraph and practice introducing him or her to the class.

This is _____. He or she is _____ years old.
He or she is from _____. He or she speaks
_____. His or her favorite food
is _____.

**Figure 41.3** Partner Introductions

My summer was _____ (great, good, okay, bad). I did _____ (many, a few) things.

One thing I did was _____. Another thing I did was _____.

My favorite part of the summer was _____ _____. The worst part of my summer was _____ _____.

I practiced my English _____ (a lot, some, a little) over the summer. I practiced it by _____ (reading books, using Duolingo, watching TV, going to summer school). I think my English is _____ (better, worse, the same) as it was when school ended in June.

I feel _____ (happy, feeling okay, sad) about being back in school. The best part about school is_____ (seeing friends, learning new things, seeing Mr. Ferlazzo).

My big goal for this year is to _____ (work hard, work harder than I did last year, practice speaking English more, behave better in class, do my best).

I think it's going to be a _____ (great, good, okay, bad) year.

**Figure 41.4** My Summer

# STRATEGY 42

# Ending the School Year

## What Is It?

The end of the school year can be a challenging time for students to stay engaged in learning and for teachers to maintain their energy. Incorporating end-of-year activities that encourage ELLs to celebrate their growth can be energizing and can keep students learning up until the last bell rings.

## Why We Like It

Teachers and students may feel like they are limping across the finish line at the end of the school year. During the last quarter, when testing is finished and spring is in the air, teachers and students can be tempted to go on cruise control. However, this attitude can result in a loss of valuable learning and practice time, especially for ELLs who benefit from as many language-learning opportunities as possible. Although these last several weeks definitely present challenges, they also provide opportunities for students to consider what it means to finish strong, set goals and plan to make it happen, and experience success.

## Supporting Research

As we mentioned earlier in Strategy 17: Using Photos or Other Images in Reading and Writing, research by Daniel Kahneman, a Nobel Prize winner, has found that we tend to make future decisions based on the peak-end rule (Holt, 2011)—that we primarily remember how particular events and time periods *ended* along with the best moments that we experienced during those times (Ferlazzo, 2010, March 8). Those memories then influence our future decision making. From this perspective, asking students at the end of the year to reflect on the positive learning experiences they've had (the peaks) and the progress they've made can influence their feelings about—and future decisions related to—school and learning.

## Common Core Connections

Depending on how the activities described in this strategy are structured, they can support multiple Standards in all four domains.

# Application

This section will share ideas for encouraging ELLs to finish strong during the *last few months* of school and to boost learning in the *last few days* of school.

### ACTIVITIES FOR THE LAST FEW MONTHS OF SCHOOL

### Finishing Strong Goal-Setting Activity

ELLs can be taught the concept of a strong finish by using simple sports metaphors to illustrate the idea of pushing through fatigue and other difficulties in order to play our best until the end of the school year (e.g., runners don't slow down at the end of a race, basketball teams don't stop playing defense or shooting the ball in the last quarter, etc.). Understanding this concept is easier than actually applying it, however! One of the ways we help students do this is through a goal-setting activity.

After students understand the concept of finishing strong, we ask them to think about what they would like to accomplish in order to finish the school year strong (ideas may be related to learning English, academic skills, behavior, etc.). We pass out Figure 42.1: Finishing Strong Goal Sheet, put a copy under the document camera, and model writing down three goals for ourselves using the sentence frame "I want to _____" (e.g., "I want to finish two books by the end of the school year" or "I want to call three parents a week for positive reasons").

We then model writing down the actions we will need to take in order to accomplish these goals using the sentence frame "To do this, I will" (e.g., "To do this, I will ask my friends to recommend a book that will keep me interested and I will read 20 minutes each night before bed" or "I will make a note when a student does something positive that I want to share with his or her family").

Students are given time to write down their goals and what actions they can take to accomplish them. We circulate and help students who may need ideas for action steps. We also allow students to work together and to share their goals with each other in order to generate more ideas. For beginners, their goals and action steps might be "I want to learn to talk to my counselor about college. To do this, I will make a list of questions and translate them into English" or "I want to get better at writing sentences in English. To do this, I will write about my book every day and ask my teacher to check it."

We have students glue or staple this sheet in their writer's notebooks. Then, every Friday for the last several weeks of school, students are given time to reflect on their progress and fill out one row of the weekly goal check-in chart on the bottom half of Figure 42.1. They use the chart to reflect on how they did in terms of each goal during that week, what changes they will make the next week if needed, and what help they may need to do this. We complete our weekly check-in on our copy of Figure 42.1 on the document camera. Students love holding us accountable for our goals! See the Technology Connections section for links to multiple other examples of student goal-setting sheets.

### Free-Choice Unit

A great way to keep engagement high and to promote language learning is to have students work in pairs or small groups to create a unit on a topic of their choice and teach it to their classmates. Students can select any topic that they want to learn more about or the class could vote on a category to choose from (e.g., famous people, cities, cultures, etc.). The teacher can ask students to generate a list of questions they have about the topic and incorporate time for Internet research. Students can use a graphic organizer (such as a KWL chart) to capture new learnings.

Students can teach their classmates about their topic in a number of ways, depending on how extensive the teacher wants the project to be. For example, students could use higher-order teaching strategies described in this book—inductive data sets, clozes, and sequencing activities—to teach their peers about their topic. Student instructions for creating these activities can be found in Figure 6.5: Strip Story Instructions in Strategy 6: Sequencing, Figure 7.15: Instructions for Making a Cloze in Strategy 7: Clozes, and Figure 11.6: Data Set Instructions in Strategy 11: Inductive Learning. Of course, students should be asked to use these instructional strategies only if they have applied them on multiple occasions throughout the year. Students can also be asked to create a visual aid or to use technology (a slideshow, video, infographic) to teach their topic. The teacher can provide students with a lesson plan format (see Figure 42.2: Lesson Plan) so students can think through how they will teach their classmates about their topic. These lessons can be taught in small groups with groups taking turns to teach each other, or small groups can teach the whole class over a several day period.

A modified version of this activity could be done with a beginning class. Students could work in groups to identify a topic and five questions they want to research. Then they could be given time to look online for the answers and write them down in English (with teacher or peer tutor assistance if needed). Each group could then create a poster containing the information they learned about the topic with images or drawings.

Students could teach their classmates about their topic using the poster and teacher-provided sentence frames (e.g., "We learned that _____" or "One interesting fact about is _____"). Another option is to use the student-led lesson plan described in Strategy 45: Using Technology.

**Visual Displays of Learning**

The final quarter is a great time to ask ELLs to reflect on the progress they've made throughout the year. In our experience, asking them to create visual displays of their learning makes this process even more creative and engaging.

In Strategy 1: Independent Reading, we describe an activity we do with students to celebrate the reading they've done during the year. Students design a visual representation of their reading journey (a chart, a time line, a map, a bookshelf, etc.) that contains the titles of the books they've read. See Figure 1.2: My Year of Reading Visual Project for the directions and Figure 1.3: My Year of Reading Student Example.

There are many other ways for students to visually represent what they've learned (here are just a few):

- Students can make a top-ten list (most important skills or content learned).

- Students can be divided into groups with each one being assigned a topic the class has studied. Students then work as a group to create a poster containing the five most important things they learned about this topic, along with an image to represent each one.

- Each student can draw a picture or create a storyboard of their best moment in class during the year. This could then be used as a springboard for writing about the experience.

- Students could create a map or time line of the school year on a large sheet of paper. It could include important learning topics, memorable activities, school events, field trips, when new students entered the class, holidays, and so on.

- See the year-in-review activity in the upcoming Reflecting on Growth section for another visual project.

**Visiting Other Classes**

Making arrangements to visit an elective teacher's classroom at the end of the year can be another way to increase engagement and to encourage ELL and English-only students to learn from each other. In the past we have taken our beginning and intermediate classes to participate in art, ceramics, and music classes. We make plans with the elective teacher for their students to teach a simple lesson to our ELLs (e.g., how to play an instrument, how to make an origami bird, how to make a simple ceramic pot, etc.). Many times, these activities turn into natural language lessons for all students involved—ELLs are learning new words in English and the non-ELLs often learn a few new words in their partner's home language. Other times, we pre-teach a set of vocabulary particular to the class we will be visiting. We have received positive feedback from our students and the student teachers in the elective classes about these activities.

### Using Technology

The last several weeks of the school year is a good time to take advantage of the instant engagement and authentic audiences that technology provides. Students can make digital book trailers (see Strategy 2: Literary Conversations) on a favorite book that can be posted on a class blog for next year's students. They could play any of the online learning games listed in Strategy 23: Learning Games for Reading and Writing. Ending the year with an oral presentation that incorporates technology can also be motivating for students. See Strategy 30: Oral Presentations for ideas on short and long student presentations.

### Field Trips

The end of the year can be a great time to get outside and take field trips. This could be an out-of-town trip or a simple one to a neighborhood store where students have to complete a scavenger hunt. See the Technology Connections section for lots of other field trip ideas.

### ACTIVITIES FOR THE LAST FEW DAYS OF SCHOOL

### Advice for Future Students

During the last week of school, we often ask students to reflect on the class (the routines, topics of study, learning strategies, projects, etc.) and think about what would be helpful information to share with new students the following year. Students can work in small groups to brainstorm ideas and can then choose from a menu of options—writing a letter to new students, making a list of tips and advice for how to be successful, creating a handbook for the class, and so on. These projects can be shared with incoming students during the first week of the new school year—and we've found that students really pay attention to what their peers have to say!

**Reflecting on Growth**

Asking ELLs to reflect on their personal and academic growth can be a powerful culminating activity. One way we do this is by having students create a year-in-review poster. We give students Figure 42.3: My Year Directions and explain that they will draw a chart like the one in the figure on a large sheet of paper (with the months of the school year on the *x*-axis and positive numbers 1 to 5 on the top of the *y*-axis and negative 1 to 5 on the bottom of the *y*-axis). We create an example based on our experiences during the year that serves as a model for students to reference.

We have students start by reflecting on their year and choosing seven important things that happened (meeting a new friend, changing into a new class, doing a project). They then plot these events on their chart. They need to think about where to place them—which month it happened and where it would go on the positive or negative *y*-axis. Once they plot the event, students need to write a short description of what happened and draw a picture to represent it. If they label an event as negative, they must describe what happened along with what they learned from this event. They could even draw a line connecting the negative event and what they learned from it up to the positive section—after all, learning from mistakes and challenges is always a good thing!

Another way we encourage ELLs to reflect on their progress is by using an improvement rubric for students to evaluate their work. This kind of rubric, unlike many others, does not contain deficit language. Instead, it emphasizes what students *have done* instead of what they *have not done*. Although this process could be used to compare any two similar pieces of work done over the course of a semester or school year, we typically use it with ELLs to analyze their growth in writing.

First, we give students time to review all the essays they've written during the year and to choose two of them—one, preferably from earlier in the year and the other a later one. Students then analyze each essay using an improvement rubric. Figure 42.4: Writing Improvement Rubric is an example of one we used with our high-beginning and low-intermediate class. Once students complete this scoring process, we give them a few reflection questions to answer (see Figure 42.5: Improvement Rubric Reflection Questions). Students can then pick one of the two essays to revise and rewrite with their reflections in mind.

**Class and Teacher Evaluations**

Asking ELLs to evaluate the class and our teaching can offer valuable feedback for us while prompting students to consider their own learning strengths and challenges. Over the years we have given students surveys about our class and our teaching in different formats (multiple-choice, question-answer, fill-in-the-blank, number rankings, etc.).

However, what they all have in common, and what makes them effective, is that they are anonymous and give students a chance to offer honest feedback. The teacher can consider in which areas he or she would like to receive feedback and then work backwards to design the questions. For example, if we want feedback on our relationship-building efforts, we might include the following fill-in-the-blank question on a survey: "My teacher cares about what is happening in my life _____ (a lot, some, a little, not at all)." If we are interested in how students felt about the level of challenge in our class we might ask, "The work in this class was _____ (too hard, just right, too easy)." Some of the questions can also be designed to prompt student reflection on their learning processes, such as "Which activities helped you learn English the most this year and why?" or "What could you do differently or better to help yourself in this class?" See the Technology Connections section for different versions of teacher and class evaluations.

### ENCOURAGING SUMMER PRACTICE

As students are taking time to reflect on and celebrate their progress at the end of the year, they can also be prompted to think about how to capitalize on these gains over the summer and not experience a summer slide. Many of us are familiar with the research on the summer slide, which shows that many young people, especially in low-income communities, experience academic losses during the time they're out of school (Ferlazzo, 2011, June 26).

We familiarize our ELLs with this research and brainstorm as a class ways to continue to build their skills over the summer. Ideas usually include reading books in English, watching movies with English subtitles, practicing their English-speaking skills out in the community, and doing online practice (see the Technology Connections section for the resources we recommend for online summer learning). We make arrangements with the teachers our students will have in the fall to give them extra credit for any work done over the summer, including online activities and reading books. We allow students to check out books from our classroom library. We also invite a librarian to come and issue library cards to our students so they can use the public library during the summer and the rest of the year. The library is a great summer resource for students who don't have easy access to computers at home. We also take students to the computer lab before they leave for the summer so they can familiarize themselves with the sites and register for them if needed.

## Student Handouts and Examples

Figure 42.1: Finishing Strong Goal Sheet
Figure 42.2: Lesson Plan

## What Could Go Wrong?

It's difficult for students to finish strong when their learning environment doesn't reflect this spirit. Don't take work off the walls and pack all your books away when you are expecting students to be engaged and learning during the final week of school. Nothing says "School's out!" like bare walls and bookshelves. Don't do a countdown of the number of days left in the school year on your board.

For some of our students, the summer doesn't represent a carefree time of rest and rejuvenation. They may already be experiencing feelings of anxiety that can be heightened by the constant reminder of how the school year is quickly coming to an end. It is not helpful when teachers talk about how much they are looking forward to their summer plans. It is important for our students to know that we *want* to be there with them (even if we have momentary dreams of vacation that we keep to ourselves).

## Technology Connections

For additional resources on ending the school year, see The Best Ways to Finish the School Year Strong (http://larryferlazzo.edublogs.org/2015/04/17/the-best-ways-to-finish-the-school-year-strong/).

Many examples of student goal sheets can be found at The Best Posts on Students Setting Goals (http://larryferlazzo.edublogs.org/2010/05/18/my-best-posts-on-students-setting-goals/).

Explore ideas for virtual and real-life field trips at The Best Resources for Organizing & Maximizing Field Trips—Both "Real" & "Virtual" (http://larryferlazzo.edublogs.org/2016/06/24/the-best-resources-for-organizing-maximizing-field-trips-both-real-virtual/).

To see many examples of teacher evaluations, along with results, visit The Best Posts on Students Evaluating Classes (and Teachers) (http://larryferlazzo.edublogs.org/2010/05/08/my-best-posts-on-students-evaluating-classes-and-teachers/).

More resources and research on the summer slide are available at The Best Resources on the "Summer Slide" (http://larryferlazzo.edublogs.org/2011/06/26/the-best-resources-on-the-summer-slide/).

For a list of updated, free online sites where teachers can easily create virtual classrooms and track student progress, see Larry's post "Updated: Here Are The Sites I'm Using for My Summer School 'Virtual Classroom'" (http://larryferlazzo

.edublogs.org/2016/05/23/updated-here-are-the-sites-im-using-for-my-summer-school-virtual-classroom/).

## Attribution

Figures 42.2, 42.4, and 42.5 were modified from Larry's book *Helping Students Motivate Themselves* (2011).

## Figures

---

Name_____

### What I Want to Do and How I Will Do It

**1.** I want to _____.

  To do this, I will _____.

**2.** I want to _____.

  To do this, I will _____.

**3.** I want to _____.

  To do this, I will _____.

### Weekly Goal Check-In

| Date | My Goal— (1, 2, or 3) | How did I do? Did I make progress? | What will I do differently next week? | What help do I need to do this? |
|------|------------------------|------------------------------------|----------------------------------------|---------------------------------|
|      |                        |                                    |                                        |                                 |
|      |                        |                                    |                                        |                                 |
|      |                        |                                    |                                        |                                 |

---

**Figure 42.1**  Finishing Strong Goal Sheet

Group Members: _____

Our Topic: _____

Make a list of the strategies you will use to teach your classmates about the topic (e.g., cloze, sequencing, data set):

*We will be using* _____ *to*

*teach about* _____ .

How will you introduce your lesson and get students' attention? (show a video clip, ask a question for students to discuss in pairs or to answer on a sticky note, etc.)?

*We will start our lesson by* _____ .

What do you want students to do during your lesson (complete a cloze, read and categorize a data set, answer a question, etc.)? How much time will students need to do each part?

*Students will* _____ .

*They will need* _____ *minutes.*

How will you give directions to students (write them on the board, say them, give them a copy of the steps, etc.)? Can students work together? Alone? With a partner?

*We will give directions by* _____ .

*Students will work* _____ .

**Figure 42.2** Lesson Plan *Source:* Modified from *Helping Students Motivate Themselves* (www .routledge.com/Helping-Students-Motivate-Themselves-Practical-Answers-to-Classroom-Challenges/ Ferlazzo/p/book/9781596671812) by Larry Ferlazzo (2011, p. 111).

What tools will you need to teach your lesson (document camera, computer, whiteboard markers, copies of activities, etc.)?

*To teach our lesson we will need* _____

_____ .

What tools will students need during your lesson (pencil, paper, colored markers, etc.)?

*During our lesson, students will need* _____

_____ .

How will you help students learn during your lesson (without giving them the answers)?

*We will help students learn by* _____

_____ .

How will you end your lesson? Will students need to turn in any work to you?

*We will end our lesson by* _____

_____ .

**Figure 42.2** *(Continued)*

1. Make a chart like this on a poster:

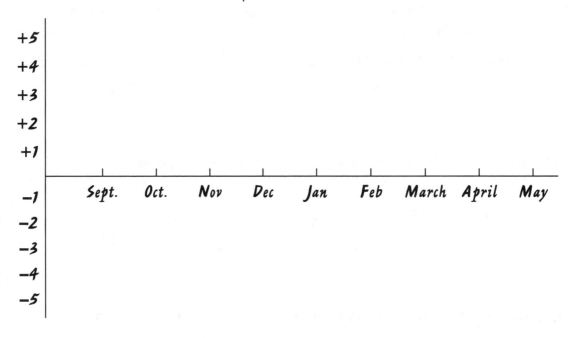

2. Think of seven important things that happended during this school year in any of your classes — a lesson, learning something new, meeting a new friend, doing a project. You can include things that were not too good, too. Plot them on your chart — describe it in words and then draw it.

**Figure 42.3** My Year Directions *Source:* Modified from Helping Students Motivate Themselves (https://www.routledge.com/Helping-Students-Motivate-Themselves-Practical-Answers-to-Classroom-Challenges/Ferlazzo/p/book/9781596671812) by Larry Ferlazzo (2011, p. 79).

| ESSAY 1: | ESSAY 2: |
|---|---|
| I opened my essay with an attention grabber (a hook). | I opened my essay with an attention grabber (a hook). |
| 1  2  3  4 | 1  2  3  4 |
| I used a thesis statement saying the main idea of the essay. | I used a thesis statement saying the main idea of the essay. |
| 1  2  3  4 | 1  2  3  4 |
| I wrote a list in the introduction paragraph saying what topics I would cover in the essay. | I wrote a list in the introduction paragraph saying what topics I would cover in the essay. |
| 1  2  3  4 | 1  2  3  4 |
| I organized my essay into paragraphs. | I organized my essay into paragraphs. |
| 1  2  3  4 | 1  2  3  4 |
| I used topic sentences in all my paragraphs. | I used topic sentences in all my paragraphs. |
| 1  2  3  4 | 1  2  3  4 |
| I used the correct verb tenses (past or present). | I used the correct verb tenses (past or present). |
| 1  2  3  4 | 1  2  3  4 |
| Punctuation was correct throughout the essay, including in dialogues. | Punctuation was correct throughout the essay, including in dialogues |
| 1  2  3  4 | 1  2  3  4 |
| I wrote a conclusion in which I summarized my main points and left the reader with something to think about. | I wrote a conclusion in which I summarized my main points and left the reader with something to think about. |
| 1  2  3  4 | 1  2  3  4 |

**Figure 42.4** Writing Improvement Rubric *Source: Modified from Helping Students Motivate Themselves* (https://www.routledge.com/Helping-Students-Motivate-Themselves-Practical-Answers-to-Classroom-Challenges/Ferlazzo/p/book/9781596671812) *by Larry Ferlazzo (2011, p. 79).*

1. Look at the scores you gave yourself on both essays. Overall, which essay was your strongest? Why?

2. Look at the scores on your strongest essay. What did you do well?

3. Look at the scores on your strongest essay. What are three things you need to get better at next year?

4. In what areas of your writing would you like your teacher to help you with next year?

**Figure 42.5** Improvement Rubric Reflection Questions *Source:* Reproduced with permission of Routledge Company.

# STRATEGY 43

# Beginning and Ending of Class

## What Is It?

As educators know, what happens during the first and the last few minutes of class can have a big impact on student learning. *Do nows, walk-in procedures, bell ringers,* or *warm-ups* are all names for activities that students do right at the beginning of class or, as we try to do in our schools, a minute or two prior to the bell ringing. For our purposes, we will refer to these types of openers as *do nows*.

Closure activities are designed to wrap up the lesson in the last few minutes of class and provide students the opportunity to respond to their learning in some way.

## Why We Like It

Do nows can take many forms (which we will discuss in the Application section). In our experience, the most-effective do nows for ELLs share two features—they are meaningful activities connected to student learning *and* students can do them independently as part of a routine. Establishing a daily routine—one in which students come into class and immediately know what to do—sets the tone for learning and is a great management tool. Having all students engaged in a learning activity gives us the opportunity to check in with individuals who may need extra support or direction. We also make a point to periodically share with students how the do-now activity can benefit them (e.g., how improving their reading skills in English and in their home language can directly help them in school and in life). Ultimately, we like this practice because it sets a focused and supportive tone in the classroom where students know what they are expected to do, when to do it, and why they are doing it.

Closure activities, which can also include a variety of options, give students a chance to process, summarize, and reflect on their learning. As teachers, we can use them for formative assessment and to gather valuable student feedback. We like closure activities because we can get a lot of bang for our buck. Taking just a few minutes to do one of these activities can yield a wealth of information about our students, our teaching, our curriculum, and ourselves!

## Supporting Research

Research shows that do nows can be used to create a sense of purpose. Sharing with students not only what they will be learning about that day but also *how it can benefit them* has been found to increase student learning, motivation, and engagement (Busch, 2017). Beginning class with a do now further serves as an excellent classroom management technique when incorporated as part of a daily routine. Students can immediately be engaged and on task from the moment they enter class. This effectively sets the tone for the rest of the lesson (Shen & Frances, n.d.).

In Strategy 17: Using Photos or Other Images in Reading and Writing and in Strategy 42: Ending the School Year, we shared research on Daniel Kahneman's peak-end rule, which can also be applied to closure activities. This research stresses the importance of good endings, because we tend to primarily remember the *endings* of events and time periods, and these memories can shape our feelings and decisions in the future (Ferlazzo, 2010, March 8).

## Common Core Connections

Depending on which do nows and closure activities are included in a lesson, they can support multiple Standards in all four domains.

## Application

This section is divided into two parts—ideas for how to *start* and how to *end* class.

### DO-NOW ACTIVITIES

As we stated previously, effective do nows in our experience share two key qualities—they are meaningful activities connected to student learning *and* students can do them independently as part of a routine. The do nows included here best meet these criteria. They can also be modified for use with all proficiency levels and, even though they are part of our classroom routine, they don't feel routine. They allow for student choice and take students' diverse interests into account. This list is not long, but the three main activities described here encompass all of these qualities and have worked best for our students.

We tend to use the following three do nows with our intermediate ELL students or if we have a combination intermediate and beginners class. When we have a class of beginners only, our do now often looks slightly different and doesn't necessarily fit our criteria. In that situation, we display a worksheet or a textbook page on the document camera that reinforces a theme we are studying (home, school, etc.). We model the first few exercises and then students spend ten minutes working on it individually or with a partner. We then review it as a class.

**Independent Reading**

Strategy 1: Independent Reading, describes how we support our ELLs in reading books of their choice in class on a daily basis. This practice becomes an established routine in the first few weeks of school as we help students select books, familiarize them with the classroom and school library, and begin to share with them the research on the positive impacts of reading on the brain and on learning (see Strategy 1: Independent Reading for this research).

Once independent reading is an established routine it serves as an excellent do-now activity. When students enter the room, they can immediately get their book and begin reading. Some students keep their books in their backpacks, and others leave them in plastic crates which we have labeled for each class and are placed near the door for easy access. We give students who have demonstrated responsibility the option of reading a book on the computer or on their phone. Most students are engaged in their reading because we encourage them to read books that interest them. For the few students who are struggling to stay engaged, we can use this independent reading time to help them find a new book or to read one-on-one with them. If we are fortunate enough to have a peer tutor or two in the class, we'll have each of them take a student to a quiet corner or outside. The ELL student can then read his or her book to the peer tutor.

This do now works for students at all English proficiency levels because they can read a book at their level or even in their home language. Our classroom library is leveled and contains a section of books in other languages (but we never restrict which levels students can choose from). This type of organization does, however, make it easier for students to quickly find books on their own.

**Partner Reading**

As we described in Strategy 2: Literary Conversations, we do a partner reading activity as a do now in our beginner-intermediate class once a week. Students enter to see the directions posted on the document camera (Figure 2.3: Partner-Reading Instructions). They form partners (or we have the names of pairs listed on the front board), choose a book, and start reading. They then complete the rest of the steps listed on Figure 2.3. Of course, the first few times we do this activity, it requires teacher modeling and support. Once students are familiar with the process, it becomes another do-now routine that actively engages students in learning within a few minutes of entering class. Students enjoy it because they are working together and are free to choose any book they like.

### Writer's Notebook Prompts

Though our main do-now activity for ELLs is reading, we have also used writer's notebook prompts to engage students at the start of a lesson. We usually teach our ELLs in two-hour block classes. Often times we will have students read at the start of the first hour and then respond to a prompt in their writer's notebook at the beginning of the second hour. The prompts can vary with students responding to their reading, answering questions related to the upcoming lesson, or choosing a topic from their heart map or writing territories to write about (all of these ideas are described in Strategy 18: Writer's Notebook).

We post the prompt on the document camera during the break between classes and students get their notebooks as they enter the room. Then when they go to their seat, they can immediately begin thinking and responding to the prompt. Because we want them to be able to work independently, we are careful to write the prompt in simple language and provide any synonyms for challenging words. Beginners can translate the question with the help of a higher-level English-proficient classmate or Google Translate and can respond in their home language if needed.

### An Additional Note on Do Nows

Some educators suggest that do nows should directly connect to the lesson being taught that day or review concepts from the previous lesson. We agree with them but may have a broader definition of connect than they have in mind. Literacy skills relate to everything that students are doing. And, we know these reading and writing do nows are engaging our students because many times they don't want to stop doing them!

Some also suggest that do nows must be assessed and feedback must be provided to students in order for them to be effective so they don't become, as educator David Ginsburg (2011) says, "do laters" or "do nevers." We agree that assessment and feedback are important to inform our practice and enhance students' learning.

However, we've also found that attaching points to enjoyable literacy practices (such as free reading and journaling) can make them less enjoyable for students, thus decreasing motivation and engagement. We seek to find a balance by periodically collecting students' notebooks to check their progress and to offer brief written feedback.

## CLOSURE ACTIVITIES

Meaningful closure activities only need to take a few minutes, yet they are so hard to do! Before we know it, the class period has whizzed by and our closure consists of calling out "Have a good day everybody!" The most effective closure activities, in our experience, share the following characteristics—they are short, they involve student reflection, and they require active processing from all students. The activities described here contain these elements.

### Shining Moments

This activity was introduced to us by secondary teacher Paige Price (Your Shining Moment, n.d.) and involves asking students to think about what they did best on an assignment, an essay, or in class that day. They then write down this shining moment on a notecard or at the bottom of the assignment and turn it in before they leave. We like to use this as a closing activity with ELLs because it encourages them to reflect on their progress and to leave the classroom on a positive note (remember the research about good endings!). It also gives us valuable information about our students and their confidence levels. We usually have students write on notecards and may provide sentence frames such as "My shining moment today was _____" or "Today, what I did best was _____." Sometimes, we leave a few extra minutes so students can share their shining moments with a partner or in a small group.

   A variation on this activity that we use when students are doing a longer piece of writing is to stop a few minutes before the end of class and ask students to read over what they've written. We then ask them to highlight or underline what they believe is their best sentence—a shining sentence. They also have to think about *why* it is the best and be prepared to share their sentence and reasoning with a partner. We provide the sentence frames: "My best sentence is _____." I think it is the best because _____."

### Question Menu

One way to ensure that you always have a closing activity on hand is to create a menu of reflection questions and tasks that students can choose from. This question menu can be stapled into their notebooks for easy reference. There are numerous options to include on the menu—students can be asked to summarize their learning, make connections, reflect on their learning processes, list something they did well and something that was a challenge, draw a quick sketch to represent their learning, write a new word they learned, and many others. The Technology Connections section contains resources for many more closure questions.

**Everybody Think . . .**

This quick closure activity is short and can be done on the fly, but it is highly effective. At the end of the class, the teacher simply asks a closure question (about content, the learning process, etc.) and says he or she will give all the students 45 seconds to think of their answers and then will call on three students to share.

**Self-Assessment Exit Tickets**

Exit tickets, or exit slips, are typically responses that students write on a card, slip of paper, or sticky note and hand in as they exit the classroom. We frequently use this type of closing activity as a quick and easy way for students to assess their comprehension. At the end of class, we ask students to reflect on their understanding of the lesson and to choose from a list of responses on the board. Examples could include "I've got it!"; "I need more practice"; "I don't get _____"; or "I still need help with _____." Students can quickly write down the response that is closest to how they're feeling. The teacher can review these responses and address any needs the following day.

We generally have students put their names on exit tickets, but sometimes we make them anonymous. This works when we want to confirm or not confirm our gut feelings about how the class is doing on a specific project or comprehending a specific concept. Even though we emphasize often that mistakes are opportunities for learning, some students might still be hesitant to disclose their lack of understanding. For example, if we're in the middle of a project and feel that students are not being entirely candid with us about how they're doing ("I got it! I got it!"), we will have them complete an anonymous exit ticket rating their feelings about the project (1 = excellent, 2 = okay, 3 = lost). We can then plan next steps based on the results. For example, maybe we need to give students additional time to complete it or provide further scaffolding.

**Sticky Note Compliments**

This activity encourages student reflection while cultivating positive student-student relationships. At the end of the lesson, the teacher quickly passes out sticky notes to each student and displays the following prompt on the document camera:

> On your sticky note, write something you learned from a classmate today or write a positive comment about one of your classmates.

The teacher then collects student responses as they leave. The next day, the teacher can share the positive comments that students have written about each other with the whole class.

**3–2–1**

The 3–2–1 activity described in Strategy 9: Jigsaw can be varied in multiple ways. One way to use it as a closing activity is to have students write down on a notecard three things they learned from the day's lesson, two questions they still have about the topic, and one thing they did well during the lesson.

**One-Minute Reports**

Another activity we've previously described that could work for closure is the one-minute report in Strategy 30: Oral Presentations. In this activity, students work together to develop a short oral report (no more than one minute long) summarizing what they learned from the day's lesson. The teacher then calls on five or six (could be more or less depending on time) students from various groups to share their one-minute report with the class or in small groups. Everyone must participate and have his or her report ready to go because students will be chosen at random by the teacher.

# What Could Go Wrong?

Do nows are meant to engage students as they walk in the door for a short period of time (usually 5 to 10 minutes, a bit longer with independent reading). Stick to the time limit and move on while students are still engaged. Don't sabotage this time by telling students all about your weekend or asking them to run errands for you. Do circulate to offer support and encourage students who seem less engaged. It is tempting to use this time (and we sometimes succumb to this temptation) to attend to our own business (checking e-mail, stapling copies, etc.), but we will see better results when we stay tuned in.

As we said, we are sometimes guilty of closing our lesson as the bell is ringing and we are shouting our good-byes or clean up instructions. Try to avoid this by devoting some thought to each lesson's closing activity. Using a question menu (such as the one previously described in the Application section) for students to reference in their folders on any day can help address this challenge. Asking students to be in charge of reminding you when it is time to close the lesson or of developing and implementing their own closure ideas can also work well.

# Technology Connections

For more on do nows, see The Best Resources for "Do Now" Activities to Begin a Class (http://larryferlazzo.edublogs.org/2016/09/10/the-best-resources-for-do-now-activities-to-begin-a-class/).

For further information on closure activities, including a long list of sample questions, see The Best Questions to Use for Class Closing Activities—What Are Yours? (http://larryferlazzo.edublogs.org/2013/09/19/here-are-some-questions-i-use-for-class-closing-activities-what-are-yours/).

# Attribution

Thank you to Paige Price for her helpful ideas in the Teaching Channel video "Your Shining Moment" (www.teachingchannel.org/videos/celebrating-student-achievement).

# STRATEGY 44

# Textbooks

## What Is It?

Many school districts have adopted textbooks of varying quality as part of the curriculum for ELLs. Unfortunately, teachers may be given only the textbook without any professional development or additional curriculum resources. It can be challenging, especially for newer teachers, to figure out how to use the textbook to meet the needs of culturally and linguistically diverse students who may be at different levels of English proficiency. It can also be difficult if the textbook is outdated or not well designed in terms of instructional practice.

## Why We Like It

Textbooks do have some advantages. They can provide a guide for effective language teaching, contain helpful models, save teachers time, and are usually leveled and aligned to standards. However, they can also present a danger when they are viewed (by teachers, administrators, or districts) as the only curriculum or one that must be followed precisely. It is also highly problematic if they are used as a substitute for instruction.

In our experience, textbooks can be practical tools when used as a *resource,* not as a curriculum. And, sometimes, their use allows us to focus on other pressing pedagogical concerns. Educator John T. McCrann (2017) explains this idea in his thought-provoking blog post "Teaching from a Textbook Makes My Class More Student-Centered." He writes how his view of textbook use has evolved over the years. Although he used to spend hours creating his own curriculum, he now feels his time is better spent deepening his relationships with students and developing the peda- gogical moves to support their thinking and learning. If using the textbook as part of the next day's lesson is going to give you more time to make that parent phone call, talk with a colleague about an intervention for a student, or allow you to more thoughtfully plan a group activity, then we say go for it!

## Supporting Research

As we discussed, there can be advantages to using textbooks, especially when their use can free up time for teachers to focus on addressing other critical pedagogical issues. However, textbooks are not a silver bullet. Researcher Robert E. Slavin (2016) points out that although content is important, numerous research studies reveal that "changing textbooks almost never changes outcomes on achievement tests." He goes on to say, "What does work, in contrast, are programs, ones that provide a great deal of professional development on well-defined models of teaching, such as cooperative learning and teaching of metacognitive skills" (para. 5).

Nothing can act as a substitute for good teaching and good professional development that can support that good teaching. We hope you will keep this in mind as you read the suggestions offered here.

## Common Core Connections

One of the advantages of textbooks touted by publishers is that they are clearly aligned to the Common Core Standards or other state standards. Sometimes this is the case, but research has also found that these claims are not always accurate ("Polikoff Study...," 2014). As with everything, trust, but verify.

## Application

The suggestions in this section can be used to make textbook activities more engaging and effective for students—whether teachers are using textbooks occasionally or on a daily basis. Some of the ideas here appeared in *The ESL/ELL Teacher's Survival Guide* (Ferlazzo & Sypnieski, 2012) and some are new.

Many textbooks for ELLs, especially for beginners, are organized thematically. Teachers can build on these themes and incorporate any of the following suggestions to increase student engagement, critical thinking skills, and language learning:

- Turn textbook passages into sequencing activities or clozes for students to complete or have students create them. See Strategy 6: Sequencing and Strategy 7: Clozes for information on these strategies and instructions for students to create their own versions.

- Use information from the text to create an inductive data set for students to read and categorize or have students create their own. Have students convert the information from the data set categories into sentences, paragraphs, or an essay. See Strategy 11: Inductive Learning for an explanation of data sets, including instructions for student-created ones.

- Supplement the activities in the text by adding engaging texts on the same theme. These could include written texts, photos, video clips, infographics, and so on.

- Turn a textbook chapter or a set of questions at the end of a chapter into a Jigsaw activity in which students work in small groups (see Strategy 9: Jigsaw). Each jigsaw group could read one section of a chapter or answer a few of the questions and work to prepare a short presentation for the class on their assigned part.

- Use graphic organizers to assist students in comprehending the textbook and organizing new information (e.g., KWL charts, Venn diagrams, etc.). See Strategy 3: Graphic Organizers for ideas.

- Convert textbook passages into read alouds or think alouds with follow-up speaking or writing prompts (see Strategy 10: Reading Comprehension for more on these strategies).

- Take dialogues contained in the textbook and personalize them based on student interests and experiences. Have students work in pairs to use a textbook dialogue as a model to write and perform their own dialogue.

- Select pictures from the textbook to use for picture word inductive model lessons (see Strategy 11: Inductive Learning for a description of this method).

- Choose a picture from the textbook for students to use with a partner for picture dictation (see Strategy 24: Dictation). One partner can describe the picture while the other partner draws on a piece of paper or mini-whiteboard. The roles can then be reversed using a different picture from the textbook.

- Convert grammar or phonics lessons from the textbook into concept attainment lessons such as the ones explained in Strategy 11: Inductive Learning.

- As suggested by teacher Russel Tarr, have students complete an activity in which they choose a topic that isn't covered in depth in the textbook or that they want to learn more about. Students can then research the topic and create a new page for the textbook containing this information along with any visuals (pictures, graphs, maps, etc.). Students can do a low-tech version on paper or can create one using technology.

- Have students review the textbook by selecting what they think is the best page or chapter and the worst. Students can support their opinion with reasons and examples from the selected page or chapter.

- Have higher-level English-proficient students choose an activity from the textbook to teach to less-proficient students. See Strategy 37: Peer Teaching and Learning for resources on students teaching each other.

- Take advantage of the online learning resources that usually come with textbooks that are often more engaging and current than the print version.

## What Could Go Wrong?

As we stated previously, a textbook *cannot* act as a substitute for good teaching. It *can* be a practical resource that provides a thematic framework, model texts, and a base of activities that teachers can modify to meet the needs and interests of their students.

## Technology Connection

For more resources on textbooks, see The Best Resources for Adapting Your Textbook So It Doesn't Bore Students to Death (http://larryferlazzo.edublogs.org/ 2011/05/14/the-best-resources-for-adapting-your-textbook-so-it-doesnt-bore-students-to-death/).

## Attribution

Versions of some of these ideas appeared in our book, *The ESL/ELL Teacher's Survival Guide* (Ferlazzo & Sypnieski, 2012, p. 264–265).

Thanks to Russel Tarr for his helpful ideas at Tarr's Toolbox (www.classtools.net/ blog/design-a-new-page-for-your-textbook/). Russel has developed what we think is the best collection of free tools for ELLs and all students to create online content (a slideshow, an annotated picture, etc.) at www.classtools.net/.

# STRATEGY 45

# Using Technology

## What Is It?

When we say *technology* in this strategy, we are specifically talking about smartphones, desktops, laptops, and tablets. Most strategies in this book have featured Technology Connections. The point of this particular strategy is to discuss broader issues about tech use and share some specific tech projects we've done with ELLs.

## Why We Like It

In Strategy 25: Conversation Practice, we briefly discussed the four pillars that promote intrinsic motivation:

1. **Autonomy:** having a degree of control over what needs to happen and how it can be done
2. **Competence:** feeling that one has the ability to be successful in doing it
3. **Relatedness:** doing the activity helps students feel more connected to others and feel cared about by people whom they respect
4. **Relevance:** work must be seen by students as interesting and useful to their present lives and hopes and dreams for the future (Ryan & Deci, 2000)

Not every lesson must have the maximum level of all four of these elements, but we don't think it's too difficult, or too much to ask, to suggest that most lessons have some degree of all of these qualities. When they are combined, these qualities promote a sense of *student agency*, when students feel that they have and, in fact, do have a greater ability to proactively determine their life's path. Student agency, in turn, also encourages a higher likelihood of being able to transfer what they learn to other contexts (Lindgren & McDaniel, 2012).

Technology—used well—can provide superior opportunities to integrate these four qualities with language instruction and particularly create possibilities to personalize learning. In other words, it can assist students to pursue highly relevant topics to their lives while connecting them to strong academic challenges.

The three main activities we highlight in this strategy clearly make those connections. We feel it is important to include the fourth one—learning to type or keyboard—because it is often overlooked in secondary classrooms (the assumption is students have developed that ability in earlier grades). This is an important skill our ELL students need to develop if they haven't already done so in their countries of origin.

As the ability to comfortably use technology becomes essential in our social, academic, and professional worlds, our ELLs can benefit by using it in ways we suggest here and in previous Technology Connections sections.

## Supporting Research

Extensive research has documented the positive impact the use of technology can have on ELLs' reading abilities (Sullivan, 2007); motivation and engagement (Baker et al., 2015; Diallo, 2014, p. 6; Lee, 2012); and writing, speaking, and listening skills (Kasapoğlu-Akyol, 2010, p. 237).

## Common Core Connections

The first three activities listed in the Application section support many different Standards. They involve reading, Writing, Speaking and Listening, and teachers need to be mindful that students are regularly increasing the complexity of the work being done. Autonomy can be a two-edged sword, and though most of our students are eager to challenge themselves, left to their own devices they may not know *how* to go about doing so.

Student skill in typing and keyboarding is important so they can meet the Standard of using "technology, including the Internet, to produce and publish writing and to interact and collaborate with others."

## Application

We will discuss specific recommendations on how students can use technology to teach their classmates, how tech can be used to promote independent learning, and how online resources can provide opportunities for meaningful homework. In addition, we'll be discussing ways to effectively teach typing and keyboarding.

## TEACHING OTHERS

In a multilevel English language learner class (and what ELL class *isn't multilevel?*), it's not always easy to keep all students engaged all the time. Periodically, we have a group (usually two or three) of more advanced ELLs choose a topic and, using computers or smartphones, work together to prepare a lesson they then teach to the entire class (see Figure 45.1: Student-Led Lesson Plan). Using Figure 45.2: Lesson Guide and teacher guidance, students identify a short and simple read aloud of four to seven sentences from online text about a topic of interest, identify several new vocabulary words from it that they will need to pre-teach the class, and find a related image they can use for a picture word inductive model (see Strategy 11: Inductive Learning) mini-lesson. We give them time to practice teaching their lesson, and then they give it a try with the entire class. Though the quality tends to be mixed, the teachers and the students seem to benefit from this change-of-pace activity.

Substantial research shows many benefits to students teaching their classmates—in motivation and academic achievement (Ferlazzo, 2012, April 22). These lessons usually take 20 minutes or so. If you want to use less time, have students only do one or two of the steps.

## INDEPENDENT STUDY

As you might note from all of our previous sections on Technology Connections, we are often very specific in the technology-related assignments we give to our students. However, we also provide them time to pursue their own choices to study. This freedom, though, comes with some guidance from us.

Researchers have found that providing different kinds of choice in learning encourages autonomy. Teachers are familiar with organizational choice (in this case, for example, it might be letting students choose which computer they would like to use and where they would like to sit) and procedural choice (e.g., providing a list of final presentation options). However, a third kind—*cognitive choice*—is thought by some researchers to stimulate even more self-motivation (Stefanou et al., 2010). Both of these independent projects try to promote cognitive choice so students are given a wide latitude in determining what they learn and how they are assessed.

We use these next two activities to promote disciplined independent study—one on a weekly basis, the other for individual days. Of course, this schedule assumes that teachers and students have regular access to technology.

### Weekly Independent Project

Every other Monday, ELL students in our class complete a form (Figure 45.3: Weekly Computer Independent Study Plan) on which they can identify anything they want to learn so long as it promotes their language development: verbs, the history of Mexico, vocabulary about food, and so on. They also choose how their learning will be assessed on that Friday—through a test (see Figure 45.4: Personalized Learning Weekly Test), a class presentation, or a student-generated assessment idea. For the most part, students research their topics using the wide variety of resources on our class blog (accessible during class and at home), but they are free to visit other online sites as well.

**Daily Independent Work**

We sometimes give students a class period to use their choice of study activities available on our class blog (which has hundreds of links). As we've previously discussed, online tools can help students reinforce their sense of competence by promoting risk-taking. Making mistakes in grammar, articulating new knowledge, or experimenting with pronunciation feels less scary when we know that our missteps will remain a secret between us and our computer.

In fact, immediate feedback from a computer program can serve as a limited form of coaching—a crucial component of deliberate practice that supports mastery. Deliberate practice is intentional goal-oriented repetition with regular reflection and subsequent readjustment of one's study (Ferlazzo, 2012, July 21). Effective practice also requires feedback and coaching. Such support might be adequately provided by a combination of feedback from the computer program and regular conversations between a student and teacher. But it also requires constant reflection by the learner on what he or she is doing right, could be doing better, and must do in order to reach the next level.

Online tools seldom provide this reflective space, so we need to consider how we can make students' work on the computer more comparable to deliberate practice. With ELL students, we provide a simple form (Figure 45.5: Daily Computer Plan and Reflection) they can use, in combination with our one-on-one conversations, for goal setting and reflection on their work online. It contains three sentence starters or guidelines (the figure also includes multiple examples and models):

- [Before you log in] Today, I want to . . .
- [At the end of class] Did I achieve my goal? (yes or no)
- [At the end of class] What things helped me learn today or didn't help me learn today?

For example, after using the reflection form and thinking about additional questions we had discussed in class, Rodrigo realized that although he had enjoyed using a site filled with English language-learning games the most, he had learned more when he used an independent reading tool that provided audio and visual support. His realization didn't mean that he never played the language games again, but he began spending more time—at home and at school—on the reading site to reach his goal of being able to read more-challenging text in English.

## HOMEWORK

In our classes, students probably have a little non-online homework once or twice a week if they don't complete some of the writing tasks we do in class. But that's pretty minimal. Online homework is a different kettle of fish and first requires some prep work with our students.

As part of more than one personal conversation we have with each student, we learn their goals, their personal situations (including age, work schedules, family and living situations, and access to the Internet). We discuss the difficulties of learning a new language, what the research says about the length of time it takes, and how much time they have left in high school. We explain that we make individual contracts with students about online homework based on their goals, age, and access to the Internet. We also tell them that our school library is open for two and one-half hours after school each day so, if they don't have a smartphone or service at home, they can use computers there (and receive tutoring).

At the end of our conversation(s), we ask each student how much time they think they can spend on one of the sites we use (we have this conversation after students have become familiar with using them during class time). Sixty percent of the time, students say an unreasonably high amount, and we say, "That's great, but why don't we start at a lower amount and then build up to that time?" We're happy with 30 minutes a day, five days a week. However, that amount can be challenging for students who are working full-time or who have had minimal prior school experience or who don't have a smartphone or Internet access at home. In those situations, we make different agreements.

In each case, we make a joint call home to talk with a family member (if a family member is not available during school hours, we'll call home at night if the family is Spanish-speaking) and explain the agreement. We do this to support the student if there's only one computer in the house or if there is a limited data plan and to help ensure there's a little more accountability support at home.

All the sites students can use—and choice is important—provide teachers with reports on student progress. Students know this and we show the reports to them. The atmosphere, however, that we work hard at creating in our classroom is not one of "If you don't do it, then your grade will go down." Instead, it's more of "What's going on? Has something changed? Do we need to readjust the time expectation?" We use a system in which students have a major influence in grading themselves and grades don't function as a big motivator in our classrooms. But it's clear that most students want us to believe that they do follow through on what they say they are going to.

Links to the homework sites our students use can be found in the Technology Connections section. In addition, we've included a link there to more details about our thoughts and practices on grading.

### LEARNING TO TYPE AND USE THE KEYBOARD

Many of our students come to us with limited typing or keyboarding skills. This can be yet another challenge to writing and test-taking success in school, so we believe it's important to help them develop this ability.

We have a link in the Technology Connections sections to free online typing and keyboarding sites. All of them are good, though Dance Mat typing from the BBC is far and above the best for ELLs because of the audio and visual support it provides to users. The link to the list that includes all of the typing sites is in the Technology Connections section.

# Student Handouts and Examples

Figure 45.1: Student-Led Lesson Plan

Figure 45.2: Lesson Guide

Figure 45.3: Weekly Computer Independent Study Plan

Figure 45.4: Personalized Learning Weekly Test

Figure 45.5: Daily Computer Plan and Reflection

# What Could Go Wrong?

Students, like all of us, can find it hard to resist the siren call of Internet distractions (social media, YouTube music and sports videos, games, etc.) when they are supposed to be working on other more academic or professional projects online. One way we try to preempt these challenges is by teaching a lesson on the famous "marshmallow test" so students can see the long-term value of self-control. A link in the Technology Connections section will lead you to that lesson. Then, prior to each time we use technology, we are able to remind students to not "eat the marshmallow."

Sometimes, prior to working on a tech task, we will also just ask students to raise their hands if they agree to not use other sites while working on their devices. Does this mean that all our students will show self-control? No, of course not. But usually a gentle reminder (or two or three) will take care of the problem. As always, teachers should not be sitting behind their desks catching up on other tasks while students are working. We need to be constantly circulating, checking in with students, offering encouragement, asking and answering questions and, yes, checking computer screens.

In Strategy 14: Writing Frames and Writing Structures, we discussed the benefits and challenges Google Translate offers to our students. Please see that strategy if you'd like to review the suggestions we offered there.

A final point we'd like to make in this section is recognizing that not all teachers and students have adequate access to school technology. If that is the case for you, and your school or district is strapped for cash, you might want to consider grant sources, including Donors Choose. We have included links to resources and advice in the Technology Connections section on seeking those kinds of funds.

## Technology Connections

For even more research on technology and language learning, you can explore The Best Places to Find Research on Technology & Language Teaching/Learning (http://larryferlazzo.edublogs.org/2011/02/23/the-best-places-to-find-research-on-technology-language-teachinglearning/).

You can find links to the online sites our students use for homework at The Best Online Homework Sites for English Language Learners (http://larryferlazzo .edublogs.org/2017/07/30/the-best-online-homework-sites-for-english-language-learners-please-offer-your-own-suggestions/).

If you'd like more information on how we handle grading, check out The Best Resources on Grading Practices (http://larryferlazzo.edublogs.org/2013/01/09/the-best-resources-on-grading-practices/).

We've listed links to typing and keyboarding sites at The Best Sites Where Students Can Learning Typing/Keyboarding (http://larryferlazzo.edublogs.org/2017/07/30/the-best-sites-where-students-can-learning-typingkeyboarding/).

For lesson plans on the marshmallow test and other ideas on how to encourage our students to develop more self-control, go to The Best Posts About Helping Students Develop Their Capacity for Self-Control (http://larryferlazzo.edublogs .org/2010/06/03/my-best-posts-about-helping-students-develop-their-capacity-for-self-control/).

If you need to raise your own funds for classroom technology (or for anything else), visit The Best Resources On Advice—& Advice for Using—for Using Donors Choose (http://larryferlazzo.edublogs.org/2015/04/05/the-best-resources-on-advice-for-using-donors-choose-please-share-your-experiences/).

## Attribution

Portions of the text in this strategy originally appeared in Larry's article in ASCD *Educational Leadership*, "Student Engagement: Key to Personalized Learning" (Ferlazzo, 2017, www.ascd.org/publications/educational-leadership/mar17/vol74/num06/Student-Engagement@-Key-to-Personalized-Learning.aspx) and is used with permission.

# Figures

Names of Teachers: _____

Lesson Topic: _____

Six words your students need to know: Write the word, definition, and how you will teach it (gesture, picture, acting, etc.). Remember, the words need to come from the read aloud:

**1.**

**2.**

**3.**

**4.**

**5.**

**6.**

Copy your read aloud here:

Show a picture on the whiteboard about your topic. Ask students to tell you words about the picture. Add at least four new words to the picture. Write one sentence on the board about the picture. Then, ask students to write one or more sentences about the picture and share with the class.

**Figure 45.1** Student-Led Lesson Plan

1. Choose a topic.

2. Ask the teacher for advice on what to read or watch online to learn about the topic.

3. Find a written passage of four to seven sentences about the topic. Copy and paste it on a document to print out and write at the bottom the URL address of where you found it.

4. Choose six words that students need to know so they can understand the read aloud.

5. Decide who will be teaching the six words and how they will teach them.

6. Decide who is going to read the read aloud.

7. Choose a picture online that relates to the topic and print it out.

8. Decide who is going to teach about the picture and what words you are going to use to label the picture.

9. Practice teaching the entire lesson at least two times.

**Figure 45.2** Lesson Guide

Name _____

This week, when you are working on the computer, think about what you would like to learn about or do. Examples could be "learn 20 words used in construction and how to use them"; "learn eight irregular verbs and how to use them"; "learn more about the history of Mexico—in English"; "read enough books in Raz-Kids to increase two levels"; "earn 600 points in Duolingo"; and so on. List them here:

**1.**

**2.**

**3.**

**4.**

How do you want to show what you have learned at the end of the week (check one; if you check more than one, you will get extra credit):

_____ Taking a test
_____ Making a presentation to the class
_____ Creating a poster
_____ Writing a song and performing it
_____ Creating and performing a short play
_____ Other (write your idea here _____)

**Figure 45.3**  Weekly Computer Independent Study Plan

Name _____

# Vocabulary

Write six new words in the area you studied and use them in sentences.

The area I studied was _____.

**1.** Word _____

Sentence _____

**2.** Word _____

Sentence _____

**3.** Word _____

Sentence _____

**4.** Word _____

Sentence _____

**5.** Word _____

Sentence _____

**6.** Word _____

Sentence _____

**Figure 45.4** Personalized Learning Weekly Test

# Conversation

If you practiced conversations on the computer, write them here:

*First Conversation:*

You: "_____
_____"

Someone else: "_____
_____"

You: "_____
_____"

Someone else: "_____
_____"

*Second Conversation:*

You: "_____
_____"

Someone else: "_____
_____"

You: "_____
_____"

Someone else: "_____
_____"

**Figure 45.4** *(Continued)*

Name _____

Date _____

# Examples

[Before you log-in] Today, I want to:

- ☐ Learn about clothes words
- ☐ Read a new level of books on Raz-Kids
- ☐ Try a new site on the class blog

[At the end of class] Did I achieve my goal? yes or no_____

[At the end of class] What things helped me learn today or didn't help me learn today:

- ☐ Working with someone else helped me learn better.
- ☐ Working with someone else did not help me learn better.
- ☐ I liked a new site called _____ because _____ _____.
- ☐ I played some games, but they didn't really help because they were too easy. I should have gone to the site called _____.

# Today's Plan and Reflection

[Before you log-in] Today, I want to:



[At the end of class] Did I achieve my goal? _____

[At the end of class] These things helped me learn today or didn't help me learn today:

**Figure 45.5** Daily Computer Plan & Reflection

# Appendix: English Language Arts Standards—Anchor Standards

## College and Career Readiness Anchor Standards for Reading

*Key Ideas and Details*

**CCSS.ELA-LITERACY.CCRA.R.1**

Read closely to determine what the text says explicitly and to make logical inferences from it; cite specific textual evidence when writing or speaking to support conclusions drawn from the text.

**CCSS.ELA-LITERACY.CCRA.R.2**

Determine central ideas or themes of a text and analyze their development; summarize the key supporting details and ideas.

**CCSS.ELA-LITERACY.CCRA.R.3**

Analyze how and why individuals, events, or ideas develop and interact over the course of a text.

*Craft and Structure*

## CCSS.ELA-LITERACY.CCRA.R.4

Interpret words and phrases as they are used in a text, including determining technical, connotative, and figurative meanings, and analyze how specific word choices shape meaning or tone.

## CCSS.ELA-LITERACY.CCRA.R.5

Analyze the structure of texts, including how specific sentences, paragraphs, and larger portions of the text (e.g., a section, chapter, scene, or stanza) relate to each other and the whole.

## CCSS.ELA-LITERACY.CCRA.R.6

Assess how point of view or purpose shapes the content and style of a text.

*Integration of Knowledge and Ideas*

## CCSS.ELA-LITERACY.CCRA.R.7

Integrate and evaluate content presented in diverse media and formats, including visually and quantitatively, as well as in words.[1]

## CCSS.ELA-LITERACY.CCRA.R.8

Delineate and evaluate the argument and specific claims in a text, including the validity of the reasoning as well as the relevance and sufficiency of the evidence.

## CCSS.ELA-LITERACY.CCRA.R.9

Analyze how two or more texts address similar themes or topics in order to build knowledge or to compare the approaches the authors take.

*Range of Reading and Level of Text Complexity*

## CCSS.ELA-LITERACY.CCRA.R.10

Read and comprehend complex literary and informational texts independently and proficiently.

---

[1] Please see "Research to Build and Present Knowledge" in **Writing** and "Comprehension and Collaboration" in **Speaking and Listening** for additional standards relevant to gathering, assessing, and applying information for print and digital resources.

# College and Career Readiness Anchor Standards for Writing

## *Text Types and Purposes*

### CCSS.ELA-LITERACY.CCRA.W.1

Write arguments to support claims in an analysis of substantive topics or texts using valid reasoning and relevant and sufficient evidence.

### CCSS.ELA-LITERACY.CCRA.W.2

Write informative/explanatory texts to examine and convey complex ideas and information clearly and accurately through the effective selection, organization, and analysis of content.

### CCSS.ELA-LITERACY.CCRA.W.3

Write narratives to develop real or imagined experiences or events using effective technique, well-chosen details, and well-structured event sequences.

## *Production and Distribution of Writing*

### CCSS.ELA-LITERACY.CCRA.W.4

Produce clear and coherent writing in which the development, organization, and style are appropriate to task, purpose, and audience.

### CCSS.ELA-LITERACY.CCRA.W.5

Develop and strengthen writing as needed by planning, revising, editing, rewriting, or trying a new approach.

### CCSS.ELA-LITERACY.CCRA.W.6

Use technology, including the Internet, to produce and publish writing and to interact and collaborate with others.

## *Research to Build and Present Knowledge*

### CCSS.ELA-LITERACY.CCRA.W.7

Conduct short as well as more sustained research projects based on focused questions, demonstrating understanding of the subject under investigation.

## CCSS.ELA-LITERACY.CCRA.W.8

Gather relevant information from multiple print and digital sources, assess the credibility and accuracy of each source, and integrate the information while avoiding plagiarism.

## CCSS.ELA-LITERACY.CCRA.W.9

Draw evidence from literary or informational texts to support analysis, reflection, and research.

### *Range of Writing*

## CCSS.ELA-LITERACY.CCRA.W.10

Write routinely over extended time frames (time for research, reflection, and revision) and shorter time frames (a single sitting or a day or two) for a range of tasks, purposes, and audiences.

# College and Career Readiness Anchor Standards for Speaking and Listening

### *Comprehension and Collaboration*

## CCSS.ELA-LITERACY.CCRA.SL.1

Prepare for and participate effectively in a range of conversations and collaborations with diverse partners, building on others' ideas and expressing their own clearly and persuasively.

## CCSS.ELA-LITERACY.CCRA.SL.2

Integrate and evaluate information presented in diverse media and formats, including visually, quantitatively, and orally.

## CCSS.ELA-LITERACY.CCRA.SL.3

Evaluate a speaker's point of view, reasoning, and use of evidence and rhetoric.

### *Presentation of Knowledge and Ideas*

## CCSS.ELA-LITERACY.CCRA.SL.4

Present information, findings, and supporting evidence such that listeners can follow the line of reasoning and the organization, development, and style are appropriate to task, purpose, and audience.

**CCSS.ELA-LITERACY.CCRA.SL.5**

Make strategic use of digital media and visual displays of data to express information and enhance understanding of presentations.

**CCSS.ELA-LITERACY.CCRA.SL.6**

Adapt speech to a variety of contexts and communicative tasks, demonstrating command of formal English when indicated or appropriate.

# College and Career Readiness Anchor Standards for Language

*Conventions of Standard English*

**CCSS.ELA-LITERACY.CCRA.L.1**

Demonstrate command of the conventions of standard English grammar and usage when writing or speaking.

**CCSS.ELA-LITERACY.CCRA.L.2**

Demonstrate command of the conventions of standard English capitalization, punctuation, and spelling when writing.

*Knowledge of Language*

**CCSS.ELA-LITERACY.CCRA.L.3**

Apply knowledge of language to understand how language functions in different contexts, to make effective choices for meaning or style, and to comprehend more fully when reading or listening.

*Vocabulary Acquisition and Use*

**CCSS.ELA-LITERACY.CCRA.L.4**

Determine or clarify the meaning of unknown and multiple-meaning words and phrases by using context clues, analyzing meaningful word parts, and consulting general and specialized reference materials, as appropriate.

**CCSS.ELA-LITERACY.CCRA.L.5**

Demonstrate understanding of figurative language, word relationships, and nuances in word meanings.

## CCSS.ELA-LITERACY.CCRA.L.6

Acquire and use accurately a range of general academic and domain-specific words and phrases sufficient for reading, writing, speaking, and listening at the college and career readiness level; demonstrate independence in gathering vocabulary knowledge when encountering an unknown term important to comprehension or expression.

# Technological Connections
## Web Resources

### STRATEGY 1: Independent Reading

Ferlazzo, L. (2008, January 22). The best websites to help beginning readers. http://bit.ly/elltoolbox1

Ferlazzo, L. (2008, January 23). The best websites for beginning older readers. http://bit.ly/elltoolbox2

Ferlazzo, L. (2008, December 6). The best online resources for teachers of preliterate ELLs. http://bit.ly/elltoolbox3

Ferlazzo, L. (2008, January 26). The best websites for intermediate readers. http://bit.ly/elltoolbox4

Ferlazzo, L. (2009, July 31). The best sources for free and accessible printable books. http://bit.ly/elltoolbox5

### STRATEGY 2: Literary Conversations

Martin, T.M. (2016, August 23). *#BookSnaps—Snapping for Learning.* http://bit.ly/elltoolbox6

Sharp, C. (2017, April 17). *15 Second Book Talks Take 1.* http://bit.ly/elltoolbox7

Ferlazzo, L. (2010, May 30). The best posts on books: Why they're important & how to help students select, read, write & discuss them. http://bit.ly/elltoolbox8

Ferlazzo, L. (2013, February 18). The best resources for learning to use the video apps "Vine" & Instagram. http://bit.ly/elltoolbox9

Ferlazzo, L. (2008, March 17). The best sites to practice speaking English. http://bit.ly/elltoolbox10

Ferlazzo, L. (2014, November 7). Here's a new reading activity I tried out today that went pretty well. http://bit.ly/elltoolbox11

Ferlazzo, L. (2017, April 6). Apple's new video-editing app "Clips". http://bit.ly/elltoolbox12

Ferlazzo, L. (2017, January 24). Video: "Adobe Spark" is excellent tool for ELLs. http://bit.ly/elltoolbox13

Ferlazzo, L. (2012, May 19). The best resources for teaching "what if" history lessons. http://bit.ly/elltoolbox14

## STRATEGY 3: Graphic Organizers

Ferlazzo, L. (2009, February 9). The best list of mindmapping, flow chart tools, & graphic organizers. http://bit.ly/elltoolbox15

## STRATEGY 4: Vocabulary

Ferlazzo, L. (2013, February 18). The best resources for learning to use the video apps "Vine" & Instagram. http://bit.ly/elltoolbox9

Dweck, C. (2010). Even geniuses work hard. *Educational Leadership*, *68*(1), 16–20. http://bit.ly/elltoolbox16

*Test Your Vocab*. (n.d.). http://testyourvocab.com/

Ferlazzo, L. (2013, January 5). A collection of "best" lists on vocabulary development. http://bit.ly/elltoolbox18

Ferlazzo, L. (2008, November 13). The best reference websites for English language learners. http://bit.ly/elltoolbox19

Ferlazzo, L. (2008, April 6). The best websites for developing academic English skills & vocabulary. http://bit.ly/elltoolbox20

## STRATEGY 5: Activating Prior Knowledge

Ferlazzo, L. (2014, November 16). The best places to get the "same" text written for different "levels." http://bit.ly/elltoolbox21

Ferlazzo, L. (2008, October 3). The best multilingual & bilingual sites for math, social studies, & science. http://bit.ly/elltoolbox22

Ferlazzo, L. (2009, August 11). The best resources for finding and creating virtual field trips. http://bit.ly/elltoolbox23

Ferlazzo, L. (2017, February 27). A beginning list of the best resources on virtual reality in education. http://bit.ly/elltoolbox24

## STRATEGY 6: Sequencing

Ministry of Education. (n.d.). Strip stories. *ESOL Online*. http://bit.ly/elltoolbox25

Ferlazzo, L. (2010, March 29). The best sites for creating sentence scrambles. http://bit.ly/elltoolbox26

Ferlazzo, L. (2008, June 4). The best ways to make comic strips online. http://bit.ly/elltoolbox27

## STRATEGY 7: Clozes

Ferlazzo, L. (2012, April 30). The best tools for creating clozes (gap-fills). http://bit.ly/elltoolbox28

## STRATEGY 8: Language Experience Approach (LEA)

Ferlazzo, L. (2008, May 6). The best ways to create online slide shows. http://bit.ly/elltoolbox29

## STRATEGY 9: Jigsaw

*edHelper.com*. (n.d.). https://edhelper.com/

Welcome to Enchanted Learning. (n.d.). www.enchantedlearning.com/Home.html

*ESL Jigsaws*. (n.d.). www.esljigsaws.com

Ferlazzo, L. (2015, September 19). The best ways to use "3–2–1" as an instructional strategy. http://bit.ly/elltoolbox33a

Ferlazzo, L. (2014, November 16). The best places to get the "same" text written for different "levels." http://bit.ly/elltoolbox21

## STRATEGY 10: Reading Comprehension

Ferlazzo, L. (2008, December 18). Best applications for annotating websites. http://bit.ly/elltoolbox34

Ferlazzo, L. (2008, May 21). The best sites that students can use independently and let teachers check on progress. http://bit.ly/elltoolbox35

Ferlazzo, L. (2015, August 5). The best resources on close reading paintings, photos & videos. http://bit.ly/elltoolbox36

Ferlazzo, L. (2013, May 13). The best resources on "close reading"—Help me find more. http://bit.ly/elltoolbox37

Ferlazzo, L., & Sypnieski, K.H. (2012). *The ESL/ELL Teacher's Survival Guide.* Jossey-Bass, San Francisco, CA. http://bit.ly/elltoolbox38

Ferlazzo, L., & Sypnieski, K.H. (2016). *Navigating the Common Core with English Language Learners.* Jossey-Bass, San Francisco, CA. http://bit.ly/elltoolbox39

Ferlazzo, L. (2013, July 13). The best videos & articles where athletes explain how reading & writing well has helped their career—Help me find more. http://bit.ly/elltoolbox40

Ferlazzo, L. (2016, August 13). The best resources on the study finding that reading books makes you live longer. http://bit.ly/elltoolbox41

## STRATEGY 11: Inductive Learning

Ferlazzo, L. (2011, March 30). The best online virtual "corkboards" (or "bulletin boards"). http://bit.ly/elltoolbox42

Ferlazzo, L. (2017, May 26). How my ELL students used Padlet to create a "picture data set." http://bit.ly/elltoolbox43

Ferlazzo, L. (2016, August 14). The "all-time" best sources of online images. http://bit.ly/elltoolbox44

Ferlazzo, L. (2015, January 16). The best resources about inductive learning & teaching. http://bit.ly/elltoolbox45

## STRATEGY 12: Concept Attainment—Plus!

Ferlazzo, L. (2009, April 1). The best places where students can write for an "authentic audience." http://bit.ly/elltoolbox46

Ferlazzo, L. (2008, December 26). The best sources for advice on student blogging. http://bit.ly/elltoolbox47

Ferlazzo, L. (2009, August 10). The best teacher resources for online student safety & legal issues. http://bit.ly/elltoolbox48

## STRATEGY 13: Sentence Navigators and Sentence Builders

Ferlazzo, L. (2014, April 19). "Sentence navigator" is Jason Renshaw's gift to ESL/EFL/ELL teachers everywhere! http://bit.ly/elltoolbox49

## STRATEGY 14: Writing Frames and Writing Structures

Ferlazzo, L. (2016, December 1). The best scaffolded writing frames for students. http://bit.ly/elltoolbox50

Ferlazzo, L. (2009, April 1). The best places where students can write for an "authentic audience." http://bit.ly/elltoolbox46

Ferlazzo, L. (2015, July 5). "They Say, I Say" is a great writing resource. http://bit.ly/elltoolbox51

Barnabel, G. (n.d.). What is a kernel essay? *Trail of Breadcrumbs.* http://bit.ly/elltoolbox52

## STRATEGY 15: Quoting, Summarizing, and Paraphrasing

Ferlazzo, L. (2009, September 21). The best online resources to teach about plagiarism. http://bit.ly/elltoolbox53

## STRATEGY 16: Cooperative Writing

Ferlazzo, L. (2009, August 10). The best teacher resources for online student safety & legal issues. http://bit.ly/elltoolbox48

Ferlazzo, L. (2010, December 29). The best sites for collaborative storytelling. http://bit.ly/elltoolbox54

Ferlazzo, L. (2008, March 2). The best online tools for real-time collaboration. http://bit.ly/elltoolbox55

Ferlazzo, L. (2008, April 10). The best online tools for collaboration—NOT in real time. http://bit.ly/elltoolbox56

## STRATEGY 17: Using Photos or Other Images in Reading and Writing

Ferlazzo, L. (2012, October 19). The best online tools for using photos in lessons. http://bit.ly/elltoolbox57

Ferlazzo, L. (2015, August 1a). The best resources for using "If this animal or image could talk" lesson idea in class. http://bit.ly/elltoolbox58

Ferlazzo, L. (2015, August 5). The best resources on close reading paintings, photos & videos. http://bit.ly/elltoolbox59

## STRATEGY 18: Writer's Notebook

Ferlazzo, L. (2008, October 19). The best places where students can write online. http://bit.ly/elltoolbox60

## STRATEGY 19: Error Correction Strategies

Ferlazzo, L. (2008, December 7). The best sites for grammar practice.

http://bit.ly/elltoolbox61

Ferlazzo, L. (2013, November 7). The best ways to use mistakes when teaching writing. http://bit.ly/elltoolbox62

Ferlazzo, L. (2011, July 28). The best posts, articles & videos about learning from mistakes and failures. http://bit.ly/elltoolbox63

Ferlazzo, L. (2012, October 13). The best resources on helping our students develop a growth mindset. http://bit.ly/elltoolbox64

Ferlazzo, L., & Sypnieski, K.H. (2016). *Navigating the Common Core with English Language Learners*. Jossey-Bass, San Francisco, CA.

http://bit.ly/elltoolbox65

## STRATEGY 20: Revision

Ferlazzo, L. (2015, July 23). The best resources on getting student writers to "buy-into" revision—Help me find more. http://bit.ly/elltoolbox66

Ferlazzo, L. (2015, April 16). The "all-time" best 2.0 tools for beginning English language learners. http://bit.ly/elltoolbox67a

Ferlazzo, L. (2015, June 29). The best online tools that can help students write an essay. http://bit.ly/elltoolbox68

Ferlazzo, L. (2017, March 6). Resources from all my blogs. http://bit.ly/elltoolbox69

Ferlazzo, L. (n.d.). Mr. Ferlazzo's ELD class blog. *Edublogs*.

http://bit.ly/elltoolbox70

Ferlazzo, L. (2009, June 3). The best sources of advice for teachers (and others!) on how to be better bloggers. http://bit.ly/elltoolbox71

Ferlazzo, L. (2008, December 26). The best sources for advice on student blogging. http://bit.ly/elltoolbox47

## STRATEGY 21: Problem-Posing

Ferlazzo, L. (2011, October 10). The best resources for learning about teacher home visits. *Edublogs*. http://bit.ly/elltoolbox72

Ferlazzo, L. (2013, November 1). Using Freire & Fotobabble with English language learners. http://bit.ly/elltoolbox73

Ferlazzo, L. (2016, September 21). A look back: Combining an "assets" perspective with an authentic audience. http://bit.ly/elltoolbox74

## STRATEGY 23: Learning Games for Reading and Writing

Ferlazzo, L. (n.d.). "All-time" best web tools for English language learners.

http://bit.ly/elltoolbox75

Ferlazzo, L. (2011, September 19). The best beginner, intermediate & advanced English language learner sites. http://bit.ly/elltoolbox76

*duoLingo.* (n.d.). www.duolingo.com

*LingoHut.* (n.d.). http://lingohut.com

*Draw a Stickman.* (n.d.). www.drawastickman.com

Ferlazzo, L. (2008). Pointing and clicking for ESL: Using video games to promote English language development. *Technology and Learning Educator's eZine.* http://bit.ly/elltoolbox80

Ferlazzo, L. (2013, April 21). Video games and walkthroughs used in class. http://bit.ly/elltoolbox81

Ferlazzo, L. (2008, April 21). The best websites for creating online learning games. http://bit.ly/elltoolbox82

*ClassTools.* (n.d.). www.classtools.net

*Kahoot!* (n.d.). https://kahoot.com/

*Quizalize.* (n.d.). www.quizalize.com/

*Quizizz.* (n.d.). https://quizizz.com/

Ferlazzo, L. (2013, October 27). The best ideas for using games in the ESL/EFL/ELL classroom. http://bit.ly/elltoolbox87

Ferlazzo, L. (2010, August 28). A collection of "the best" lists on learning games. http://bit.ly/elltoolbox88

## STRATEGY 24: Dictation

Ferlazzo, L. (2017, July 15). The best sites for ELLs to practice online dictation. http://bit.ly/elltoolbox89

Ferlazzo, L. (2011, September 6). The best online resources for "information gap" activities. http://bit.ly/elltoolbox90

Ferlazzo, L. (2009, July 31). The best sources for free & accessible printable books. http://bit.ly/elltoolbox91

Ferlazzo, L. (2014, November 16). The best places to get the "same" text written for different "levels." http://bit.ly/elltoolbox92

## STRATEGY 25: Conversation Practice

Ferlazzo, L. (2008, March 17). The best sites to practice speaking English. http://bit.ly/elltoolbox93

Ferlazzo, L. (2008, April 6). The best sites for developing English conversational skills. http://bit.ly/elltoolbox94b

Ferlazzo, L. (2008, March 31). The best sites for learning English pronunciation. http://bit.ly/elltoolbox95

Ferlazzo, L. (2009, October 7). The best resources for using puppets in class. http://bit.ly/elltoolbox96

Ferlazzo, L., & Sypnieski, K.H. (2012). *The ESL/ELL Teacher's Survival Guide* (Exhibit 4.3). Jossey-Bass, San Francisco, CA.

http://bit.ly/elltoolbox97

## STRATEGY 26: Total Physical Response (TPR)

Ferlazzo, L. (2016, September 10b). The best resources for learning about total physical response (TPR). http://bit.ly/elltoolbox98

Jellema, H. (n.d.). *For English as a Second Language: TPR Exercises.*

http://bit.ly/elltoolbox100

Ferlazzo, L. (2010, July 3). The best "When I say jump" online sites for practicing English. http://bit.ly/elltoolbox101

## STRATEGY 27: Music

Ferlazzo, L. (2008, January 30). The best music websites for learning English. http://bit.ly/elltoolbox102

Ferlazzo, L. (2008, October 15). The best online karaoke sites for English language learners. http://bit.ly/elltoolbox103

Ferlazzo, L. (2016, November 18). The mannequin challenge, ELLs & a frozen tableau. http://bit.ly/elltoolbox104

Ferlazzo, L. (2015, May 10). Here's a successful music lesson we did with beginning ELLs (hand-outs & student examples included).

http://bit.ly/elltoolbox105

Ferlazzo, L. (2013, February 23b). The best tools for creating visually attractive quotations for online display. http://bit.ly/elltoolbox106

Ferlazzo, L. (2011, July 28). The best sites (& videos) for learning about jazz chants. http://bit.ly/elltoolbox107

## STRATEGY 28: Using Photos or Other Images in Speaking and Listening

Ferlazzo, L. (2010, June 27). The best ways to use photos in lessons. http://bit.ly/elltoolbox108

Ferlazzo, L. (2015, August 1a). The best resources for using "If this animal or image could talk" lesson idea in class. http://bit.ly/elltoolbox109

ELTpics. (n.d.). www.eltpics.com/

ELTpics. (n.d.). *Flickr.* http://bit.ly/elltoolbox111

## STRATEGY 29: Video

Ferlazzo, L. (2008, April 26). The best popular movie/tv shows for ESL/EFL (& how to use them). http://bit.ly/elltoolbox112

Ferlazzo, L. (2017, May 21). The best fun videos for English language learners in 2017—so far. http://bit.ly/elltoolbox113

Ferlazzo, L. (2010, February 1). The best movie scenes to use for English-language development. http://bit.ly/elltoolbox114

Ferlazzo, L. (2014, February 23). The "all-time" best ways to create online content easily & quickly. http://bit.ly/elltoolbox115

*Tildee: You explain, they understand.* (n.d.). www.tildee.com/

Ferlazzo, L. (2008, May 14). The best ways for students to create online videos (using someone else's content). http://bit.ly/elltoolbox117

Ferlazzo, L. (2012, November 6). A potpourri of the best & most useful video sites. http://bit.ly/elltoolbox118

Ferlazzo, L. (2008, July 24). The best online instructional video sites. http://bit.ly/elltoolbox119

Ferlazzo, L. (2013, February 18). The best resources for learning to use the video apps "Vine" & Instagram. http://bit.ly/elltoolbox120

Ferlazzo, L. (2013, August 13). If you don't have teacher access to YouTube at your school, then this search engine is a "must." http://bit.ly/elltoolbox121

Ferlazzo, L. (2015, October 16). The best ways to deal with YouTube's awful safety mode. http://bit.ly/elltoolbox122

Ferlazzo, L. (2017, February 27). A beginning list of the best resources on virtual reality in education. http://bit.ly/elltoolbox123

## STRATEGY 30: Oral Presentations

Ferlazzo, L. (2015, September 19). The best ways to use "3–2–1" as an instructional strategy. http://bit.ly/elltoolbox33a

Ferlazzo, L. (2017, August 1a). The best resources for teaching students the differences between a good & bad slide. http://bit.ly/elltoolbox125

Ferlazzo, L. (2009, May 25). The best sources of advice for making good presentations. http://bit.ly/elltoolbox126

Ferlazzo, L. (2014, January 20). Home culture presentations with English language learners. http://bit.ly/elltoolbox127

## STRATEGY 31: Listening

Ferlazzo, L. (2012, July 23). The best ideas to help students become better listeners—Contribute more. http://bit.ly/elltoolbox128

Ferlazzo, L. (2008, May 28). The best listening sites for English language learners. http://bit.ly/elltoolbox129

Ferlazzo, L. (2009, May 2). The best places to read & write "Choose your own adventure" stories. http://bit.ly/elltoolbox130

Ferlazzo, L. (2012, May 13). The best posts on metacognition. http://bit.ly/elltoolbox131

## STRATEGY 32: Debate

Ferlazzo, L. (2009, October 24). The best sites for students to create & participate in online debates. http://bit.ly/elltoolbox132

## STRATEGY 33: Learning Games for Speaking and Listening

Ferlazzo, L. (2008, March 17). The best sites to practice speaking English. http://bit.ly/elltoolbox93

Ferlazzo, L. (2017, July 20). The best resources & ideas for using sound effects in ELL lessons. http://bit.ly/elltoolbox133

Ferlazzo, L. (2016, July 12). "Guess what" is a great "new" game—Plus, ELLs can create a video for an authentic audience. http://bit.ly/elltoolbox134

*Drawception*. (n.d.). https://drawception.com/

Ferlazzo, L. (2009, February 10). The best online games students can play in private virtual "rooms." http://bit.ly/elltoolbox135

## STRATEGY 34: Differentiation for ELLs in Mainstream Classes

Ferlazzo, L. (2017, July 14). The best videos for content teachers with ELLs in their classes—please suggest more. http://bit.ly/elltoolbox136

Ferlazzo, L. (2011, September 7). The best sites for learning strategies to teach ELLs in content classes. http://bit.ly/elltoolbox137

Ferlazzo, L. (2014, November 22a). The best resources for teaching Common Core math to English language learners. http://bit.ly/elltoolbox138

Ferlazzo, L. (2014, November 22b). The best resources for teaching the Next Generation Science Standards to English language learners.

http://bit.ly/elltoolbox139

Ferlazzo, L. (2008, October 3). The best multilingual & bilingual sites for math, social studies, & science. http://bit.ly/elltoolbox140

Ferlazzo, L. (2014, November 16). The best places to get the "same" text written for different "levels." http://bit.ly/elltoolbox141

Ferlazzo, L. (2009, July 31). The best sources for free & accessible printable books. http://bit.ly/elltoolbox142

Ferlazzo, L. (2009, February 9). The best places to buy ESL/EFL books, software & multimedia. http://bit.ly/elltoolbox143

Ferlazzo, L. (2008, April 19). The best books for teaching & learning ESL/EFL. http://bit.ly/elltoolbox144

Ferlazzo, L. (2015, June 23). The best resources on effective note-taking strategies—Help me find more. http://bit.ly/elltoolbox145

Ferlazzo, L. (2014, June 14). The best research demonstrating that lectures are not the best instructional strategy. http://bit.ly/elltoolbox146

Ferlazzo, L. (2016, November 24). Ways that a mainstream teacher can support an ELL newcomer in class. http://bit.ly/elltoolbox147

Ferlazzo, L. (n.d.). *Online tools.* Teaching English.org. http://bit.ly/elltoolbox148

Ferlazzo, L. (2017, January 5). The best resources on providing scaffolds to students. http://bit.ly/elltoolbox149

## STRATEGY 35: Supporting ELL Students with Interrupted Formal Education (SIFEs)

Ferlazzo, L. (2008, December 6). The best online resources for teachers of pre-literate ELL's & those not literate in their home language.

http://bit.ly/elltoolbox150

Ferlazzo, L. (2011, March 1). The best articles & sites for teachers & students to learn about phonics. http://bit.ly/elltoolbox151

## STRATEGY 36: Culturally Responsive Teaching

Ferlazzo, L. (2016, June 10). The best resources about "culturally responsive teaching" & "culturally sustaining pedagogy"—Please share more! http://bit.ly/elltoolbox152

Ferlazzo, L. (2016, June 11). The best resources on the importance of correctly pronouncing student names. http://bit.ly/elltoolbox153

Ferlazzo, L. (2016, July 14). A collection of advice on talking to students about race, police & racism. http://bit.ly/elltoolbox154

Ferlazzo, L. (2017, March 22). A beginning list of the best resources for fighting Islamophobia in schools. http://bit.ly/elltoolbox155

Ferlazzo, L. (2017, February 26). The best practical resources for helping teachers, students & families respond to immigration challenges.

http://bit.ly/elltoolbox156

## STRATEGY 37: Peer Teaching and Learning

Ferlazzo, L. (2017, April 21). Guest post: What ELLs taught our school in a week-long empathy project. http://bit.ly/elltoolbox157

Ferlazzo, L. (2017, June 17). This is a must-watch video for any volunteer or peer tutor working with ELLs. http://bit.ly/elltoolbox158

Ferlazzo, L. (2009, February 18). The best sites for free ESL/EFL hand-outs & worksheets. http://bit.ly/elltoolbox159

Ferlazzo, L. (2015, August 1b). Links to the joint projects my ELL geography class did with classes around the world. http://bit.ly/elltoolbox160

Ferlazzo, L. (2009, May 30). The best ways to find other classes for joint online projects. http://bit.ly/elltoolbox161

Ferlazzo, L. (2012, April 22). The best posts on helping students teach their classmates—Help me find more. http://bit.ly/elltoolbox162

## STRATEGY 38: Co-Teaching

Ferlazzo, L. (2017, July 7). The best resources on co-teaching with ELLs—Please suggest more. http://bit.ly/elltoolbox163

## STRATEGY 39: Working with Parents and Guardians

Ferlazzo, L. (2017, August 6). The best parent engagement resources for immigrant families. http://bit.ly/elltoolbox164

Ferlazzo, L. (2011, October 10). The best resources for learning about teacher home visits. *Edublogs: Engaging Parents in School*. http://bit.ly/elltoolbox165

Ferlazzo, L. (2011, March 19). The best resources for learning about schools providing home computers & Internet access to students. http://bit.ly/elltoolbox166

Ferlazzo, L. (2013, May 16). The best multilingual resources for parents. *Edublogs: Engaging Parents in School*. http://bit.ly/elltoolbox167

Ferlazzo, L. (2013, February 23a). My best posts on parent "academies" & "universities." *Edublogs: Engaging Parents in School.* http://bit.ly/elltoolbox168

Ferlazzo, L. (2017, February 26). The best practical resources for helping teachers, students & families respond to immigration challenges. http://bit.ly/elltoolbox156

Ferlazzo, L. (2016, October 12). The best places where students can tell their—and/or their families—immigration story. http://bit.ly/elltoolbox169

Ferlazzo, L. (2014, February 9). The best student projects that need family engagement—Contribute your lessons! *Edublogs: Engaging Parents in School.* http://bit.ly/elltoolbox170

## STRATEGY 40: Learning Stations

Ferlazzo, L. (2017, August 14). The best resources for planning "learning stations." http://bit.ly/elltoolbox171

## STRATEGY 41: Beginning the School Year

Ferlazzo, L. (2017, July 18). The best resources on developing a sense of community in the classroom. http://bit.ly/elltoolbox172

Ferlazzo, L. (2011, August 8). The best resources for planning the first days of school. http://bit.ly/elltoolbox173

## STRATEGY 42: Ending the School Year

Ferlazzo, L. (2015, April 17). The best ways to finish the school year strong. http://bit.ly/elltoolbox174

Ferlazzo, L. (2010, May 18). The best posts on students setting goals. http://bit.ly/elltoolbox175

Ferlazzo, L. (2016, June 24). The best resources for organizing & maximizing field trips—both "real" & "virtual." http://bit.ly/elltoolbox176

Ferlazzo, L. (2010, May 8). The best posts on students evaluating classes (and teachers). http://bit.ly/elltoolbox177

Ferlazzo, L. (2011, June 26). The best resources on the "summer slide." http://bit.ly/elltoolbox178

Ferlazzo, L. (2016, May 23). Updated: Here are the sites I'm using for my summer school "virtual classroom." http://bit.ly/elltoolbox179

## STRATEGY 43: Beginning and Ending of Class

Ferlazzo, L. (2016, September 10a). The best resources for "do now" activities to begin a class. http://bit.ly/elltoolbox180

Ferlazzo, L. (2013, September 19). The best questions to use for class closing activities—What are yours? http://bit.ly/elltoolbox181

## STRATEGY 44: Textbooks

Ferlazzo, L. (2011, May 14). The best resources for adapting your textbook so it doesn't bore students to death. http://bit.ly/elltoolbox182

## STRATEGY 45: Using Technology

Ferlazzo, L. (2011, February 23). The best places to find research on technology & language teaching/learning. http://bit.ly/elltoolbox183

Ferlazzo, L. (2017, July 30a). The best online homework sites for English language learners. http://bit.ly/elltoolbox184

Ferlazzo, L. (2013, January 9). The best resources on grading practices. http://bit.ly/elltoolbox185

Ferlazzo, L. (2017, July 30b). The best sites where students can learn typing/keyboarding. http://bit.ly/elltoolbox186

Ferlazzo, L. (2010, June 3). The best posts about helping students develop their capacity for self-control. http://bit.ly/elltoolbox187

Ferlazzo, L. (2015, April 5). The best resources on—& advice for using—Donors Choose. http://bit.ly/elltoolbox188

# REFERENCES

Aguilar, E. (2015, February 25). Making connections: Culturally responsive teaching and the brain. *Edutopia*. Retrieved from www.edutopia.org/blog/making-connections-culturally-responsive-teaching-and-brain-elena-aguilar

Albano, L. (2017, April 11). *The Dice Game: A Fun, Low-Prep Speaking Game*. Larissa's Language Studio. Retrieved from http://larissaslanguages.blogspot.com.es/2017/04/the-dice-game-fun-low-prep-speaking-game.html

Alkire, S. (2002). Dictation as a language learning device. *The Internet TESL Journal, VIII*(3). Retrieved from http://iteslj.org/Techniques/Alkire-Dictation.html

Almurashi, W.A. (2016). The effective use of YouTube videos for teaching English language in classrooms as supplementary material at Taibah University in Alula. *International Journal of English Language and Linguistics Research*, 4(3), 32–47. Retrieved from www.eajournals.org/wp-content/uploads/The-Effective-Use-of-Youtube-Videos-for-Teaching-English-Language-in-Classrooms-as-Supplementary-Material-at-Taibah-University-in-Alula.pdf

American English equivalent of "revise" (as in studying). (n.d.). *English Language & Usage*. Retrieved from https://english.stackexchange.com/questions/139918/american-english-equivalent-of-revise-as-in-studying

AnthonyTeacher.com. (n.d.a). *The Power of PechaKucha*. Retrieved from www.anthonyteacher.com/blog/the-power-of-pechakucha

AnthonyTeacher.com. (n.d.b). *Research Bites: Corrective Feedback—A Meta-Analysis*. Retrieved from www.anthonyteacher.com/blog/researchbites/research-bites-the-mother-of-all-corrective-feedback-studies

Appel, T., & Ferlazzo, L. (n.d.). *The Positive Impact of English Language Learners at an Urban School*. Retrieved from http://larryferlazzo.com/Positiveimpact.html

Ariely, D. (2016, December 12). How the "IKEA effect" can motivate people to work harder. *YouTube.* Retrieved from www.youtube.com/watch?v=D5hD1uAg1N4

Arvin, R. (1987). *Application of the Language Experience Approach for Secondary Level Students.* Master's thesis, University of North Florida, Jacksonville. Retrieved from http://digitalcommons.unf.edu/cgi/viewcontent.cgi?article=1319&context=etd

Ashraf, H., Motlagh, F.G., & Salami, M. (2014). The impact of online games on learning English vocabulary by Iranian (low-intermediate) EFL learners. *Procedia— Social and Behavioral Sciences, 98,* 286–291. Retrieved from www.sciencedirect .com/science/article/pii/S1877042814025099

Association for Psychological Science. (2013, May 28). *Picking up a Second Language is Predicted by Ability to Learn Patterns.* Retrieved from www.psychologicalscience .org/news/releases/picking-up-a-second-language-is-predicted-by-the-ability- to-learn-statistical-patterns.html

Atwell, N. (2014). *In the Middle* (3rd ed.). Heinemann, Portsmouth, NH.

Atwell, N. (2017). *Lessons That Change Writers.* Heinemann, Portsmouth, NH.

Baecher, L. (2011). Differentiated instruction for English language learners: Strategies for the secondary English teacher. *Wisconsin English Journal, 53*(2), 64–73. Retrieved from http://journals.library.wisc.edu/index.php/wej/article/viewFile/ 378/479

Baker, R., Do, D.M., & Mailand, S. (2015). *The Use of Technology to Enhance English Language (ESL) Teaching.* Bachelor's qualifying project, Worcester Polytechnic Institute, Worcester, MA. Retrieved from https://web.wpi.edu/Pubs/E-project/ Available/E-project-030515–211609/unrestricted/CIHE_IQP_Report_C15.pdf

Banville, S. (n.d.). People who read live longer. *Breaking News English.* Retrieved from www.breakingnewsenglish.com/1608/160810-reading.html

Bashir, S. (2014). A study of second language-speaking anxiety among ESL intermediate Pakistani learners. *International Journal of English and Education, 3,* 216–229.

Bassano, S. (2002). *Sounds Easy! Phonics, Spelling, and Pronunciation Practice.* Alta Book Company, Palm Springs, CA.

Bedee, S. (2010). *The Impact of Literature Circles on Reading Motivation and Comprehension for Students in a Second Grade Classroom.* Master's thesis, Bowling Green State University, Bowling Green, OH. Retrieved from https://etd.ohiolink.edu/rws_ etd/document/get/bgsu1269222677/inline

Bennett, C.M. (2013). *Close Reading Constable's "The Hay Wain" and Turner's "The Fighting Temeraire."* Retrieved from https://usedbooksinclass.com/2013/10/03/close- reading-constables-the-hay-wain-and-turners-the-fighting-temeraire/

Boonkit, K. (2010). Enhancing the development of speaking skills for non-native speakers of English. *Procedia—Social and Behavioral Sciences, 2*(2), 1305–1309. Retrieved from www.sciencedirect.com/science/article/pii/S1877042810002314

Boulware-Gooden, R., Carreker, S., Thornhill, A., & Joshi, M. (n.d.). Instruction of metacognitive strategies enhances reading comprehension and vocabulary achievement of third-grade students. *Reading Rockets*. Retrieved from www.readingrockets.org/article/instruction-metacognitive-strategies-enhances-reading-comprehension-and-vocabulary

Boyles, N. (2012/2013). Closing in on close reading. *Educational Leadership, 70*(4), 36–41. Retrieved from www.ascd.org/publications/educational-leadership/dec12/vol70/num04/Closing-in-on-Close-Reading.aspx

Brady-Myerov, M. (2015, July 21). Closed captioning gives literacy a boost. *Education Week*. Retrieved from www.edweek.org/ew/articles/2015/07/21/closed-captioning-gives-literacy-a-boost.html?utm_source=fb&utm_medium=rss&utm_campaign=mrss

Brain Pop. (n.d.). *Movie of the Week*. Retrieved from https://jr.brainpop.com/

Brown, M. (2011). *Effects of Graphic Organizers on Student Achievement in the Writing Process*. Retrieved from https://eric.ed.gov/?id=ED527571

Bruner, J.S., Goodnow, J.J., & Austin, G.A. (1956). *A Study of Thinking*. Chapman & Hall, London, UK.

Budden, J. (2008). *Chain Drawings. BBC British Council*. Retrieved from www.teachingenglish.org.uk/article/chain-drawings

Burgess, M. (2011). *Best Practices for Collaboration Between ESL and General Education Teachers*. Master's thesis, Minnesota State University, Mankato, MN. Retrieved from http://cornerstone.lib.mnsu.edu/cgi/viewcontent.cgi?article=1269&context=etds

Busch, B. (2017, June 7). Teachers: Here's how to get your lessons off to a flying start. *The Guardian*. Retrieved from www.theguardian.com/teacher-network/2017/jun/07/teachers-heres-how-to-get-your-lessons-off-to-a-flying-start

Byers-Heinlein, K., & Garcia, B. (2015). Bilingualism changes children's beliefs about what is innate. *Developmental Science, 18*(2), 344–350. Retrieved from http://onlinelibrary.wiley.com/doi/10.1111/desc.12248/abstract

Cabal, C. (2016, September 21). 10 creative ways to use the *Wheel of Fortune* to teach English. *Blog de Cristina*. Retrieved from www.cristinacabal.com/?p=5269

Calet, N., Gutiérrez-Palma, N., & Defior, S. (2017). Effects of fluency training on reading competence in primary school children: The role of prosody. *Learning and Instruction*. Retrieved from www.sciencedirect.com/science/article/pii/S0959475217302530

Calhoun, E.F. (1999). *Teaching Beginning Reading and Writing with the Picture Word Inductive Model*. Association for Supervision and Curriculum Development, Alexandria, VA.

Calkins, L., & Ehrenworth, M. (n.d.). *What Does Research Say Adolescent Readers Need? A Preview from a Guide to the Reading Workshop*: Middle Grades. Retrieved from www.heinemann.com/blog/what-does-research-say-adolescent-readers-need/?utm_campaign=Calkins&utm_content=56491188&utm_medium=social&utm_source=twitter

Carnegie Mellon University. (2015, August 13). New information is easier to learn when composed of familiar elements. *EurekAlert!* Retrieved from www.eurekalert.org/pub_releases/2015–08/cmu-nii081315.php

Carpenter, S.K., & Toftness, A.R. (2017). The effect of prequestions on learning from video presentations. *Journal of Applied Research in Memory and Cognition, 6*(1), 104–109. Retrieved from www.sciencedirect.com/science/article/pii/S2211368116301103?dgcid=raven_sd_via_email

Carthew, M., & Scitt, C. (2015). An investigation into the use of writing frames and writing structures to overcome boys' reluctance to write in geography lessons. *The STeP Journal, 2*(4), 17–27. Retrieved from http://194.81.189.19/ojs/index.php/step/article/viewFile/271/396

Clark, S.K., & Andreason, L. (2014). Examining sixth grade students' reading attitudes and perceptions of teacher read aloud: Are all students on the same page? *Literacy Research and Instruction, 53*(2), 162–182. Retrieved from www.tandfonline.com/doi/abs/10.1080/19388071.2013.870262

Cole, J., & Feng, J. (2015, April 15–16). *Effective Strategies for Improving Writing Skills of Elementary English Language Learners*. Paper presented at the Chinese American Educational Research and Development Association Annual Conference, Chicago, IL. Retrieved from http://files.eric.ed.gov/fulltext/ED556123.pdf

Coleman, D., & Pimentel, S. (2012). *Revised Publisher's Criteria for the Common Core State Standards in English Language Arts and Literacy, Grades 3–12*. Retrieved from www.corestandards.org/wp-content/uploads/Publishers_Criteria_for_Literacy_for_Grades_3-12.pdf

Common Core State Standards Initiative. (n.d.a). *Common Core Standards for English Language Arts & Literacy in History/Social Studies, Science, and Technical Subjects. Appendix A*. Retrieved from www.corestandards.org/assets/Appendix_A.pdf

Common Core State Standards Initiative. (n.d.b). *English Language Arts Standards: Anchor Standards: College and Career Readiness Anchor Standards for Reading*. Retrieved from www.corestandards.org/ELA-Literacy/CCRA/R/

Common Core State Standards Initiative. (n.d.c). *English Language Arts Standards: Anchor Standards: College and Career Readiness Anchor Standards for Speaking and Listening*. Retrieved from www.corestandards.org/ELA-Literacy/CCRA/SL/

Common Core State Standards Initiative. (n.d.d). *Media*. Retrieved from www.corestandards.org/search/?f=ela&t=media

Common Core State Standards Initiative. (n.d.e). *Patterns*. Retrieved from www.corestandards.org/search/?f=ela&t=pattern

Comprehend. (n.d.). *Online Etymology Dictionary*. Retrieved from www.etymonline.com/index.php?allowed_in_frame=0&search=comprehend

Conti, G. (2015, May 7). Why teachers should not bother correcting errors in their students' writing (not the traditional way at least). *The Language Gym*. Retrieved from https://gianfrancoconti.wordpress.com/2015/05/07/why-teachers-should-not-bother-correcting-errors-in-their-students-writing

Conti, G. (2015, May 20). Why asking our students to self-correct the errors in their essays is a waste of time… *The Language Gym*. Retrieved from https://gianfrancoconti.wordpress.com/2015/05/20/why-asking-our-students-to-self-correct-the-errors-in-their-essay-a-waste-of-valuable-teacher-time

Conti, G. (2017, February 4). Why marking students' books should be the least of a language teacher's priorities. *The Language Gym*. Retrieved from https://gianfrancoconti.wordpress.com/2017/02/04/why-marking-your-students-books-should-be-the-least-of-your-priorities

Cooper, R. (2015, December 1). (Almost) paperless literature circles. *Edutopia*. Retrieved from www.edutopia.org/blog/almost-paperless-literature-circles-ross-cooper?utm_source=twitter&utm_medium=socialflow

Corbitt, A. (2016, September 17). KWHLAQ for the 21st century [Twitter post]. Retrieved from https://twitter.com/Alex_Corbitt/status/777327034150322176

Council of Chief State Officers and the National Governors Association. (n.d.). *Application of Common Core State Standards for English Language Learners*. Retrieved from www.corestandards.org/assets/application-for-english-learners.pdf

Crawford-Lange, L.M. (1983). Review of "Language and culture in conflict: Problem-posing in the ESL classroom." *TESOL Quarterly*, *17*(4), 673–676. Retrieved from http://onlinelibrary.wiley.com.sci-hub.cc/doi/10.2307/3586619/abstract

Csikszentmihalyi, M. (2008). *Flow: The Psychology of Optimal Experience*. HarperCollins, New York, NY.

Dahlman, A., Hoffman, P., & Brauhn, S. (n.d.). *Classroom Strategies for Differentiating Instruction in the ESL Classroom*. Retrieved from http://citeseerx.ist.psu.edu/viewdoc/download?doi=10.1.1.943.291&rep=rep1&type=pdf

Dean, J. (n.d.a). The emotion that does motivate behaviour after all. *PsyBlog*. Retrieved from www.spring.org.uk/2017/06/emotion-change-behaviour.php

Dean, J. (n.d.b). The Zeigarnik effect. *PsyBlog*. Retrieved from www.spring.org.uk/2011/02/the-zeigarnik-effect.php

Decades of scientific research that started a growth mindset revolution. (n.d.). *Mindset Works*. Retrieved from www.mindsetworks.com/science

Dewi, R.K. (2011). *Improving Students' Speaking Skills Through Dialogue*. Master's thesis, Sabelas Maret University, Surakarta, Indonesia. Retrieved from Arvin, R. (1987). *Application of the language Experience Approach for Secondary Level Students*. Master's thesis, University of North Florida, Jacksonville. Retrieved from http://digitalcommons.unf.edu/cgi/viewcontent.cgi?article=1319&context=etd

Diallo, A. (2014). *The Use of Technology to Enhance the Learning Experience of ESL Students*. Master's thesis, Concordia University, Portland, OR. Retrieved from www.academia.edu/7123140/TECHNOLOGY_ENHANCES_ESL_STUDENTS_LEARNING_EXPERIENCE

*Drawception*. (n.d.). Retrieved from https://drawception.com/

Du, X. (2009). The affective filter in second language teaching. *Asian Social Science*, 5(8), 162–165. Retrieved from www.ccsenet.org/journal/index.php/ass/article/viewFile/3457/3131

Dunlosky, J., Rawson, K.A., & Marsh, E.J., Nathan, M.J., & Willingham, D.T. (2013). Improving students' learning with effective learning techniques: Promising directions from cognitive and educational psychology. *Psychological Science in the Public Interest*, 14(1), 4–58. Retrieved from http://journals.sagepub.com/stoken/rbtfl/Z10jaVH/60XQM/full

Education Endowment Foundation. (n.d.). *Reading Comprehension Strategies*. Retrieved from https://educationendowmentfoundation.org.uk/resources/teaching-learning-toolkit/reading-comprehension-strategies/?utm_content=buffer9058e&utm_medium=social&utm_source=twitter.com&utm_campaign=buffer

ELT Brewery. (2016, October 17). *Beyond Gap Fills. Using Songs to Learn a Language. Why, How and Which?* Retrieved from https://myeltbrewery.wordpress.com/2016/10/17/beyond-gap-fills-using-songs-to-learn-a-language-why-how-and-which/

ELTpics. (n.d.). *Flikr*. Retrieved from www.flickr.com/photos/eltpics/albums

ELTpics. (n.d.). Retrieved from www.eltpics.com/

Error (linguistics). (n.d.). *Wikipedia*. Retrieved from https://en.wikipedia.org/wiki/Error_(linguistics)#Difference_between_error_and_mistake

Fehér, J. (2015). From everyday activities to creative tasks. In A. Maley & N. Peachey (Eds.), *Creativity in the English Language Classroom* (pp. 64–72). British Council, London, UK. Retrieved from www.teachingenglish.org.uk/sites/teacheng/files/F004_ELT_Creativity_FINAL_v2%20WEB.pdf

Feldman, K., & Kinsella, K. (2005). *Narrowing the Language Gap: The Case for Explicit Vocabulary Instruction*. Scholastic Inc., New York, NY. Retrieved from http://teacher.scholastic.com/products/authors/pdfs/Narrowing_the_Gap.pdf

Felix, R. (2013). *Jazz Chants for ELT Cued Pronunciation Readings: A Materials Portfolio*. Terminal project, University of Oregon, Eugene. Retrieved from http://linguistics.uoregon.edu/wp-content/uploads/2015/08/Felix-Ryan-Aug-13.pdf

Ferlazzo, L. (2008, January 30). The best music websites for learning English. *Larry Ferlazzo's Websites of the Day*. Retrieved from http://larryferlazzo.edublogs.org/2008/01/30/the-best-music-websites-for-learning-english/

Ferlazzo, L. (2008, March 2). The best online tools for real-time collaboration. *Larry Ferlazzo's Websites of the Day*. Retrieved from http://larryferlazzo.edublogs.org/2008/03/02/the-best-online-tools-for-real-time-collaboration

Ferlazzo, L. (2008, March 17). The best sites to practice speaking English. *Larry Ferlazzo's Websites of the Day*. Retrieved from http://larryferlazzo.edublogs.org/2008/03/17/the-best-sites-to-practice-speaking-english/

Ferlazzo, L. (2008, March 31). The best sites for learning English pronunciation. *Larry Ferlazzo's Websites of the Day*. Retrieved from http://larryferlazzo.edublogs.org/2008/03/31/the-best-websites-for-learning-english-pronunciation/

Ferlazzo, L. (2008, April 6). The best sites for developing English conversational skills. *Larry Ferlazzo's Websites of the Day*. Retrieved from http://larryferlazzo.edublogs.org/2008/04/05/the-best-sites-for-developing-english-conversational-skills/

Ferlazzo, L. (2008, April 10). The best online tools for collaboration—NOT in real time. *Larry Ferlazzo's Websites of the Day*. Retrieved from http://larryferlazzo.edublogs.org/2008/04/10/the-best-online-tools-for-collaboration-not-in-real-time

Ferlazzo, L. (2008, April 21). The best websites for creating online learning games. *Larry Ferlazzo's Websites of the Day*. Retrieved from http://larryferlazzo.edublogs.org/2008/04/21/the-best-websites-for-creating-online-learning-games/

Ferlazzo, L. (2008, April 19). The best books for teaching & learning ESL/EFL. *Larry Ferlazzo's Websites of the Day*. Retrieved from http://larryferlazzo.edublogs.org/2008/04/19/the-best-books-for-teaching-learning-eslefl/

Ferlazzo, L. (2008, April 26). The best popular movie/tv shows for ESL/EFL (& how to use them). *Larry Ferlazzo's Websites of the Day*. Retrieved from http://larryferlazzo.edublogs.org/2008/04/26/the-best-popular-moviestv-shows-for-eslefl/

Ferlazzo, L. (2008, May 6). The best ways to create online slide shows. *Larry Ferlazzo's Websites of the Day*. Retrieved from http://larryferlazzo.edublogs.org/2008/05/06/the-best-ways-to-create-online-slideshows

Ferlazzo, L. (2008, May 14). The best ways for students to create online videos (using someone else's content). *Larry Ferlazzo's Websites of the Day*. Retrieved from http://larryferlazzo.edublogs.org/2008/05/14/the-best-ways-for-students-to-create-online-videos-using-someone-else%E2%80%99s-content/

Ferlazzo, L. (2008, May 21). The best sites that students can use independently and let teachers check on progress. *Larry Ferlazzo's Websites of the Day*. Retrieved from http://larryferlazzo.edublogs.org/2008/05/21/the-best-sites-that-students-can-use-independently-and-let-teachers-check-on-progress/

Ferlazzo, L. (2008, May 28). The best listening sites for English language learners. *Larry Ferlazzo's Websites of the Day*. Retrieved from http://larryferlazzo.edublogs.org/2008/05/28/the-best-listening-sites-for-english-language-learners/

Ferlazzo, L. (2008, July 24). The best online instructional video sites. *Larry Ferlazzo's Websites of the Day*. Retrieved from http://larryferlazzo.edublogs.org/2008/07/24/the-best-online-instructional-video-sites/

Ferlazzo, L. (2008, October 3). The best multilingual & bilingual sites for math, social studies, & science. *Larry Ferlazzo's Websites of the Day*. Retrieved from http://larryferlazzo.edublogs.org/2008/10/03/the-best-multilingual-bilingual-sites-for-math-social-studies-science/

Ferlazzo, L. (2008, October 15). The best online karaoke sites for English language learners. *Larry Ferlazzo's Websites of the Day*. Retrieved from http://larryferlazzo.edublogs.org/2008/10/15/the-best-online-karaoke-sites-for-english-language-learners/

Ferlazzo, L. (2008, October 19). The best places where students can write online. *Larry Ferlazzo's Websites of the Day*. Retrieved from http://larryferlazzo.edublogs.org/2008/10/19/the-best-places-where-students-can-write-online/

Ferlazzo, L. (2008, December 6). The best online resources for teachers of pre-literate ELL's & those not literate in their home language. *Larry Ferlazzo's Websites of the Day*. Retrieved from http://larryferlazzo.edublogs.org/2008/12/06/the-best-online-resources-for-teachers-of-pre-literate-ells/

Ferlazzo, L. (2008, December 7). The best sites for grammar practice. *Larry Ferlazzo's Websites of the Day*. Retrieved from http://larryferlazzo.edublogs.org/2008/12/07/the-best-sites-for-grammar-practice

Ferlazzo, L. (2008, December 18). Best applications for annotating websites. *Larry Ferlazzo's Websites of the Day*. Retrieved from http://larryferlazzo.edublogs.org/2008/12/18/best-applications-for-annotating-websites/

Ferlazzo, L. (2008, December 26). The best sources for advice on student blogging. *Larry Ferlazzo's Websites of the Day*. Retrieved from http://larryferlazzo.edublogs.org/2008/12/26/the-best-sources-for-advice-on-student-blogging/

Ferlazzo, L. (2009, February 9). The best places to buy ESL/EFL books, software & multimedia. *Larry Ferlazzo's Websites of the Day*. Retrieved from http://larryferlazzo.edublogs.org/2009/02/09/the-best-places-to-buy-eslefl-books-software-multimedia

Ferlazzo, L. (2009, February 10). The best online games students can play in private virtual "rooms." *Larry Ferlazzo's Websites of the Day*. Retrieved from http://larryferlazzo.edublogs.org/2009/02/10/the-best-online-games-students-can-play-in-private-virtual-rooms/

Ferlazzo, L. (2009, February 18). The best sites for free ESL/EFL hand-outs & worksheets. *Larry Ferlazzo's Websites of the Day*. Retrieved from http://larryferlazzo.edublogs.org/2009/02/18/the-best-sites-for-free-eslefl-hand-outs-worksheets/

Ferlazzo, L. (2009, March 12). The best tools to help develop global media literacy. *Larry Ferlazzo's Websites of the Day*. Retrieved from http://larryferlazzo.edublogs.org/2009/03/12/the-best-tools-to-help-learn-global-media-literacy/

Ferlazzo, L. (2009, April 1). The best places where students can write for an authentic audience. *Larry Ferlazzo's Websites of the Day*. Retrieved from http://larryferlazzo.edublogs.org/2009/04/01/the-best-places-where-students-can-write-for-an-authentic-audience/

Ferlazzo, L. (2009, May 2). The best places to read & write "choose your own adventure" stories. *Larry Ferlazzo's Websites of the Day*. Retrieved from http://larryferlazzo.edublogs.org/2009/05/02/the-best-places-to-read-write-choose-your-own-adventure-stories/

Ferlazzo, L. (2009, May 25). The best sources of advice for making good presentations. *Larry Ferlazzo's Websites of the Day*. Retrieved from http://larryferlazzo.edublogs.org/2009/05/25/the-best-sources-of-advice-for-making-good-presentations/

Ferlazzo, L. (2009, May 30). The best ways to find other classes for joint online projects. *Larry Ferlazzo's Websites of the Day*. Retrieved from http://larryferlazzo.edublogs.org/2009/05/30/the-best-ways-to-find-other-classes-for-joint-online-projects/

Ferlazzo, L. (2008, June 4). The best ways to make comic strips online. *Larry Ferlazzo's Websites of the Day*. Retrieved from http://larryferlazzo.edublogs.org/2008/06/04/the-best-ways-to-make-comic-strips-online/

Ferlazzo, L. (2008, November 13). The best reference websites for English language learners. *Larry Ferlazzo's Websites of the Day*. Retrieved from http://larryferlazzo .edublogs.org/2008/11/13/the-best-reference-websites-for-english-language-learners-2008

Ferlazzo, L. (2009, June 3). The best sources of advice for teachers (and others!) on how to be better bloggers. *Larry Ferlazzo's Websites of the Day*. Retrieved from http://larryferlazzo.edublogs.org/2009/06/03/the-best-sources-of-advice-for-teachers-and-others-on-how-to-be-better-bloggers

Ferlazzo, L. (2009, July 31). The best sources for free & accessible printable books. *Larry Ferlazzo's Websites of the Day*. Retrieved from http://larryferlazzo.edublogs .org/2009/07/31/the-best-sources-for-free-accessible-printable-books

Ferlazzo, L. (2009, August 10). The best teacher resources for online student safety & legal issues. *Larry Ferlazzo's Websites of the Day*. Retrieved from http:// larryferlazzo.edublogs.org/2009/08/10/the-best-teacher-resources-for-online-student-safety-legal-issues/

Ferlazzo, L. (2009, August 11). The best resources for finding and creating virtual field trips. *Larry Ferlazzo's Websites of the Day*. Retrieved from http://larryferlazzo .edublogs.org/2009/08/11/the-best-resources-for-finding-and-creating-virtual-field-trips/

Ferlazzo, L. (2009, September 21). The best online resources to teach about plagiarism. *Larry Ferlazzo's Websites of the Day*. Retrieved from http://larryferlazzo .edublogs.org/2009/09/21/the-best-online-resources-to-teach-about-plagiarism

Ferlazzo, L. (2009, October 7). The best resources for using puppets in class. *Larry Ferlazzo's Websites of the Day*. Retrieved from http://larryferlazzo.edublogs.org/ 2009/10/07/the-best-resources-for-using-puppets-in-class/

Ferlazzo, L. (2009, October 24). The best sites for students to create & participate in online debates. *Larry Ferlazzo's Websites of the Day*. Retrieved from http:// larryferlazzo.edublogs.org/2009/10/24/the-best-sites-for-students-to-create-participate-in-online-debates/

Ferlazzo, L. (2010, February 1). The best movie scenes to use for English-language development. *Larry Ferlazzo's Websites of the Day*. Retrieved from http:// larryferlazzo.edublogs.org/2010/02/01/the-best-movie-scenes-to-use-for-english-language-development/

Ferlazzo, L. (2010, March 8). The importance of good endings. *Larry Ferlazzo's Websites of the Day*. Retrieved from http://larryferlazzo.edublogs.org/2010/03/08/the-importance-of-good-endings/

Ferlazzo, L. (2010, March 29). The best sites for creating sentence scrambles. *Larry Ferlazzo's Websites of the Day*. Retrieved from http://larryferlazzo.edublogs.org/ 2010/03/29/the-best-sites-for-creating-sentence-scrambles/

Ferlazzo, L. (2010, May 8). The best posts on students evaluating classes (and teachers). *Larry Ferlazzo's Websites of the Day*. Retrieved from http://larryferlazzo .edublogs.org/2010/05/08/my-best-posts-on-students-evaluating-classes-and-teachers/

Ferlazzo, L. (2010, May 17a). The best posts & articles on "motivating" students. *Larry Ferlazzo's Websites of the Day*. Retrieved from http://larryferlazzo.edublogs .org/2010/05/17/my-best-posts-on-motivating-students/

Ferlazzo, L. (2010, May 17b). More on the importance of home libraries. *Larry Ferlazzo's Websites of the Day*. Retrieved from http://larryferlazzo.edublogs.org/ 2010/05/17/more-on-the-importance-of-home-libraries/

Ferlazzo, L. (2010, May 18). The best posts on students setting goals. *Larry Ferlazzo's Websites of the Day*. Retrieved from http://larryferlazzo.edublogs.org/2010/05/18/ my-best-posts-on-students-setting-goals/

Ferlazzo, L. (2010, June 3). The best posts about helping students develop their capacity for self-control. *Larry Ferlazzo's Websites of the Day*. Retrieved from http:// larryferlazzo.edublogs.org/2010/06/03/my-best-posts-about-helping-students-develop-their-capacity-for-self-control/

Ferlazzo, L. (2010, June 27). The best ways to use photos in lessons. *Larry Ferlazzo's Websites of the Day*. Retrieved from http://larryferlazzo.edublogs.org/2010/06/27/ the-best-ways-to-use-photos-in-lessons/

Ferlazzo, L. (2010, July 3). The best "When I say jump" online sites for practicing English. *Larry Ferlazzo's Websites of the Day*. Retrieved from http:// larryferlazzo.edublogs.org/2010/07/03/the-best-when-i-say-jump-online-sites-for-practicing-english/

Ferlazzo, L. (2010, August 28). A collection of "the best . . . " lists on learning games. *Larry Ferlazzo's Websites of the Day*. Retrieved from http://larryferlazzo.edublogs .org/2010/08/28/a-collection-of-the-best-lists-on-games

Ferlazzo, L. (2010, December 29). The best sites for collaborative storytelling. *Larry Ferlazzo's Websites of the Day*. Retrieved from http://larryferlazzo.edublogs.org/ 2010/12/29/the-best-sites-for-collaborative-storytelling/

Ferlazzo, L. (2011). *Helping Students Motivate Themselves: Practical Answers to Classroom Challenges*. Routledge, New York, NY.

Ferlazzo, L. (2011, February 23). The best places to find research on technology & language teaching/learning. *Larry Ferlazzo's Websites of the Day*. Retrieved from http://larryferlazzo.edublogs.org/2011/02/23/the-best-places-to-find-research-on-technology-language-teachinglearning/

Ferlazzo, L. (2011, February 26). The best resources documenting the effectiveness of free voluntary reading. *Larry Ferlazzo's Websites of the Day*. Retrieved from http://larryferlazzo.edublogs.org/2011/02/26/the-best-resources-documenting-the-effectiveness-of-free-voluntary-reading/

Ferlazzo, L. (2011, March 1). The best articles & sites for teachers & students to learn about phonics. *Larry Ferlazzo's Websites of the Day*. Retrieved from http://larryferlazzo.edublogs.org/2011/03/01/the-best-articles-sites-for-teachers-students-to-learn-about-phonics/

Ferlazzo, L. (2011, March 19). The best resources for learning about schools providing home computers & internet access to students. *Larry Ferlazzo's Websites of the Day*. Retrieved from http://larryferlazzo.edublogs.org/2011/03/19/the-best-resources-for-learning-about-schools-providing-home-computers-internet-access-to-students/

Ferlazzo, L. (2011, March 30). The best online virtual "corkboards" (or "bulletin boards"). *Larry Ferlazzo's Websites of the Day*. Retrieved from http://larryferlazzo.edublogs.org/2011/03/30/the-best-online-virtual-corkboards-or-bulletin-boards/

Ferlazzo, L. (2011, May 14). The best resources for adapting your textbook so it doesn't bore students to death. *Larry Ferlazzo's Websites of the Day*. Retrieved from http://larryferlazzo.edublogs.org/2011/05/14/the-best-resources-for-adapting-your-textbook-so-it-doesnt-bore-students-to-death/

Ferlazzo, L. (2011, June 2). The best resources on students using gestures & physical movement to help with learning. *Larry Ferlazzo's Websites of the Day*. Retrieved from http://larryferlazzo.edublogs.org/2011/06/02/the-best-resources-on-students-using-gestures-physical-movement-to-help-with-learning/

Ferlazzo, L. (2011, June 26). The best resources on the "summer slide." *Larry Ferlazzo's Websites of the Day*. Retrieved from http://larryferlazzo.edublogs.org/2011/06/26/the-best-resources-on-the-summer-slide/

Ferlazzo, L. (2011, July 28). The best sites (& videos) for learning about jazz chants. *Larry Ferlazzo's Websites of the Day*. Retrieved from http://larryferlazzo.edublogs.org/2011/07/28/the-best-sites-videos-for-learning-about-jazz-chants

Ferlazzo, L. (2011, August 8). The best resources for planning the first days of school. *Larry Ferlazzo's Websites of the Day*. Retrieved from http://larryferlazzo.edublogs.org/2011/08/08/the-best-resources-for-planning-the-first-day-of-school/

Ferlazzo, L. (2011, August 16). Five questions that will improve your teaching. *Education Week*. Retrieved from www.edweek.org/tm/articles/2011/08/16/ferlazzo_fiveways.html

Ferlazzo, L. (2011, September 6). The best online resources for "information gap" activities. *Larry Ferlazzo's Websites of the Day*. Retrieved from http://larryferlazzo.edublogs.org/2011/09/06/the-best-online-resources-for-information-gap-activities/

Ferlazzo, L. (2011, September 7). The best sites for learning strategies to teach ELLs in content classes. *Larry Ferlazzo's Websites of the Day*. Retrieved from http://larryferlazzo.edublogs.org/2011/09/07/the-best-sites-for-learning-strategies-to-teach-ells-in-content-classes/

Ferlazzo, L. (2011, September 19). The best beginner, intermediate & advanced English language learner sites. *Larry Ferlazzo's Websites of the Day*. Retrieved from http://larryferlazzo.edublogs.org/2011/09/19/the-best-beginner-intermediate-advanced-english-language-learner-sites/

Ferlazzo, L. (2011, October 10). The best resources for learning about teacher home visits. *Edublogs: Engaging Parents in School*. Retrieved from http://engagingparents inschool.edublogs.org/2011/10/10/the-best-resources-for-learning-about-teach er-home-visits/

Ferlazzo, L. (2011, October 30). The best research available on parent engagement. *Edublogs: Engaging Parents in School*. Retrieved from http://engagingparents inschool.edublogs.org/2011/10/30/the-best-research-available-on-parent-engagement/

Ferlazzo, L. (2011, November 26). The best resources for showing students that they make their brain stronger by learning. *Larry Ferlazzo's Websites of the Day*. Retrieved from http://larryferlazzo.edublogs.org/2011/11/26/the-best-resources-for-showing-students-that-they-make-their-brain-stronger-by-learning/

Ferlazzo, L. (2012, March 27). Response: The difference between parent "involvement" & parent "engagement." *Education Week*. Retrieved from http://blogs.edweek.org/teachers/classroom_qa_with_larry_ferlazzo/2012/03/response_the_difference_between_parent_involvement_parent_engagement.html

Ferlazzo, L. (2012, April 22). The best posts on helping students teach their classmates—Help me find more. *Larry Ferlazzo's Websites of the Day*. Retrieved from http://larryferlazzo.edublogs.org/2012/04/22/the-best-posts-on-helping-students-teach-their-classmates-help-me-find-more/

Ferlazzo, L. (2012, May 19). The best resources for teaching "what if" history lessons. *Larry Ferlazzo's Websites of the Day*. Retrieved from http://larryferlazzo.edublogs.org/2012/05/19/the-best-resources-for-teaching-what-if-history-lessons/

Ferlazzo, L. (2012, May 13). The best posts on metacognition. *Larry Ferlazzo's Websites of the Day*. Retrieved from http://larryferlazzo.edublogs.org/2012/05/13/my-best-posts-on-metacognition/

Ferlazzo, L. (2012, July 21). The best resources for learning about the 10,000 rule & deliberate practice. *Larry Ferlazzo's Websites of the Day*. Retrieved from http://larryferlazzo.edublogs.org/2012/07/21/the-best-resources-for-learning-about-the-10000-hour-rule-deliberative-practice

Ferlazzo, L. (2012, July 23). The best ideas to help students become better listeners—Contribute more. *Larry Ferlazzo's Websites of the Day*. Retrieved from http://larryferlazzo.edublogs.org/2012/07/23/the-best-ideas-to-help-students-become-better-listeners-contribute-more/

Ferlazzo, L. (2012, October 13). The best resources on helping our students develop a "growth mindset." *Larry Ferlazzo's Websites of the Day*. Retrieved from http://larryferlazzo.edublogs.org/2012/10/13/the-best-resources-on-helping-our-students-develop-a-growth-mindset

Ferlazzo, L. (2012, October 19). The best online tools for using photos in lessons. *Larry Ferlazzo's Websites of the Day*. Retrieved from http://larryferlazzo.edublogs.org/2012/10/19/the-best-online-tools-for-using-photos-in-lessons/

Ferlazzo, L. (2012, November 6). A potpourri of the best & most useful video sites. *Larry Ferlazzo's Websites of the Day*. Retrieved from http://larryferlazzo.edublogs.org/2012/11/06/a-potpourri-of-the-best-most-useful-video-sites/

Ferlazzo, L. (2013, January 9). The best resources on grading practices. *Larry Ferlazzo's Websites of the Day*. Retrieved from http://larryferlazzo.edublogs.org/2013/01/09/the-best-resources-on-grading-practices/

Ferlazzo, L. (2013, February 18). The best resources for learning to use the video apps "Vine" & Instagram. *Larry Ferlazzo's Websites of the Day*. Retrieved from http://larryferlazzo.edublogs.org/2013/02/18/the-best-resources-for-learning-to-use-the-video-app-twine/

Ferlazzo, L. (2013, February 23a). My best posts on parent "academies" & "universities." Edublogs: *Engaging Parents in School*. Retrieved from http://engagingparentsinschool.edublogs.org/2013/02/23/my-best-posts-on-parent-academies-universities/

Ferlazzo, L. (2013, February 23b). The best tools for creating visually attractive quotations for online sharing. *Larry Ferlazzo's Websites of the Day*. Retrieved from http://larryferlazzo.edublogs.org/2013/02/23/the-best-tools-for-creating-visually-attractive-quotations-for-online-display/

Ferlazzo, L. (2013, April 21). *Video games and walkthroughs used in class*. Retrieved from www.sacschoolblogs.org/larryferlazzo/category/games/

Ferlazzo, L. (2013, May 13). The best resources on "close reading"—Help me find more. *Larry Ferlazzo's Websites of the Day*. Retrieved from http://larryferlazzo.edublogs.org/2013/05/13/the-best-resources-on-close-reading-help-me-find-more

Ferlazzo, L. (2013, May 16). *The best multilingual resources for parents*. Edublogs: *Engaging Parents in School*. Retrieved from http://engagingparentsinschool.edublogs.org/2013/05/16/the-best-multilingual-resources-for-parents/

Ferlazzo, L. (2013, July 13). The best videos & articles where athletes explain how reading & writing well has helped their career—Help me find more. *Larry Ferlazzo's Websites of the Day*. Retrieved from http://larryferlazzo.edublogs .org/2013/07/13/the-best-videos-articles-where-athletes-explain-how-reading-writing-well-has-helped-their-career-help-me-find-more/

Ferlazzo, L. (2013, August 13). If you don't have teacher access to YouTube at your school, then this search engine is a "must." *Larry Ferlazzo's Websites of the Day*. Retrieved from http://larryferlazzo.edublogs.org/2013/08/13/if-you-dont-have-teacher-access-to-youtube-at-your-school-then-this-search-engine-is-a-must

Ferlazzo, L. (2013, September 19). The best questions to use for class closing activities—What are yours? *Larry Ferlazzo's Websites of the Day*. Retrieved from http://larryferlazzo.edublogs.org/2013/09/19/here-are-some-questions-i-use-for-class-closing-activities-what-are-yours/

Ferlazzo, L. (2013, September 25). "Lyrics videos" on YouTube & English language learners. *Larry Ferlazzo's Websites of the Day*. Retrieved from http://larryferlazzo .edublogs.org/2013/09/25/lyrics-videos-on-youtube-english-language-learners/

Ferlazzo, L. (2013, October 27). The best ideas for using games in the ESL/EFL/ELL classroom. *Larry Ferlazzo's Websites of the Day*. Retrieved from http://larryferlazzo .edublogs.org/2013/10/27/the-best-ideas-for-using-games-in-the-esleflell-classroom/

Ferlazzo, L. (2013, November 1). Using Freire & Fotobabble with English language learners. *Larry Ferlazzo's Websites of the Day*. Retrieved from http://larryferlazzo .edublogs.org/2013/11/01/using-freire-fotobabble-with-english-language-learners-2

Ferlazzo, L. (2013, November 7). The best ways to use mistakes when teaching writing. *Larry Ferlazzo's Websites of the Day*. Retrieved from http://larryferlazzo .edublogs.org/2013/11/07/the-best-ways-to-use-mistakes-when-teaching-writing

Ferlazzo, L. (2014, January 20). Home culture presentations with English language learners. *Larry Ferlazzo's Websites of the Day*. Retrieved from http://larryferlazzo .edublogs.org/2014/01/20/home-culture-presentations-with-english-language-learners/

Ferlazzo, L. (2014, February 9). The best student projects that need family engagement—Contribute your lessons! *Edublogs: Engaging Parents in School*. Retrieved from http://engagingparentsinschool.edublogs.org/2014/02/09/the-best-student-projects-that-need-family-engagement-contribute-your-lessons/

Ferlazzo, L. (2014, February 23). The "all-time" best ways to create online content easily & quickly. *Larry Ferlazzo's Websites of the Day*. Retrieved from http://larryferlazzo.edublogs.org/2014/02/23/the-all-time-ways-to-create-online-content-easily-quickly/

Ferlazzo, L. (2014, June 14). The best research demonstrating that lectures are not the best instructional strategy. *Larry Ferlazzo's Websites of the Day*. Retrieved from http://larryferlazzo.edublogs.org/2014/06/14/the-best-research-demonstrating-that-lectures-are-not-the-best-instructional-strategy/

Ferlazzo, L. (2014, November 7). Here's a new reading activity I tried out today that went pretty well… *Larry Ferlazzo's Websites of the Day*. Retrieved from http://larryferlazzo.edublogs.org/2014/11/07/heres-a-new-reading-activity-i-tried-out-today-that-went-pretty-well/

Ferlazzo, L. (2014, November 16). The best places to get the "same" text written for different "levels." *Larry Ferlazzo's Websites of the Day*. Retrieved from http://larryferlazzo.edublogs.org/2014/11/16/the-best-places-to-get-the-same-text-written-for-different-levels/

Ferlazzo, L. (2014, November 22a). The best resources for teaching Common Core math to English language learners. *Larry Ferlazzo's Websites of the Day*. Retrieved from http://larryferlazzo.edublogs.org/2014/11/22/the-best-resources-for-teaching-common-core-math-to-english-language-learners/

Ferlazzo, L. (2014, November 22b). The best resources for teaching the Next Generation Science Standards to English language learners. *Larry Ferlazzo's Websites of the Day*. Retrieved from http://larryferlazzo.edublogs.org/2014/11/22/the-best-resources-for-teaching-the-next-generation-science-standards-to-english-language-learners/

Ferlazzo, L. (2015, April 5). The best resources on—& advice for using—donors choose (Please share your experiences!). *Larry Ferlazzo's Websites of the Day*. Retrieved from http://larryferlazzo.edublogs.org/2015/04/05/the-best-resources-on-advice-for-using-donors-choose-please-share-your-experiences/

Ferlazzo, L. (2015, April 17). The best ways to finish the school year strong. *Larry Ferlazzo's Websites of the Day*. Retrieved from http://larryferlazzo.edublogs.org/2015/04/17/the-best-ways-to-finish-the-school-year-strong/

Ferlazzo, L. (2015, May 10). Here's a successful music lesson we did with beginning ELLs (hand-outs & student examples included). *Larry Ferlazzo's Websites of the Day*. Retrieved from http://larryferlazzo.edublogs.org/2015/05/10/heres-a-successful-music-lesson-we-did-with-beginning-ells-hand-outs-student-examples-included/

Ferlazzo, L. (2015, June 19). Study: Inductive learning promotes "transfer of knowledge" better than direct instruction. *Larry Ferlazzo's Websites of the Day*. Retrieved from http://larryferlazzo.edublogs.org/2015/06/19/study-inductive-learning-promotes-transfer-of-knowledge-better-than-direct-instruction

Ferlazzo, L. (2015, June 23). The best resources on effective note-taking strategies—Help me find more. *Larry Ferlazzo's Websites of the Day*. Retrieved from http://larryferlazzo.edublogs.org/2015/06/23/the-best-resources-on-effective-note-taking-strategies-help-me-find-more/

Ferlazzo, L. (2015, June 29). The best online tools that can help students write an essay. *Larry Ferlazzo's Websites of the Day*. Retrieved from http://larryferlazzo.edublogs.org/2015/06/29/am-i-missing-something-or-are-there-very-few-online-tools-than-can-help-students-write-an-essay

Ferlazzo, L. (2015, July 5). "They Say, I Say" is a great writing resource. *Larry Ferlazzo's Websites of the Day*. Retrieved from http://larryferlazzo.edublogs.org/2015/07/05/they-say-i-say-is-a-great-writing-resource

Ferlazzo, L. (2015, July 23). The best resources on getting student writers to "buy-into" revision—Help me find more. *Larry Ferlazzo's Websites of the Day*. Retrieved from http://larryferlazzo.edublogs.org/2015/07/23/the-best-resources-on-getting-student-writers-to-buy-into-revision-help-me-find-more

Ferlazzo, L. (2015, August 1a). The best resources for using "If this animal or image could talk" lesson idea in class. *Larry Ferlazzo's Websites of the Day*. Retrieved from http://larryferlazzo.edublogs.org/2015/08/01/the-best-resources-on-using-if-this-animal-or-image-could-talk-lesson-idea-in-class/

Ferlazzo, L. (2015, August 1b). Links to the joint projects my ELL geography class did with classes around the world—Want to join us this year? *Larry Ferlazzo's Websites of the Day*. Retrieved from http://larryferlazzo.edublogs.org/2015/08/01/links-to-the-joint-projects-my-ell-geography-class-did-with-classes-around-the-world-want-to-join-us-this-year/

Ferlazzo, L. (2015, August 5). The best resources on close reading paintings, photos & videos. *Larry Ferlazzo's Websites of the Day*. Retrieved from http://larryferlazzo.edublogs.org/2015/08/05/the-best-resources-on-close-reading-paintings-photos-videos/

Ferlazzo, L. (2015, September 14). Strategies for helping students motivate themselves. *Edutopia*. Retrieved from www.edutopia.org/blog/strategies-helping-students-motivate-themselves-larry-ferlazzo

Ferlazzo, L. (2015, September 19). The best ways to use "3–2–1" as an instructional strategy. *Larry Ferlazzo's Websites of the Day*. Retrieved from http://larryferlazzo.edublogs.org/2015/09/19/the-best-ways-to-use-3-2-1-as-an-instructional-strategy

Ferlazzo, L. (2015, October 16). The best ways to deal with YouTube's awful safety mode. *Larry Ferlazzo's Websites of the Day*. Retrieved from http://larryferlazzo.edublogs.org/2015/10/16/the-best-ways-to-deal-with-youtubes-awful-safety-mode/

Ferlazzo, L. (2016, April 30). Great news for California students—Undocumented children become eligible for free medical insurance in May. *Larry Ferlazzo's Websites of the Day*. Retrieved from http://larryferlazzo.edublogs.org/2016/04/30/great-news-for-california-students-undocumented-children-become-eligible-for-free-medical-insurance-in-may

Ferlazzo, L. (2016, May 23). Updated: Here are the sites I'm using for my summer school "virtual classroom." *Larry Ferlazzo's Websites of the Day*. Retrieved from http://larryferlazzo.edublogs.org/2016/05/23/updated-here-are-the-sites-im-using-for-my-summer-school-virtual-classroom/

Ferlazzo, L. (2016, June 10). The best resources about "culturally responsive teaching" & "culturally sustaining pedagogy"—Please share more! *Larry Ferlazzo's Websites of the Day*. Retrieved from http://larryferlazzo.edublogs.org/2016/06/10/the-best-resources-about-culturally-responsive-teaching-culturally-sustaining-pedagogy-please-share-more/

Ferlazzo, L. (2016, June 11). The best resources on the importance of correctly pronouncing student names. *Larry Ferlazzo's Websites of the Day*. Retrieved from http://larryferlazzo.edublogs.org/2016/06/11/the-best-resources-on-the-importance-of-correctly-pronouncing-student-names/

Ferlazzo, L. (2016, June 24). The best resources for organizing & maximizing field trips—Both "real" & "virtual." *Larry Ferlazzo's Websites of the Day*. Retrieved from http://larryferlazzo.edublogs.org/2016/06/24/the-best-resources-for-organizing-maximizing-field-trips-both-real-virtual/

Ferlazzo, L. (2016, July 12). "Guess what" is a great "new" game—Plus, ELLs can create a video for an authentic audience. *Larry Ferlazzo's Websites of the Day*. Retrieved from http://larryferlazzo.edublogs.org/2016/07/12/guess-what-is-a-great-new-game-plus-ells-can-create-a-video-for-an-authentic-audience/

Ferlazzo, L. (2016, July 14). A collection of advice on talking to students about race, police & racism. *Larry Ferlazzo's Websites of the Day*. Retrieved from http://larryferlazzo.edublogs.org/2016/07/14/a-collection-of-advice-on-talking-to-students-about-race-police-racism/

Ferlazzo, L. (2016, August 13). The best resources on the study finding that reading books makes you live longer. *Larry Ferlazzo's Websites of the Day*. Retrieved from http://larryferlazzo.edublogs.org/2016/08/13/the-best-resources-on-the-study-finding-that-reading-books-makes-you-live-longer

Ferlazzo, L. (2016, August 14). The "all-time" best sources of online images. *Larry Ferlazzo's Websites of the Day*. Retrieved from http://larryferlazzo.edublogs.org/2016/08/14/the-all-time-best-sources-of-online-images/

Ferlazzo, L. (2016, September 10a). The best resources for "do now" activities to begin a class. *Larry Ferlazzo's Websites of the Day*. Retrieved from http://larryfer lazzo.edublogs.org/2016/09/10/the-best-resources-for-do-now-activities-to-begin-a-class/

Ferlazzo, L. (2016, September 10b). The best resources for learning about Total Physical Response (TPR). *Larry Ferlazzo's Websites of the Day*. Retrieved from http://larryferlazzo.edublogs.org/2016/09/10/the-best-resources-for-learning-about-total-physical-response-tpr/

Ferlazzo, L. (2016, September 21). A look back: Combining an "assets" perspective with an authentic audience. *Larry Ferlazzo's Websites of the Day*. Retrieved from http://larryferlazzo.edublogs.org/2016/09/21/a-look-back-combining-an-assets-perspective-with-an-authentic-audience

Ferlazzo, L. (2016, September 23). Here's how we modified the picture word inductive model today. *Larry Ferlazzo's Websites of the Day*. Retrieved from http://larryferlazzo.edublogs.org/2016/09/23/heres-how-we-modified-the-picture-word-inductive-model-today

Ferlazzo, L. (2016, October 2). A look back: Is this the most important research study of the year? Maybe. *Larry Ferlazzo's Websites of the Day*. Retrieved from http://larryferlazzo.edublogs.org/2016/10/02/a-look-back-is-this-the-most-important-research-study-of-the-year-maybe

Ferlazzo, L. (2016, October 12). The best places where students can tell their—and/or their families—immigration story. *Larry Ferlazzo's Websites of the Day*. Retrieved from http://larryferlazzo.edublogs.org/2016/10/12/the-best-places-where-stude nts-can-tell-their-andor-their-families-immigration-story/

Ferlazzo, L. (2016, November 18). The mannequin challenge, ELLs & a frozen tableau. *Larry Ferlazzo's Websites of the Day*. Retrieved from http://larryferlazzo .edublogs.org/2016/11/18/the-mannequin-challenge-ells-a-frozen-tableau/

Ferlazzo, L. (2016, November 24). Ways that a mainstream teacher can support an ELL newcomer in class. *Larry Ferlazzo's Websites of the Day*. Retrieved from http://larryferlazzo.edublogs.org/2016/11/24/ways-a-mainstream-teacher-can-support-an-ell-newcomer-in-class/

Ferlazzo, L. (2016, December 1). The best scaffolded writing frames for students. *Larry Ferlazzo's Websites of the Day*. Retrieved from http://larryferlazzo.edublogs .org/2016/12/01/the-best-scaffolded-writing-frames-for-students

Ferlazzo, L. (2017). Student engagement: Key to personalized learning. *Educational Leadership*, 74(6), 28–33. Retrieved from www.ascd.org/publications/educational-leadership/mar17/vol74/num06/Student-Engagement@-Key-to-Personalized-Learning.aspx

Ferlazzo, L. (2017, January 5). The best resources on providing scaffolds to students. *Larry Ferlazzo's Websites of the Day*. Retrieved from http://larryferlazzo.edublogs .org/2017/01/05/the-best-resources-on-providing-scaffolds-to-students/

Ferlazzo, L. (2017, February 26). The best practical resources for helping teachers, students & families respond to immigration challenges. *Larry Ferlazzo's Websites of the Day*. Retrieved from http://larryferlazzo.edublogs.org/2017/02/26/the-best-practical-resources-for-helping-teachers-students-families-respond-to-immigration-challenges/

Ferlazzo, L. (2017, February 27). A beginning list of the best resources on virtual reality in education. *Larry Ferlazzo's Websites of the Day*. Retrieved from http://larryferlazzo.edublogs.org/2017/02/27/a-beginning-list-of-the-best-resources-on-virtual-reality-in-education/

Ferlazzo, L. (2017, March 6). Resources from all my blogs. *Larry Ferlazzo's Websites of the Day*. Retrieved from http://larryferlazzo.edublogs.org/2017/03/06/resources-from-all-my-blogs-10

Ferlazzo, L. (2017, March 8). Sacramento City Unified School District launches campaign to assist undocumented students. *Larry Ferlazzo's Websites of the Day*. Retrieved from http://larryferlazzo.edublogs.org/2017/03/08/sacramento-city-unified-school-district-launches-campaign-to-assist-undocumented-students/

Ferlazzo, L. (2017, March 22). A beginning list of the best resources for fighting Islamophobia in schools. *Larry Ferlazzo's Websites of the Day*. Retrieved from http://larryferlazzo.edublogs.org/2017/03/22/a-beginning-list-of-the-best-resources-for-fighting-islamophobia-in-schools/

Ferlazzo, L. (2017, April 10). The best resources explaining why we need to support the home language of ELLs. *Larry Ferlazzo's Websites of the Day*. Retrieved from http://larryferlazzo.edublogs.org/2017/04/10/the-best-resources-explaining-why-we-need-to-support-the-home-language-of-ells/

Ferlazzo, L. (2017, April 21). Guest post: What ELLs taught our school in a week-long empathy project. *Larry Ferlazzo's Websites of the Day*. Retrieved from http://larryferlazzo.edublogs.org/2017/04/21/guest-post-what-ells-taught-our-school-in-a-week-long-empathy-project/

Ferlazzo, L. (2017, May 5). The best resources for learning about the value of "self-explanation." *Larry Ferlazzo's Websites of the Day*. Retrieved from http://larryferlazzo.edublogs.org/2017/05/05/the-resources-for-learning-about-the-value-of-self-explanation/

Ferlazzo, L. (2017, May 21). The best fun videos for English language learners in 2017—So far. *Larry Ferlazzo's Websites of the Day*. Retrieved from http://larryferlazzo.edublogs.org/2017/05/21/the-best-fun-videos-for-english-language-learners-in-2017-so-far/

Ferlazzo, L. (2017, May 26). How my ELL students used Padlet to create a "picture data set." *Larry Ferlazzo's Websites of the Day*. Retrieved from http://larryferlazzo.edublogs.org/?s=padlet

Ferlazzo, L. (2017, June 17). This is a must-watch video for any volunteer or peer tutor working with ELLs. *Larry Ferlazzo's Websites of the Day*. Retrieved from http://larryferlazzo.edublogs.org/2017/06/17/this-is-a-must-watch-video-for-any-volunteer-or-peer-tutor-working-with-ells/

Ferlazzo, L. (2017, July 7). The best resources on co-teaching with ELLs—Please suggest more. *Larry Ferlazzo's Websites of the Day*. Retrieved from http://larryferlazzo.edublogs.org/2017/07/07/the-best-resources-on-co-teaching-with-ells-please-suggest-more/

Ferlazzo, L. (2017, July 14). The best videos for content teachers with ELLs in their classes—Please suggest more. *Larry Ferlazzo's Websites of the Day*. Retrieved from http://larryferlazzo.edublogs.org/2017/07/14/the-best-videos-for-content-teachers-with-ells-in-their-classes-please-suggest-more

Ferlazzo, L. (2017, July 15). The best sites for ELLs to practice online dictation. *Larry Ferlazzo's Websites of the Day*. Retrieved from http://larryferlazzo.edublogs.org/2017/07/15/the-best-sites-for-ells-to-practice-online-dictation

Ferlazzo, L. (2017, July 18). The best resources on developing a sense of community in the classroom. *Larry Ferlazzo's Websites of the Day*. Retrieved from http://larryferlazzo.edublogs.org/2017/07/18/the-best-resources-on-developing-a-sense-of-community-in-the-classroom/

Ferlazzo, L. (2017, July 20). The best resources & ideas for using sound effects in ELL lessons. *Larry Ferlazzo's Websites of the Day*. Retrieved from http://larryferlazzo.edublogs.org/2017/07/20/the-best-resources-ideas-for-using-sound-effects-in-ell-lessons/

Ferlazzo, L. (2017, July 30a). The best online homework sites for English language learners—Please offer your own suggestions. *Larry Ferlazzo's Websites of the Day*. Retrieved from http://larryferlazzo.edublogs.org/2017/07/30/the-best-online-homework-sites-for-english-language-learners-please-offer-your-own-suggestions/

Ferlazzo, L. (2017, July 30b). The best sites where students can learn typing/keyboarding. *Larry Ferlazzo's Websites of the Day*. Retrieved from http://larryferlazzo.edublogs.org/2017/07/30/the-best-sites-where-students-can-learning-typingkeyboarding

Ferlazzo, L. (2017, August 1a). The best resources for teaching students the differences between a good & bad slide. *Larry Ferlazzo's Websites of the Day*. Retrieved from http://larryferlazzo.edublogs.org/2017/08/01/the-best-resources-for-teaching-students-the-differences-between-a-good-bad-slide/

Ferlazzo, L. (2017, August 1b). Guest post: "Co-teaching dos and don'ts." *Larry Ferlazzo's Websites of the Day*. Retrieved from http://larryferlazzo.edublogs.org/2017/08/01/guest-post-co-teaching-dos-and-donts/

Ferlazzo, L. (2017, August 6). The best parent engagement resources for immigrant families. *Larry Ferlazzo's Websites of the Day*. Retrieved from http://larryferlazzo.edublogs.org/2017/08/06/the-best-parent-engagement-resources-for-immigrant-families/

Ferlazzo, L. (2017, August 14). The best resources for planning "learning stations"—Please add more. *Larry Ferlazzo's Websites of the Day*. Retrieved from http://larryferlazzo.edublogs.org/2017/08/14/the-best-resources-for-planning-learning-stations-please-add-more/

Ferlazzo, L. (n.d.). "All-time" best web tools for English language learners. *Larry Ferlazzo—Online tools*. www.teachingenglish.org.uk/blogs/larry-ferlazzo/larry-ferlazzo-online-tools

Ferlazzo, L., & Sypnieski, K.H. (2012). *The ESL/ELL Teacher's Survival Guide: Ready-to-Use Strategies, Tools, and Activities for Teaching English Language Learners of All Levels*. Jossey-Bass, San Francisco, CA.

Ferlazzo, L., & Sypnieski, K.H. (2016). *Navigating the Common Core with English Language Learners: Practical Strategies to Develop Higher-Order Thinking Skills*. Jossey-Bass, San Francisco, CA.

Fisher, D., & Frey, N. (2012). Close reading in elementary schools. *The Reading Teacher*, 66(3), 179–188. Retrieved from https://s3-us-west-1.amazonaws.com/fisher-and-frey/documents/close_reading_elem.pdf

Fisher, D., & Frey, N. (2016, February 15). Questioning that deepens comprehension. *Edutopia*. Retrieved from www.edutopia.org/blog/questioning-that-deepens-comprehension-douglas-fisher-nancy-frey?utm_source=twitter&utm_medium=socialflow

Ford, K. (n.d.). Differentiated instruction for English language learners. *¡Colorín Colorado!* Retrieved from www.colorincolorado.org/article/differentiated-instruction-english-language-learners

Ford-Connors, E., & Paratore, J.R. (2015). Vocabulary instruction in fifth grade and beyond: Sources of word learning and productive contexts for development. *Review of Educational Research*, 85(1), 50–91. Retrieved from http://journals.sagepub.com/doi/abs/10.3102/0034654314540943

Gallagher, K. (2006). *Teaching Adolescent Writers*. Stenhouse, Portland, ME.

Gallagher, K. (2015, July 20). [Twitter post]. Retrieved from https://twitter.com/KellyGToGo/status/623122274938261504

Gay, G. (2002). Preparing for culturally responsive teaching. *Journal of Teacher Education*, *53*(2), 106–116. Retrieved from http://journals.sagepub.com/doi/abs/10.1177/0022487102053002003?journalCode=jtea

Genesee, F. (n.d.). The home language: An English language learner's most valuable resource. *¡Colorín Colorado!* Retrieved from www.colorincolorado.org/article/home-language-english-language-learners-most-valuable-resource

Genesisd. (n.d.). 10 quick and easy ESL listening games to fill extra time. *FluentU English Educator Blog*. Retrieved from www.fluentu.com/blog/educator-english/esl-listening-games/

George, S.G.K. (2011). *Academic Writing Strategies for Secondary ELLs in Social Studies*. Master's thesis, Hamline University, Saint Paul, MN.

Ginsburg, D. (2011, March 27). The "do now" or "do never"? *Education Week*. Retrieved from http://blogs.edweek.org/teachers/coach_gs_teaching_tips/2011/03/the_do_now_or_do_never_1.html

Goh, C.C.M. (2014). Exploring the relationship between metacognitive awareness and listening performance with questionnaire data. *Language Awareness*, *23*(3), 255–274.

Gold, J., & Gibson, A. (n.d.). Reading aloud to build comprehension. *Reading Rockets*. Retrieved from www.readingrockets.org/article/reading-aloud-build-comprehension

Goldenberg, C. (2013, Summer). Unlocking the research on English learners: What we know—and don't yet know—about effective instruction. *American Educator*. Retrieved from www.aft.org/sites/default/files/periodicals/Goldenberg.pdf

González, N., Moll, L., & Amanti, C. (2005). *Funds of Knowledge: Theorizing Practices in Households, Communities, and Classrooms*. Lawrence Erlbaum, Mahwah, NJ.

Graff, G., & Birkenstein, C. (2015). *They Say, I Say: Movies That Matter in Academic Writing (3rd ed.)*. W. W. Norton, New York, NY.

Grundman, J. (2002). *Cooperative Learning in an English as a Second Language Classroom*. Master's thesis, Hamline University, Saint Paul, MN.

Guo, P.J., Kim, J., & Rubin, R. (2014). How video production affects student engagement: An empirical study of MOOC videos. *Proceedings of the First ACM Conference on Learning @ Scale Conference*, Atlanta, GA. Retrieved from http://dl.acm.org/citation.cfm?id=2566239

Hammond, Z. (2015). *Culturally Responsive Teaching and the Brain: Promoting Authentic Engagement and Rigor Among Culturally and Linguistically Diverse Students*. Corwin Press, Thousand Oaks, CA.

Hans, D.M. (n.d.). *The Effectiveness of Paraphrasing Strategy in Increasing University Students' Reading Comprehension and Writing Achievement*. Retrieved from http://

download.portalgaruda.org/article.php?article=298291&val=6797&title=THE %20EFFECTIVENESS%20OF%20PARAPHRASING%20STRATEGY%20IN %20INCREASING%20UNIVERSITY%20STUDENTS%C3%A2%E2%82%AC %E2%84%A2%20READING%20COMPREHENSION%20AND%20WRITING %20ACHIEVEMENT

Harmon, J.M., Wood, K.D., Hedrick, W.B., Vintinner, K., & Willeford, T. (2009). Interactive word walls: More than just reading the writing on the walls. *Journal of Adolescent & Adult Literacy, 52*(5), 398–408. doi:10.1598/JAAL.52.5.4

Hendrick, C. (2015, March 22). Engagement: Just because they're busy, doesn't mean they're learning anything. *Chronotype.* Retrieved from https://chronotopeblog .com/2015/03/22/engagement-just-because-theyre-busy-doesnt-mean-theyre-learning-anything/

Hendrickson, D.V. (2011). *ESL and Mainstream Co-teaching Practices in One Elementary School.* Retrieved from www.google.com/url?sa=t&rct=j&q=&esrc= s&source=web&cd=1&cad=rja&uact=8&ved=0ahUKEwictZCDpLnVAhVni1QK HTyXBG8QFggtMAA&url=https%3A%2F%2Fwww.hamline.edu%2FWorkArea% 2FDownloadAsset.aspx%3Fid%3D2147516348&usg=AFQjCNGrAizyhiNA_BQG tjiZCs6agdKdow

Holt, J. (2011, November 25). Two brains running. *New York Times.* Retrieved from www.nytimes.com/2011/11/27/books/review/thinking-fast-and-slow-by-daniel-kahneman-book-review.html

Honigsfeld, A., & Dove, M. (2008, Winter). Co-teaching in the ESL classroom. *The Phi Delta Kappa Bulletin* (pp. 8–14). Retrieved from http://citeseerx.ist.psu.edu/ viewdoc/download?doi=10.1.1.601.3487&rep=rep1&type=pdf

Honigsfeld, A., & Dove, M.G. (2010). *Collaboration and Co-Teaching: Strategies for English Learners.* Corwin, Newbury Park, CA.

Howard Research. (2009, October). *Kindergarten to Grade 12 English as a Second Language Literature Review Update.* Howard Research, Calgary, Edmonton, Canada. Retrieved from https://education.alberta.ca/media/1477345/K–12-esl-literature-review-update-2009.pdf

Ingham, J. (n.d.). Clines in language teaching. *Recipes for the EFL Classroom.* Retrieved from https://eflrecipes.com/2014/03/18/clines/

International Reading Association. (2014). *Leisure Reading: A Joint Position Statement on the International Reading Association, The Canadian Children's Book Centre, and the National Council of Teachers of English.* International Reading Association, Newark, NJ.

Jellema, H. (n.d.). *For English as a Second Language: TPR Exercises.* Retrieved from http:// static.digischool.nl/oefenen/hennyjellema/engels/tpr/voorbladtpr.htm

Jensen, E. (2001, June 1). Music tickles the reward centers in the brain. *Brain-Based Jensen Learning.* Retrieved from www.jensenlearning.com/news/music-tickles-the-reward-centers-in-the-brain/brain-based-learning

Just Read, Florida! (n.d.). Literacy centers. *Reading Rockets.* Retrieved from www.readingrockets.org/article/literacy-centers

Kagan, M. (2013, March 18). *7 Public Speaking Tips from the World's Best Speakers & Presenters* [Slideshare]. *Hubspot.* Retrieved from https://blog.hubspot.com/blog/tabid/6307/bid/34274/7-Lessons-From-the-World-s-Most-Captivating-Presenters-SlideShare.aspx

Kasapoğlu-Akyol, P. (2010). Using educational technology tools to improve language and communication skills of students. *Novitas-ROYAL (Research on Youth and Language)*, 4(2), 225–241. Retrieved from www.dphu.org/uploads/attachements/books/books_4761_0.pdf

Keppler, L. (2016, May 23). *The Background Building Controversy and the Common Core State Standards.* Retrieved from www.paridad.us/single-post/2016/05/23/The-Background-Building-Controversy-and-The-Common-Core-State-Standards-1

Khathayut, P., & Karavi, P. (2011). Summarizing techniques: The effective indicators of reading comprehension? In: *Proceedings of the 3rd International Conference on Humanities and Social Sciences*, 1–12. Songkia University, Hat Yai, Thailand. Retrieved from http://fs.libarts.psu.ac.th/research/conference/proceedings-3/3pdf/004.pdf

Kiany, G.R., & Shiramiry, E. (2002). The effect of frequent dictation on the listening comprehension ability of elementary EFL learners. *TESL Canada Journal*, 20(1), 57–63.

Kidd, R. (1992). Teaching ESL grammar through dictation. *TESL Canada Journal*, 10(1), 49–61. Retrieved from www.teslcanadajournal.ca/index.php/tesl/article/view/611

Kietlinska, K. (n.d.). *Revision and ESL Students.* Retrieved from https://wac.colostate.edu/books/horning_revision/chapter5.pdf

Kiftiah, S. (n.d.). *Literature Review of Strip Story.* Retrieved from www.academia.edu/7741637/Literature_reviews_of_Strip_story

Kit, C.O. (2004). Report on the action research project on English dictation in a local primary school. *Hong Kong Teachers' Centre Journal*, 2, 1–10. Retrieved from http://edb.org.hk/hktc/download/journal/j2/P1-10.pdf

Krashen, S.D. (1981). *Second Language Acquisition and Second Language Learning.* Pergamon Press, Oxford, UK. Retrieved from www.sdkrashen.com/content/books/sl_acquisition_and_learning.pdf

Krashen, S.D., & Terrell, T.D. (1983). *The Natural Approach: Language Acquisition in the Classroom*. The Alemany Press, San Francisco, CA. Retrieved from https://eric.ed.gov/?q=ED230069&id=ED230069

Krasnoff, B. (2016, March). *Culturally Responsive Teaching: A Guide to Evidence-Based Practices for Teaching All Students Equitably*. Region X Equity Assistance Center at Education Northwest, Portland, OR. Retrieved from http://educationnorthwest.org/sites/default/files/resources/culturally-responsive-teaching.pdf

Kung, F.-W. (2013). Rhythm and pronunciation of American English: Jazzing up EFL teaching through Jazz chants. *The Asian EFL Journal, 70*, 4–27. Retrieved from http://asian-efl-journal.com/wp-content/uploads/mgm/downloads/77667900.pdf

Ladson-Billings, G. (1995). But that's just good teaching! The case for culturally relevant pedagogy. *Theory into Practice, 34*(3), 159–165.

Lavery, C. (n.d.). *Short Projects to Get Them Talking. Teaching English.org*. Retrieved from www.teachingenglish.org.uk/article/short-projects-get-them-talking?utm_source=facebook&utm_medium=social&utm_campaign=bc-teachingenglish

Leaf, M. (1977). *The Story of Ferdinand*. Penguin Books, London, UK.

Lee, H.-G. (2012). *ESL Learners' Motivation and Task Engagement in Technology Enhanced Language Learning Contexts*. Doctoral dissertation, Washington State University, Pullman, WA. Retrieved from https://research.wsulibs.wsu.edu:8443/xmlui/bitstream/handle/2376/4277/Lee_wsu_0251E_10499.pdf?sequence=1&isAllowed=y and https://web.wpi.edu/Pubs/E-project/Available/E-project-030515-211609/unrestricted/CIHE_IQP_Report_C15.pdf

Lee, S.H. (2008). Beyond reading and proficiency assessment: The rational cloze procedure as stimulus for integrated reading, writing, and vocabulary instruction and teacher-student interaction in ESL. *System, 36*, 642–660. Retrieved from https://eric.ed.gov/?id=EJ819333

Li, X., & Brand, M. (2009). Effectiveness of music on vocabulary acquisition, language usage, and meaning for mainland Chinese ESL learners. *Contributions to Music Education, 36*(1), 73–84. Retrieved from http://krpb.pbworks.com/f/music-esl.pdf

Liebtag, E. (n.d.). Culturally responsive pedagogy. *Global Teacher Education*. Retrieved from www.globalteachereducation.org/culturally-responsive-pedagogy

Lin, O.P., & Maarof, N. (2013). Collaborative writing in summary writing: Student perceptions and problems. *Procedia—Social and Behavioral Sciences, 90*, 599–606. Retrieved from www.sciencedirect.com/science/article/pii/S1877042813020193

Lindahl, K. (2015, November 2). *Tap into Funds of Knowledge*. TESOL International Association. Retrieved from http://blog.tesol.org/tap-into-funds-of-knowledge/

Lindgren, R., & McDaniel, R. (2012). Transforming online learning through narrative and student agency. *Educational Technology & Society*, *15*(4), 344–355. Retrieved from www.academia.edu/3973171/Transforming_Online_Learning_through_Narrative_and_Student_Agency

Lin-Siegler, X., Shaenfield, D., & Elder, A.D. (2015). Contrasting case instruction can improve self-assessment of writing. *Educational Technology Research and Development*, *63*(4), 517–537. Retrieved from https://link.springer.com/article/10.1007/s11423-015-9390-9

Lorenzutti, N. (2014). Beyond the gap fill: Dynamic activities for song in the EFL classroom. *English Teaching Forum*, *1*, 14–21. Retrieved from https://americanenglish.state.gov/files/ae/resource_files/52_1_4_lorenzutti.pdf

Lundgren, C., & Lundy-Ponce, G. (n.d.). Cultural responsive instruction for holiday and religious celebrations. *¡Colorín Colorado!* Retrieved from www.colorincolorado.org/article/culturally-responsive-instruction-holiday-and-religious-celebrations

Martin, J. (2016, December 13). Research shows how gaming can support language learning. *Pearson English Blog*. Retrieved from www.english.com/blog/gaming-research

Marzano, R.J. (2004). *Building Background Knowledge for Academic Achievement: Research on What Works in Schools*. Association for Supervision and Curriculum Development, Alexandria, VA.

Marzano, R. (2009). The art and science of teaching: Six steps to better vocabulary instruction. *Educational Leadership*, *67*(1), 83–84. Retrieved from www.ascd.org/publications/educational-leadership/sept09/vol67/num01/Six-Steps-to-Better-Vocabulary-Instruction.aspx

Marzano, R.J. (2010). The art and science of teaching/using games to enhance student achievement. *Educational Leadership*, *67*(5), 71–72. Retrieved from www.ascd.org/publications/educational-leadership/feb10/vol67/num05/Using-Games-to-Enhance-Student-Achievement.aspx

Mathewson, T.G. (2016, July 2). Schools are under federal pressure to translate for immigrant parents. *The Hechinger Report*. Retrieved from http://hechingerreport.org/schools-federal-pressure-translate-immigrant-families/

McCrann, J.T. (2017, July 29). Teaching from a textbook makes my class more student-centered. *Education Week*. Retrieved from http://blogs.edweek.org/teachers/prove-it-math-and-education-policy/2017/07/textbook-makes-class-student-centered.html

Miller, D. (2015, February 8). *I've Got Research. Yes, I Do. I've Got Research. How About You?* Retrieved from https://bookwhisperer.com/2015/02/08/ive-got-research-yes-i-do-ive-got-research-how-about-you/

Millin, S. (2013). *Writing Bingo.* Retrieved from https://sandymillin.wordpress.com/2013/10/15/writing-bingo/

Millington, N.T. (n.d.). *Ask-Answer-Add—A Speaking Activity to Help Learners Maintain a Natural Conversation. British Council.* Retrieved from www.teachingenglish.org.uk/blogs/neil-t-millington/ask-answer-add-a-speaking-activity-help-learners-maintain-a-natural?utm_source=facebook&utm_medium=social&utm_campaign=bc-teachingenglish

Mogahed, M.M. (2011). To use or not to use translation in language teaching. *Translator Journal, 15*(4). Retrieved from http://translationjournal.net/journal/58education.htm

Morat, B.N.B., Shaari, A., & Abidin, M.J.Z. (2016). *Facilitating ESL Learning Using YouTube: Learners' Motivational Experiences.* Retrieved from http://ijeisr.net/wp-content/uploads/2016/10/Isu-1.pdf

Morrow, L.M., Shanahan, T., & Wixson, K.K. (2012). *Teaching with the Common Core Standards for English Language Arts, PreK–2.* Guilford Press, New York, NY.

Moses, E. (2015, January 17). *3-2-1 and the Common Core Writing Book: Cues from Ekuwah Moses.* Retrieved from http://ekuwah.blogspot.com/2015/01/3–2–1-and-common-core-writing-book.html

Movitz, A.P., & Holmes, K.P. (2007). Finding center: How learning centers evolved in a secondary, student-centered classroom. *The English Journal, 96*(3), 68–73. Retrieved from www.jstor.org/stable/30047298?seq=1#page_scan_tab_contents

Mubaslat, M.M. (2011/2012). *The Effect of Using Educational Games on the Students' Achievement in English Language for the Primary Stage.* Retrieved from http://files.eric.ed.gov/fulltext/ED529467.pdf

Mulligan, C., & Garofalo, R. (2011). A collaborative writing approach: Methodology and student assessment. *The Language Teacher, 35*(3), 5–10. Retrieved from www.google.com/url?sa=t&rct=j&q=&esrc=s&source=web&cd=8&cad=rja&uact=8&ved=0ahUKEwjMy6rSo-PUAhWjiVQKHUVYC84QFghjMAc&url=http%3A%2F%2Fwww.jalt-publications.org%2Ffiles%2Fpdf-article%2Fart1_13.pdf&usg=AFQjCNFr4l2x8V4FdlJAGSvoN1NL7jujIA

Nation, P. (2007). The four strands. *Innovation in Language Teaching, 1*(1), 1–12. Retrieved from www.victoria.ac.nz/lals/staff/Publications/paul-nation/2007-Four-strands.pdf

National Association of Geoscience Teachers. (n.d.). *Teaching Methods: A Collection of Pedagogic Techniques and Example Activities.* Retrieved from https://serc.carleton.edu/NAGTWorkshops/teaching_methods/jigsaws/why.html

National Center for Education Statistics. (2017). *The Condition of Education: Racial/Ethnic Enrollment in Public Schools.* Retrieved from https://nces.ed.gov/ programs/coe/indicator_cge.asp

National Reading Panel. (2000). *Teaching Children to Read: An Evidence-Based Assessment of the Scientific Research Literature on Reading and Its Implications for Reading Instruction.* National Reading Panel, Bethesda, MD. Retrieved from www.nichd.nih.gov/ publications/pubs/nrp/Documents/report.pdf

National Reading Technical Assistance Center. (2010). *A Review of the Current Research on Vocabulary Instruction.* Retrieved from www.academia.edu/33523216/ A_Review_of_the_Current_Research_on_Comprehension_Instruction

Nestojko, J.F., Bui, D.C., Kornell, N., & Bjork, E.L. (2014, August 8). Expecting to teach enhances learning recall. *EurekAlert!* Retrieved from www.eurekalert.org/ pub_releases/2014-08/wuis-ett080814.php

Nordin, N.M., Rashid, S.M., Zubir, S.I.S.S., & Sadjirin, R. (2013). Differences in reading strategies: How ESL learners really read. *Procedia—Social and Behavioral Sciences, 90*(10), 468–477. Retrieved from https://doi.org/10.1016/j.sbspro.2013.07.116

Northwest Regional Educational Laboratory. (2012, March 24). Focus on effectiveness: Research-based strategies. *Icebreaker Ideas.* Retrieved from https:// icebreakerideas.com/researched-based-education-strategies/#Key_Research_ Findings

Nowogrodski, A. (2015, February 23). Why listening might be the most important skill to hire for. *Fast Company.* Retrieved from www.fastcompany.com/3042688/ why-listening-might-be-the-most-important-skill-to-hire-for

Pak, S.S., & Weseley, A.J. (2012). The effect of mandatory reading logs on children's motivation to read. *Journal of Research in Education, 22*(1), 251–265. Retrieved from http://media.wix.com/ugd/baaa29_daccad9c8acb49d095e3a0c2c2b378ae.pdf

Paris, D. (2012). Culturally sustaining pedagogy: A needed change in stance, terminology, and practice. *Educational Researcher, 41*(3), 93–97. Retrieved from http:// journals.sagepub.com/doi/abs/10.3102/0013189X12441244

Paul, A.M. (2013, January 9). Highlighting is a waste of time: The best and worst learning techniques. *Time.* Retrieved from http://ideas.time.com/2013/01/09/ highlighting-is-a-waste-of-time-the-best-and-worst-learning-techniques

Peck, C. (2012, September 17). Flyswatter. *Melting Teacher.* Retrieved from http:// eslcarissa.blogspot.com/2012/09/flyswatter.html

Perkins, D.N., & Salomon, G. (1992). *Transfer of learning.* In T.N. Postelthwaite & T. Husen (eds.), *The International Encyclopedia of Education* (2nd ed.). Pergamon

Press, Oxford, UK. Retrieved from https://pdfs.semanticscholar.org/fb86/245e6623502017940c796c01ed508c3d8208.pdf

Perkins, D.N., & Salomon, G. (n.d.). *The Science and Art of Transfer*. Retrieved from https://pdfs.semanticscholar.org/aea8/9351b6eba09d9fee5af02b8bef9ce53bbe0f.pdf

Petrie, G.M. (2003). ESL teachers' views on visual language: A grounded theory. *The Reading Matrix*, 3(3), 137–168. Retrieved from www.readingmatrix.com/articles/petrie/article.pdf

*Polikoff Study Finds Textbooks Not Aligned to Common Core Standards*. (2014, February 25). USC Rossier School of Education, Los Angeles, CA. Retrieved from http://rossier.usc.edu/polikoff-study-finds-textbooks-not-aligned-to-common-core-standards/

Pollard, L., & Hess, N. (1997). *Zero Prep: Ready-to-Go Activities for the Language Classroom*. Alta Book Center, Palm Springs, CA.

Prince, M., & Felder, R. (2007, February 15). The many faces of inductive teaching and learning. *NSTA WebNews Digest*. Retrieved from www.nsta.org/publications/news/story.aspx?id=53403

Public Broadcasting System. (n.d.). *Wit and wisdom*. Retrieved from www.pbs.org/benfranklin/l3_wit_self.html

Qiu, Y. (2016). Research on the application of Total Physical Response approach to vocabulary teaching in primary schools. *International Journal of Arts and Commerce*, 5(7), 18–24. Retrieved from www.ijac.org.uk/images/frontImages/gallery/Vol._5_No._7/3._18-24.pdf

Rahayu, D.S. (2013). The use of language experience approach in teaching reading for young learners. *Journal of English Education*, 1(1), 43–53. Retrieved from www.google.com/url?sa=t&rct=j&q=&esrc=s&source=web&cd=15&cad=rja&uact=8&ved=0ahUKEwia9Pay4J_VAhUCilQKHcoQCP8QFghqMA4&url=http%3A%2F%2Fejournal.upi.edu%2Findex.php%2FL-E%2Farticle%2Fdownload%2F324%2F213&usg=AFQjCNFQ8ChcDQ9ze_HU97EydBvY1g2Zhg

*Random Name Picker*. (n.d.). ClassTools.net. Retrieved from www.classtools.net/random-name-picker/

Reischer, E. (2016, June 3). Can reading logs ruin reading for kids? *The Atlantic*. Retrieved from ww.theatlantic.com/education/archive/2016/06/are-reading-logs-ruining-reading/485372/

Reyes Jr., J.P. (2015). *The Impact of Sentence Frames on Student Readers Workshop Responses*. Master's thesis, Hamline University, Saint Paul, MN.

Rich, M. (2015, April 11). Where are the teachers of color. *New York Times*. Retrieved from www.nytimes.com/2015/04/12/sunday-review/where-are-the-teachers-of-color.html

Roberts, C.A. (1994). Transferring literacy skills from L1 to L2: From theory to practice. *The Journal of Education Issues of Language Minority Students, 13*, 209–221. Retrieved from www.edtechpolicy.org/ArchivedWebsites/transf13.htm

Roberts, K., & Roberts, M.B. (2016). *DIY Literacy: Teaching Tools for Differentiations, Rigor, and Independence*. Heinemann, Portsmouth, NH.

Roberts, K., & Roberts, M.B. (n.d.). *Videos: DIY Literacy*. Retrieved from www.kateandmaggie.com/videos-diy-literacy/

Robertson, K., & Lafond, S. (n.d.). How to support ELL students with interrupted formal education (SIFEs). *¡Colorín Colorado!* Retrieved from www.colorincolorado.org/article/how-support-ell-students-interrupted-formal-education-sifes

Rodgers, T.S., Palmer, A.S., & Olsen, J.W. (1985). *Back & Forth: Photocopiable Cooperative Pair Activities for Language Development*. Alta English Publishers, Palm Springs, CA. Retrieved from https://altaenglishpublishers.com/product/back-forth-photocopiable-cooperative-pair-activities-for-language-evelopment

Rodriguez, T. (2012, November 1). How to use your ears to influence people. *Scientific American*. Retrieved from www.scientificamerican.com/article/how-to-use-your-ears-to-influence-people/

Rossiter, M.J., Abbott, M.L., & Kushnir, A. (2016). L2 vocabulary research and instructional practices: Where are the gaps? *Teaching English as a Second or Foreign Language, 20*(1). Retrieved from www.tesl-ej.org/wordpress/issues/volume20/ej77/ej77a6/

Russ on Reading. (2016, October 16). Independent Reading: *A Research-Based Defense*. Retrieved from http://russonreading.blogspot.com/2016/10/independent-reading-research-based.html

Ryan, R.M., & Deci, E.L. (2000). Intrinsic and extrinsic motivations: Classic definitions and new directions. *Contemporary Educational Psychology, 25*, 54–67. Retrieved from http://mmrg.pbworks.com/f/Ryan,+Deci+00.pdf

Sabbah, S.S. (2016). The effect of jigsaw strategy on ESL students' reading achievement. *Arab World English Journal, 7*(1), 445–458. Retrieved from www.academia.edu/25090010/The_Effect_of_Jigsaw_Strategy_on_ESL_Students_Reading_Achievement_The_Effect_of_Jigsaw_Strategy_on_ESL_Students_Reading_Achievement_Sabbah

Salva, C., & Matis, A. (2017). *Boosting Achievement*. Canter Press, San Antonio, TX.

Sam D. P., & Rajan, P. (2013). Using graphic organizers to improve reading comprehension skills for the middle school ESL students. *English Language Teaching, 6*(2),

155–170. Retrieved from www.ccsenet.org/journal/index.php/elt/article/view/23823/15121

Savaşçı, M. (2014). Why are some students reluctant to use L2 in EFL speaking classes? An action theory at tertiary level. *Procedia—Social and Behavioral Sciences, 116*, 2682–2686. Retrieved from www.sciencedirect.com/science/article/pii/S1877042814006521

Schenk, C. (2012, January 4). Silent post-it chats. *Mr. Schenk's Summer School.* Retrieved from https://mrschenk.net/2012/01/04/silent-post-it-chats

Schleppegrell, M.J., & Bowman, B. (1995). Problem-posing: A tool for curriculum renewal. *ELT Journal, 49*(4), 297–306. Retrieved from https://academic.oup.com/eltj/article-abstract/49/4/297/498125/Problem-posing-a-tool-for-curriculum-renewal

Schoepp, K. (2001). Reasons for using songs in the ESL/EFL classroom. *The Internet TESL Journal, VII*(2). Retrieved from http://iteslj.org/Articles/Schoepp-Songs.html

Schwartz, K. (2017, June 14). How do you know when a teaching strategy is most effective? John Hattie has an idea. *KQED News.* Retrieved from www2.kqed.org/mindshift/2017/06/14/how-do-you-know-when-a-teaching-strategy-is-most-effective-john-hattie-has-an-idea/

Serravallo, J. (2015, July 26). Expanding our approach to reading strategies. *MiddleWeb.* Retrieved from www.middleweb.com/23839/expanding-our-approach-to-reading-strategies/

Shanahan, T. (2013, Fall). Letting the text take center stage: How the Common Core Standards will transform English language instruction. *American Educator, 4*(11), 43. Retrieved from http://files.eric.ed.gov/fulltext/EJ1021044.pdf

Shanahan, T. (n.d.). Common Core: Close reading. *Teacher.* Retrieved from www.scholastic.com/teachers/articles/teaching-content/common-core-close-reading-0/

Shapiro, J. (2014, June 27). Games in the classroom: What the research says. *KQED News.* Retrieved from www2.kqed.org/mindshift/2014/06/27/games-in-the-classroom-what-the-research-says

Shen, D. (n.d.). Debate. *ABL Connect.* Retrieved from https://ablconnect.harvard.edu/debate-research

Shen, D., & Frances, H. (n.d.). *Do now.* ABL Connect. Harvard University. Retrieved from https://ablconnect.harvard.edu/do-now-research

Shernoff, D.J. (2013). *Optimal Learning Environments to Promote Student Engagement.* Springer, New York, NY.

Short, D., & Echevarria, J. (2004–2005). Teachers skills to support English language learners. *Educational Leadership*, 62(4), 8–13. Retrieved from www.ascd.org/publications/educational-leadership/dec04/vol62/num04/Teacher-Skills-to-Support-English-Language-Learners.aspx

Slavin, R.E. (2016, August 26). Do textbooks matter? *Huffpost*. Retrieved from www.huffingtonpost.com/robert-e-slavin/do-textbooks-matter_b_11694856.html

Smith, J.E. (2005). *Factors That Inhibit School Involvement of Hispanic Parents*. Doctoral dissertation, Oklahoma State University, Stillwater, OK. Retrieved from http://digital.library.okstate.edu/etd/umi-okstate-1557.pdf

Snyder, E., Witmer, S.E., & Schmitt, H. (2016). English language learners and reading instruction: A review of the literature. *Preventing School Failure: Alternative Education for Children and Youth*. Retrieved from www.tandfonline.com/doi/abs/10.1080/1045988X.2016.1219301?src=recsys&journalCode=vpsf20

Southerland, L. (2011). *The Effects of Using Interactive Word Walls to Teach Vocabulary to Middle School Students*. Doctoral Dissertation, University of North Florida, Jacksonville, FL.

Sparks, S.D. (2015, March 31). "Middle" students find success tutoring peers, in N.Y.C. study. *Education Week*. Retrieved from www.edweek.org/ew/articles/2015/04/01/middle-students-find-success-tutoring-peers-in.html?cmp=ENL-EU-NEWS2-RM

Sparks, S.D. (2017, June 14). Even for late learners, starting to read changes the brain fast. *Education Week*. Retrieved from http://blogs.edweek.org/edweek/inside-school-research/2017/06/learning_to_read_changes_your_brain_fast.html

Spiering, C. (2015, April 30). Kid interviewer cuts off Obama for going on too long. *YouTube*. Retrieved from www.youtube.com/watch?v=e7C8vEDhhVQ

Stafford, T. (2011, October 24). Make study more effective, the easy way. *Mind Hacks*. Retrieved from https://mindhacks.com/2011/10/24/make-study-more-effective-the-easy-way

Stefanou, C.R., Perencevich, K.C., DiCintio, M., & Turner, J.C. (2010). Supporting autonomy in the classroom: Ways teachers encourage student decision making and ownership. *Educational Psychologist*, 39(2), 97–110. Retrieved from www.tandfonline.com/doi/abs/10.1207/s15326985ep3902_2#.VQiF_mTF-nR

Strangman, N., Vue, G., Hall, T., & Meyer, A. (2004). *Graphic Organizers and Implications for Universal Design for Learning: Curriculum Enhancement Report*. National Center on Accessible Materials, Wakefield, MA. Retrieved from www.google.com/url?sa=t&rct=j&q=&esrc=s&source=web&cd=2&cad=rja&uact=8&ved=0ahUKEwiD-oCKwtjLAhUY1mMKHfvyAgoQFgghMAE&url=http%3A%2F%2Faem.cast.org%2Fbinaries%2Fcontent%2Fassets%2Fcommon%2Fpublications%2Faem%2Fncac-

graphic-organizers-udl-2014–10.docx&usg=AFQjCNGjBKkuZhbskavKn_pIRi7 x5SnRZA&sig2=KlQmcdco1AI-0kCUaAhs_g&bvm=bv.117868183,d.cGc

Strategy. (n.d.). *Online Etymology Dictionary*. Retrieved from www.etymonline.com/ index.php?term=strategy

Suarez-Orozco, C., Pimentel, A., & Martin, M. (2009). The significance of relationships: Academic engagement and achievement among newcomer immigrant youth. *Teachers College Record, 111*(3), 712–749. Retrieved from https://eric.ed .gov/?id=EJ829126

Sullivan, J. (2007). *The Use of Technology to Enhance Comprehension and Fluency of ESL Students in the Elementary School Classroom.* Paper for university class, California State University, Northridge, CA. Retrieved from www.google .com/url?sa=t&rct=j&q=&esrc=s&source=web&cd=8&cad=rja&uact=8& ved=0ahUKEwj0iK3lnbLVAhXsyVQKHcxtC8IQFghgMAc&url=http%3A%2F %2Fwww.csun.edu%2F˜jms22462%2F616%2FResearch%2520Paper%2520EED %2520616.doc&usg=AFQjCNFQwcpkqxl-VcdM8K59yPj_qK1cMQ

Tarr, R. (2015). *Design a New Page for Your Textbook.* Retrieved from www.classtools .net/blog/design-a-new-page-for-your-textbook/

Tayib, A.-M. (2015). The effect of using graphic organizers on writing (A case study of preparatory college students at UMM-AL-QURA University). *International Journal of English Language and Linguistics Research, 3*(1), 15–36. Retrieved from www .eajournals.org/wp-content/uploads/The-Effect-of-Using-Graphic-Organizers-on-Writing.pdf

Tedick, D. (2001, Summer). *Dictogloss Procedure.* Retrieved from http://carla.umn .edu/cobaltt/modules/strategies/Dictogloss.pdf

Tennant, A. (n.d.). *Listening Matters: Active Listening. One Stop English.* Retrieved from www.onestopenglish.com/skills/listening/teaching-tips/listening-matters/ listening-matters-active-listening/554465.article

Terrell, S. (2012, March 5). *20+ Activities and Resources for Teaching Language Through Song Lyrics.* ESL *Library.* Retrieved from http://blog.esllibrary.com/2012/03/05/ 20-tips-language-through-song-lyrics

Thaler, M. (2000). *The Teacher from the Black Lagoon.* Cartwheel Books, New York, NY.

Thornbury, S. (2013, February 6). V is Vocabulary Teaching. *An A-Z of ELT.* Retrieved from https://scottthornbury.wordpress.com/2013/06/02/v-is-for-vocabulary-teaching/

Thornbury, S. (2017, March 4). S is for speaking. *An A-Z of ELT.* Retrieved from https://scottthornbury.wordpress.com/2017/04/30/s-is-for-speaking/

*Tildee: You explain, they understand.* (n.d.). Retrieved from www.tildee.com/

Toppel, K. (2017, April 13). [Twitter post]. Retrieved from https://twitter.com/Toppel_ELD/status/852598723779493892

Trang, N.T.H. (n.d.). *Using Pictures as Motivating Factors in Speaking Lessons.* Retrieved from www.vnseameo.org/TESOLConference2015/Materials/Fullpaper/Ms.%20Nguyen%20Thi%20Huyen%20Trang.pdf

Truscott, J. (1996). The case against grammar correction in L2 writing classes. *Language Learning, 46*(2), 327–369.

Truscott, J. (2005). The continuing problems of oral grammar correction. *The International Journal of Foreign Language Teaching, 1*(2), 17–22. Retrieved from http://ijflt.com/images/ijflt/IJFLTSpring05.pdf

Tuan, N.H., & Mai, T.N. (2015). Factors affecting students' speaking performance at Le Thanh Hien High School. *Asian Journal of Educational Research, 3*(2), 8–23. Retrieved from www.multidisciplinaryjournals.com/wp-content/uploads/2015/03/FACTORS-AFFECTING-STUDENTS%E2%80%99-SPEAKING.pdf

University of Kansas. (2017, May 31). *Relating Curriculum to Culture Key in Educating English Language Learners with Disabilities, Researchers Argue.* Retrieved from https://news.ku.edu/2017/05/12/relating-curriculum-culture-key-educating-english-language-learners-disabilities

University of Sydney. (2016, May 5). Pattern learning key to children's language development. *Science Daily.* Retrieved from www.sciencedaily.com/releases/2016/05/160505222938.htm

US Department of Justice and US Department of Education. (2015, January 7). *Dear Colleague Letter.* Retrieved from www2.ed.gov/about/offices/list/ocr/letters/colleague-el-201501.pdf

Vandergrift, L. (n.d.). *Listening: Theory and Practice in Modern Foreign Language Competence.* Centre for Languages Linguistics & Area Studies. Retrieved from www.llas.ac.uk/resources/gpg/67

Vandergrift, L., & Goh, C.C.M. (2011). *Teaching and Learning Second Language Listening: Metacognition in Action, ESL & Applied Linguistics Professional Series.* Routledge, New York, NY. Retrieved from https://eric.ed.gov/?id=ED525538

VanderMolen, M.A. (2011). *Does the Use of Dialogue Journals Affect the Writing Fluency of Low-Literacy Adult Somali Students?* Master's thesis, Hamline University, Saint Paul, MN.

Warwick, P., Stephenson, P., Webster, J., & Bourne, J. (2010). Developing pupils' written expression of procedural understanding through the use of writing frames in science: Findings from a case study approach. *International Journal of Science Education, 25*(2), 173–192. Retrieved from www.tandfonline.com/doi/abs/10.1080/09500690210163251

Washington University, St. Louis. (2014, August 8). Expecting to teach enhances learning, recall. *EurekAlert!* Retrieved from www.eurekalert.org/pub_releases/2014–08/wuis-ett080814.php

WIDA Consortium. (2015, May). *SLIFE: Students with Limited or Interrupted Formal Education.* Retrieved from www.google.com/url?sa=t&rct=j&q=&esrc=s&source=web&cd=16&cad=rja&uact=8&ved=0ahUKEwjH0rjvwbnVAhWKgFQKHQBPAI0QFgh7MA8&url=https%3A%2F%2Fwww.wida.us%2Fget.aspx%3Fid%3D848&usg=AFQjCNFNl8xrS1TIkOXQCUYvWEGKbc5pCA

Williams, C., & Roberts, D. (2011). *Strategic Oral Language Instruction in ELD: Teaching Oracy to Develop Literacy.* Ballard & Tighe, Brea, CA. Retrieved from www.cwellresources.com/Strategic_Oral_Language_Instruction_in_ELD.pdf

Williams, J.J., & Lombrozo, T. (2010). The role of explanation in discovery and generalization: Evidence from category learning. *Cognitive Science, 34,* 776–806. doi: 10.1111/j.1551–6709.2010.01113.x

Willams, J.P., & Atkins, J.G. (2009). The role of metacognition in teaching reading comprehension to primary students. In D.J. Hacker, J. Dunlosky, & A.C. Graesser (Eds.), *Handbook of Metacognition in Education* (pp. 26–43). Routledge, New York, NY. Retrieved from www4.ncsu.edu/~jlnietfe/Metacog_Articles_files/Williams%20%26%20Atkins%20%282009%29.pdf

Willingham, D. (2012, April 30). *Collateral Damage of Excessive Reading Comprehension Strategy Instruction.* Retrieved from www.danielwillingham.com/daniel-willingham-science-and-education-blog/collateral-damage-of-reading-comprehension-strategy-instruction

Willingham, D. (2016, October 7). [Twitter post]. Retrieved from https://twitter.com/DTWillingham/status/784391011527196672

Willingham, D. (2017, April 9). Should teachers use prequestions? *Daniel Willingham—Science & Education.* Retrieved from www.danielwillingham.com/daniel-willingham-science-and-education-blog/should-teachers-use-prequestions

Wilson III, E.J. (2015, June 10). 5 skills employers want that you won't see in a job ad. *Fortune.* Retrieved from http://fortune.com/2015/06/10/5-skills-employers-want-that-you-wont-see-in-a-job-ad/?xid=timehp-popular

Wisconsin Center for Education Research. (n.d.). *Collaborative Learning for English Language Learners.* Retrieved from www.google.com/url?sa=t&rct=j&q=&esrc=s&source=web&cd=2&cad=rja&uact=8&ved=0ahUKEwjYkdaYpOPUAhXo5IMKHaC3DE4QFggwMAE&url=https%3A%2F%2Fwww.wida.us%2Fget.aspx%3Fid%3D752&usg=AFQjCNHXHTAoCoJ6udNLTVY2Ndbu9pLhUA

Wong, W., & Van Patten, B. (2003, October). The evidence is in: Drills are out. *Foreign Language Annals, 36*(3), 403–423. Retrieved from http://onlinelibrary.wiley.com/doi/10.1111/j.1944-9720.2003.tb02123.x/full

Wormeli, R. (2016). What to do in week one? *Educational Leadership, 74*(1), 10–15. Retrieved from www.ascd.org/publications/educational-leadership/sept16/vol74/num01/What-to-Do-in-Week-One%C2%A2.aspx

Wright, T.S., & Cervetti, G.N. (2016). A systematic review of the research on vocabulary instruction that impacts text comprehension. *Reading Research Quarterly, 52*(2), 203–226. doi: 10.1002/rrq.163

Yip, F., & Kwan, A.C.M. (2006). Online vocabulary games as a tool for teaching and learning English vocabulary. *Educational Media International, 43*, 233–249. Retrieved from www.tandfonline.com/doi/abs/10.1080/09523980600641445?src=recsys&journalCode=remi20

Your shining moment. (n.d.). *Teaching Channel*. Retrieved from www.teachingchannel.org/videos/celebrating-student-achievement

Zare, P. (2012). Language learning strategies among EFL/ESL learners: A review of literature. *International Journal of Humanities and Social Science, 2*(5), 162–169. Retrieved from www.ijhssnet.com/journals/Vol_2_No_5_March_2012/20.pdf

Živković, S. (2014). The importance of oral presentations for university students. *Mediterranean Journal of Social Sciences, 5*(19), 468–475. Retrieved from www.mcser.org/journal/index.php/mjss/article/viewFile/4278/4184

# Index